YA
920.02
Bio

95-70

ZEELAND PUBLIC LIBRARY
14 S. CHURCH STREET
ZEELAND, MI 49464
PHONE: 616-772-0874

Biography Today

Profiles of People of Interest to Young Readers

1994
Annual
Cumulation

Laurie Lanzen Harris
Editor

Omnigraphics, Inc.

Penobscot Building
Detroit, Michigan 48226

Laurie Lanzen Harris, *Editor*
Cherie D. Abbey and Margaret W. Young, *Contributing Editors*
Barry Puckett, *Research Associate*

Omnigraphics, Inc.

* * *

Matthew Barbour, *Production Manager*
Laurie Lanzen Harris, *Vice President & Editorial Director*
Peter E. Ruffner, *Vice President, Administration*
James A. Sellgren, *Vice President, Operations and Finance*
Jane Steele, *Vice President, Research*

* * *

Frederick G. Ruffner, Jr., *Publisher*

Copyright © 1995 Omnigraphics, Inc.

ISBN 0-7808-0022-2

The information in this publication was compiled from the sources cited and from other sources considered reliable. While every possible effort has been made to ensure reliability, the publisher will not assume liability for damages caused by inaccuracies in the data, and makes no warranty, express or implied, on the accuracy of the information contained herein.

This book is printed on acid-free paper meeting the ANSI Z39.48 Standard. The infinity symbol that appears above indicates that the paper in this book meets that standard.

Printed in the United States

Contents

Preface 9

Tim Allen   1953- 15
   American Comedian and Star of "Home Improvement"

Marian Anderson (Obituary)   1897-1993 22
   American Classical, Opera, and Spiritual Singer

Mario Andretti   1940- 31
   Italian-Born American Professional Race Car Driver

Ned Andrews (Brief Entry)   1980- 39
   American Winner of the 1994 National Spelling Bee

Yasir Arafat   1929- 41
   Palestinian Chairman of the Palestine Liberation Organization

Bruce Babbitt   1938- 50
   American Secretary of the Interior

Mayim Bialik   1975- 57
   American Actress and Star of "Blossom"

Bonnie Blair   1964- 63
   American Speed Skater and Winner of Five Olympic
   Gold Medals

Ed Bradley   1941- 70
   American Journalist and Correspondent for "60 Minutes"

John Candy (Obituary)   1950-1994 77
   Canadian Actor and Comedian

Mary Chapin Carpenter   1958- 84
   American Singer and Songwriter

Benjamin Chavis   1948- 91
   American Civil Rights Leader and Former Head of the NAACP

Connie Chung 1946- 98
American Broadcast Journalist and Co-Anchor of
"CBS Evening News"

Beverly Cleary 1916- 105
American Writer and Author of the *Ramona* Series, *The Mouse and the Motorcycle,* and *Dear Mr. Henshaw*

Kurt Cobain (Obituary) 1967-1994 115
American Musician and Songwriter

F.W. de Klerk 1936- 123
Former South African President

Rita Dove (Brief Entry) 1952- 131
American Poet Laureate

Linda Ellerbee 1944- 133
American Broadcast Journalist and Host of "Nick News"

Sergei Fedorov 1969- 141
Russian Professional Hockey Player with the Detroit Red Wings

Zlata Filipovic 1980- 148
Bosnian Author of *Zlata's Diary*

Daisy Fuentes (Brief Entry) 1966- 153
Cuban-Born American MTV Broadcaster

Ruth Bader Ginsburg 1933- 155
American Associate Justice, U.S. Supreme Court

Whoopi Goldberg 1949(?)- 162
American Actress and Star of *Sister Act*

Tonya Harding 1970- 170
American Figure Skater

Melissa Joan Hart 1976- 178
American Actress and Star of "Clarissa Explains It All"

Geoff Hooper (Brief Entry) 1979- 183
American Winner of the 1993 National Spelling Bee

Whitney Houston   1963- 185
    American Singer

Dan Jansen   1965- 192
    American Speed Skater and Olympic Gold Medalist

Nancy Kerrigan   1969- 199
    American Figure Skater and Olympic Silver Medalist

Alexi Lalas (Brief Entry)   1970- 206
    American Professional Soccer Player

Charlotte Lopez   1976- 209
    Puerto Rican-Born American, Miss Teen USA 1993

Wilma Mankiller   1945- 215
    Native American Principal Chief of the Cherokee Nation
    of Oklahoma

Shannon Miller   1977- 224
    American Gymnast and World Champion

Toni Morrison   1931- 230
    American Writer and Winner of the 1993 Nobel Prize
    in Literature

Richard Nixon (Obituary)   1913-1994 240
    American Former President

Greg Norman   1955- 250
    Australian Professional Golfer

Severo Ochoa (Brief Entry—Obituary)   1905-1993 259
    Spanish-Born American Scientist

River Phoenix (Obituary)   1970-1993 261
    American Actor

Elizabeth Pine (Brief Entry)   1975- 267
    American Winner of the 1993 Science Talent Search

Jonas Salk   1914- 269
    American Scientist Who Developed the First Polio Vaccine

Richard Scarry (Obituary)   1919-1994 277
   American Writer and Author of *Cars and Trucks and Things
   That Go, Richard Scarry's Best Word Book Ever,* and *What Do
   People Do All Day?*

Emmitt Smith   1969- 284
   American Professional Football Player with the Dallas Cowboys

Will Smith   1968- 292
   American Actor and Star of "The Fresh Prince of Bel-Air"

Steven Spielberg   1947- 299
   American Filmmaker and Director of *Jurassic Park*

Patrick Stewart   1940- 309
   English Actor and Star of "Star Trek: The Next Generation"

R.L. Stine   1943- 317
   American Writer and Author of "Goosebumps" and "Fear
   Street" Series

Lewis Thomas (Brief Entry—Obituary)   1913-1993 323
   American Scientist, Educator, Writer, and Physician

Barbara Walters   1931- 326
   American Broadcast Journalist and Host of "20/20"

Charlie Ward (Brief Entry)   1970- 334
   American Football and Basketball Player and Winner of
   the 1993 Heisman Trophy

Steve Young   1961- 337
   American Professional Football Player with the
   San Francisco 49ers

Kim Zmeskal   1976- 344
   American Gymnast

Photo and Illustration Credits 351

Appendix: Updates 353

Name Index 359

General Index 363

Places of Birth Index 379

Birthday Index (by month and day) 385

People to Appear in Future Issues 389

Preface

Biography Today is a publication designed and written for the young reader—aged 9 and above—and covers individuals that librarians and teachers tell us that young people want to know about most: entertainers, athletes, writers, illustrators, cartoonists, and political leaders.

Biography Today is available as a magazine and as a hardbound annual. In its first year (Volume 1, 1992) *Biography Today* was published four times. Beginning with Volume 2, 1993, *Biography Today* will be published three times a year, in January, April, and September. We have made this change to adapt our publishing schedule more closely to the school year. Despite this change in frequency, the total number of pages will not change. We had initially planned to produce four issues of approximately 100 pages each; now we plan three issues of approximately 150 pages each, with a hardbound cumulation of approximately 400 pages.

The Plan of the Work

The publication was especially created to appeal to young readers in a format they can enjoy reading and readily understand. Each issue contains approximately 20 sketches arranged alphabetically; this annual cumulation contains 51 entries. Each entry provides at least one picture of the individual profiled, and bold-faced rubrics lead the reader to information on birth, youth, early memories, education, first jobs, marriage and family, career highlights, memorable experiences, hobbies, and honors and awards. Each of the entries ends with a list of easily accessible sources designed to lead the student to further reading on the individual and a current address. Obituary entries are also included, written to provide a perspective on the individual's entire career. Obituaries are clearly marked in both the table of contents and at the beginning of the entry.

New Feature—Brief Entries

Beginning with Volume 3, *Biography Today* will include Brief Entries of approximately two pages each. These entries cover people who may not have had as much extensive media coverage as the subjects of our other profiles. Examples of people profiled in Brief Entries in Volume 3 include scientist and writer Lewis Thomas, Heisman winner Charlie Ward, and U.S. World Cup Soccer player Alexi Lalas. All brief entries are clearly marked in the table of contents and at the beginning of the entry.

Biographies are prepared by Omni editors after extensive research, utilizing the most current materials available. Those sources that are generally available to students appear in the list of further reading at the end of the sketch.

Updates

This annual cumulation contains a special Appendix featuring updates for those people covered in Volumes 1, 2, and 3 whose careers have changed significantly since we included them. For the 1994 cumulation, these individuals include Nelson Mandela, who is now the president of South Africa, Michael Jordan, who is now a minor league baseball player, and Steven Spielberg, who won an Oscar in 1994 for his film *Schindler's List*. Updates to entries are noted in the cumulative indexes.

Indexes

To provide easy access to entries, each issue of *Biography Today* contains a Name Index, a General Index covering occupations, organizations, and ethnic and minority origins, a Places of Birth Index, and a Birthday Index. These indexes cumulate with each succeeding issue. The three yearly issues are cumulated annually in the hardbound volume, with cumulative indexes.

Our Advisors

Biography Today was reviewed by an Advisory Board comprised of librarians, children's literature specialists, and reading instructors so that we could make sure that the concept of this publication—to provide a readable and accessible biographical magazine for young readers—was on target. They evaluated the title as it developed, and their suggestions have proved invaluable. Any errors, however, are ours alone. We'd like to list the Advisory Board members, and to thank them for their efforts.

Sandra Arden	Assistant Director, Retired Troy Public Library Troy, MI
Gail Beaver	Ann Arbor Huron High School Library and the University of Michigan School of Information and Library Studies Ann Arbor, MI
Marilyn Bethel	Pompano Beach Branch Library Pompano Beach, FL
Eileen Butterfield	Waterford Public Library Waterford, CT
Linda Carpino	Detroit Public Library Detroit, MI
Helen Gregory	Grosse Pointe Public Library Grosse Pointe, MI
Jane Klasing	School Board of Broward County Fort Lauderdale, FL
Marlene Lee	Broward County Public Library System Fort Lauderdale, FL

Judy Liskov	Waterford Public Library Waterford, CT
Sylvia Mavrogenes	Miami-Dade Public Library System Miami, FL
Carole J. McCollough	Wayne State University School of Library Science Detroit, MI
Deborah Rutter	Russell Library Middletown, CT
Barbara Sawyer	Groton Public Library and Information Center Groton, CT
Renee Schwartz	School Board of Broward County Fort Lauderdale, FL
Lee Sprince	Broward West Regional Library Fort Lauderdale, FL
Susan Stewart	Birney Middle School Reading Laboratory Southfield, MI
Ethel Stoloff	Librarian, Birney Middle School Library, Retired Southfield, MI

Our Advisory Board stressed to us that we should not shy away from controversial or unconventional people in our profiles, and we have tried to follow their advice. The Advisory Board also mentioned that the sketches might be useful in reluctant reader and adult literacy programs, and we would value any comments librarians and teachers might have about the suitability of our magazine for those purposes.

New Series

In response to the growing number of suggestions from our readers, we have decided to expand the *Biography Today* family of publications. *Biography Today Author Series*, to be published in 1995, will be a 200-page hardbound volume covering 20 authors of interest to the reader aged 9 and above. The length and format of the entries will be like those found in the regular issues of *Biography Today*, but there will be *no* duplication between the two publications.

Your Comments Are Welcome

Our goal is to be accurate and up-to-date, to give young readers information they can learn from and enjoy. Now we want to know what you think. Take a look at this volume of *Biography Today*, on approval. Write or call me with your comments. We want to provide an excellent source of biographical information for young people. Let us know how you think we're doing.

And here's a special incentive: review our list of people to appear in upcoming issues. Use the bind-in card to list other people you want to see in *Biography Today*. If we include someone you suggest, your library wins a free issue, with our thanks. Please see the bind-in card for details.

And take a look at the next page, where we've listed those libraries and individuals who received a free copy of *Biography Today* in 1994 for their suggestions.

Laurie Harris
Editor, *Biography Today*

CONGRATULATIONS!

Congratulations to the following individuals and libraries, who received a free copy of *Biography Today* in 1994 for suggesting people who appeared in Volume 3:

Champion R. Avecilla
San Jose, CA

Tiffany-Jenelle Bates
Machesney Park, IL

Brownsburg Public Library
Brownsburg, IN
Nancy Gwin

Camden Fairview Middle School
Camden, AR
Marva M. Marks

Central Junior High School Library,
Sand Springs, OK
Sherry Chesbro

Emily Chan
San Francisco, CA

Cimarron Middle School
Media Center
Edmond, OK

City of Inglewood Public Library
Inglewood, CA
Kay Ikuta

Joann and Ruth Collier
San Jose, CA

Alina Degtyar
Kew Gardens, NY

East China Schools
East China, MI
Janelle Cavis

East Liberty Branch Library
Pittsburgh, PA
Amy G. Korman

Eastover Elementary School
Charlotte, NC

Edmunds Middle School
Burlington, VT
Jan Hughes

Linda Eveleth
Valencia, CA

Fairfield Center Elementary
Baraboo, WI
Molly K. Fitzgerald

Fairview Elementary School
Milwaukee, WI
Dana Reinoos

Fauquier County Public Library
Warrenton, VA
Sharon Hanlon

First Colony Middle School
Sugar Land, TX
G. Jones
K. Penrod

Grace A. Dow Memorial Library
Midland, MI
Cheryl Levy

Shaquana M. Green
Hampton, VA

Highland Park Public Schools
Instructional Materials Center
Highland Park, MI
Sheila Jones

Hillcrest Elementary
Holland, PA
Terri Napierkowski

Keigwin School
Middletown, CT

Lucas Krolak
Brooklyn, NY

Laurel Springs School Library
Laurel Springs, NJ
Andrew Gersham

Anthony Litchfield
Hartford, CT

Serena Liu
Woodhaven, NY

Morrison Regional Library
Charlotte, NC
Michele L. Bowling
Ingrid Kasbo

North Miami Beach Library
North Miami Beach, FL
Sylvia Freireich

North Pocono S.D.
Moscow, PA
Marianne Cummings

Northwest Regional Library
Tampa, FL
Susan Oliver

Michelle O'Donnell
Euclid, OH

Paschal High School
Ft. Worth, TX
Cheryll Falcone

Ben Pennewell
Lawrence, KS

Matt Phelps
Niskayuna, NY

Tara Quell
Cedar Rapids, IA

River Valley Middle School
Jeffersonville, IN
Eden Kuhlenschmidt

Marianne Robinson
Butler, PA

Dana Rufo
Berwyn, IL

St. Benedict Joseph Labre
School Library
Queens, NY
Patricia Singh

Saratoga Public Library
Saratoga, NY
Rebecca O'Dunne

Scarsdale Library
Scarsdale, NY
Charlene Chan

Jo-Lin Shih
Woodhaven, NY

Stevenson Elementary
Lathrup Village, MI
Chris Jackson

Roel Suasin
Stockton, CA

Rose Talbert
Laytonville, CA

Tinker Elementary
Media Center
TAFB, OK

University City Public Library
University City, MO
Marilyn Phillips

Watertown Public Library
Watertown, WI
Kelly Raatz

Wayland Free Public Library
Wayland, MA
C. Behr

Wiley Elementary School
Hutchinson, KS
Tyler Gates

Tim Allen 1953-
American Comedian and Actor
Star of the Hit TV Series "Home Improvement"

BIRTH

Timothy Allen Dick, now known professionally as Tim Allen, was born on June 13, 1953, in Denver, Colorado. His father, Gerald, was a real estate salesman, while his mother, Martha, was a homemaker caring for a large family. Tim was the third of their six children. It was his mother who first taught him about being a man: when she would get frustrated taking care of the boys, Tim claims, "she'd insist that men were only good for two things—lawn care and vehicle maintenance."

YOUTH

Tim's early years were uneventful, spent hanging out with his father and brothers in the tool department at Sears. All that changed in November 1964, when Tim was eleven. The whole family piled into the car to attend a University of Colorado football game, but for once, Tim decided not to go along. A drunk driver hit them, crushing the driver's side of the car. His father was killed. If Allen had been sitting in his usual seat, up in front between his parents, he would have been killed as well.

It was a tough time for the family, and they all relied on one another for support. After two years, his mother married her high school boyfriend, and Tim gained a stepfather. It was a big adjustment, at first. "My stepfather came in when I was at that obstinate stage," Allen now says. "We had problems getting on the right track." Eventually, though, things worked out, and Allen now says, "He's been a terrific father."

In 1967, the new blended family, with seven boys and two girls, moved to Birmingham, Michigan, an affluent suburb of Detroit. His interests from that time come as no great surprise to his fans today: he loved all types of cars and trucks, goofing off at school, and shop class. "I loved making stuff and the smell of those places, but I hated the teachers," he once told *People* magazine. "If there was no opportunity for me to be a smart ass, then I wouldn't be happy."

EDUCATION

Voted "Class Clown" in his senior year, Allen graduated in 1971 from Seaholm High School in Birmingham, Michigan. He went on to college, first at Central Michigan University in Mount Pleasant and then at Western Michigan University in Kalamazoo. To earn spending money, Allen and a friend began to sell small amounts of drugs—a decision that he now calls "really stupid" and one that soon got him in a lot of trouble. In 1976, Allen graduated from Western Michigan University with a B.S. degree in communications.

SELLING DRUGS—AND GETTING CAUGHT

After graduation, Allen stayed in Kalamazoo and continued selling drugs, adding cocaine to his inventory. As he now says, "I didn't have any idea what I was going to do with my life, and the money was right. I was floundering, actually. That's how I got into trouble. By 1979 I was getting very worried about where I was going."

He had good reason to worry. That same year, Allen and 20 others were caught in an undercover sting operation at a Kalamazoo airport. He was arrested, charged with possession and distribution of narcotics, and thrown in jail. After 60 days in a holding cell at the county jail, Allen pleaded guilty at his arraignment and was then released on his own recognizance to await sentencing. He returned home to wait, working at a sporting goods store and hanging out at a local comedy club. One amateur night, on a dare from a friend, he got up the courage to go on stage and tell a few jokes. He was hooked, telling the club owner, "I want to do this the rest of my life."

PRISON

First, though, came the little matter of his prison term. In November 1980, Allen was sentenced to seven-and-a-half years at Sandstone Federal Correctional Institution in northern Minnesota, a minimum security prison. He was shocked—he had hoped to receive a shorter sentence because he was a first-time offender and a college graduate. Still, he was a model prisoner. He took classes, attended a rehabilitation program (even though he wasn't using drugs any more), and worked hard to maintain a positive attitude, to plan for the future, and to avoid becoming angry like so many of the other prisoners. He also quickly learned to use humor to defuse some tough situations: "Humor was the only defense I had." With time off for good behavior, he served a total of 28 months. He left prison determined to clean up his life: "Being in a penitentiary realigned everything. Sometimes you have to hit bottom to know where to go."

CHOOSING A CAREER

Where Allen went next was back home to Detroit, working first at a sporting goods store and then at an advertising agency from 1983 to 1984. At the same time he started appearing in comedy clubs and in commercials for Ford, Chevrolet, Kmart, and others, soon getting enough work to quit his advertising job. He has, to date, written, produced, or acted in more than 500 commercials. Allen spent the next decade developing a successful routine as a stand-up comedian, living on the road and traveling to different clubs on the comedy circuit.

It was at one such club, in Akron, Ohio, that Allen had the inspiration that has made him famous. At that time, much of his routine was based on jokes about prison. But one night, Allen was bombing on stage, so he started to improvise. "I was in Akron, Ohio, and the Goodyear Tire and Rubber Company was having a man's night at a comedy club. And they wouldn't listen to me because they were eating. So I said, 'Let's get in the garage, guys!' And I started this run about tools and pliers and dadohead cutting. And they just went *'Yaaah!'* and listened to me." They not only listened, they loved it; and Allen went to work on a new routine.

As Allen explains, his comedy then and now "celebrates what's cool about guys"—but without insulting or degrading women. "I have a very feminist upbringing, and I wish there was a thing called 'masculinist.' I'm starting the movement. It's a celebration of men's stuff: Gunk, gaskets, Lava soap, aluminum boats, bass fishing, big V-8s, blowing your nose with your thumb over a nostril . . . men's stuff. It doesn't represent anything anti-woman, it's just things women would never, ever think of doing or enjoying. And these things make women laugh, because they're just hysterically stupid. They go, 'If this is all you want, go ahead.'" Men's stuff, as Allen calls it, soon became the focus of his new routines—and grunting, power tools, cars, and motors of all kinds featured prominently. He joked about rewiring things, like his grandfather's hearing aid ("On a clear night, he can pick up shuttle conversations") and his grandmother's lift chair: "I must admit, I misjudged Nana's weight a little on the first shot," Allen says. "I fired her 60, 62 knots. . . . She was grabbing doilies as she went."

CAREER HIGHLIGHTS

It was that act that executives at Disney Studios caught in 1990, and they were impressed. First they offered him the lead in a couple of other sitcoms, which Allen refused. But when they developed the idea for "Home Improvement," based on the character he created for his own comedy routine, Allen was hooked.

The show went into development in early 1991 for ABC. But for a time it seemed doomed before it even aired. A newspaper got hold of the story about Allen's drug bust and imprisonment and planned to tell all. Although Allen hadn't tried to keep it a secret, he also hadn't made an effort to inform the network executives or the show's producers. Allen told the TV brass and then went public with his story. His forthrightness paid off. Impressed with his honesty, most people seemed to feel that he had made a youthful mistake which he clearly regretted, had paid his debt to society, and had earned a second chance.

"HOME IMPROVEMENT"

That chance came in September 1991, when "Home Improvement" first aired. Originally sandwiched into the Tuesday night lineup between "Full House" and "Roseanne," the show was a hit from the start. It features Allen as Tim "The Toolman" Taylor, the host of a local TV do-it-yourself show, his wife Jill (Patricia Richardson), their three sons, Brad (Zachary Ty Bryan), Randy (Jonathan Taylor Thomas), and Mark (Taran Smith), their neighbor, Wilson (Earl Hindman), and their friend Al Borland (Richard Karn), Tim's assistant on his cable TV show, "Tool Time." For some viewers, its classic family values are its greatest appeal, "a comedy where the father is a hero," according to executive producer Matt Williams, "a dad who has a good relationship with his sons." For others, its best feature is its depiction of what it means to be a man in America today.

A celebration and parody of maleness, "Home Improvement" portrays both the work life and home life of Tim Taylor, giving the audience a splendidly balanced view. At work, on his show "Tool Time," Taylor is almost a parody of the swaggering, macho male, grunting and calling for "More power!" At home with his family, though, a different side emerges. Though he tries to act cool and always in control, he is sometimes uncertain in his relationships with his young sons and his good-humored, self-assured, and well-grounded wife. And he is also obsessed with power tools, although, unfortunately, Tim's projects around the house often end badly, with either a visit from the fire department or a trip to the hospital emergency room. But throughout these adventures it is always clear that this family loves and cherishes one other.

Allen's genius as a comedian brings together a diverse audience to laugh at his antics. "Home Improvement" has consistently demonstrated its broad appeal to male, female, and younger viewers: kids watch it for the silliness, while their parents enjoy the relationship between Jill and Tim. The show did so well in the ratings that the network changed its time slot in its second season, to be the anchor show for their Wednesday night lineup. Even though it first aired opposite the critically acclaimed and popular series "Seinfeld," it proved to be a phenomenal success. Since its premiere, "Home Improvement" has consistently ranked in the Top 10 hits, and it currently ranks No. 1, the most watched show in the country.

MARRIAGE AND FAMILY

Allen was married on April 7, 1984, to Laura Deibel, his college girlfriend. Throughout the tough times earlier in his life—being arrested, going to prison, spending years on the road trying to make it as a comedian—Laura stood behind him and supported him, and Allen frequently expresses gratitude, love, and bewilderment at her support. According to Laura, "We loved each other. It was that simple." They have one daughter, Kady, now age four.

The irony that Mr. Toolman himself has a daughter and no

sons is not lost on him. When asked about it, Allen responded, "When we did the ultrasound and they said 'It's a little girl,' I went, 'Ohhh.' I actually made that sound. Like I'd opened the wrong Christmas present. Three people in the room said, 'What was that all about?' My wife goes, 'what's ohhh for?' I went, 'Oh, I was clearing my throat. Oh, look! A girl! Dresses and parties and a friend to you! Look at that!' I was very disappointed. And now, of course, I feel guilty in front of God. This girl is so much pleasure to me that it's incredible. I go to other guys' houses and their little boys are . . . monsters. The difference is night and day. . . . I keep thinking that she—any kid—could potentially ruin or rule the world. What a responsibility. And there's no manual."

The family has two homes. Until recently they lived in Beverly Hills, Michigan, near Birmingham, where Allen grew up. Although they still consider Michigan their true home, they have also purchased a house in the San Fernando Valley in Southern California, where they live when Tim is taping "Home Improvement." What clinched the deal on their new four-bedroom, 5,500 square foot house, according to Allen, was the barbecue patio: "There's a rotisserie, a fireplace, two grills, a sink, and a meat locker. A meat locker. So you don't have to walk four steps into the kitchen. I loved that."

HOBBIES AND OTHER INTERESTS

Unlike his alter ego Tim "The Toolman" Taylor, Tim Allen really is handy at home repairs, including spending about ten years remodeling his house in Michigan. But in other respects Allen is, in fact, quite similar to the character he plays—he loves men's stuff. Allen likes to read do-it-yourself magazines like *Popular Mechanics* and to work on his collection of high performance cars which, at last count, included a Ferrari, a couple of Cadillacs, two Jeeps, and a big, souped-up GMC Typhoon truck that's perfect for hauling supplies for home projects. Lately he's been working on a high-powered 1993 Mustang with nearly 600 horsepower—"the more horsepower the better," according to Allen. "As a kid, I used to go to auto shows and look at prototype cars and wonder what it would be like to build them. Now some of my dreams are coming true." His current TV success, of course, has given him the financial means to make those dreams come true and to buy all the toys he ever wanted, like his collection of high-tech audio and video equipment and his collection of power tools. His tool shed alone contains nine with combustion motors: a big John Deere tractor, a mulcher, a blower, a Rototiller, two weed whackers, and three lawn mowers.

These days, of course, Allen doesn't have much time for yard work. But he does take every opportunity, whenever "Home Improvement" has a break in filming, to do stand-up comedy shows. The comedy in his live shows, according to reviewers, has a sharper edge than that on his TV series, featuring a lot of explicit language and sexual innuendo that he saves for an adult audience.

CREDITS

"Men Are Pigs," 1990 (cable special)
"Home Improvement," 1991- (TV series)
"Tim Allen Rewires America," 1991 (cable special)

HONORS AND AWARDS

American Comedy Awards: 1989, Best Male Comic
ACE Award: 1990, for Best Performance in a Comedy Special in "Just for Laughs: The Montreal International Comedy Festival"
People's Choice Awards: 1992, Favorite Male Performer in a New TV Series; 1993, 1994 (2 awards), Favorite Male TV Performer

FURTHER READING

BOOKS

Who's Who in America, 1994

PERIODICALS

Ladies Home Journal, Feb. 1992, p.46; Dec. 1992, p.44; Dec. 1993, p.112
People, July 6, 1992, p.105
TV Guide, Nov. 9, 1991, p.8
US, Nov. 1991, p.65
USA Today, Aug. 16, 1991, p.D1

ADDRESS

Disney Studios
"Home Improvement"
500 South Buena Vista Street
Burbank, CA 91521-2215

OBITUARY

Marian Anderson 1897-1993
American Classical, Opera, and Spiritual Singer
First Black American to Sing at the White
House and to Sing with the Metropolitan Opera

BIRTH

Marian Anderson was born February 17, 1897, in Philadelphia, Pennsylvania. (Throughout her professional career she gave her birth date as February 27, 1902, but the earlier date and year were verified on her birth certificate after her death.) She was the first child of John Anderson, who sold ice and coal, and Anna Anderson, who had been a school teacher before the birth of her children. Marian had two younger sisters, Alyce and Ethel.

EARLY MEMORIES

Anderson always loved music and began to sing at three. In her autobiography, *My Lord, What a Morning*, she tells of how she "sat at the table or on a little bench, beating out some sort of rhythm with my hands and feet and la-la-la-ing a vocal accompaniment. Some people might say that these were the first signs of music in me. I would only say that I felt cozy and happy."

EARLY MUSIC BACKGROUND

Marian was singing in the choir at the Union Baptist Church in Philadelphia by the time she was six. By the time she was eight, she had earned her first fee—50 cents—for singing at church. Flyers circulated in her neighborhood bid audiences to "Come and hear the baby contralto" at Union Baptist.

Even as a child, Marian Anderson had an incredible range—three octaves—and she was able to sing all four parts in hymns—soprano, alto, tenor, and bass. In her career as a singer, Anderson sang as a contralto, the range between the tenor and the alto voice, but even as a young girl, she sang well outside that range. By the time she was 13, she was singing in the adult choir at her church, and if one of the soloists in any voice part couldn't perform, Marian sang the piece.

She loved instrumental music, too. When she was eight, her father bought a piano from his brother, and Marian began to play. She also bought a violin, saving her earnings from scrubbing steps (five cents for a whole set), and buying a violin for $3.98 that the owner claimed was "just short of being a Stradivarius." She played it till it fell apart.

YOUTH

John Anderson died of a brain tumor when Marian was 12, and the deeply grieving family moved in with John's parents. Anderson said in her autobiography that she knew at her father's death that "tragedy had moved into our house." She remembered her strong-willed paternal grandmother as "a large woman used to being the boss of her own house and the people in it," who was a domineering force in the lives of her grandchildren and their mother.

Marian's mother went to work right after her husband died, working as a domestic laborer, cleaning stores, and taking in laundry. The children helped whenever they could, delivering laundry or pitching in at home. Anderson remained devoted to her mother and credited this humble, hardworking woman with giving her the strength to face all the challenges of life.

EDUCATION—SCHOOL AND MORE MUSIC

Anderson attended local grade schools in Philadelphia. She did well in school, enjoying spelling bees and speech classes and joining the Camp Fire Girls. She first attended high school at William Penn High School, taking commercial courses like typing and shorthand to prepare her for a clerical job. But she knew that most of all she wanted to study music. She sang in the school chorus and once, when performing a solo, so impressed an influential member of the community that he claimed "I don't understand why this girl is taking shorthand and typewriting. She should have a straight college preparatory course and do as much as possible in music." Anderson was transferred to South Philadelphia High School, where the principal, Dr. Lucy Wilson, took a special interest in her.

When she was 15, Anderson first encountered the racism that was to plague her career. She was denied the right to apply to a Philadelphia music school because, the clerk told her, "we don't take colored." The experience stunned her. "It was my first contact with the blunt, brutal words, and this school of music was the last place I expected to hear them. True enough, my skin was different, but not my feelings."

But further music education was to come her way. When she was 16, Roland Hayes, a distinguished black tenor, sang with Marian at a concert at Union Baptist, and he encouraged her to take lessons. Unfortunately, her grandmother's response was that Marian already knew how to sing and didn't need lessons, and her mother felt she couldn't fight the decision of the grandmother. Still, others pressed the issue. John Thomas Butler, a Philadelphia actor, also heard Marian and introduced her to Mary S. Patterson, a well-known soprano in Philadelphia who took Marian as a student, waiving her usual fee for her promising pupil.

With Patterson, Anderson began to truly study music, to train her voice and develop the technique on which all professional vocal performance depends. She learned how to breathe properly so that air circulates in the head to create a resonant effect. She performed vocal exercises to develop her range and to help her to sound each note correctly. She learned how to enunciate words so that they could be clearly heard. Above all, she learned "that the purpose of all the exercises and labors was to give you a thoroughly reliable foundation and to make sure you could do your job under any circumstances There is no shortcut. You must understand the how and why of what you are doing."

Anderson began performing in local clubs, churches, and YMCAs, sometimes receiving fees, sometimes not. When she made $5 for a performance, she gave her mother two, her sisters one dollar each, and kept one for expenses.

Anderson's next teacher was Agnes Reifsnyder, a contralto, who helped her with the lower tones in her voice. Her high school principal then arranged an audition with the well-known voice teacher Giuseppe Boghetti, who at first claimed he had no time or room for a new pupil. But after hearing Anderson sing "Deep River," he made time. He was her vocal teacher for years.

Under Boghetti, Anderson developed both the voice and repertoire for which she became famous. He introduced her to the *lieder,* or songs, of Franz Schubert, which became lifelong favorites, as well as the works of Johannes Brahms, Robert Schumann, George Friedrich Handel, Hugo Wolf, Richard Strauss, and Claude Debussy. She began to tour with her first accompanist, Billy King. They played churches, colleges, and schools throughout the Mid-Atlantic states, including the South, earning from $50 to $100 per performance. By the time she was 20, she was able to buy a house for her family in Philadelphia.

It was while touring the South with Billy King that Anderson once again came face to face with the racism that severely and cruelly limited the lives of blacks in the U.S. at the time. The South was then under what were known as "Jim Crow" laws, which designated separate facilities for blacks and whites. These laws allowed businesses—hotels, concert halls, trains, etc.—to discriminate against blacks and to deny them service solely because of their skin color. With the dignity and sense of fortitude that became her trademark, Anderson continued to perform.

At this time in her career, she thought she was ready for the additional challenge of a debut in New York, and she prepared a performance for the Town Hall. The concert didn't go well—there were few people in the hall, and she was not in good voice. The bad reviews and other aspects of the experience almost made Anderson give up her career. But she persevered.

CAREER HIGHLIGHTS

In 1923, Anderson won first prize in the Philadelphia Philharmonic Society vocal contest. She was the first black to win, and the event gained her a larger audience. In 1925, she won another, and more significant, vocal contest, the National Music League competition in New York City. The first prize winner, chosen from a field of 300 singers, won the chance to give a performance with the New York Philharmonic. Her concert with the Philharmonic was greeted with great reviews, including this notice from the *New York Times*: "Miss Anderson made an excellent impression. She is endowed by nature with a voice of unusual compass, color, and dramatic capacity. The lower tones have a warm contralto quality, but the voice has the range and resources of the mezzo-soprano."

TO EUROPE

But the National Music League prize didn't bring Anderson an increased demand for her performances. She decided to realize a long-held goal to study in Europe, which she was able to do through a scholarship given by the National Association of Negro Musicians. She studied music, and particularly languages, in her first year abroad. She returned to the U.S. briefly, and then, with funds provided by a Rosenwald scholarship, she returned to Europe for more training and concerts.

In 1933, while studying in Germany, she was approached by a German music promoter, who offered to produce a concert for her at a cost to the singer of $500. She agreed, and the concert was a success. In particular, it proved to be an important moment in her career, for it garnered the attention of a Scandinavian promoter, who scheduled her for a series of concerts in Norway, Finland, and Sweden, where she was a smashing success. She continued to tour Europe for several years. Her accompanist at this time was a Finnish pianist named Kosti Vehanen, who encouraged her to learn the songs of the contemporary Finnish composer Jean Sibelius. It was also Vehanen who encouraged her to perform for the maestro.

They were invited to coffee at Sibelius's home, where she sang one of his songs. When she was finished, Anderson recalled, Sibelius "strode to my side, and threw his arms around me in a hearty embrace. 'My roof is too low for you,' he said, and then he called out in a loud voice to his wife, 'Not coffee, but champagne.'"

Accolades came from other famous members of the music community during that tour. While in Salzburg, Austria, to sing a concert, she was visited by the great conductor Arturo Toscanini, who claimed "Yours is a voice such as one hears once in a hundred years." On that same tour, Anderson came to the attention of Sol Hurok, the famed impresario, who offered to manage her career. She accepted.

TRIUMPHANT RETURN TO THE U.S.

Anderson returned to the United States in 1935, where she also reappeared at the scene of one of her earlier failures, New York City's Town Hall. But this time the hall, and the town, were hers. Despite the fact that her foot was in a cast—she had fallen down stairs on the ship on the way home—she triumphed. "Let it be said," wrote Howard Taubman of the *New York Times*, "Marian Anderson has returned to her native land one of the great singers of our time."

Her career firmly established, Anderson began a grueling concert schedule, often giving as many as 100 recitals a year. She traveled all over the world, drawing from a repertoire that included some 200 songs in 9 languages and always featuring operatic arias and spirituals.

Continuing to break new ground, she became the first black to sing at the White House, when First Lady Eleanor Roosevelt invited her to perform before the King and Queen of England in 1936. Her name would be linked to Roosevelt's again, under very different circumstances.

CONSTITUTION HALL AND THE D.A.R.

This great singer, whose strength and humility marked everything she did, became the center of controversy in 1939, when her manager tried to book her for a performance in Constitution Hall in Washington, D.C. The hall, one of the most important in the country, was run by the D.A.R. (Daughters of the American Revolution), a conservative women's group that did not allow blacks to perform in the hall. As noted in the *New York Times*, "it was a particularly unfortunate display of prejudice that helped to make Miss Anderson a household name." Outraged at the decision, Eleanor Roosevelt resigned from the D.A.R., and Interior Secretary Harold Ickes arranged for Anderson to sing at the Lincoln Memorial.

On Easter Sunday, April 9, 1939, Anderson gave a concert on the steps of the Lincoln Memorial for 75,000 adoring fans, including members of congress, cabinet secretaries, justices of the Supreme Court, the head of the NAACP (National Association for the Advancement of Colored People), and religious leaders from the Washington area. She reached the platform amidst the tumultuous applause, closed her eyes, folded her hands, and began with "America." She followed with Schubert's "Ave Maria," operatic arias, and closed with the spirituals for which she was so deservedly famous. These special songs created a hush over the audience, "a silence instinctive, natural and intense," wrote Vincent Sheean, "so that you were afraid to breathe."

Anderson wrote about the matter in her autobiography: "What were my own feelings? I was saddened and ashamed. I was sorry for the people who had precipitated the affair. I felt that their behavior stemmed from a lack of understanding. They were not persecuting me personally or as a representative of my people so much as they were doing something that was neither sensible nor good." Despite the uproar in the press, this humble, private woman stayed above the fray. "I did not feel that I was designed for hand-to-hand combat," was the way she phrased it. The concert was later immortalized in a mural that can be seen in the office of the Department of the Interior.

Four years later, Marian Anderson did sing in Constitution Hall, at the invitation of the D.A.R., for a relief effort during the Second World War. Yet she continued to face prejudice: she was once given the key to Atlantic City, but couldn't stay in a hotel there. She also continued to fight back. She refused to allow the segregated seating mandated in many Southern towns for her concerts, insisting instead on a system known as "vertical seating," where blacks were allowed to sit in every part of the performance hall.

MET DEBUT

In 1955, Anderson broke another racial barrier, becoming the first black to sing with the Metropolitan Opera in New York. It is hard to believe today, when the talents of such great black divas as Jessye Norman, Leontyne Price, and Kathleen Battle grace the world's opera stages, that just forty years ago there were no black singers at the Met. When Anderson, singing the role of Ulrica in Giuseppe Verdi's "Un Ballo en Maschera," appeared on stage on opening night, January 7, 1955, she was greeted with a standing ovation that went on and on before she even sang a note.

MUSICAL AMBASSADOR

In 1957, Anderson sang at the inauguration of President Dwight D. Eisenhower. That same year, under the sponsorship of the State Department, she began a 12-nation tour of the Far East, during which she became the first black to sing for the Japanese Imperial court in its 2,600-year history. She was greeted everywhere with acclaim. Her tour became the subject of a television special entitled "The Lady from Philadelphia," produced and broadcast by Edward R. Murrow on his famous news show, "See It Now." In 1958, Anderson was named a special delegate to the United Nations Human Rights Committee by Eisenhower.

In 1961, she sang at another presidential inauguration, this time for the newly elected John F. Kennedy. In 1964, she began her farewell tour at Constitution Hall, which concluded in 1965 in a final concert at Carnegie Hall that marked her retirement from the stage. But she continued to give occasional benefit concerts for such groups as the NAACP, the Congress of Racial Equality, and for the Jobs and Freedom March on Washington.

HOBBIES AND OTHER INTERESTS

Anderson funded a major musical award, the Marian Anderson Award, in the 1940s. It began when she was awarded the Bok Prize in 1941, which at that time was given to Philadelphia's most outstanding citizen. She was the first black and only the second woman to receive it. With the $10,000 prize money she began the scholarship program that continues to bear her name. It is given annually to a promising young vocalist and carries a monetary award of $25,000. It has furthered the careers of such great black opera singers as Grace Bumbry and Florence Quivar.

MEMORABLE EXPERIENCES

Anderson recalled in her autobiography that "the happiest day in my life was when I told my mother she didn't need to work any more." Anderson was finally making enough money to support her family, and she called her mother's supervisor at the department store where she cleaned in the evenings and told her, politely but firmly, that her mother would not be back.

MARRIAGE AND FAMILY

Anderson married Orpheus Fisher, whose nickname was King, in 1943. They had no children. They lived on a 100-acre farm in Danbury, Connecticut. King died in 1986, and in 1992, Anderson went to live with her nephew, James DePriest, who is the music director of the Oregon Symphony. She died in Portland of congestive heart failure on April 8, 1993.

LEGACY AND INSPIRATION

The opera star Jessye Norman said this at Anderson's death: "Marian Anderson was the personification of all that is wonderful, simple, pure, and majestic in the human spirit. She wore the glorious crown of her voice with the grace of an empress. I have loved her all my life."

HONORS AND AWARDS

Spingarn Medal (NAACP): 1939
Bok Prize (City of Philadelphia): 1941
Presidential Medal of Freedom: 1963
Kennedy Center Award for Lifetime Achievement in the Arts: 1978
Eleanor Roosevelt Human Rights Award of the City of New York: 1984
National Arts Medal: 1986
Grammy Lifetime Achievement Award: 1991

SELECTED RECORDINGS

Marian Anderson Sings Beloved Schubert, 1951
Marian Anderson: Songs and Arias by Bach, Handel, Schubert, Schumann, Brahms, Strauss, Verdi; Negro Spirituals, 1954

Marian Anderson, 1964
Jus' Keep on Singin', 1965
Spirituals, 1976
Marian Anderson: Bach, Brahms, Schubert, 1989
Marian Anderson, 1990
Tribute: Marian Anderson, 1993

WRITINGS

My Lord, What a Morning, 1956

FURTHER READING

BOOKS

Anderson, Marian. *My Lord, What a Morning,* 1956
Richardson, Ben, and William A. Fahey. *Great Black Americans,* 1976
Story, Rosalyn M. *And So I Sing: African-American Divas of Opera and Concert,* 1990
Tedards, Anne. *Marian Anderson,* 1988 (juvenile)

PERIODICALS

Current Biography Yearbook 1950
New York Times, Apr. 9, 1993, p.A1; Apr. 18, 1993, p.23
New York Times Biographical Service, Feb. 1977, p.177
Opera News, July 1993, p.54
Smithsonian, June 1993, p.14
Variety, Apr. 19, 1993, p.59

Mario Andretti 1940-
Italian-Born American Professional
Race Car Driver
One of the Greatest Drivers of All Time
The Only Driver Ever to Win the Indy 500,
the Daytona 500, and the Formula One
World Championship

BIRTH

Mario Gabriele Andretti was born on February 28, 1940, in Montona, Italy, a small town near Trieste. His parents were Alvise Luigi (called Gigi) and Rina (Giovanelli) Andretti. Mario has an identical twin brother, Aldo, and an older sister, Anna Maria.

YOUTH

When Mario and Aldo were born, the Andretti family lived on a farm in Montona, near the Adriatic Sea on the border between Italy and what was then Yugoslavia. Gigi Andretti's family owned a large tract of land, and he worked as an administrator on the family farm, managing the farm and supervising the 21 families that lived and worked there.

But World War II was just starting in Europe then, and the family soon lost everything. Following the war, their land became part of Yugoslavia, and their town, Montona, became Motovun (in what is now Croatia). Yugoslavia was then under Communist rule, and the family land was taken over by the state. Gigi Andretti, who as manager of the family farm had essentially worked for himself, now worked for the government. At first they had no choice, but in 1948 they were offered the option to leave. Both to escape Communist rule and to keep their Italian citizenship, the family decided to leave their home.

Taking just what they could carry, the Andrettis moved back to Italy in 1948. Along with hundreds of other refugee families from all over central Europe, they stayed in a relief camp for displaced persons in Lucca, in west/central Italy. For four years, they shared their rooms with 17 other families. Over time, the family moved into what was considered, under the circumstances, luxurious quarters: two small adjoining rooms, one for the grandparents, and one for Gigi, Rina, and their three children.

EARLY MEMORIES

Even when he was very young, Andretti was aware of the family's difficult circumstances. As he recalls, "There are some things you never forget, no matter how hard you try. For instance, one of my earliest memories is of my mother crying. I was too young to comprehend, but since the young live by instinct, I didn't need to know why. To me it was simple. My mother was crying; therefore the situation was bad."

CHOOSING A CAREER

It was while living at the refugee camp in Lucca that Andretti first fell in love with racing. With no toys, he and his brother Aldo used to create their own imaginary games. They liked to climb into the top bunk, pull the covers over their heads, and pretend they were race car drivers. And after a while, some of those imaginary games started to come true. They started out by hanging around a garage in Lucca, talking the owners into letting them park cars—even though they were only 13 and could barely see over the dashboard.

The owners were also race fans, and one year they took the boys to the Mille Miglia, a 1,000-mile race around Italy that passed near Florence, some 70 miles away. For Andretti, "I really don't think I can describe my feeling. It was as if I was *living* for the first time." Others shared this feeling. In Italy, racing is phenomenally popular, and drivers are national heroes. One of the most famous drivers at the Mille Miglia, Alberto Ascari, soon became his idol. As Andretti later recalled, "I can even tell you when it all fell into place, when I knew beyond a shadow of a doubt that my future would be chained to racing. It was after the 1954 Grand Prix of Monza. Ascari drove against Juan Manuel Fangio in a thrilling wheel-to-wheel duel that lasted for most of the race; the entire nation talked of nothing else.

"Before that race I *wanted* to be a race driver. After that race I *had* to be a race driver."

He soon got his chance. The Italian government was funding a new program called Formula Junior Racing, using small copies of Formula One cars, similar to go-karts. The plan was to train and develop young Italian drivers for Grand Prix racing. Mario and Aldo convinced the garage owners to let them use a car and entered the world of auto racing. Every other weekend they swapped driving and crewing their little single seater, with an 85 horsepower engine whose top speed was about 90 miles per hour. Their father hated racing, and they had to make up stories to explain their absences. Still, as Mario recalls, "We had a ball."

MOVING TO THE UNITED STATES

The boys were happy—unlike the rest of the family. In the impoverished economy of post-war Italy, Gigi Andretti had been unable to find steady work during their seven years in Lucca, and they lived on a government subsidy plus occasional odd jobs. When their request for a visa to the United States was approved in 1955, three years after they first applied, the choice was clear. To many Europeans struggling to rebuild their lives after the devastation of war, America was the promised land. Hoping to create a better life for their children, Rina and Gigi Andretti decided to move to Nazareth, Pennsylvania, where Rina's uncle lived. They arrived in New York Harbor on June 16, 1955, steaming past the Statue of Liberty.

Of course, the boys were crushed, thinking they were leaving their dreams of auto racing behind. What they didn't know was that they were moving to a local racing center. The oval dirt track at Nazareth Speedway hosted events that attracted national racing stars. And for two poor teenagers, it proved to be a far more accessible entree into the world of auto racing than European Grand Prix racing ever would have been. "It was the first time we had seen oval racing," Andretti recalls. "We were impressed—mainly because it looked like something we could do. From that moment, the master plan was conceived. We were going to build a stock car and go racing, American-style."

Mario and Aldo went to work in a service station and started meeting all the local drivers. The stock car they built was a modified 1948 Hudson Hornet, assembled with advice from all who offered. With Aldo driving, they entered their first race on April 25, 1959—and won. Mario's turn to drive came the following week, and he also won. Despite a growing reputation for wildness, the brothers continued to race their own car, and even started getting offers to drive other cars as well. Their luck gave out in the last race of the 1959 season. Aldo was involved in a dreadful crash that fractured his skull and put him in the hospital in a coma for about two weeks. It was the first of two serious wrecks that eventually forced Aldo to retire from racing in 1969.

EDUCATION

School was never Andretti's first love. While still in Italy, he had attended a technical school in Lucca, studying auto mechanics. When he enrolled in school in the U.S., he expected to be placed as a high-school sophomore. But with his poor English-language skills, the school district decided to bump him back to seventh grade. It was humiliating, and Andretti ended up dropping out of school. He later completed his high school requirements, earning his diploma through correspondence courses. He had the help of a tutor, Dee Ann Hoch, who became his wife in 1961.

CAREER HIGHLIGHTS

Throughout his 35-year racing career, Andretti has demonstrated his intense competitive spirit in all areas of auto racing. "I love race cars and that's why I get involved with so many different types of them," he once said. "I admire versatility more than any other skill in racing. I always wanted to be an all-around driver, a man who can handle any kind of equipment on any kind of track." And racing enthusiasts agree that Andretti has proven himself to be one of the most versatile drivers in racing history, winning on all types of surfaces—dirt tracks, ovals, city streets, even mountain peaks—and in all types of races—stock cars, sprints, midgets, Indy cars, and Formula One.

After starting out with modified stock cars in the late 1950s, Andretti switched to sprint and midget cars from 1961 to 1963. He won his first important victory on March 3, 1962, in a 35-lap midget race in New Jersey. In 1964, he caught the attention of Clint Brawner, chief mechanic and pit boss for Al Dean, a major race car sponsor. Brawner was so impressed with Andretti's driving skill, his knowledge of cars, and his ability to work with the crew that he hired Andretti to drive for Al Dean. This was Andretti's big break. It meant that he would be driving on the U.S. Auto Club (USAC) Championship Trail, a year-long series of big-money events for full-size race cars, or Indy cars. The cars are expensive and well-maintained, the mechanics are the best, and the money prizes are lucrative. The best known of these races is the Indianapolis 500, the world's most prestigious oval-track race for Indy cars. In his first Indy car event, a 100-mile race late in the 1964 season in Trenton, New Jersey, Andretti finished eleventh.

The following year, 1965, marked the start of a string of successful seasons. In addition to six second-place finishes and three thirds, he won his first Indy-car race, the Hoosier Grand Prix, a 150-mile race at Indianapolis Raceway Park. In his first appearance at the Indianapolis 500, he placed third—an outstanding finish for a rookie driver. His record that season won him the Rookie of the Year award and the national USAC Indy Car championship, calculated from the number of points earned throughout the season on the U.S. Auto Club trail. He won the championship title again in 1966, with eight wins out of fifteen, and was the fastest qualifier that year at Indianapolis.

During the next three years alone, he won 21 Indy car events, the 1967 Daytona 500 stock car race, and the 1967 Sebring Twelve-Hour Endurance race. He also took the pole at his first Formula One Grand Prix, at Watkins Glen, New York, in 1968. The following year proved to be his best racing season ever. In 1969, for what would be his only success in 29 attempts, Andretti won the Indianapolis 500 and finished off the season by again

taking the championship. For these accomplishments, he was named Driver of the Year.

Soon afterward, Andretti changed his emphasis a bit. He continued to compete on the USAC trail, but primarily focused on his first love, road racing, driving in endurance races and Formula One events. He racked up two more wins at Sebring in 1970 and 1972 and won his first Formula One event in 1971 in South Africa. In 1974, he won the USAC Dirt Track championship. In 1977 he became the first U.S. driver to win a Formula One race in America, at the U.S. Grand Prix West in Long Beach, California. The following year, 1978, Andretti won the biggest prize in international auto racing, the Formula One world championship. He was the first driver ever to win both the Indianapolis and Formula One championships, again earning the Driver of the Year award.

After several more seasons of international competition, Andretti returned to full-time Indy car racing. Since 1980, he has won 19 Indy car races. In 1984, he won the Indy car championship and was again named Driver of the Year, the only person to ever win this award in three consecutive decades. He was honored as Driver of the Quarter Century in 1992. With his 1993 Indy car win in the Phoenix 200, Andretti became the first driver to win races in five decades. The 1994 season, called the "Arrivederci, Mario" tour, marks Andretti's final year in Indy car racing. While he plans to retire at the end of the season from the Indy car circuit, he has expressed interest in driving in the LeMans, a 24-hour endurance event.

It is perhaps too early to judge Andretti's place in history. While racing fans typically praise his drive, intensity, fearlessness, determination, and competitive spirit, they differ in their evaluations of his career. His detractors point to his repeated unsuccessful attempts to win the Indianapolis 500. Andretti's bad luck at the Brickyard, as the Indy Raceway is known, is legendary. Faulty equipment, engine breakdowns, accidents, fuel problems, spinouts—he's seen it all. The Indy 500 is such an important race that his single win in 29 starts disqualifies him, according to some, from the front rank of his sport. His supporters, meanwhile, call him the greatest race car driver of his time. They emphasize the sheer magnitude of his wins—52 Indy car wins (second on the all-time list to A.J. Foyt's 67), 12 Formula One wins, 36 other major wins, 4-time Indy car champion, Grand Prix champion, and USAC Dirt Track champion. He is still the only driver to win the Indy 500, the Daytona 500, and the Formula One world championship.

Let's leave it to his own son Michael, now a famous race car driver himself, to reflect on Andretti's career: "There's nobody who has achieved what he has achieved, and nobody ever will. There are some who might equal him in some categories, but when you spread it out over different types of race cars, there's nobody who's going to achieve what he did.

"Sprint cars, midgets, Pike's Peak, Daytona 500, Indy 500, world championship. . . . He's always been my hero."

MAJOR INFLUENCES

Andretti considers Italian race car driver Alberto Ascari, who he saw as a child in Italy, to be his most important influence. "Ascari was a national hero," he says. "And he was my man. For me, no other driver existed. I read everything I could find about him and lived and died through every one of his races. If I had to pick the person who had the strongest influence on my life, it would be Ascari—a man I never met."

MARRIAGE AND FAMILY

Mario married Dee Ann Hoch on November 25, 1961. They have three children: Michael, Jeffrey, and Barbra Dee, and three grandchildren: Marco, Marissa, and Miranda. The family home is a five-bedroom split-level in Nazareth, Pennsylvania, but they spend much of their time on their 640-acre vacation retreat, a former resort in the Poconos Mountains, complete with a lake.

HOBBIES AND OTHER INTERESTS

For the most part, Andretti's hobbies reflect his love of speed. In addition to fishing and golf, he enjoys water skiing, power boating, snowmobiling, motorcycling, and flying ultra-light airplanes. He also flies a Lockheed Jetstar 731 and his personal cars include a Lamborghini Diablo and Countach, a Mercedes 600 SEL, a Chevy Corvette, a Ford Bronco, and a Ford van.

WRITINGS

What's It Like Out There? 1970 (with Bob Collins)

HONORS AND AWARDS

- 1965: USAC Indy Car World Series champion; Indianapolis 500 Rookie of the Year
- 1966: USAC Indy Car World Series champion; Indianapolis 500 pole winner
- 1967: Indianapolis 500 pole winner; Daytona 500 winner
- 1969: USAC Indy Car World Series champion; Indianapolis 500 winner; Driver of the Year
- 1974: USAC Dirt Track champion
- 1978: World Grand Prix champion (Formula I); Driver of the Year
- 1979: International Race of Champions (IROC VI) titlist
- 1984: CART/PPG Indy Car World Series champion; Driver of the Year

1987: Indianapolis 500 pole winner
1989: Indy Car "Triple Crown" winner
1992: Driver of the Quarter Century

CAREER TOTALS

52 Indy Car wins, second on all-time list behind A.J. Foyt's 67
12 Formula One wins
36 Other Major wins, including USAC sprint cars, USAC midgets, NASCAR stock cars, sports cars, USAC stock cars, drag racing, Formula One, USAC dirt cars, Formula 5000, and IROC

FURTHER READING

BOOKS

Andretti, Mario, with Bob Collins. *What's It Like Out There?* 1970
Burchard, Marshall. *Sports Hero: Mario Andretti,* 1977
Great Athletes: The Twentieth Century, Vol. 1, 1992
Grolier Library of North American Biographies: Athletes, Vol. 2, 1994
Lincoln Library of Sports Champions, Vol. 1, 1985
Who's Who in America, 1994

PERIODICALS

Car and Driver, Sep. 1989, p.145
Current Biography Yearbook 1968
Esquire, Oct. 24, 1978, p.39
The National, May 23, 1990, p.17
New York Times Biographical Service, May 1984, p.591
People, Aug. 28, 1978, p.37; May 28, 1984, p.60
Sports Illustrated, June 30, 1986, p.58; May 11, 1992, p.78

ADDRESS

Mario Andretti
Nazareth, PA 18064

BRIEF ENTRY

Ned Andrews 1980-
American Winner of the 1994 National Spelling Bee

EARLY YEARS

Ned G. Andrews was born November 12, 1980, in Oakridge, Tennessee, to Carolyn Andrews, a technical editor, and Andy Andrews, an electrical engineer. Ned has two brothers.

MAJOR ACCOMPLISHMENTS

THE NATIONAL SPELLING BEE

The National Spelling Bee is sponsored by the Scripps Howard media organization. Spellers can compete through their eighth grade year. More than nine million students take part in regional contests each year, and competitors come from the U.S., Mexico, Guam, Puerto Rico, the Virgin Islands, and Defense Department Schools in Germany.

Ned had already competed in the 1992 and 1993 National Spelling Bees when he made the final in the 1994 competition, while he was in the seventh grade. Having made it through two days of competition that included some 1,068 words, with such mind-benders as "dyskinesia, proboscis, and naiad," Ned was in the 15th and final round. The 13-year-old stood up and with full authority spelled "antediluvian" to win the title, beating out 237 other contenders.

Afterwards, he met with reporters to talk about himself and his victory. How did he triumph this time, after two losses? "That's a good question," the young champ replied. "I guess it's just like me to keep trying on something like this." He names his parents as his heroes, and says that, although he has no professional coach, his mother helps. "And," he added, "she ought to be paid." He said that his good spelling "helped getting the teachers to be nice to me." His advice to other Spelling Bee hopefuls is to "read everything," but suggested that "extremely, awfully bad spellers give it up."

As champion, Ned wins $5,000, a $1,000 savings bond, and a trip to Disney World.

Ned will begin eighth grade this year at Webb School in Knoxville, Tennessee. He also likes geography and placed 11th at this year's National Geography Bee. His favorite subject is Latin, and he would like to be a doctor or a lawyer.

FURTHER READING

Commercial Appeal, June 3, 1994, p.B10
New Orleans Time Picayune, June 3, 1994, p.A16
Oregonian, June 4, 1994, p.A18

ADDRESS

Scripps Howard National Spelling Bee
P.O. Box 5380
Cincinnati, OH 45201

Yasir Arafat 1929-
Palestinian Chairman of the Palestine Liberation Organization

BIRTH

Yasir Arafat (YAH-sir AH-ra-fat) was born August 24, 1929, as Rahman Abdul Rauf al-Qudwa al-Husayni. (He took both the names "Yasir" and "Arafat" later in life, as evidence of his political and religious convictions. He was given the name "Yasir" in honor of a young Palestinian who had died in the Arab-Israeli conflict. He later took the name "Arafat" in honor of Mt. Arafat, a site near Mecca where Muslims believe God made Muhammad his prophet.) As with so much of Arafat's life, the place of his birth remains a question. He has claimed he was born in Jerusalem, in the Gaza section of modern-day Israel, and in Cairo, Egypt.

Most sources state that he was born in Cairo, and that he was the sixth of seven children of Hamida Khalifa al-Husayni, a descendent of a prestigious Islamic family, and Abdul Rauf al-Qudwa, a wealthy merchant. He had three sisters—Inam, Yosra, and Khadiga—and three brothers—Gamal, Moustapha, and Fathe.

PALESTINE

Every aspect of Yasir Arafat's life has been influenced by the Arab-Israeli conflict that has disrupted the Middle East for years. The Palestinian people have lived in the area that is now Israel for more than 10,000 years. The area of modern Israel contains land that is sacred to three of the world's major religions—Christianity, Judaism, and Islam. Each group claims to be the rightful heirs to the land that has been contested for centuries.

In the nineteenth century, Zionists, people of the Jewish faith who believed that a separate nation for Jews should be established in Palestine, began to immigrate to the area. In the 1920s, the conflict between the Jews and Arabs in the area of Palestine had reached the point of armed conflict. Under the directive of the League of Nations, England had been given the task of governing Palestine and trying to keep the peace among the warring factions.

EARLY YEARS

The story of Arafat's life mirrors the struggles of the Palestinian people throughout much of this century. In 1928, the year prior to Yasir's birth, his father had been forced to flee Palestine. Even though he was staunchly anti-Jewish, Abdul Rauf was threatened by anti-Zionist extremists because he sold items to Jews, and the family had to live in Egypt for several years for safety. Arafat's mother died when he was four, and he and his younger brother Fathe were sent to live with relatives in Jerusalem. When his father remarried four years later, Yasir and his brother returned to the family in Egypt. But his father's new wife could not get along with her step-children, and Abdul Rauf divorced her within several months. He married a third time and placed Yasir's eldest sister, Inam, in charge of the younger siblings, an arrangement that worked out much better for the children.

By most accounts Arafat was a withdrawn child, who showed an early interest in his religion, Islam. His mother, Hamida, was a direct descendent of Fatima, one of the daughters of Muhammad, the prophet and founder of the Islamic faith. As a young boy, Arafat came under the influence of his maternal great-uncle, Yusuf Awad al-Akbar, who nurtured his interest in religion; he also encouraged Yasir to share his contempt for Yasir's father. The great-uncle felt that the mother's family, with its illustrious religious heritage, was superior to the father's, and he fostered the young boy's feelings of rebellion and disobedience.

Meanwhile, Arafat's father, Abdul Rauf, had joined the Moslem Brotherhood, an organization of militant Arabs committed to establishing Islamic states in the Middle East and rejecting Western values and influence. Arafat was growing more contemptuous of his father, and Abdul Rauf was furious with Yusuf Awad for cultivating his son's scorn. Yusuf Awad was murdered in 1939 by the Moslem Brotherhood. Young Arafat didn't know of his father's complicity in his revered teacher's death, but the family was forced to move from Egypt to Gaza in 1939, in part, it is believed, so that Abdul Rauf could escape police questioning over his former kinsman's murder.

YOUTH

Moving to Gaza, Abdul Rauf began to organize another unit of the Moslem Brotherhood. Among his new recruits was Majid Halaby, a schoolteacher, who now took over young Arafat's education. According to some reports, it was Halaby who gave Arafat the name "Yasir." Drawn to his new teacher as he had been to his great-uncle, Arafat accepted Halaby's creed that the Palestinian cause was the single most important thing in life. Halaby taught young Yasir and his other young charges the elements of guerilla warfare and planned to lead them on an attack in Jerusalem. The older members of the Moslem Brotherhood tried to stop Halaby; when he defied them, they had him murdered.

Now young Yasir had lost two of his most important early teachers. Although he had been told that Halaby died while fighting for the cause, he guessed the truth. After a period of mourning and confusion, he recommitted himself to the Palestinian cause, which was becoming more violent.

The British, still in charge of Palestine in the 1940s, met with armed resistance from both Arab and Jewish groups. The situation worsened when, in the aftermath of World War II, a huge mass of Jews immigrated to the area. The world was outraged and shocked as the horrors of the Holocaust, the Nazis' systematic murder of some six millions Jews during World War II, came to light, gaining sympathy for the Zionist cause. In 1947, the United Nations created the nation of Israel by dividing Palestine into separate Arab and Jewish states. Prior to that time, there was no legally established Jewish country, in the Middle East or anywhere else in the world.

The Arab world soon declared war on the new Jewish nation, but in 1948-49, Israel waged and won what it calls its War of Independence against Egypt, Syria, Lebanon, Jordan, and Iraq. Arafat fought with the Egyptian forces during the war, and was part of the defeated troops who were forced back within the borders of their own countries. Some 1.5 million Arab Palestinians also fled. Without a homeland, they became exiles, scattered in cities and refugee camps in neighboring Arab countries. It is these Palestinian refugees that the PLO represents today. Despite the U.N.'s proclaimed intention, no new Arab nation in Palestine was ever created; instead, that land was absorbed by surrounding Arab nations.

EDUCATION AND CONTINUING POLITICAL ACTIVITY

After the Arab-Israeli War, in which he smuggled guns to Arab forces, Arafat returned to Cairo to take courses in explosives at a technological school. He returned to Gaza after some training and was involved in guerilla activities for several years, leading groups who attacked and murdered both Israelis and Palestinians who did not share their beliefs.

In 1950, Arafat began to take courses in civil engineering at Cairo University. But once again his political activities took precedent, as he founded the Palestinian Student Federation, a group devoted to the aim of reclaiming Palestine. In 1953, he lost control of the organization, but formed another student political group. Throughout the fifties, Arafat continued to consolidate his power as a leader within the various and warring groups of exiled Palestinians. As power shifted in the Middle East, Arafat would ascertain a new leader's willingness to help the Palestinian cause, then offer his support. For instance, when Gamal Abdal Nasser became president of Egypt after overthrowing the monarchy in 1952, Arafat continued his guerilla training under the Egyptian army and took part in raids on Israel sponsored by Nasser.

FIRST JOBS

After receiving his engineering degree, Arafat found work in Kuwait, which in the 1950s was one of several Middle Eastern nations with a large population of Palestinian exiles. He started a construction company and was very successful, but was still actively involved in the Palestinian cause. He started an anti-Zionist newspaper, *Our Palestine,* toured refugee camps, and formed the political organization al-Fatah, which would later form the nucleus of his Palestine Liberation Organization, or PLO. Al-Fatah was involved in commando raids against selected targets in Israel, often aided and armed by various Arab governments. Arafat has said in recent years that he could have continued in his role as a successful and wealthy engineer in Kuwait, but he felt he had to carry on in his quest to regain the Palestinian homeland. At this time, he and his group had fallen out of favor with Nasser, who had uncovered a plot by the Moslem Brotherhood to assassinate him, and who believed that Arafat was involved in the conspiracy. He ordered his secret police to assassinate Arafat, the first of some 50 known plots against the Palestinian leader's life. Arafat was also at times out of favor with the governments of the Middle East, and spent time in jails in Egypt, Lebanon, and Syria.

CAREER HIGHLIGHTS

By the mid-1960s, Arafat was continuing to lead raids into Israel, aided and sponsored by various Arab governments. In June of 1967, the Israelis struck back during the Six-Day War, in which they resoundingly defeated the armies of Jordan, Syria, and Egypt, including battalions of PLO soldiers. In the war's humiliating aftermath, the Arab states lost valuable territory, as Israel annexed the Sinai Peninsula from Egypt, the Golan Heights from Syria, and the Old City of Jerusalem.

In February 1969, Arafat was named chairman of the PLO, continuing to gain power and prestige in the Arab world. When the PLO was headquartered in Jordan, he would take journalists to a hill overlooking Jerusalem and say: "This is my beloved Jerusalem, my beloved country. I stand here to smell the air that keeps me alive." By the mid-1970s, the Arab states had recognized the PLO as the sole representative of the Palestinian people, and as such Arafat was asked to speak at the UN. His address in November 1974 is remembered for his words: "Today I have come bearing an olive branch and a freedom fighter's gun. Do not let the olive branch fall from my hand. I repeat: Do not let the olive branch fall from my hand." As reported in the *New York Times*, whether Arafat was a "terrorist or moderate nation-builder may depend on how one reads recent history of the Middle East." Arafat condemned the horrible acts of terrorism—the hijacking of planes, the murder of Israeli athletes at the 1972 Olympics—that had taken place under the command of rival Palestinian factions. And yet some of those extremist organizations had long-standing ties to Arafat and al-Fatah. "Whether he gave the orders or not," *Time* magazine wrote in January 1994, "his organization has always been linked to some of the bloodiest acts of terrorism in the Arab-Israeli conflict."

This two-sided view of Arafat has continued over the years he has held power and become a pivotal figure on the international political stage. Although often reviled in the Western press as a dangerous, callous terrorist, Arafat is a hero to the Palestinian people, especially those in the refugee camps. He is known to those within the cause as "Abu Amar," from the Arabic "to build," and is also affectionately called "the Old Man." His life and lifestyle reveal a man devoted to his cause. He has no permanent residence, spending most of his time on the move, visiting refugee camps, meeting with heads of state, and raising money for the PLO. He works 12 to 18 hour days, seven days a week, without vacations. He is recognized the world over with his characteristic *kaffiyeh*, or traditional Arab headdress, and his stubbly beard. He is a devout Muslim and neither drinks nor smokes. His one vice is supposedly his terrible temper—described as "pure, naked anger" by a colleague.

This controversial figure also keeps on the move because of the constant threats to his life. He has been the target of numerous assassination attempts—Arafat once said that Ariel Sharon of Israel had "tried to have me killed 13 times." His own security head told an English journalist why he thinks Arafat is still alive: "Sixty per cent is Arafat himself—his nose or smell for danger. Thirty percent is good luck. Ten per cent we can put down to the effectiveness of our own security agencies." Arafat must also continually battle the divisiveness within the Palestinian community, for many of the threats against him have come from the more militant factions.

In the early 1980s, the PLO was concentrated in Lebanon. Israel invaded Lebanon in 1982 in an attempt to wipe the PLO out. After Arafat and other leaders fled, hundreds of Palestinians still in the camps of Sabra and Shatila were massacred by Lebanese Christians, with many suspecting the complicity of the Israelis. The world was outraged, and the PLO began to gain recognition and sympathy.

In 1982, rebels led a revolt against Arafat and he fought to remain in control. Headquartered in Tunis, Arafat was reelected chairman in 1983. 1988 brought a major breakthrough in negotiations, as Arafat agreed to renounce terrorism and recognized Israel's right to exist. But in the 1990 Gulf War, Arafat made what many thought was a fatal mistake by aligning himself with Saddam Hussein of Iraq against the powerful and overwhelmingly successful forces of the U.N., which drove back Hussein's forces in Iraq's attempt to invade and control Kuwait. After years of receiving large sums from the Arab states as well as from the Soviet Union, Arafat and the PLO were faced with political and economic collapse.

In 1992, Mideast peace talks began, without Arafat. Then word came that Arafat had survived an airplane crash that had killed the plane's crew. His miraculous survival, compounded with the knowledge that the negotiators at the peace talks were indeed taking their directives from Arafat, despite his absence, led the political powers brokering peace to know that Arafat could not be ignored nor forgotten.

By that time, the effects of the "intifada" were also making the case for the Palestinians known. Begun in the late 1980s, the intifada was an uprising by the Palestinian residents in the occupied territories against the Israelis forces in Gaza and the West Bank. Based on the concept of civil disobedience, the intifada was characterized by strikes, protests, and rock-throwing, but not armed violence. The Israelis responded by deporting Palestinians and destroying their homes. But world pressure to recognize the rights of the Palestinians, as well as the knowledge that they were facing a perpetual confrontation that showed no sign of abating, led the Israelis to seek peace.

A BREAKTHROUGH FOR PEACE

In September 1993, after months of secret negotiations, Arafat and Israeli Prime Minister Yitzhak Rabin stunned the world by announcing that a preliminary accord had been reached between Israel and the Palestinians. The accord outlined that the 1.7 million Palestinians who now live in the West Bank and Gaza will be given home rule, the right to self-government.

In March of 1994, the peace process took a terrible blow when a Jewish extremist massacred more than 50 people at a holy shrine in Hebron in the West Bank. Rioting and protest broke out immediately, and the bloodshed proved to be the worst in the occupied territories since the 1967 war. Anxiously, the Israeli government worked with the PLO to try to preserve the peace.

In July of 1994, Arafat returned to Gaza for the first time since the Six-Day War in 1967, met by thousands of Palestinian supporters, but also by disgruntled political factions who felt he had sold out his people. There are also groups, like Hammas and other violent, extremist sects, who refuse to accept Arafat as their leader and who see their purpose as the extermination of Arafat and his organization. Currently, plans are for elections to be held within the year.

Now, as Israel pursues peace with each of its neighbors, the future of Arafat and his organization is unclear. What is certain is that he has fought for and gained worldwide recognition for the Palestinian people. With elections scheduled to occur soon, Arafat may become the first president of the new Palestine. He outlines his plans this way: "What is important

for me is to fix my people on the map of the Middle East and not to be like those who have been canceled out in international agreements, like many communities after World War I and II. It is the continuous tragedy of my people that I cannot forgive. We have paid a very high price." [See Appendix for Update on Arafat.]

MARRIAGE AND FAMILY

It was a surprise to everyone when Yasir Arafat, who had claimed to be "married to the Palestinian revolution," announced that he had married Suha Tawil in November 1991. She is 35 years younger than Arafat, the daughter of a prominent Christian Palestinian family and Arafat's former secretary. The marriage proved to be very unpopular with the more hard-line Muslim factions, who believe he should not have married outside the faith. But Arafat himself was very happy: "I have been looking for a long time," he said, "and at last I found someone who wanted me."

HOBBIES AND OTHER INTERESTS

Although he has little time for anything but politics, Arafat is a fan of American cartoons, particularly "Bugs Bunny" and "Tom and Jerry." He also likes to drive fast cars and has supposedly been involved in several car accidents.

HONORS AND AWARDS

Man of the Year (*Time* magazine, shared with Yitzhak Rabin, F.W. de Klerk, and Nelson Mandela): 1994

FURTHER READING

BOOKS

Hart, Alan. *Arafat: Terrorist or Peacemaker?* 1984
Haskins, James. *Leaders of the Middle East*, 1985
Reich, Bernard, ed. *Political Leaders of the Contemporary Middle East and North Africa*, 1990
Stefoff, Rebecca. *Yasir Arafat*, 1988

PERIODICALS

Current Biography Yearbook 1971
Interview, Dec. 1988, p.113
New York Times, June 30, 1994, p.A1; July 2, 1994, p.A1; July 3, 1994, p. A1; July 27, 1994, p.A1
New York Times Biographical Service, Nov. 1974, p.1526; Mar. 1975, p.257
Newsweek, May 4, 1992, p.40; Mar. 14, 1994, p.32

Progressive, Dec. 1993, p.22
Time, Oct. 15, 1990, p.55; Jan 3, 1994, p.40; Mar. 7, 1994, p.48
Vanity Fair, Feb. 1989, p.111

ADDRESS

PLO Affairs Center
1730 K Street NW
Suite 703
Washington, D.C. 20006

Bruce Babbitt 1938-
American Politician
United States Secretary of the Interior
and Former Governor of Arizona

BIRTH

Bruce Edward Babbitt was born in Los Angeles, California, June 27, 1938, the second child of Paul J. and Frances Perry Babbitt. His father was legal counsel to the Babbitt Brothers Trading Company, and his mother was a concert violinist. Bruce Babbitt has four brothers, Kenneth, Paul, James, and Charles, and one sister, Christine.

YOUTH

The Babbitt family was the wealthiest and most influential in all of Arizona, controlling nearly a million acres of ranchland. They also owned much of Flagstaff, the town Paul returned to with his wife and children when Bruce was seven. Five Babbitt brothers, Bruce's grandfather among them, had arrived in frontier Arizona at the end of the 1880s, and there they set up an Indian trading post and began to build a mercantile and ranching empire. "It was [still] all wooden sidewalks and dirt roads," recalls Frances Babbitt in describing Flagstaff of the mid-1940s. "The church was two blocks away, the high school was three blocks, Father's office [here she refers to her late husband] was two blocks . . . and everybody came home for lunch every day."

The Babbitts attempted to give their children a well-rounded life despite their privileged circumstances. They hiked, hunted, and explored nature together, and Bruce fondly remembers growing up in what he calls a "large and close family." His ideal boyhood in the American West was lyrically portrayed by writer Timothy Egan in a recent *New York Times* article: "With the sunset-colored breach of the Grand Canyon as his backyard . . . he chased deer, caught snakes, built tree forts, floated rivers, scavenged for arrowheads, fought forest fires, fished with Indians . . . followed dinosaur tracks, skied the first snow of November and dreamed about it all at night."

EARLY MEMORIES

Babbitt recently described his teenage experiences fighting forest fires. In an interview with *Audubon* magazine last year, he recalled that he had always had a romantic view of the U.S. Forest Service and told of going to a mountain town during the summer dry season to work in the fire lines. "I was fifteen years old and my high school biology teacher was the recruiting officer," he relates. "He looked me in the eye and said 'Bruce, how old are you? Are you eighteen?' And I said, 'Mr. Mickey, yes I am.' He had me sign the paper. And then they loaded us on to the back of the truck and took us up."

He remembers now the exhausting, miserable work, and the nights "that were so cold that if you stepped back from the fire, you felt like you were freezing to death." Babbitt tells of how he would move in close to the fire that was crowning across the treetops, and then "run like hell to get back from it." In all, it was an awesome experience, he says. "You came away from it feeling that you had been next to the raw power of nature."

EDUCATION

Babbitt, who once described himself as "hopelessly overeducated," graduated from Flagstaff High School in 1956. He then attended Indiana's

Notre Dame University, where he served as student body president and became immersed in the Catholic social activism of those years. He earned a B.S. degree, *magna cum laude*, in geology from Notre Dame in 1960. After graduation, Babbitt went to the University of Newcastle in northern England as part of the Marshall Scholars program, and there he was awarded a master's in geophysics in 1962.

To these scientific credentials, he added a J.D. (juris doctor) from Harvard Law School in 1965.

FIRST JOBS

During law school, Babbitt spent one summer doing social work in a Venezuelan *barrio* and another at a student work camp in Peru. After graduation, he worked for the federal antipoverty program in Texas and in Washington, D.C. While he values this experience, he claims to have become skeptical about "efforts to force change from the top down."

CHOOSING A CAREER

Bruce Babbitt's career path included several changes of direction. The turning point came in 1962 during a geological field trip to the Amazon River basin in Bolivia, where he decided to give up academic geology for a career in law and politics. "It was the apotheosis of my childhood fantasy," he says of the university trip that had taken him into the copper mining fields of Bolivia. "Virgin jungle, research, flying across mountaintops in a helicopter. But at one point we were out setting up base camps, where we had those tents and cooks and martinis at night. And somehow I was just so struck by the contrast between a landscape of people starving to death and me sitting in the lap of this frontier luxury, that it started eating at me. I had found the Amazon, and discovered that it wasn't what I was all about. Watching these people in rags in Bolivia, I realized I'm more a part of the world and people problems than this extravagant adventure." The experience motivated him to enroll in law school, join the 1965 civil rights march on Selma, Alabama, and, upon graduation, to enlist in President Lyndon Johnson's War on Poverty.

Disillusionment with the federal bureaucracy again changed his course, and Babbitt returned to Arizona to join a corporate law firm, where he received another shock. Arizona business was virtually unregulated and highly corrupt, with crooked land deals, antitrust violations, bribery, and white-collar crime considered business as usual. Outraged, Babbitt ran for state attorney general in 1974, beginning a political career that has now spanned twenty years.

BRUCE BABBITT

CAREER HIGHLIGHTS

After his election, Babbitt proved that his "clean up the mess" platform had been no empty slogan. He vigorously prosecuted the kingpins of Arizona corruption, convicting more than fifty land-fraud artists. His aggressive tactics so enraged the criminals that he reportedly ended up on a mob "hit" list, the same one that included slain Phoenix reporter Don Bolles, who had been exposing that felonious activity. Babbitt successfully prosecuted Bolles's killers, but their convictions were overturned by the Supreme Court. Nevertheless, his reputation as a fearless fighter against crime—no matter how wealthy and powerful its perpetrators—was sealed. His allies were both the state's patrician families and its new, poor immigrants. This dual support allowed a liberal Democrat to be the most popular politician in the nation's most conservative and Republican state.

Babbitt was contemplating a run for the U.S. Senate when an uncommon turn of events caused a career shift. Arizona's incumbent governor, Raul H. Castro, had stepped down when President Jimmy Carter appointed him ambassador to Argentina, and his replacement, Secretary of State Wesley A. Bolin, died after only five weeks in office. Babbitt, as attorney general, was next in line and became governor on March 4, 1978. He quickly proved that he would let neither his unelected status nor his office's reputation as "weak" allow him to work as a figurehead. He vetoed several bills and aggressively campaigned for a full, elected term in office. In November of that same year, he narrowly defeated the far-right Evan Mecham in an election that gave him 52 percent of the vote.

Always underestimated by his political opponents, Babbitt served a first term that was highlighted by one startling demonstration of courage and one "virtuoso display of leadership" [*Time*], both relating to the environment. First, he caused a stir in 1979 by calling in the Arizona National Guard to seize the Tuscon plant of American Atomics Corporation because the company refused to remove radioactive tritium from its premises. A year later, Babbitt showed that he was no more intimidated by political gridlock than by corporate power when he tackled what had long been the state's most pressing problem—the depletion of groundwater caused by decades of urban growth and agricultural irrigation. Babbitt convened and chaired a commission that brought miners, farmers, environmentalists, community leaders, and land developers to the table to hammer out a solution. His astonishing patience and command of detail led to the drafting and passage of a landmark conservation bill that is expected to stabilize Arizona's water table by the year 2225. He succeeded where others had despaired of trying, and he made friends, or at least admirers, of many political enemies. "Bruce Babbitt," commented Wesley Stiner, a water commissioner who has served under five governors, "is undoubtedly the best governor I have ever worked for. It would be impossible for anyone to make a larger, more significant contribution to a state than to help manage its most important resource."

Babbitt's second term, which he won in 1982 with 62 percent of the vote, was somewhat more controversial. He alienated organized labor by again calling in the National Guard, this time to break a strike at a Phelps-Dodge plant. The move earned for him the nickname "Governor Scabbit," a caustic play on the derogatory word "scab," used to describe a person who accepts employment when the regular work force is on strike. On a less controversial note, he devoted his entire State of the State address to the issue of child welfare. The education and health reforms he was able to institute now serve as a model for delivering top-notch social services on a limited budget.

When Democrat Walter Mondale, a classic liberal, was defeated by Ronald Reagan in a landslide in the 1984 presidential election, Babbitt and other centrists (Bill Clinton among them) decided to form the Democratic Leadership Council. This group's mission has been to redefine the party's vision in order to compete nationally in an era of changing expectations. Babbitt argued that such programs as Social Security and Medicare should be evaluated for their purpose and fairness, and that state and local governments should take a more active role in these issues. His point of view was tested with the electorate in 1988, when he sought the Democratic nomination for president. Observers are divided on whether Babbitt's campaign was derailed because voters rejected his ideas, or because they objected to his rather wooden stage and television presence. He withdrew from the race after a weak showing in the New Hampshire primary, and returned to the private sector.

AMERICA'S LANDLORD

When the like-minded Bill Clinton won the presidency in 1992, the way was paved for Bruce Babbitt's return to public life. The new president appointed Babbitt Secretary of the Interior: overseer of 500 million acres of federal lands—parks, forests, rangelands, wildlife refuges, and recreation areas. The man dubbed "America's landlord" by the press was sworn in as the forty-seventh Secretary of the Interior on January 22, 1993. As Secretary, Babbitt splits his time between his Washington office and trips into the field to examine what is happening on public lands. Calling the department "a mess," Babbitt has vowed to end the ideological warfare begun in the 1980s by the Reagan administration's arch-conservative secretary James Watt, and to implement a more environmentally sensitive land-use policy. Environmental groups were generally pleased with

Babbitt's appointment, but some expressed concern that he had recently lobbied for a hazardous-waste incinerator in Arizona. Business and conservation leaders agree that he will be more moderate than the political right fears, and more pragmatic than environmentalists might hope.

Babbitt's 1993 attempt to raise grazing fees on federal lands was turned back by pressure from Western senators, dealing the current administration a stinging defeat. Babbitt vows that he will not back down on this or on his support for the reauthorization of the Endangered Species Act. On the latter issue, his goal is to focus less on individual species and to examine ecosystems as a whole. Time will tell whether Babbitt's skills at negotiation can succeed at the federal level as well as they did at the state level.

MARRIAGE AND FAMILY

Babbitt is married to an attorney, the former Hattie Coons, whom he met in Texas while he was working in the antipoverty program. She is nine years younger than he is and was in college in Virginia when they met. She studied in Spain during her junior year, then transferred to Arizona State University as a senior, confides her mother, "saying that she couldn't run this romance from Sweet Briar." After her graduation and marriage, she enrolled in law school at Arizona State. Currently, Mrs. Babbitt serves as ambassador to the Organization of American States.

The Babbitts have two young sons, Christopher and T.J. (Thomas Jeffrey), and have recently moved to Washington from their ranch house in Phoenix.

HOBBIES AND OTHER INTERESTS

Beyond his work at Interior, Babbitt indulges mainly in outdoor recreational activities. He hikes, rafts, backpacks, bicycles and, whenever he can find a quiet moment, spreads his sleeping bag under the Arizona night sky. His reading habits are said to be concentrated mainly on social issues and the environment.

WRITINGS

Color and Light: The Southwest Canvases of Louis Akin, 1973
Grand Canyon: An Anthology, 1978 (editor)

HONORS AND AWARDS

Don Bolles Award (media presentation in memory of the murdered Arizona crime reporter): 1976
Thomas Jefferson Award (National Wildlife Federation): 1981
Special Conservation Award (National Wildlife Federation): 1983

FURTHER READING

BOOKS

Osborne, David. *Laboratories of Democracy,* 1988
Who's Who in America, 1992-93

PERIODICALS

Arizona Republic, Jan. 26, 1988, p.B1; Jan. 18, 1993, p.A1
Audubon, May-June 1993, p. 78
Commonweal, Feb. 22, 1985, p.109
Current Biography Yearbook 1987
Inc., Aug. 1987, p.34
New Republic, May 27, 1985, p.9; Jan. 4 & 11, 1988, p.20; Mar. 8, 1993, p.21
New York Times Magazine, Aug. 1, 1993, p.21
Newsweek, Mar. 29, 1993, p.25
Rolling Stone, July 8-22, p.46
Time, Jan. 4, 1988, p.43
U.S. News & World Report, May 17, 1993, p.63

ADDRESS

U.S. Department of the Interior
1849 C. Street NW
Washington, DC 20240

Mayim Bialik 1975-
American Actress
Star of the Hit TV Series "Blossom"

BIRTH

Mayim Bialik [MY-im be-AL-ik] was born on December 12, 1975, in San Diego, California. Her unusual first name, which means "water" in Hebrew, comes from her great-grandmother, who was named Miriam but called Mayim. Her parents, Barry and Beverly Bialik, are former New Yorkers and independent filmmakers who used to make movies denouncing the Vietnam war for the public television series "Great American Dream Machine." They eventually moved to California and became educators, Barry as an English teacher at a performing arts junior high and Beverly as a nursery school teacher and director. Beverly Bialik later left her own work to manage her daughter's acting career. Mayim has one older brother, Isaac, who recently graduated from UCLA (University of California at Los Angeles) and now works as a graphic designer.

YOUTH

Bialik grew up in a close-knit family in Los Angeles. Her parents were determined to raise their children to be responsible, independent, and concerned about social issues. The dinner hour was a time to discuss major social and political topics, with her father often taking the role of devil's advocate to sharpen Mayim and Isaac's debating skills. But they also encouraged Mayim's creative interests. From an early age she was involved in a wide range of activities, appearing in all her school plays as well as taking ballet lessons beginning at age four, piano lessons at six, and trumpet lessons at ten. The trumpet was her second choice, though, as she explains: "I wanted to play the trombone, but my arms weren't long enough." She has recently taken up bass guitar as well.

EDUCATION

Bialik, who just graduated from high school in the spring of 1993, has refused to divulge the school's name for fear that it would attract journalists and photographers. She has said, though, that she attended a magnet school for gifted students in the Los Angeles public school system. Throughout much of high school, she split her time between being tutored on the "Blossom" set during filming and then returning to school to attend classes when the show went on hiatus. Yet Bialik doesn't feel that she missed out on anything by spending part of the year away from school. "I really don't feel I'm any different from any other kid in my school," she once said. "Oh, I may have more fun, because I have a lot of fun when I work. But I'm not missing anything a normal teen-age girl does. . . . I keep in touch with the kids at my school when the show is taping, and I also see other kid actors when they come on the show. So I'm always meeting new kids. It's not like I'm deprived of anything I'd have if I were in school all the time. I get that, and more besides."

After finishing high school, Bialik applied to colleges and was accepted by several, including UCLA, Yale University, and her first choice, Harvard University in Massachusetts. She has delayed her admission there to continue working on "Blossom," but as she says, "I have a feeling that some time in the future, college will be for me." Psychobiology, philosophy, and literature are her major academic interests.

CHOOSING A CAREER

Mayim was six when she announced to her parents that she wanted to start acting. "It interested me for the same reasons it interests everybody else. Acting seemed glamorous and fun." At first, her "strict but supportive" parents tried to discourage her. They worried that she was too young and wanted to protect her from the rejections they knew she would suffer. Finally, they decided that she was mature enough to handle it. "I always wanted to be an actress," Mayim recalls. "I was always active in school plays and things like that. But my parents didn't want me to be an actress, because it is very hard for a little kid. So finally when I was eleven-and-a-half they let me. I think they realized that I was old enough at eleven-and-a-half to kind of deal with things like rejection and things that can be very hard for a little kid. And I was very persistent, and I still am."

That persistence eventually paid off. When her parents finally agreed that Mayim could try acting, her mother quit her job as a nursery school director to help her daughter. They started off by sending letters to talent agents describing Mayim as a "Bette Midler/Barbra Streisand type." It may have seemed an odd attention-getting device for an eleven year old, but it worked. She found an agent, started out in a few television commercials, went on to a five-line part in the horror film *Pumpkinhead* ("I didn't get butchered or anything"), and had roles in the TV series "Beauty and the Beast," "Webster," "MacGyver," "Doogie Howser, M.D.," "Murphy Brown," and "Facts of Life."

CAREER HIGHLIGHTS

In less than two years, Bialik won her first big part—a role in *Beaches* (1988), starring Bette Midler and Barbara Hershey. Bialik played the young version of Midler's character, CC Bloom. The audition process was tough. With her long straight brown hair and green eyes, Bialik doubted anyone could picture her as the red-haired, brown-eyed Midler. So Bialik showed up for the audition with director Garry Marshall wearing a curly red wig and smoking a cigarette. It wasn't the costume that caught the director's attention as much as her cocky attitude—just like Midler's. According to Marshall, "Mayim was shy at first, but the second time we saw her, she was cooking. In the film she went flat out." After an audition with Midler, she won the part.

The movie's opening scene finds Bialik lounging under the Atlantic City boardwalk, smoking a cigarette and wearing a red satin bodysuit, black fishnet stockings, a feather boa, and tap shoes. Her self-assured and flamboyant performance won raves from critics and quickly captured the attention of other filmmakers. She soon found herself in an enviable position: screenwriters wanted to create parts specifically for her, a rarity for a relative newcomer. She didn't even need to audition for new parts; instead, people came to her with ideas. Bialik next appeared in the short-lived sitcom "Molloy" before finding success on a long-running TV series.

"BLOSSOM"

Now in its fourth season, "Blossom" depicts family life and teenage concerns through the eyes of an intelligent, sensitive young woman. Blossom Russo, played by Bialik, is growing up in a household of all men—her father (Ted Wass), a musician, and two older brothers, Anthony (Michael Stoyanov), a recovering substance abuser, and Joey (Joey Lawrence), a school jock and teen heartthrob. Blossom's relationship with her mother, who left the family intent on pursuing her dream to become a singer in Paris, has been a recurring storyline. Since its debut in January 1991, the series has changed somewhat, reflecting Blossom's growth into young adulthood. Recent shows have included such topics as alcohol and drug use, troubles at school, staying out all night, running away, relationships, sex, and contraceptives. But such issues are always mixed with a little humor and a lot of clothes. As fans know, Blossom's unique look features creative, colorful, and offbeat layered combinations of oversize pants, leggings, vests, boots, and hats. With her spunky attitude and her funky clothes, Blossom has become a role model for many teens. Ironically, Blossom's efforts to create a unique look for herself as an individual have been widely copied by her fans.

Much of the show's appeal derives from Bialik's portrayal of its title character. Blossom Russo in many ways seems similar to Mayim Bialik, and some of her fans seem to confuse the two. But Bialik is quick to point out the distinction between herself and the character she plays. First, their clothes. Bialik favors simpler outfits, wearing lots of black, jeans, and vintage pieces. But there is certainly more to it than just clothes. As a young actress, Bialik is often called confident, well-adjusted, mature, intense, assertive, articulate, and self-possessed, "a blend of savvy sophistication and youthful sensibility," according to one critic. "Mayim is an exceptional person," producer Paul Junger Witt explains. "One of the things we wanted to do in

having a young female protagonist—which is very unusual in television—from whose point of view we're seeing life, was to not have some cute airhead, which television is covered with. We wanted to have a young woman who is capable of articulating herself and is capable of thinking, perhaps confusedly, but thinking deeply. And we happened to get the whole package in one person."

Bialik's own description of her approach to the series best sums it up: "The show is about a young woman, which is so rarely done. I might as well try to be a positive role model. I don't want my character to be the typical bimbo who is just interested in shopping and boys. Basically, I want to break down the stereotypes." And she has been able to do just that. When one early episode contained flat-chested jokes about Blossom, Bialik, then only 15, had the courage to object to the producer, who changed the script. As she said then, "I'm a little feminist. So when it comes to things like that, you don't have to go along. Especially with the 'flat-chested' jokes. I think that's sexist. I think it was very insulting to me as a woman, and as a human being. I never make any compromises in my life. If there's something I believe in, I say it. I turn a lot of people off."

With this sort of background, "Blossom" has prompted many critics to discuss issues of sexism in TV programming. Many have commented on its emphasis on a female lead, a rarity in the world of TV. In the television industry, which like any business needs to make a profit, decisions about programming are based on demographics. The number of viewers each show attracts determines how much advertisers are willing to pay to put their commercials on a show. TV shows have been dominated by males, according to critics, for two reasons: because some studies have shown that girls will watch a show about boys while boys won't watch one about girls, but also because most TV executives are male themselves and are therefore more interested in stories about experiences that are similar to their own. Eventually, according to some critics, girls come to believe TV's underlying message: that boys and their concerns are more important than girls. "Blossom" challenges that message, empowering young women by giving voice and granting validity to their concerns.

HOME AND FAMILY

Bialik lives in Los Angeles with her family and their pets—a few cats, some fish, and a one-legged parakeet.

HOBBIES AND OTHER INTERESTS

Bialik enjoys a wide range of creative, physical, and political activities. She likes to write poetry, read J.D. Salinger, do what she calls "political painting," and work with beads, especially making one-of-a-kind jewelry pieces for her friends and decorating clothing with beads and embroidery. Music also plays a big role in her life. She enjoys playing her musical instruments and listening to alternative music like Elvis Costello and Violent Femmes, with whom she once appeared on stage. Bialik is also physically active: she has always participated in sports like basketball, baseball, softball, running, and swimming, and she has more recently added gymnastics, racquetball, and jazz, tap, and hip-hop dancing. "Exercise is fun for me," she says. "It keeps me feeling good. I think sports are really important for kids—it keeps them happy and healthy." Bialik also spends time promoting political and social issues, including funding for pediatric AIDS research, the environment, animal rights, and homelessness. "I like to use the visibility that I have to help others," she explains.

FURTHER READING

PERIODICALS

Baltimore Morning Sun, Apr. 5, 1992, p.
People, Feb. 6, 1989, p.63
Sassy, Nov. 1992, p.58
TV Guide, Mar. 30, 1991, p.16

ADDRESS

"Blossom"
NBC
3000 Alameda Avenue
Burbank, CA 91523

Bonnie Blair 1964-
American Speed Skater
Olympic Gold Medalist in 1988, 1992, and 1994
First American Woman to Win Five Olympic Gold Medals

BIRTH

Bonnie Kathleen Blair was born March 18, 1964, in Cornwall, New York. She is the youngest of six children born to Eleanor Blair, a real estate agent, and Charlie Blair, a civil engineer. Bonnie's sisters and brothers are Mary, Susie, Angela, Charlie Jr., and Rob.

The story of Bonnie's birth is a favorite with her many fans: when Eleanor went into labor, Charlie dropped her off at the hospital, then went on to a local rink where the older children were competing in a skating match and he was a timer. He thought he'd make it back in time for Bonnie's birth, but several hours into the competition, the following announcement was made: "Looks like the Blairs have another skater."

YOUTH

Bonnie was born when the oldest sibling was 23 and the youngest was seven. Eleanor Blair was 46 when she had Bonnie, and she used to call her "my do-it-yourself grandchild." All the kids loved to skate, and four of Bonnie's five siblings were national speed skating champs. (Although the older kids first tried figure skates, the Blairs all quickly declared their love for speed over figure eights, and Bonnie has never been on a pair of figure skates.)

The Blairs moved to Champaign, Illinois, when Bonnie was two so that Charlie could take a job as a sales manager for a concrete company. That same year Bonnie first took to the ice when her sisters shoved her little feet—with baby shoes still on—into a pair of skates. "I can't even remember learning how to skate. It comes almost as naturally as walking," says Blair. She was competing by the age of four, and by the age of seven was racing in the state championships.

Nearly every weekend the Blair kids would pile into the family station wagon and go to meets. Bonnie would go, too, and sometimes would nap right through her race. For years Bonnie participated in what is called "pack" skating: a group of skaters starts together, battling for the inside position. Skating commentators think that this gave Bonnie an advantage early on in her training and helped to develop her fierce competitiveness. As a teenager, she began to race as they do in the Olympics, where athletes skate two at a time, racing against the clock rather than each other.

EDUCATION

Bonnie attended the public schools in Champaign, and while in high school added track and gymnastics to her sporting activities. She graduated from Centennial High School in Champaign, but not in the traditional fashion. Due to the demands of her sport, she completed the work required for her diploma through correspondence courses while traveling the international speed skating circuit.

CAREER HIGHLIGHTS

One of the benefits of growing up in Champaign was the chance to train and compete in an area where speed skating was an important sport. Blair's first coach was Cathy Priestner Faminow, a former silver medalist with the Canadian Olympic team. Under her direction, Blair developed into a powerful skater, particularly in what were to become her signature events, the 500-meter and 1,000-meter races. In 1979, at the age of 15, she tried out for the national team. She qualified for the Olympic trials that year, where she was up against the best in the world: Beth Heiden and Leah Poulos. Narrowly missing a spot on the 1980 Olympic team, Blair set her sights on the next Olympics.

RAISING MONEY TO TRAIN

Faminow knew that Blair needed to go to Europe to race the World Cup circuit to continue to improve and to have a shot at the 1984 Olympic team. But that kind of training takes money. Blair's father had just retired, so her parents couldn't help her. She found a main source of funding through the Champaign Police Department, on whose softball team she had pitched. They sponsored her for years, selling bumper stickers that read "Bonnie Blair: Champaign Policemen's Favorite Speeder." Another important early backer was Milwaukee Bucks' star Jack Sikma, a college friend of her brother Rob, who also helped Bonnie out financially.

1984 OLYMPICS

Blair made the 1984 U.S. Olympic team and went to Sarajevo, in what was then Yugoslavia, for what would be her very first international competition. "I was totally in awe at Sarajevo," she recalls. "I'd sit in the dining hall with [figure skater] Scott Hamilton and [skiers] the Mahre brothers, Steve and Phil. My mouth would be on the ground." She skated well enough to finish eighth in the 500 meters. She learned in that competition that even though she was smaller than the women who then dominated the sport, she could beat them based on superior technique. That was her strength, and she just got better and better. Her coach at that time, Mike Crowe, said this about Blair: "If I were to do a textbook on sprinting, she would be the model."

One of the realities of speed skating is the strenuous training program it requires. At 5'5" and 130 pounds, Blair is not as large as some competitors in her sport, and she has worked for years to develop strength. In addition to hours on the ice, her workout includes bicycle riding, weight lifting, roller skating, and "imitation," exercises done in skating positions. Blair is known for her low skating style and swift, powerful stroke and glide. In order to move rapidly on the ice, a speed skater must stay in a low crouch position to avoid wind resistance. This is hard to do, because as the body tires during a race, it is a natural reflex to want to rise up to a standing position. That's what the years of strength and endurance training are for: to discipline the body to respond with a machine-like regularity when the starting gun is fired. Throughout all the years of training, Blair has insisted she skates for the sheer fun of it. "Skating has always been a pleasure and a joy. I love to go fast and create the wind. It's fun to set goals, reach goals, reset goals. I don't see any torture in this at all."

By 1985 Blair was ranked second in the world in the 500. In the National Sport Festival that year Blair placed first in individual events. She was also a last-minute replacement in the men's 5,000 meter relay. She won again, calling it a "blast."

1988 OLYMPICS

At the 1988 Olympics in Calgary, Alberta, Canada, Blair won her first gold medal, defeating her rival, East German skater Christa Rothenburger, by .002 of a second—10 1/2 inches—in the 500 meters, and breaking the world record. Before the race, feeling a bit jittery, she ate a snack that has become part of her trademark—a peanut butter and jelly sandwich. It fueled her to victory. "I think it was the happiest moment of my life," she said. "When they were playing the National Anthem, it was the second happiest."

It was a moment shared by the entire family, who have become rather famous themselves in accompanying Bonnie to her several Olympic triumphs. Her sister had hung a sign in the stands that said "Go Baby Bear" (based on Bonnie's nickname) and the family cheered her on in her next race, the 1,000 meters. She won a bronze medal, finishing behind Rothenburger and Karin Kania, both of East Germany. She also raced in the 1,500 meters, where she placed fourth. "I tried," she said of the 1,500, "and it was hard. I was tired right off the bat."

The Blair clan also offered a positive moment in an Olympics whose happiness was marred by the tragic death of the sister of Dan Jansen, fellow U.S. speed skater and one of Bonnie's close friends. Jansen had fallen twice earlier in the week, after hearing of his sister's death from cancer. The Blairs have a special closeness to Jansen, for one of their family, Rob, has battled cancer for years.

In the aftermath of the '88 Olympics, Blair became something of a celebrity at home, although the attention was nothing compared to what she received in Europe. In countries like Holland and Norway, speed skaters are treated like stars. "It's funny," Blair says, "but I'm more likely to be recognized on the street in Norway that I am in New York." Her Dutch fans began a tradition of greeting her victories with a rousing chorus of "My Bonnie Lies Over the Ocean," a tribute that has caught on wherever she skates. In another anecdote loved by her fans, two Dutch skating enthusiasts vacationing in the U.S. showed up on her parent's doorstep one day, hoping to catch a glimpse of Bonnie Blair's home. Her brother let them in and gave them tea.

She also was invited to dinner at the White House. Then-Vice President George Bush came up to her after dinner and said, "You know, I saw you just kind of looking around the room. Sometimes I do that same exact thing. I just can't believe I'm here, either."

In 1989, Blair began her college studies at Montana Technical University, one of three locations in the U.S. with an oval speed-skating track. Also in 1989, she became the first American in a decade to win the World Sprint Championships. In that same year, she embarked on a new career as a bicycle racer, joining the Sundance Juice Sparkler team. Because cycling is a part of their training, several world-class speed skaters have combined skating with cycling. In 1988 Christa Rothenburger of East Germany became the first athlete to earn a medal in both the Summer and Winter Olympics, as a cyclist and a skater. Blair raced on the cycling circuit for one year, then concentrated solely on skating.

Blair's 1990 and 1991 seasons were disappointing; she was only able to place fifth in the world rankings in her major events. Blair and Dan Jansen began to call for a coaching change for the American team, and they got it. Both began to train under Peter Mueller, a former Olympian, who helped both skaters improve. Of Blair he said, "Bonnie is a killer. She gets them down and keeps them there."

1992 OLYMPICS

Blair went into the 1992 Olympics in Albertville, France, as the favorite in the 500 and 1,000 meter races, fresh from victories in both events at the World Cup Championships. She raced to a gold medal in both matches, becoming the first American woman to win a gold medal in consecutive Winter Olympics. Her family—now called "Team Blair"—cheered her on, without her father, who had died of cancer in 1989. Bonnie remembered her father during the races. After she won the 500, she said, "This medal I definitely won for him." "He knew I would go to the Olympics before I would," she told reporters at a press conference. "I always thought my father was crazy, but somehow he knew I'd get here."

She raced in the 1,500 again and finished 21st, after Mueller signalled her during the race to slow down when it became obvious that she couldn't win. But her overall performance was enough to garner a number of endorsements from companies like Visa, Xerox, Mizuno sportswear, Evian, Mars candy, Kraft, and Jeep.

Blair changed coaches again in 1993, training under former U.S. speed skating champ Nick Thometz, in preparation for her fourth and final Olympics, held in Lillehammer, Norway, in 1994.

1994 OLYMPICS

Blair had determined that the 1994 Olympics would be her last, and she went out in a blaze of glory. Just one month shy of her thirtieth birthday,

Blair made sports history. In the words of *New York Times* columnist Jere Longman, "She is as dependable as a light switch, flipping on her power at every Winter Olympics, skating with such aggressiveness and impeccable technique that her victories have become devoid of suspense." It might not have been suspenseful, but it was sweet. She won her fourth gold medal on February 18, posting her third fastest time in the 500 meters.

Blair won her fifth and final gold medal in the 1,000 meters in an amazing race. Her time was a full 1.38 seconds ahead of the second place finisher. And with that fifth gold medal, Blair entered the record books again. She became the first American woman to win five gold medals, outdistancing swimmer Janet Evans, runner Evelyn Ashford, and diver Pat McCormick, each of whom had earned four. She was also the first American to win five gold medals in the Winter Olympics.

Knowing that these Olympics would be her last, Blair felt "almost sad" when she heard the National Anthem the night of her victory in the 1,000. As she listened, her eyes filled with tears, and she thought, "I'm never going to hear the anthem like this again." That chapter in her life was over.

FUTURE PLANS

Blair plans to retire after the 1995 World Championships, which will take place in her current hometown of Milwaukee. She likes the idea of retiring after racing at home. She plans to finish college—she has taken courses in physical education and business, but she has not completed her degree. She hopes to stay involved with skating in some way, maybe as a speaker, fund raiser, or coach. "It is a sport I thoroughly love. It has brought me a lot of happiness, and I want to return that."

HOME AND FAMILY

Nearly everyone who has met or interviewed Bonnie Blair remarks on her warm personality and down-to-earth nature. She isn't impressed with herself or her accomplishments. She lives in a condominium in Milwaukee, close to her sister Angela. The two share a golden retriever. She and her boyfriend, U.S. speed skater David Cruikshank, have been going together for several years, although they have no definite plans to marry at this time. When reporters at Lillehammer pressed her regarding gossip about a wedding date, she joked that it was just "rumors started by my mother." Actually, Angela had just announced her engagement, and with characteristic Blair humor Bonnie said, "there are so many of us, maybe Mom got us confused."

HOBBIES AND OTHER INTERESTS

Blair is an avid water and snow skier, and also loves golf and softball. She also likes to read Danielle Steele novels and enjoys watching "Seinfeld" and "Home Improvement" on TV.

HONORS AND AWARDS

Olympic Speed Skating, 500 meters: 1988, gold medal; 1992, gold medal; 1994, gold medal
Olympic Speed Skating, 1,000 meters: 1988, bronze medal; 1992, gold medal; 1994, gold medal
James E. Sullivan Award, as top amateur athlete in U.S.: 1993
World Cup Speed Skating, 500 meters: 1992, first place
World Cup Speed Skating, 1,000 meters: 1992, first place

FURTHER READING

BOOKS

Who's Who in America, 1994

PERIODICALS

Boston Globe, Feb. 23, 1988, p.10; Feb. 9, 1992, p.14
Chicago Tribune, Feb. 4, 1992, Sports, p.8.
Current Biography Yearbook 1992
Newsday, Jan 17, 1988, p.32
New York Times, Feb. 20, 1994, p.A20
People, Feb. 15, 1988, p.34
Philadelphia Daily News, Feb. 10, 1988, p.76.
Sporting News, Mar 7, 1994, p.15
Sports Illustrated, Feb. 9, 1988, p.166; Feb. 27, 1988; Feb. 24, 1992, p.18; Feb. 28, 1994, p.43
Women's Sports, Jan. 1984, p.52

ADDRESS

Advantage International Management, Inc.
1025 Thomas Jefferson St., NW
Washington, DC 20007-3825

Ed Bradley 1941-
American Journalist
Coeditor of and Correspondent on "60 Minutes"

BIRTH

Edward R. (Ed) Bradley was born June 22, 1941, in Philadelphia, Pennsylvania. He was the only child of Edward and Gladys (Gaston) Bradley, who separated when he was an infant.

YOUTH

After they split up, Gladys stayed in Philadelphia, while Edward Senior moved to Detroit, where he owned a vending-machine business and a small restaurant. As a boy, Ed Bradley lived with his mother in a tough Philadelphia neighborhood, spending part of every summer with his father in Detroit. Both parents, he says, "worked twenty-hour days at two jobs each. They had middle-class values, but no middle-class money." Neither father nor mother ever let him think that he could not make a better life for himself. He was told again and again that he could be anything he wanted to be, and hearing that challenge often enough gave him reason to believe it—even though most black role models of his boyhood experience were sports heroes. "There were no Walter Cronkites in my world," he says.

Bradley remembers happy, but never idle, teen summers. He had what a friend called a "beat-up old Chevrolet," and he was enterprising enough to use it for more than recreational purposes. He delivered phone books during school breaks, starting at dawn and working until 8 or 9 at night. He would then return to the warehouse to pick up another load for the next day. Even after Bradley enrolled in college classes, his car gave him some financial return with the half-dollar he charged his fellow students for rides.

EDUCATION

Bradley attended neighborhood parochial school until fourth grade before being sent to a Roman Catholic boarding school "that took charity cases," he says with an edge of bitterness. "My mother worked at night, and she didn't want me to be running the streets." Bradley then boarded for three years at a high school in Rhode Island run by an order of Catholic brothers whose "unreasonable" rules young Bradley followed with passive resistance. He was away from home more years than he cares to discuss, a captive of circumstances beyond his, or his mother's, control.

After boarding school, Bradley attended Cheyney University of Pennsylvania, a small, black commuter college close to home. In an uncommonly revealing *Men's Journal* profile on the newsman, writer John Anderson tells that "Choosing [Cheyney] was an act of subtle rebellion against the brothers. Not Catholic, not private, not rich, not prestigious, not white. Definitely not Notre Dame."

Newsman Jim Vance, a close friend from Bradley's old neighborhood and college days, gives us a sense of what their years at Cheyney were like. Several years ago the two friends reminisced about their youth and about what *Philadelphia Daily News* columnist Chuck Stone characterized as their "shared passion for success." They played football at Cheyney, which then offered neither suitable facilities nor financial aid. Undaunted, they scrambled to improvise. "We were just a bunch of dudes . . . most of us commuters," Vance told Stone. "Conditions were so bad that we would pull our cars up to the field and put the lights on so we could practice late. Other teams would come out on the field with forty-five. We had nineteen." Despite such hardships, Bradley persevered, earning his B.S. degree in education in 1964.

FIRST JOBS

Full-time teaching was Ed Bradley's first job after college, but radio work had already become his consuming interest when he joined the faculty at Mann Elementary School in Philadelphia. He had been hanging around WDAS-FM since 1963 with a disc-jockey friend and managed to ease his way into air time by working evenings at the station without pay. Eventually, he was hired for a part-time news slot, at $1.25 per hour, and he moonlighted in that job while continuing to teach sixth grade during the day.

CHOOSING A CAREER

But that couldn't last. Eventually, "[I] reached the point where I had to decide between two careers," Bradley once revealed in an interview. "I had thought about black stations, but I said, 'Why confine myself?'" With that decision behind him, the would-be newsman moved to New York in 1967 and took a job at WCBS Radio, the CBS affiliate station. Within a few years, however, he was restless and anxious to change his routine.

In 1971, Bradley left behind the security of a regular paycheck and moved to Paris, with his sights set on writing a novel—perhaps some poetry—and listening to the jazz that remains to this day an integral part of his being. "I didn't go to Paris for a career," he remarked years later. "I went to Paris for my life." He bought a motorbike, lived frugally by "crashing" with musician friends, and managed to get along surprisingly well without learning much of the French language. His only source of income at first was from voice-overs he did for commercials; then, when his funds were nearly depleted, he signed on again with CBS. He worked this time for the TV news division as a stringer (a reporter who works for a news agency on a part-time basis) during the Paris peace talks on ending the Vietnam War. Within the year, Ed Bradley had returned to the network in New York, ready for a second shot.

CAREER HIGHLIGHTS

Back in the fold and angling for a meaty assignment, Bradley asked for a transfer to Southeast Asia. From 1972 to 1974 he was a familiar figure on television as he delivered the news from war-torn Vietnam and Cambodia. At one point, he narrowly escaped serious injury himself when he was wounded by shrapnel in a mortar attack. He returned to the States, but his assignment in the CBS Washington News Bureau paled in light of the action he had seen and reported over the previous eighteen months. In March 1975, Bradley volunteered to go back to Indochina. There, broadcasting every day during the fall of Saigon (now Ho Chi Minh City) and Phnom Penh, the capitals of South Vietnam and Cambodia, he was one of the last Americans to be ferried out of the danger zone.

The newsman's next stint was coverage of the 1976 presidential campaign. He was initially assigned to an early hopeful, Indiana Senator Birch Bayh. When Bayh dropped out of the race, CBS moved Bradley over to Jimmy Carter's press entourage. Carter won the presidency, and Bradley, on the strength of his solid reporting, landed a prestigious post as CBS White House correspondent. Once again, though, he felt boxed in. "You go to the same place every day and check in," he later complained, adding, "It wasn't the kind of work I wanted to do." Before two years had elapsed in what the self-described "footloose gypsy" considered a confining job, he had moved on to assignments with more drama and exposure. During this period, and until May 1981, Bradley continued to anchor the "CBS Sunday Night News," as he had done since late November 1976.

Bradley became a principal correspondent for "CBS Reports" in 1978, and soon was widely acclaimed for his insightful and analytical documentaries that reflected life at home in America and in the far corners of the earth. As a correspondent for "CBS Reports," Bradley won commendation for his vastly diverse segments. In 1979 alone, he followed the Boston Symphony Orchestra on its historic visit to communist China, developed the compelling segment "Blacks in America: With All Deliberate Speed?" and created "The Boat People," all award-winning reports. One of his most memorable stories, "The Boat People" was a heart-wrenching report on the plight of Vietnamese who lived in small boats stranded off the Malaysian coast. The documentary was aired in January 1979, and "Those who have seen it," said *TV Guide*, "will not forget the image of Bradley carrying refugees ashore through the breaking surf." The segment was later excerpted on a "60 Minutes" broadcast, and few doubt that its excellence was a deciding factor in Bradley's eventual bid to join television's most highly rated news program.

"60 MINUTES"—AND THIRTEEN YEARS

In 1981, he was named successor to Dan Rather on "60 Minutes," one of television's most honored programs and now in its third decade. "Bradley's as good a reporter as I've met in my life," executive producer Don Hewitt told the *Philadelphia Daily News* soon after the hiring. "His presence on the screen is big and important. He is what he purports to be. He doesn't just look the part, he *is* the part."

Bradley joined a resourceful Sunday-night team that already took justifiable pride in the talents of Mike Wallace, Morley Safer, and Harry Reasoner (who died in 1991). Since then, Diane Sawyer has come and gone (to another network) and been replaced by longtime Washington correspondent Lesley Stahl. Steve Kroft also has been added to the list of principal correspondents, and Andy Rooney contributes his wry commentary at the end of each program. "60 Minutes" is the "stuff of TV legend," says the *Los Angeles Times,* and most observers agree that Bradley has been an unqualified part of its success.

In his thirteen seasons with "60 Minutes," Ed Bradley has proven his skill in developing both colorful and controversial stories. He is instinctive in his approach to a subject, sensitive and compassionate in almost every instance, but tough-minded enough to lean hard in less-cordial interviews. His work has brought him nearly every significant broadcasting award, many of them repeated several times over the years. Among his noteworthy stories for "60 Minutes" is his Emmy award-winning profile, "Lena," a 1983 television portrait of singer Lena Horne that Bradley himself counts as his most satisfying piece. He has developed and narrated numerous other impressive segments, from "Schizophrenia," an examination of a perplexing and tragic brain disorder; to "In the Belly of the Beast," a prison interview with Jack Henry Abbott, convicted murderer and author; to "Made in China," a look at forced labor camps inside that country.

Bradley's frenetic pace in search of a story has not diminished, even as middle age has set in. He is seen often on CBS news specials, and he has been an imposing presence among floor correspondents at all but one national political convention since 1976 (he was on another assignment during the Republican gathering in 1984). In addition, Bradley anchored "Street Stories," the CBS prime-time weekly magazine, from its premiere in January 1992 through August 1993. That program is about to leave the network schedule for revision.

Ed Bradley will begin his fourteenth season with "60 Minutes" in September 1994. He recently signed a lucrative four-year deal with the network and will concentrate on the Sunday broadcast and on coverage of special events.

MAJOR INFLUENCES

Often asked about those who have inspired him, Bradley says simply, "My mother, Gladys Bradley, was the biggest influence in my life." Her challenge to him to be everything that he *could* be has kept Bradley from seeing himself as defined by race. He says, "The challenge we all face is to be judged by the body of our work rather than by the color of our bodies."

Bradley mentions one other role model, too: "Leuis Roundtree. I called him my uncle though we weren't blood. He was our neighbor in West Philly, he and his wife, Mildred. He taught me to play ball. He taught me to tie a tie. He taught me just about everything a boy needs to know in life." Usually reticent about sharing his innermost feelings, Bradley uncharacteristically tells about a dream he had after Leuis died, where he saw him in the place they used to live. "I walked up to him and hugged him, and I cried and cried. It was the most beautiful dream I ever had."

MARRIAGE AND FAMILY

Bradley has been married and divorced twice. Few details are available on his 1964 marriage, which ended after only five months. His second wife, to whom he was married from the summer of 1980 until January 1984, was Priscilla Coolidge, sister of singer Rita Coolidge and a performer in her own right. There are no children from either union.

Home to Ed Bradley is a co-op apartment on Manhattan's Central Park West, where photographs, wooden Mandalay Buddhas, and other art objects are mementos of his days as a war correspondent in Southeast Asia. He also owns a retreat in the ski country of Aspen, Colorado. Bradley has said that he would marry again, but concedes that he may not be the ideal mate. Restless by nature and constantly crisscrossing the world to meet the demands of his profession, he has yet to make room in his life for domesticity.

HOBBIES AND OTHER INTERESTS

Journalism has been Bradley's professional commitment for thirty years, but jazz is his lifelong delight. He readily admits that there are two very different sides to his personality. Scott Minerbrook explains Bradley's alter ego in a 1989 *Emerge* cover story: "His best friends have taken to joking with him about 'Eddie' and 'Teddy.' Eddie is the serious journalist. . . . Teddy, on the other hand—the name was given to Bradley by his close friend, Florida Keys musician Jimmy Buffet—is the one who likes to play, . . . wear an earring, let off steam while hanging out with musicians. He likes to climb onstage with the Buffet band or the Neville Brothers and shake the tambourine or a cowbell."

At home in New York, Bradley loves to cook, and friends say his apartment has a magnificent kitchen. Athletic since boyhood, Bradley is an avid skier as well, and he takes to the slopes at Aspen whenever he can borrow enough leisure hours from his heavy schedule. Skiing has become so much a part of his identity that his appearance for CBS at the 1994 Winter Olympics in Lillehammer, Norway, seemed as much an affirmation of his lifestyle as the pursuit of a good story.

As for his other leisure pursuits, Bradley hikes, cycles, works out at a gym, reads thrillers, attends concerts, and listens to his vast collection of recordings.

HONORS AND AWARDS

Distinguished Commentator Award (National Association of Media Women, New York Chapter): 1975
Overseas Press Club of America Award: 1975, 1979
Association of Black Journalists Award: 1977
Emmy Awards (Academy of Television Arts and Sciences): 1979 (three awards), for "The Boat People," "The Boston Goes To China," and Blacks in America"; 1983 (two awards), for "Lena" and "In the Belly of the Beast"; 1985, for "Schizophrenia"; 1992, for "Made in China"
Alfred I. DuPont-Columbia University Award for Broadcast Journalism: 1979, 1980
George Foster Peabody Broadcasting Award (University of Georgia): 1979
Ohio State Award: 1979
George Polk Award in Journalism: 1980
Balch Institute for Ethnic Studies Award: 1991
Sol Taischoff Award (National Press Foundation): 1993

FURTHER READING

BOOKS

Contemporary Black Biography, Vol. II
Madsen, Axel. *60 Minutes: The Power and the Politics of America's Most Popular News Show,* 1984
Who's Who in America, 1994
Who's Who in Black America, 1994-95

PERIODICALS

Current Biography Yearbook 1988
Emerge, Oct. 1989, p.24
Essence, Nov. 1983, p.66; Nov. 1987, p.58; Nov. 1990, p.7
Gentlemen's Quarterly, May 1989, p.141
Los Angeles Times, Apr. 25, 1992, Calendar Section, p.1
People, Nov. 14, 1983, p.69
Philadelphia Daily News, Apr. 18, 1988, p.41; Oct. 23, 1991, p.7; Feb. 3, 1992, p.43
TV Guide, June 22, 1985, p.2; Jan. 25, 1991, p.2; May 5, 1993, p.42

ADDRESS

CBS News
524 West 57th Street
New York, NY 10019-2902

OBITUARY

John Candy 1950-1994
Canadian Actor and Comedian
Star of the Hit Films *Splash*, *Planes, Trains, and Automobiles*, *Uncle Buck*, and *Cool Runnings*

BIRTH

John Franklin Candy was born on October 31, 1950, in Newmarket, just north of Toronto, in the province of Ontario, Canada. His parents were Evangeline (Aker) Candy and Sidney James Candy, an automobile salesman. John had one older brother, Jim.

YOUTH

In 1955, when John Candy was only four years old, his father, Sidney, died of a heart ailment that apparently dated from his days as a serviceman in World War II. Sidney Candy was only 35 years old when he died. Heart disease seems to run in the family—it was the cause of brother Jim's heart attack about twelve years ago, and it was the cause of John's death on March 4, 1994, in Chupaderos, Mexico.

John was raised by his mother and aunt, who both worked in a local department store, with the help of his grandparents. He grew up in East York, a middle-class borough in Toronto. Candy, who was often characterized as an obsessive workaholic as an adult, apparently developed his work habits early. By age 10 he started doing odd jobs, like selling fish and chips and working for three drugstores at the same time.

EDUCATION

Candy attended the local parochial schools, first Holy Cross Separate School and later Neil McNeil Catholic High School, from which he graduated in 1969. His two favorite things in school were acting and sports: he performed in high school drama productions and he also played hockey and football. Sources differ on how good of an athlete he was, but it is clear that he loved to play: "His passion was football," according to Father Michael Doyle, a former principal at McNeil.

Candy attended Centennial Community College in Scarboro, Ontario, from 1969 to 1971. He had to cut his athletic career short when he injured his knee. According to Candy, that was also when he began to have trouble with his weight: "Weight has been a problem for me since I was 21, 22 years old and I was finished playing sports. I lost a kneecap in college and vowed never to go in another locker room again or do any calisthenics." While attending college, he studied journalism and acting and performed in local underground theater productions.

FIRST JOBS

After leaving college in 1971, Candy hoped to develop a professional acting carer. But work was hard to come by, so for a while he subsisted on a variety of odd jobs—selling guns and skis in a department store, mixing paint at a paint factory, and selling paper napkins on the road. His first professional experience came with a four-member group that performed for children, and he soon picked up some commercials and voiceovers.

In 1971 he met Dan Aykroyd. As Candy recalls, "I knew Dan Aykroyd from around town. He was working for the Royal Mail (the Canadian postal service), unloading sacks of mail. We hung around at parties, played improvisational games. We understood each other and had a similar sense of humor. We'd drive around town a lot together."

Soon after they met, representatives from Second City, the famed comedy troupe in Chicago, came to Toronto with plans to open a second branch there. The Chicago Second City troupe, renowned for its satirical improvisational and sketch comedy routines, has included, through the years, such comic geniuses as Mike Nichols, Elaine May, Alan Arkin, John Belushi, Gilda Radner, Bill Murray, and eventually Aykroyd himself—a training ground for many of our best comic actors. Aykroyd encouraged Candy to try out for the new Toronto group. The audition was such a success that Candy was invited to come to Chicago in 1972.

CAREER HIGHLIGHTS

Thus began a professional career that spanned over 20 years; that included live comedy shows, television series, and almost 40 films; and that earned him the love and respect of millions of fans.

EARLY CAREER

The early foundation of Candy's fame as a comedian came from his work with Second City. He spent about two years performing with the Chicago troupe before moving back home to Toronto in 1974 to work with the troupe there. Their comic ingenuity soon earned them a sizable following, and they were offered the opportunity to work on television.

"SCTV"

In 1977, the group began performing its sketches on local television under the name "Second City TV." Shortly thereafter, the show was picked up for syndication in 45 American cities. In 1981, "SCTV" was picked up the NBC network, expanded from 30 to 90 minutes, renamed "SCTV Network 90," and positioned on Friday nights at 12:30 a.m., to follow Johnny Carson on "The Tonight Show."

In all its guises, "SCTV" was an inspired satire on conventional television. Based in the fictional town of Melonville, "SCTV" offered a behind-the-scenes look at a fictional television station. In sketches that have been described as "episodes of brilliantly controlled absurdity," we meet the sleazy station owner, Guy Cabellero (Joe Flaherty), the neurotic station manager, Edith Prickley (Andrea Martin), and an oddball assortment of employees (Candy, Eugene Levy, Catherine O'Hara, Rick Moranis, Martin Short, and Dave Thomas). The "SCTV" team both wrote the sketches and performed them, and Candy, with the others, won two Emmy awards for writing. Together, they created a masterpiece of ensemble comic acting. As David Edelstein wrote in the *Village Voice*, "Individually the 'Second

City TV' performers were merely brilliant and inspired; as a group they were visionary."

Candy created a number of unforgettable characters, including Johnny La Rue, a sleazy late-night talk show host; Dr. Tongue, a creepy horror-movie star; Yosh Shmenge, an accordionist and part of the Shmenge Brothers Happy Wanderers Polka Band; and Tommy Shanks, the town's dim-witted mayor. Many critics consider these creations to be his best work ever.

Response to the show was ecstatic. Reviewers praised its irreverent and razor-sharp wit, attention to detail, and depth of character—"smashingly funny, audacious, and needlingly accurate," said James Wolcott in *New York* magazine, aptly summarizing the view of many commentators. And viewers loved it. As Ian Brown wrote in *Maclean's* magazine, "There is no such thing as an 'SCTV' fan—there are legions of fanatics who follow the show with rabid attention."

Despite such accolades, by 1983 the show was canceled, the victim of its difficult time slot and subsequent poor ratings.

FILMS, FILMS, AND MORE FILMS

Meanwhile, though, Candy had already started a second career in Hollywood. Although he appeared in several undistinguished movies in the early 1970s, his first major film was *1941* (1979), directed by Steven Spielberg. While the film was not one of Spielberg's best, it brought Candy to the attention of movie industry executives. It was *Splash* (1984), also starring Tom Hanks and Daryl Hannah, that was his breakthrough film. Just a few of his best-known films include *The Blues Brothers* (1980), *Stripes* (1981), *National Lampoon's Vacation* (1983), *Little Shop of Horrors* (1986), *Spaceballs* (1987), *Planes, Trains, and Automobiles* (1987), *Who's Harry Crumb?* (1989), *Uncle Buck* (1989), *Home Alone* (1990), *The Rescuers Down Under* (1990), *Delirious* (1991), *JFK* (1991), *Only the Lonely* (1991), and *Cool Runnings* (1993).

When he died, Candy left several films either unfinished or not-yet-released, including *Hostage for a Day*, a TV movie starring George Wendt broadcast in April 1994, his first and only directing effort; *Wagons East*, the Western comedy Candy was filming in Mexico at the time of his death, released in August 1994; and *Canadian Bacon*, in which he played a sheriff from Niagara Falls, New York, who invades Canada, currently slated for release in early 1995.

CANDY'S COMIC APPEAL

Candy's films had a very mixed success at the box office, with some hits and many more misses. He worked constantly, but his choice of roles was questionable. Reviewers repeatedly chided Candy for his choice of weak scripts, often attacking the rest of the film while praising his performance. While he appeared in many films, there are certain similarities in the roles he chose. Candy often played an ordinary guy, a loner, a loser, a slob. But these characters revealed a genuine feeling of vulnerability, sincerity, kindness, sensitivity, and tenderness that made them believable and lovable. As *People* magazine described it, he "managed to mix his own brand of slapstick blundering with a heart-wrenching sense of humility and pain." Certainly his weight was a factor in these roles, contributing to both the slapstick and the pain. But Candy always used it to his advantage. "He doesn't add weight," wrote Pauline Kael in the *New Yorker* magazine, "he adds bounce and imagination."

HEALTH

While his size certainly contributed to his appeal, it may also have contributed to his death. Many of his friends had expressed concern that his weight, combined with his smoking habit and his family history of heart trouble, would prove deadly. Candy himself acknowledged this problem, often complaining in interviews about his difficulties with diets.

MARRIAGE AND FAMILY

Candy married Rosemary Margaret Hobor, a potter, on April 27, 1979. They had two children, Jennifer Anne and Christopher Michael. Despite his success in the public eye, Candy was always fiercely protective of his family's privacy and extremely aloof from the typical Hollywood trappings of success. The family split their time between a home in southern California and a 20-acre farm near Newmarket, about 50 miles outside of Toronto, with a few horses, cows, and cats.

MAJOR INFLUENCES

Commenting once on how much he had loved to watch television as a child, Candy once said, "I loved watching Jack Benny, Jack Paar, 'The Honeymooners,' Burns and Allen, George Gobel, 'The Munsters,' 'Rocky and His Friends,' 'Howdy Doody,' 'Rin Tin Tin,' 'Lassie.' I wasn't influenced by any one show, I was influenced by the medium."

HOBBIES AND OTHER INTERESTS

Sports, and particularly football, remained one of Candy's great passions throughout his life. In addition to being a football fan, he was co-owner (with Bruce McNall, owner of the Los Angeles Kings hockey team, and Wayne Gretzky, the hockey superstar) of the Toronto Argonauts, a team in the Canadian Football League.

SELECTED CREDITS

TV

"Second City T.V.," 1977-79
"SCTV Network 90," 1981-83
"The Last Polka," 1984
"The Canadian Conspiracy," 1986
"Hostage for a Day," 1994 (as director)

MOVIES

Face of the Lady, 1971
Class of '44, 1973
It Seemed Like a Good Idea, 1975
Tunnelvision, 1976
The Clown Murders, 1976
Find the Lady, 1976
The Silent Partner, 1978
Lost and Found, 1979
1941, 1979
The Blues Brothers, 1980
Double Negative, 1980
Stripes, 1981
It Came from Hollywood, 1982
Going Berserk, 1983
National Lampoon's Vacation, 1983
Splash, 1984
Brewster's Millions, 1984
Sesame Street Presents: Follow That Bird, 1985
Summer Rental, 1985
Volunteers, 1985
Armed and Dangerous, 1986
Little Shop of Horrors, 1986
Spaceballs, 1987
Planes, Trains, and Automobiles, 1987
The Great Outdoors, 1988
Speed Zone! 1989 (also titled *Cannonball Fever*)
Uncle Buck! 1989
Who's Harry Crumb? 1989
Home Alone, 1990
Masters of Menace, 1990
The Rescuers Down Under, 1990
Nothing but Trouble, 1991
Delirious, 1991
JFK, 1991

Only the Lonely, 1991
Once Upon a Crime, 1992
Cool Runnings, 1993
Wagons East, 1994

HONORS AND AWARDS

Annual ACTRA Awards (Academy of Canadian Cinema & Television): 1978 and 1984, for Best Writer—Variety (with others)
Emmy Awards (Academy of Television Arts and Sciences): 1982 and 1983, for Outstanding Writing in a Variety or Music Program (with others)

FURTHER READING

BOOKS

McCrohan, Donna. *The Second City: A Backstage History of Comedy's Hottest Troupe*, 1987
Who's Who in America, 1994

PERIODICALS

Current Biography Yearbook 1990; May 1994, p.58 (obituary)
Entertainment Weekly, Mar. 18, 1994, p.10
Maclean's, Mar. 14, 1994, p.66
New York Times, Mar. 5, 1994, p.A12
People, July 13, 1981, p.58; Mar. 21, 1994, p.92
Toronto Star, Mar. 5, 1994, p.A1
Toronto Sun, Mar. 5, 1994, p.4

Mary Chapin Carpenter 1958-
American Singer and Songwriter

BIRTH

Mary Chapin Carpenter was born on February 21, 1958, in Princeton, New Jersey. Her father, Chapin Carpenter, was an executive with *Life* magazine, while her mother, Bowie Carpenter, worked in a private school. The third of their four children, Mary Chapin has three sisters, Mackenzie, Camilla, and Sophie.

Known as "Chapin" to her friends, Carpenter uses "Mary Chapin" as the full form of her first name. She was at first known in the music business by the hyphenated name Mary-Chapin, which she used when her first name caused confusion among fans and reporters. More recently, Carpenter reverted to her real name.

YOUTH

Carpenter had a rather unusual early life for an aspiring country singer. She spent her first years in a fairly typical suburb in New Jersey. She and her sisters are all just a few years apart in age, and they were very close growing up, especially Mary Chapin and Camilla.

As a child, Carpenter loved to ice skate, spending her summers at ice-skating camp in Colorado. Even then, according to Camilla, she was dedicated and disciplined. "Once she finds something that is important to her," Camilla explains, "she really sees it through." Music, also, was important to her from a very early age; it was a big part of their family life as well. Her father listened to jazz, her mother enjoyed opera, and her sisters liked all kinds of music: classical, Broadway show tunes, pop, Motown, and rock and roll. "When I was really young," Carpenter recalls, "I used to listen to whatever was available. I had a little Sears turntable and I'd borrow my older sister's albums, the ones she didn't care about. She'd keep the Motown, all the good stuff, but she had this Judy Collins record. . . . I was about 10 years old and [Collins] had just come out with *Wildflowers*. I fell in love with that record. I'd play it all the time." Carpenter first started making music by banging on the piano and by second grade picked up the guitar, an old hand-me-down that had belonged to her mother.

In 1969, the family moved to Japan, where her father worked as publishing director for the Asian edition of *Life*. Carpenter attended an international school in Tokyo where, for the first time, she began to develop a real passion for music. "We had a science teacher who'd hold these after-school sessions where we'd sit around and play guitar, these kids from all around the world. That's when the light bulb went on in my head. It was like, 'Ooooh, I really like this!'"

Despite her new-found passion for music, the move was really tough on her. According to Mary Chapin, "When we moved away, things changed. That's the turning point or something. Before that everything was a certain way; after that was always different. I felt very much like a loner." After two years in Tokyo, the family returned to the United States, first to New Jersey. After just a few years, though, Chapin Carpenter accepted a new job in Washington, D.C., which Mary Chapin has called home ever since.

Soon after moving to Washington in 1974, Bowie and Chapin Carpenter divorced, and their family life started to unravel. Camilla, to whom Mary Chapin felt closest, went away to college, Sophie stayed with their mother, and Mary Chapin left home to attend high school in Connecticut, returning on school vacations to stay with their father. "I thought that it would probably help me to be away," she says, "because I was just real unhappy."

EDUCATION

Carpenter attended Taft School, an exclusive private college prep school in Connecticut. Whether by inclination, or in reaction to her difficult family circumstances, she became a bit of a loner. "In high school, I wasn't ever a member of the cool group," Carpenter recalls. "I just wasn't cool enough, I wasn't pretty enough, I wasn't savvy enough or something. And I was so convinced of all these feelings that that's when I really retreated into playing music, being by myself, scribbling my thoughts on paper." Already at that point, she was starting to write her own songs.

After graduating from Taft, she took a year off to travel, and then entered Brown University, a prestigious Ivy League college in Providence, Rhode Island—and one often cited as an unexpected choice, perhaps, for a future country singer. Carpenter earned her BA there in 1981, majoring in American Civilization.

FIRST JOBS

Long before leaving college, though, she had started making music. In the summer of 1977, she got up the courage, with her father's support, to try out at an open-mike night at a club in Washington. She was scared to death: "I got a really nice response, and I couldn't even talk between songs because I thought I was going to barf." Throughout college she continued performing, at the college coffeehouse at Brown and at Washington-area clubs during school vacations. For Carpenter, who calls herself a "social dropout," music increased her self-confidence and provided a safe haven. "To me playing guitar was a refuge.... I would retreat to my guitar, sing to my walls, and be very introspective while engaging in some serious navel-gazing. Music became a place where I could express emotions that I ordinarily could not otherwise express in day-to-day life. By the time I graduated college, I was playing around in bars with my friends for fun. Before I knew it, it had evolved into something that I was doing more and more of—and getting paid for. Plus I had discovered that when I was onstage, I felt strong. I felt like *somebody*."

Returning to Washington in 1981 after graduating from Brown, Carpenter continued to appear in local clubs, singing and playing guitar. She primarily performed other people's songs—she was too shy and self-conscious to perform her own material. With no other job, it took a lot of hustling to generate enough gigs to pay the bills, and her songwriting suffered.

Working late nights in bars soon took its toll. While reluctant to speak about it in any detail, Carpenter has confirmed that she developed a problem with alcohol around 1983. "I had a big problem," she admits. "It was awful. I had to make a lifestyle change in a drastic way. It's still so painful to me to think about how I was." At first she thought she'd quit performing. Instead, she decided to stay in the music business, but on her own terms. She found a part-time day job as an administrative assistant with a local philanthropic group, one that gave her the flexibility to continue to perform. With health insurance and a steady paycheck—at that point, she was only making about $40 a night onstage—Carpenter could afford to be more selective about her club dates and freed up enough time to return to writing songs. She also quit drinking and started working only in bars where she could perform original material. It worked. Audiences responded favorably, and she became well known and respected throughout the local music community. That respect was officially acknowledged beginning in 1986, when she won the first of the 30 or so Wammies (Washington Area Music Awards), three Grammy Awards, two Academy of Country Music Awards, and two Country Music Association Awards that she has collected to date.

CHOOSING A CAREER

For Carpenter, the transition to making music her career came partly through luck, partly through talent, and wholly through being in the right place at the right time. In 1986, she decided to record a cassette tape that she could sell at her shows. With the help of guitarist and producer John Jennings, she made a tape of original material in his basement studio. "I'd get a little money together, and I'd cut a song," she says, "and I'd get a little more money together, and I'd cut another song. It was the ultimate labor of love. It had no commercial conscience."

Or so she thought. An acquaintance took the completed tape and shopped it around, playing it for music industry executives in hopes of generating interest. Carpenter was on the verge of signing a contract with Rounder Records, a small independent label specializing in folk music, when an executive from the country division of CBS Records heard the tape and signed her. Her gamble had paid off—determined to make music on her own terms, she had been signed by a major record company. The tape was released on the Columbia label as *Hometown Girl* (1987), her first recording. Sales were not spectacular, but critics raved about it. Even so she kept her day job as an administrative assistant until 1989, when she signed a song-publishing contract. "For me it was more of a validation than signing my record contract," Carpenter says. "It was somebody saying 'We believe in you as a songwriter.' I never expected to receive acknowledgment for my writing."

CAREER HIGHLIGHTS

Since the debut of *Hometown Girl*, Carpenter has released three records: State of the Heart (1989), *Shooting Straight in the Dark* (1990), and *Come*

On Come On (1992). She is scheduled to release her new album, *Stones in the Road*, in the fall of 1994. Since her first release, many have tried, without success, to assign her to a single category of music—is it really country?—while others have taken pains to point out the ways in which she differs from the traditional country approach. Yet Carpenter rejects this whole attitude. "Don't indulge in that kind of format thinking!" she demanded of one reporter. "Just stop it. That's the whole point. Those artificial parameters shouldn't be there."

Carpenter has broken through those artificial limits, creating her own unique musical style, image, and themes. Her songs, delivered in her distinctive husky alto, reflect a diverse group of stylistic influences, including country, folk, pop, rock and roll, and blues. They range from the Cajun-inspired stomp "Down at the Twist and Shout," to the spare, ironic "He Thinks He'll Keep Her," to the poignant, evocative "I Am a Town," to the contemplative, yearning "Only a Dream," to the sassy, rollicking "I Feel Lucky." Her image, also, defies traditional limits. Born in New Jersey, the daughter of a successful executive, educated at an Ivy League university, Carpenter has succeeded in country music without the external image typical of that genre—"no hair spray, no spangles," as the *New York Times Magazine* termed it. And the themes of her music have also presented a departure for country. As a songwriter, Carpenter crafts eloquent stories about women's lives, what Karen Schoemer of the *New York Times* called "succinct but deeply emotional narratives." Thoughtful, introspective, and intensely personal, her songs speak of modern women, sometimes funny, playful, or sassy, sometimes vulnerable, lonely, or sad, but always self-sufficient, independent, and in control of their own lives.

For Carpenter, country music is a broad, inclusive field, and she has succeeded in expanding its horizons—and its audience as well. "When I listen to Trisha, and Wynonna, and Emmylou Harris, I hear the melding of influences in them," Carpenter says. "They're all as different as night and day, but they all can coexist under this banner of country music. People sometimes put down country music by saying, 'Oh, it's full of cliches.' But it's like that in pop music too. I don't think any genre is immune to cliches. What I love about country is its tradition, and that's different from being predictable," Carpenter continues. "I love its simplicity, and that's different from being stupid. I love its genuine quality, which is different from being overly sentimental."

THOUGHTS ON SONGWRITING

While her fans may focus on Carpenter's skill in performing, she finds just as much satisfaction, if not more, in writing her songs. "It's a mysterious process," Carpenter once revealed. "It's a necessary outlet for me. It's therapeutic. I began writing songs as a kid, though I didn't take it seriously at first. As a teenager, I started to do so. That's a time when you really need an emotional outlet. Even now, I'd be adrift if I couldn't write."

MAJOR INFLUENCES

Carpenter has cited such diverse musical influences as The Beatles, Woody Guthrie, Motown music, Bob Dylan, the Rolling Stones, Emmylou Harris, the B-52s, Bruce Cockburn, and others. As she says, "I think artists are giant sponges, drawing from a lot of different influences."

HOME AND FAMILY

Carpenter, who is single, divides her time between life on the road, where she and her bandmates live in a luxury touring bus, and life at home, in her two-bedroom apartment in suburban Virginia, outside Washington, D.C. She lives quietly there, reading, running, renting movies, and writing songs.

For Carpenter, there is a great difference between her life at home writing songs and her life on the road. "Songwriting is very lonely; I'm all by myself when I do it—but it's very fulfilling. I find I have to work hard to balance all the time I've spent by myself doing things. I've got to interact with the world or I tie myself up in knots. It's easy for me to isolate. Out on the road, I have a wonderful band and crew that I'm with, but we're kind of [in] our own little world going from place to place. There's kind of a loneliness in that too, except for that hour-and-a-half or so that you're up on the stage each night, you're in forward motion. On the road, there is a very high level of energy and effort and work. Then you come home, and I think it happens to all of us—post-tour depression that [makes] you wish you were still out there—your routine has come to a screeching halt. It's hard to adjust quickly. I find that I have a blue period after real long tours and though I'm happy to be home, I'm kind of wailing for the first couple of days. I muddle through somehow."

FAVORITE BOOKS

Carpenter mentions two favorite books, *One Writer's Beginnings* by Eudora Welty and *One Hundred Years of Solitude* by Gabriel Garcia Marquez. Commenting on the two, she says, "I like [Welty's] compassion and humanity. After I read [Marquez's] *One Hundred Years of Solitude*, I felt I had read the most incredible story I had ever read."

HOBBIES AND OTHER INTERESTS

Carpenter has been politically active since high school, when she worked on Morris Udall's failed campaign for the 1976 Democratic presidential nomination. Through benefit performances, she has been involved in a variety of causes, including Farm Aid, Earth Day, the Voiceless Victims program of the Institute for Intercultural Understanding, and the Women's Health Environment Network of the Wilderness Society. She has also acted as co-chair of the Country Music AIDS Awareness Campaign Nashville, through which country stars have recorded public service announcements to educate radio listeners about AIDS. "It helps to feel like you're giving a little something back," she says. "It's corny, but it's the truth. It does feel like there is some sense of merging between art and belief and day-to-day life."

RECORDINGS

Hometown Girl, 1987
State of the Heart, 1989
Shooting Straight in the Dark, 1990
Come On Come On, 1992

HONORS AND AWARDS

Academy of Country Music Awards: 1990, Top New Female Vocalist; 1993, Female Vocalist of the Year
10 Best Albums of 1992 (*Time* magazine): *Come On Come On* (No. 4)
Country Music Association Awards: 1992 and 1993 (2 awards), Female Vocalist of the Year
Grammy Awards: Best Country Vocal Performance, Female (3 awards), 1992 for "Down at the Twist and Shout"; 1993 for "I Feel Lucky"; 1994 for "Passionate Kisses"
Rolling Stone Music Awards/Readers' Picks: 1993, Best Country Artists (No. 2)

FURTHER READING

BOOKS

Who's Who in America, 1994

PERIODICALS

Country Music, July/Aug. 1990, p. 42; July/Aug. 1993, p.54
Current Biography, Feb. 1994
New York Times Magazine, Aug. 1, 1993, p.36
People, Aug. 31, 1992, p.97
Rolling Stone, Mar. 21, 1991, p.22
Washington Post, June 11, 1989, p.G1

ADDRESS

Studio One Artists
7010 Westmoreland Ave., Suite 100
Tacoma Park, MD 20912

Benjamin Chavis 1948-
American Civil Rights Activist and Minister
Former Executive Director of the NAACP

BIRTH

Dr. Benjamin Franklin Chavis [CHAY-vis], Jr., was born on January 22, 1948, in Oxford, North Carolina. His father, Benjamin Sr., was a bricklayer, and his mother, Elisabeth, was a school teacher. The family had a long history of civil rights activism, as Chavis acknowledges: "The struggle for freedom, the struggle for justice, was a part of my family roots even before I was born." He grew up hearing stories about his great-great-grandfather, the Reverend John Chavis, a Greek and classics scholar. Rev. Chavis was the first black minister to be ordained by the Presbyterian church and the first black to graduate from Princeton. A freed black during the era of slavery, Rev. Chavis taught the white children of slave owners. But he also opened an underground school for the children of slaves, teaching them to read and write. For this crime, he was beaten to death. The school where Rev. Chavis taught later evolved into the University of North Carolina, the alma mater of his great-great-grandson.

YOUTH

Benjamin Chavis grew up in Oxford, North Carolina. Like the rest of the South at that time, Oxford was a segregated community with separate public facilities for blacks and whites. Even at a young age, Chavis was forced to confront racism. He started out his schooling at the North Carolina Colored Orphanage, where his mother taught. The difference between that school and the one at the white orphanage was clear—the "colored" students had few school supplies, and their only books were tattered hand-me-downs from the white students, with racist remarks scrawled inside.

EARLY MEMORIES

Once, when Chavis and his mother were shopping for Christmas presents for her students at the orphanage, they saw a young black child being harassed by a white clerk. They were both outraged. "My mother took her $100 worth of wrapped gifts and threw them up in the air," Chavis proudly remembers. "'I'll never set foot in this drugstore again as long as I live,' she said. And to this day, she never has."

BECOMING AN ACTIVIST

When Chavis was 12, his father gave him his first NAACP card at a family ceremony. Chavis began reading about the history of the NAACP, or National Association for the Advancement of Colored People. Founded in 1909, the NAACP is the nation's oldest and largest civil rights organization. Using legal challenges in the court system, demonstrations, and legislative action, the NAACP has worked for most of this century to end discrimination against blacks and other minorities. To join the NAACP "was part of my initiation into manhood," according to Chavis. "I saw it as a badge of honor. It started me on a lifelong pursuit of challenging racial injustice."

The following year marked his first foray into civil rights protest. At age 13, tired of reading only worn, hand-me-down books, Chavis walked into the whites-only library and asked to check out a book. He was told to leave. He refused, so the librarian called his parents and the police. With his parents' support, Chavis stood his ground. Soon, a crowd started to gather. The librarian gave in, Chavis got his book, and the library was soon open to blacks. At that time, it was unusual—and dangerous—for a black person to challenge a white person in this way, as one of his childhood friends, now a lawyer in Washington, D.C., explains: "He asked why. A lot of us when we were told to go away we would just do so, but Ben would always challenge, always ask why."

EDUCATION

Chavis continued such activism throughout the 1960s, in high school and later in college. As a high school student in 1965, he met Dr. Martin Luther King, Jr., while acting as youth coordinator for the Southern Christian Leadership Conference, the organization King founded. Chavis then attended the University of North Carolina, while also working as an organizer for the Commission for Racial Justice (CRJ). Chavis earned a Bachelor of Arts degree (B.A.) in chemistry in 1969.

Although he left school at that point, Chavis later returned to his studies to earn several graduate degrees, including the Master of Divinity degree (M.Div.) *magna cum laude* from Duke University Divinity School, and the Doctor of Ministry degree (D.Min.) from Howard University. Chavis has also completed the course requirements for the Doctor of Philosophy degree (Ph.D.) in systematic theology at Union Theological Seminary in New York City.

CAREER HIGHLIGHTS

EARLY CAREER

Chavis has worked for much of his life with the United Church of Christ (UCC) ministry, a predominately white, middle- and upper-class Protestant church headquartered in Cleveland, Ohio. He started while still in college, first as a volunteer organizer with the UCC's Commission for Racial Justice (CRJ), then as a part-time staffer in 1968. After graduating from college the following year, he went to work as a high-school chemistry teacher. In 1970 he was ordained as a minister with the UCC, continuing his organizing work as well.

THE WILMINGTON 10

The events that brought Chavis to national prominence as a civil rights activist began the following year. In 1971, Chavez was sent by the UCC to Wilmington, North Carolina, when the local minister requested help with a potentially volatile situation. The city's segregated school system, challenged in a lawsuit filed by the NAACP, was under a court order to desegregate. When Chavis arrived, the atmosphere was tense. The black students felt they were being treated unfairly, and they decided to boycott the schools. Chavis and his supporters were holed up in a Wilmington church, opposed by local residents as well as a racist paramilitary group called the Rights of White People. White vigilantes began shooting into the church, and the police stood by without responding. The rioting that ensued left two people dead and over one million dollars in property damage.

One year later, Chavis and nine other activists, including eight teenagers, were indicted on conspiracy, assault, and arson charges. Witnesses at the trial in September 1972 claimed that Chavis had planned the firebombing of a grocery store and had shot at police and fire fighters responding to the emergency. All ten were found guilty on October 17, 1972. Chavis received the harshest sentence, a total of 34 years, for fire bombing of property and conspiracy to assault emergency personnel. He was briefly imprisoned before being released on bond.

Steadfastly maintaining their innocence, Chavis and the other members of the Wilmington 10, as they were called, spent the next eight years fighting the verdicts. The defense team filed a series of appeals at successively higher levels of the justice system. After losing their final appeal, they were forced to return to prison in February 1976. Later that year, the main prosecution witnesses recanted their testimony, eventually admitting that they made up their stories under pressure from local police. Even after that, the Wilmington 10 were denied a new trial. Many observers saw a consistent pattern of misconduct on the part of the judges and the lawyers for the prosecution, and the case sparked national and international outrage. In 1979, the respected human rights watchdog group Amnesty International, previous winner of the Nobel Peace Prize, cited the Wilmington 10 as political prisoners—the first such case in the U.S. Chavis was paroled from prison in December 1979.

The following year, a federal appeals court unanimously reversed the convictions of all the members of the Wilmington 10. The court concluded that they were denied their constitutional right to a fair trial because their attorneys weren't given full access to the witnesses' testimony—testimony that the judges called inconsistent, full of perjured (lying) statements, and given only under coercion by the police. The appeals court overturned the convictions and exonerated the Wilmington 10 of all charges. Finally, justice—but only after almost ten years fighting the court system, the loss of freedom, and years spent enduring degrading and dangerous conditions in jail.

PRISON LIFE

Chavis spent almost four years in prison. Prison life was harsh and unrelenting. He endured handcuffs, leg irons, chains, strip-searches, a burst appendix, and a 131-day hunger strike. Because officials worried that he would organize the other prisoners, he was transferred to five different prisons. But Chavis remained unbowed. "I found an inner strength," he has said. "I realized I was not the first African-American to be imprisoned unjustly. When they put those chains about my ankles, I would think about the chains my great-grandparents wore.

"But prison was not the final chapter in my life, it was a chapter. I decided not to serve time but to make time serve me." And he succeeded. While in prison, Chavis earned his Master's degree in divinity from Duke University Divinity School. He also learned Greek and translated the New Testament from English to Greek. Although he was a model prisoner, the officials refused to bend any rules. He was taken to his classes at Duke in shackles, and the only place available for study after 10:00 p.m.—lights out—was the prison bathroom. "I can't describe to you just how filthy a prison toilet can be." Throughout, Chavis demonstrated what friends call his inner peace. The Rev. Leon White, who has known Chavis since the 1970s, described his moral growth in prison. "I never saw him crack," White said. "Ben was like an iron wall. He came out of prison a fuller dimension of himself. Like [South African political leader Nelson] Mandela, he was stronger than before. He went in as a political activist and came out as a minister of stature, a spiritual leader."

RECENT YEARS

After his release from prison in December 1979, Chavis returned to the Commission for Racial Justice, where he held a series of positions before being named Executive Director in late 1985. Throughout the 1980s and early 1990s, he also served in leadership roles in such organizations as the National Council of Churches, the National Black Leadership Roundtable, The Southern Organizing Committee for Economic and Social Justice, and the National Coalition for Peace in Angola. In addition, he was clergy coordinator for Jesse Jackson's 1984 presidential campaign.

Chavis became best known for his pioneering environmental work in the 1980s. While serving as Executive Director of the CRJ, he conducted a 1987 study that matched up zip codes, census data, and toxic sites. This landmark study found a clear link between race and pollution—toxic sites were consistently being placed in areas inhabited by blacks. To describe it, Chavis coined the term "environmental racism." "It is racial discrimination in environmental policy making," he explains. "It is the deliberate targeting of people-of-color communities for hazardous waste facilities, such as landfills and incinerators." And it was a problem that had been ignored by the traditional environmental groups, whose leaders and members are predominately white. For his work in this area, Chavis was named a senior advisor to the Clinton-Gore transition team in late 1992, charged with developing policies on environmental issues for the new presidential administration.

NAACP

In April 1993, Chavis was named Executive Director of the NAACP, replacing the retiring Benjamin Hooks. The year-long selection process for that position was often filled with strife and dissension. Many saw it as a turning point, a referendum on the future direction and purpose of the NAACP, which some critics called irrelevant, out of touch with current needs, and still living in the glory days of the early civil rights movement. Some charge that the group has concentrated too heavily on civil rights issues, which primarily concern the middle class, while ignoring the social problems of young and poor urban blacks, like crime, violence, drugs, poverty, unemployment, and dysfunctional families.

Many see Chavis as a dynamic leader ready to bring the NAACP into the present. For his part, Chavis has clarified his view of the role of the organization: "The NAACP is a social-change organization. We're not a social service. So the NAACP is not going to start having soup lines or building housing shelters. We're going to activate our 2,200 units . . . and get them to focus on impacting the public-policy agenda at the local level, the state level, and the federal level in a way that can make a difference." To that end, he has identified certain priorities: to launch an aggressive campaign to recruit new young black members; to fight neighborhood crime by increasing the organization's presence in communities; to build an endowment fund to ensure financial stability and independence; to extend membership to other minorities; to establish chapters in Africa and the Caribbean to create an international human rights organization; to fight environmental racism; and to increase lobbying efforts in Congress. It is an impressive agenda, and an ambitious one. His many supporters hope he can succeed. [See Appendix for Update on Chavis.]

MARRIAGE AND FAMILY

Chavis has been married twice. He has divulged little information about his first marriage, which took place when he was quite young and which ended in divorce. The couple had four children, now grown: Michele, Paula, Benjamin III, and Renita.

Chavis remarried in 1989. He met his second wife, Dominican-born Martha Rivera Chavis, in June of that year. Fluent in French and Portuguese, she was working at the Angolan Embassy in Paris as a translator. He was visiting the embassy en route to Africa while protesting U.S. policy toward the Angolan government. They were married just three months later. They have two young children, Franklin and Ana.

WRITINGS

An American Political Prisoner Appeals for Human Rights, 1979
Psalms from Prison, 1983
"Toxic Wastes and Race in the United States," 1987

HONORS AND AWARDS

National Community Service Award (Congressional Black Caucus): 1977
Paul Robeson National Freedom Medal (German Democratic Republic): 1977
Letelier-Moffitt International Human Rights Award (National Institute for Policy Sciences): 1978
National Courage Award (Southern Christian Leadership Conference): 1979
National Award (National Conference of Black Political Scientists): 1980
International Human Rights Award (Howard University Law School): 1980
Marcus Garvey/Steve Biko Memorial Award (University of Colorado): 1981
William Spofford Human Rights Award (Episcopal Church Publishing Company): 1982
Horrace Sudduth Award (National Business League): 1989
Gertrude E. Rush Distinguished Service Award (National Bar Association): 1991
Martin Luther King, Jr., Freedom Award (Progressive Baptist Convention)

FURTHER READING

BOOKS

Who's Who among Black Americans, 1992-93

PERIODICALS

Akron Beacon Journal, Oct. 3, 1993, Magazine Section, p.4
Audubon Magazine, Jan.-Feb. 1992, p.30
Charlotte Observer, Apr. 17, 1993, p.A15
Ebony, July 1993, p.76
Los Angeles Times, Apr. 18, 1993, p.M3
New York Times, Dec. 15, 1979, p.A10; Dec. 5, 1980, p.A20; Apr. 10, 1993, p.A6; Apr. 11, 1993, Sec. I, p.20
Newsweek, June 14, 1993, p.68
People, July 19, 1993, p.65
U.S. News and World Report, Aug. 30, 1993, p.34
Washington Post, May 16, 1993, p.A11

ADDRESS

NAACP
4805 Mt. Hope Drive
Baltimore, MD 21215-3297

Connie Chung 1946-
American Broadcast Journalist
Co-Anchor of "CBS Evening News" and
Host of "Eye To Eye With Connie Chung"

BIRTH

Constance Yu-Wha Chung was born in Washington, D.C., on August 20, 1946, the tenth and youngest child of William Ling and Margaret (Ma) Chung. She was the first in her family to be born on American soil. Before the Chungs immigrated to the United States in 1945, two daughters and three sons had died in their native China, where medical treatment for civilians was rarely obtainable in the turbulent years preceding and during World War II. Chung's surviving siblings are her four sisters—Josephine, Charlotte, June, and Mimi.

YOUTH

Connie Chung spent her childhood in the midst of a happy and boisterous brood growing up in Washington's Maryland suburbs. Her father, a former intelligence officer in the government of Chiang Kai-shek, had moved his family to the U.S. capital, where he worked at the Chinese Embassy. But political changes in China would affect the lives of the Chung family in Washington. In 1949, the Communists seized power and ousted the government of Chiang Kai-shek, which retreated to Taiwan. At that point, the elder Chung took a job in the Washington office of the United Nations.

The family lived in a modest Washington neighborhood, and Connie remembers the simple pleasures of parties and picnics and playing with the paper dolls she pressed between the pages of *Life* magazine. As the baby of the family, she was overshadowed by the vivacious older sisters who had been given the honor of choosing her name. When William Chung called from the hospital with the news of her birth, the sisters "went to their movie magazines and said 'the first page we turn to is going to be her,'" Connie tells now in mock horror. "It could have been a real disaster, but it was Constance Moore [a movie and television actress of that era]. Oh, was I lucky."

Connie was an exceptionally quiet and sensitive little girl—meek, by her own admission—and recalls a time when she ran home crying because the teacher noted on her report card that she spoke too softly. By her teen years, though, she had learned to speak up with confidence, and she began to take part in school activities. Always small and delicate of build, Chung looks back at her youthful appearance, which she describes as being as narrow as a "small letter *l* with long feet."

EARLY MEMORIES

Once the Chung family had settled in the U.S., they conformed without delay to their new culture. They did, however, continue to speak Chinese at home, and being at ease in the language of her ancestors has proved to be an advantage to Connie's career. One great societal difference, though, that was quickly put to rest in this country was the widely accepted Chinese custom of men having concubines (mistresses). Connie has a clear memory of listening to her mother reveal what life was like under such circumstances. "My mother would tell us these horrible stories," Connie says, "where she would walk into a restaurant and say, 'I'm here to meet with Mr. Chung,' and they would say, 'Oh, Mrs. Chung is already back there.' She would be livid."

EDUCATION

Chung was active in student government during her high-school years, developing a yen for politics that was further fed in the news-saturated atmosphere of Washington. She attended the University of Maryland and initially majored in biology. But after a stimulating summer internship writing speeches and press releases for New York Congressman Seymour Halpern, she promptly switched to journalism. The shift in disciplines proved both provident and timely. Chung received her bachelor of science degree in journalism from Maryland in 1969.

CHOOSING A CAREER

With a brand-new college diploma in hand, Chung was intent on breaking into television news. She took her first step in that direction with a job as secretary and copy clerk at Washington's Channel 5, WTTG-TV. Smart and engagingly aggressive, she soon worked her way up to newswriting and on-air reporting. Pressure was heavy on the networks at this time to hire more women and minorities—and Chung qualified in both categories. CBS, already impressed with what it had seen of her, was quick to sign her on in 1971 when she applied for work in its Washington affiliate.

CAREER HIGHLIGHTS

Engrossed in her new job and eager to take on any assignment, Chung covered a wide variety of news stories, from murders to air disasters to political activities on Capitol Hill. Dan Rather, now her co-anchor at CBS, remembers her dogged persistence from those early days, and once told a *New York* interviewer, "You couldn't be around her for five seconds and not know that she was willing to do anything . . . . She was literally the first person off the bench to tug at [the bureau chief's] sleeve and say 'send me in, coach.' That was very impressive."

Chung soon began to report on national and international issues. She covered George McGovern's 1972 presidential campaign, becoming an expert on the (unsuccessful) candidate in the process. After the election, she accompanied President Richard Nixon to the Middle East and the Soviet Union. She elbowed her way into the toughest assignments and was one of the most energetic and tenacious reporters in interviewing key figures of the Watergate scandal that ultimately led to Nixon's 1974 resignation.

The hard-working young reporter was assigned to CBS affiliate KNXT in Los Angeles in 1976, and there she quickly rose to anchor stardom on both local and national broadcasts. Her salary, too, escalated in relationship to her popularity, eventually reaching an estimated $700,000 before she left CBS and the West Coast in 1983 to anchor "NBC News at Sunrise" from New York. Only a little over a decade earlier she had been working for $27,000 a year. *Newsweek* noted at that time that the "ferociously indefatigable Chung began carrying the most grueling workload in the electronic press," as she simultaneously took on assignments as a reporter for "Today" and political correspondent for NBC's "Nightly News." To further burden an already demanding schedule, she also anchored the latter show's Saturday evening edition. Chung was working eighteen-hour days, running home to snatch three hours of sleep each weekday afternoon and another three hours at night. Even Saturdays were hectic as she prepared for the evening news.

In those early years with NBC, Chung appeared first as chief correspondent, then as co-anchor, with Roger Mudd in a prime-time newsmagazine that was canceled for lack of viewer interest. In March 1986, she left the "Sunrise" show to spend time on other assignments and on an expanded schedule that called for her to fill in occasionally for Tom Brokaw on the weeknight news. She co-wrote and hosted several specials, exhibiting, said a *Savvy* feature story, "her agile mastery of the broadcasting switcheroo, from the sober reportorial mode to a peppier, fluffier, eye-zapping style designed for what Chung calls 'the more populist' subjects." Some of those specials were so removed from hard news that she had to suffer harsh reviews. However, her energy and good nature helped to deflect the carping of critics.

In 1989, Chung returned to her first network home, CBS, to anchor the Sunday news and head up a weekly show called "Saturday Night with Connie Chung." Critics attacked both host and network for corrupting the newsmagazine format with staged footage of actual events, and the program made a quick exit. Undaunted, Chung was soon back on prime time with "Face to Face with Connie Chung," a revamped series that won an Emmy Award for its timely interviews and groundbreaking reports. Although successful, the new show was abandoned when its host cut back on her frenetic schedule in hopes of starting a family.

Throughout the frustration of trying to establish a surefire TV newsmagazine and to shrug off a growing reputation for covering "soft" news, Chung managed to stay focused. She served as correspondent and rotating anchor for CBS coverage of the 1991 war in the Persian Gulf, and contributed to the network's report on the 1992 political campaign. A tireless worker, in spite of her "reduced" workload, she also continued to fill in frequently for anchorman Dan Rather.

AN ANCHOR SEAT AT LAST

Connie Chung's career reached new heights in June 1993 when she was named co-anchor with Rather on the weekday "CBS Evening News." She "has been building for this moment," wrote Rick Marin in *TV Guide*, "since she started answering phones at Washington, D.C.'s Channel 5 24 years ago." Chung currently is the only woman anchor on a major network, and the second woman ever to grasp that prize assignment. Barbara Walters had an ill-fated co-anchor stint with the late Harry Reasoner (1976-78), and networks have shied away from this kind of pairing ever since. To date, no woman has been the sole regular anchor on a weeknight network news program.

Chung has one of the highest viewer popularity ratings (and highest salaries) in network news, and also is immensely well-liked by her colleagues. Driven in her career, glamorous to her public, mischievous and irreverent in her frequent celebrity appearances, she is also totally unpretentious in person. Even critics who question the weight of her authority have few doubts that she will carry the torch for her gender in changing the face of network news.

Currently, Chung plans to continue to anchor her new "Eye To Eye with Connie Chung" series as a second major assignment, but insists that her commitment to the nightly news broadcast has first priority.

MARRIAGE AND FAMILY

Married to talk-show host Maury (Maurice Richard) Povich, whom she met on her first job in Washington more than two decades ago, Chung often speaks of their long-term involvement. Their romance began while both were working in California, but they did not marry for six years. Their careers took separate paths, and they were estranged briefly. Even after their wedding on December 2, 1984, they had a "commuter" marriage for a year until Povich moved from Washington to New York to anchor "A Current Affair." He now hosts the nationally syndicated daytime talk show that bears his name.

The high-profile media couple live in a spacious co-op apartment on Manhattan's West Side during the week, and spend as many weekends as possible at their 1840 country house in New Jersey. There are no children from this union, although Povich has two grown daughters from an earlier marriage. In 1990, Chung publicly announced plans to curtail her work schedule and "take a very aggressive approach to having a baby." So far, she has been disappointed. For Chung, at age 47 and with a new and demanding job, motherhood seems to be a dwindling prospect.

MEMORABLE EXPERIENCES

Chung, who speaks Chinese, visited the land of her heritage for the first time in 1987. As part of an NBC news team broadcasting live from Beijing and other cities in China, she interviewed relatives she had not met before, learning from them about the war years of the 1940s and the Cultural

Revolution of Communist leader Mao Zedong. "I was pretty anxious about it" [going in with cameras rolling], Chung admitted, "but it was the most rewarding experience I've ever had." In a moving interview a few years ago, she told of her days in China and of visiting her grandparents' graves. "I cried a lot with my relatives . . . . My life has been much more defined by my roots since that experience."

HOBBIES AND OTHER INTERESTS

An ambitious and diligent journalist, Chung seems to have little time for interests outside her work and the reading that it entails. She is, say her husband and friends, a world-class shopper who can find relaxation in combing the stores for new fashions. "It's mental therapy to get lost in something mundane and fun," she explains. One entire bedroom in the Chung/Povich apartment has been converted into closet space for Connie's beautiful, and meticulously maintained, wardrobe.

Besides the shopping sprees, Chung enjoys weekends at her country house or, whenever she can slip away, in the Washington area with her now-widowed mother. And when the New York Knicks play at home, she and Maury often are seen cheering for their team from the sidelines.

HONORS AND AWARDS

Certificate of Achievement (U.S. Humane Society): 1969, for broadcasts promoting public awareness of the cruelty of seal harvesting
Outstanding Excellence in News Reporting and Public Service Award (Chinese-American Citizens Alliance): 1973
Outstanding Young Woman of the Year (*Ladies Home Journal*): 1975
Emmy Award (National Academy of Television Arts and Sciences): 1978, 1980, 1987, for individual achievement
Women in Communications Award (California State University): 1979
George Foster Peabody Award (Maryland Center for Public Broadcasting): 1980, for programs on the environment
First Amendment Award (Anti-Defamation League of B'nai B'rith): 1981
Silver Gavel Award (American Bar Association): 1991, for report on the controversy over testing rapists for AIDS

FURTHER READING

BOOKS

Famous Asian Americans, 1992
Who's Who in America, 1992-93

PERIODICALS

Business Week, May 31, 1993, p.33

Current Biography Yearbook 1989
Good Housekeeping, June 1993, p.112
Harper's Bazaar, Oct. 1985, p. 218; Aug. 1989, p.130
Ladies' Home Journal, Oct. 1993, p.66
New York Times, Feb. 19, 1990, p.C11; May 16, 1993, p.C18
People, June 10, 1985, p.151; Apr. 10, 1989, p.116; Aug. 2, 1990, p.74; June 21, 1993, p.59
Redbook, Oct. 1991, p.48
Savvy, Apr. 1988, p.46
TV Guide, Aug. 12, 1989, p.2; Aug. 17, 1990, p.33; June 5, 1993, p.8
Vanity Fair, Nov. 1988, p.165

ADDRESS

Office of Connie Chung
555 West 57th Street, 18th Floor
New York, NY 10019

Beverly Cleary 1916-
American Writer for Children and Young Adults
Author of the *Ramona* Series, *Henry Huggins*,
The Mouse and the Motorcycle, and
Dear Mr. Henshaw

BIRTH
Beverly Bunn Cleary was born April 12, 1916, in McMinnville, Oregon. She was the only child of Chester and Mable (Atlee) Bunn. Chester was a farmer and Mable had been a teacher before her marriage.

YOUTH
Beverly spent her early years in a 13-room farmhouse on an 80-acre farm that had been in her father's family for several generations.

She grew up near the small town of Yamhill (population 300). She loved those early years on the farm and the warmhearted people of Yamhill. Her father's family had been part of the pioneer migration that had settled Oregon in the nineteenth century, and she was always reminded: "never forget your pioneer ancestors!" She affectionately recalls that she sat on those "hard pioneer laps and felt that everyone loved me."

But life was to change for Beverly. When she was six, her father was forced to rent the farm and move the family to Portland. It was a time of financial hardship for the Bunns, as for many families across the country, and things were going to get worse. Her father had received little formal education, so after moving to the city, the only job he was able to find was as a guard in a bank. It paid poorly, and after a life outdoors, he had to stand on a hard marble floor in a basement vault area all day. Beverly loved living in a neighborhood full of playmates her own age, but her father and mother were unhappy. Her mother was glad to leave the farm; the back-breaking labor required of a farm wife did not suit her. But the financial distress of those years took its toll on both parents.

EDUCATION

GRADE SCHOOL

Beverly began grade school at Fernwood Grammar School in Portland. She had looked forward to first grade with much anticipation—she would finally learn to read! Her mother had always encouraged her love of books and had even started the first lending library in Yamhill. But what followed for Beverly was "the most terrible year of my life; the boundaries of childhood closed like a trap." She was in a first grade classroom with forty children and a teacher who "ruled by fear and shame." Beverly received the teacher's punishment for not paying attention: a rap across the hands with a bamboo stick. She remembers the tears of pain, but mostly the feeling of humiliation. She became ill, missed alot of school, and fell behind. With all those problems, and the intimidation of the teacher, she was miserable. "I could not read; I wept and begged to stay home from school." When her mother went to see for herself how Beverly was being treated, the teacher was kind and sweet. Beverly learned another "bitter lesson of childhood—an adult can be a hypocrite."

She made it to second grade where she learned to read, but it was not until third grade, at the age of eight, that she learned to *love* to read. "The accidental discovery, while looking at pictures in the library books my mother always provided, that I was reading and enjoying what I read was one of the most exciting moments of my life. I suddenly felt young, and it is a marvelous thing to feel young at the age of eight."

But she was frustrated and disappointed in much of what she found written for children. "In those important years of childhood reading that followed victory over our school readers, we wanted fun, excitement, adventure, magic. Most of all we wanted stories that would make us laugh. Laughter is reassuring, and we were in need of reassurance.... I longed for stories about my neighborhood and about my classroom. Why didn't authors write books about everyday problems that children could solve for themselves?" With the encouragement of teachers throughout her school years, she decided she would do just that.

FIRST WRITINGS

Cleary wrote her first published piece—a book review of *Dr. Doolittle*—while in the third grade. She won a free book, and she became a minor celebrity in school when her picture appeared in the *Oregon Journal*. In the fourth grade, she wrote an essay on the beaver for a writing contest sponsored by a local store. She won the first prize—two dollars—because no one else had entered the competition.

From Cleary's descriptions of herself at this age in her memoir (*A Girl from Yamhill*), a reader can see more than a passing similarity to her best-known, and by the author's own admission, favorite character, Ramona Quimby. The heroine of the books for which Cleary is most famous, Ramona is spunky, delightfully curious, and clearly puzzled by the world of grown-ups. Like Ramona's doll Chevrolet (named for her aunt's car), Cleary's first doll was named Fordson-Lafayette (for a neighbor's tractor). Like Ramona, she remembers walking through her neighborhood on stilts fashioned from old tin cans, yelling "Pieface" at the other kids. Like Ramona, Cleary remembers being referred to as a "nuisance" by a teacher, and the pain and resentment those words inspired.

And like Ramona, Cleary noticed her father's growing hopelessness at the family's financial difficulties. Mr. Bunn lost his job during the Depression, an era during the 1930s when up to 30 percent of the American workforce was unemployed. She writes that she felt "sorrow was creeping into our house." Her father, once a gentle, kind man, became angry, frustrated, and despairing. Beverly's mother became cruel and manipulative. Feeling her life was over, she tried to live through her daughter.

In part to escape the stifling atmosphere at home, Cleary became active in the Camp Fire Girls and was a constant presence at the public library, devouring all kinds of books. She remembers an assignment given by her seventh grade reading teacher and librarian, Miss Smith, to write about a favorite literary character. The assignment at first puzzled her; she finally wrote "about a girl who went to Bookland and talked to several of my favorite charcters. I wrote on and on, inventing conversations that the characters might have had with a strange girl. As rain beat against the windows, a feeling of peace came over me as I wrote far beyond the required length of the essay. I had discoverd the pleasure of writing, and to this day, whenever it rains, I have the urge to write."

When she returned the paper, Miss Smith announced to the class: "When Beverly grows up, she should write children's books." "I was dumbfounded," Cleary recalls. "Miss Smith was praising my story-essay with words that pointed to my future, a misty time I rarely even thought about. I was not used to praise. Mother did not compliment me. Now I was not only being praised in front of the whole class, but receiving approval that was to give direction to my life."

HIGH SCHOOL

Cleary attended U.S. Grant High School in Portland. She continued to do well in school, and to write well. She worked on the school literary magazine and took part in school activities, but always with the constraints of her family's financial difficulties and her mother's domineering presence. When her senior year was coming to an end, she truly didn't know what would become of her. College, because it was too expensive, was out of the question. She remembers listening to her parents discuss her future, and feeling like a burden. "What future, I wondered, and why couldn't my parents speak directly to me about it? I wanted to write; writing was expected of me, but what did I, an ordinary girl, have to write about? I could not depend on my pen and imagination for a living."

COLLEGE

But then a letter arrived from her aunt in California, offering to let Beverly stay with her family and attend a junior college, with free tuition. Against her mother's wishes, but with her father's full approval and encouragement, Beverly left Oregon for California after her senior year of high school. She attended Chaffey Junior College in Ontairo, California, for two years, and then moved on to the University of California at Berkeley, where she received her bachelor's degree in English in 1938. Cleary had always loved libraries, and the aunt she had lived with was a librarian, so she decided she would study librarianship at the University of Washington, from which she received her bachelor's degree in library science in 1939.

FIRST JOBS AND MAJOR INFLUENCES

Cleary's first job was as a children's librarian at the Yakima Public Library in Yakima, Washington. As part of her duties, she was a storyteller, and she loved to develop stories to keep the children absorbed. "Although I told folk and fairy tales, I think I learned to write for children in those Saturday afternoon story hours. When I began to write *Henry Huggins*, I did not know how to write a book, so I mentally told the stories to that remembered audience and wrote them down as I told them. This is why my first book is a collection of stories about a group of characters rather than a novel."

It was her experiences with a particularly feisty group of children that also stirred the seed of her writer's ambition. She recalls "a band of unenthusiastic readers, who came to the library once a week from one of the parochial schools for help in selecting books that might encourage them to read. They were a lively bunch and fun to work with, but the sad truth was that there was very little in the library they wanted to read. They wanted funny stories, and they wanted stories about the sort of children they knew. I sympathized because I had wanted funny stories about the sort of children I knew when I was their age."

Cleary met her husband, Clarence, in college. After their marriage in 1940, they moved to California, where she became the post librarian at a U.S. army hospital in Oakland, a position she kept until World War II ended in 1945. In 1948, Cleary worked in a bookstore in Berkeley, California, in the children's department. After a good look at the sorts of books being published for children, she thought she could do better. She decided to give it a try.

CAREER HIGHLIGHTS

Cleary recalls the setting for her first attempt at writing. "We had bought a house and had stored an old kitchen table in an empty bedroom. After the Christmas rush [at the bookstore], I found myself for the fist time in my life with free time, a quiet place in which to work and—oh joy!—confidence in myself. I sat down at that old table, wrote *Henry Huggins*, and have been at it ever since."

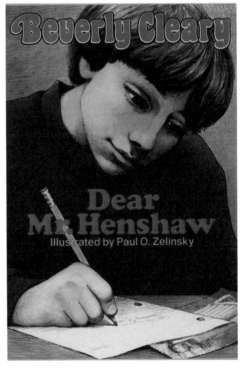

Cleary sent *Henry Huggins* to only one publisher—William Morrow in New York. The first editor who read it decided that Morrow would publish it. It was an immediate success and is still a popular book more than 40 years after its first appearance. Cleary published almost one book a year for the next two decades, producing such favorites as *Ellen Tebbits, Otis Spofford,* and *Emily's Runaway Imagination.*

Henry Huggins was the first of many books set in Portland, around Klickitat Street, and featuring Henry and Beatrice (called Beezus) and Ramona Quimbly. Many readers have noted that Cleary's characters, whether young children or teenagers, male or female, are recognizable and believable. Cleary says that even though she began *Henry Huggins* with a teenage girl in mind, Henry just sort of took over the story. Her book *Fifteen,* written almost 40 years ago, is still a favorite, despite the changes and challenges in the lives of adolescents. She receives many letters from young boys who tell her that her books, especially *The Mouse and the Motorcycle,* are the first they enjoyed reading. "I thought they were some more of the rotten boring books. Boy did I find something out!" wrote one reader.

Cleary's books have received wide praise and recognition from the start. She has been especially pleased with the awards given by young readers themselves. *Henry and Ribsy* won the Young Readers' Choice Award of the Pacific Northwest Library Association in 1957, and since then she has garnered many similar awards, such as the Dorothy Canfield Fisher Children's Book Award given by the P.T.A. and Vermont Free Library Commission for the book most popular with boys and girls grades four through eight, which she won in 1958 for *Fifteen.* In 1968 she won the William Allen White Children's Book Award, chosen every year by Kansas students in grades four through seven. Many of her books have received the highest awards in children's writing, including the Newbery Medal and the Laura Ingalls Wilder Award. And two of her Ramona books, *Ramona and Her Father* and *Ramona Quimby, Age 8,* were named Newbery Honor books.

In 1983 Cleary published one of her most popular books of recent years, *Dear Mr. Henshaw,* which won the Newbery. In her acceptance speech, Cleary said that she was responding to an often-voiced request in her mail from young readers: to write a book about a child whose parents are divorced. The book takes the form of a series of letters and diary entries from a sixth grader named Leigh Botts to his favorite author, Mr. Henshaw. The format was influenced in part by the letters that Cleary has received from readers that include lists of questions for her to answer. She gives this idea an interesting twist by having her imaginary author, Henshaw, send Leigh a list of questions for *him* to answer. Cleary's theory: "let the boy reveal his own feelings, for I believe children who want to write should look within themselves, not within the books of others." The resulting story is warm, poignant, and, like all of Cleary's books, a resounding success.

Cleary does not attribute the success of *Dear Mr. Henshaw* to its categorization as a "problem" novel, so-called because it focuses on a child dealing with divorce. In fact, she refuses to follow this popular trend of writing children's books that center on the problems or conflicts of modern life. "Writers for children should write honestly about childhood as they know it, . . . and not try to slant their writing to conform with current issues. . . . With the current fashion in problem books for children, adults forget that very small problems can loom very large for children."

Cleary has published over 30 books to date, and she continues to produce new work. In 1991, she published *Strider*, a sequel to *Dear Mr. Henshaw*. Now well into her seventies, Cleary continues to write books that children love to read by creating believable characters with honesty and humor. "Children tell me that they feel like the characters in my books," says Cleary. "They say they have the same kind of problems that the characters in my books have, and they feel better after reading them." Cleary is grateful for and respectful of her many adoring fans. "Knowing that one's books really reach young readers is the most rewarding experience that can come to a writer of children's books."

MARRIAGE AND FAMILY

Cleary was married in 1940 to Clarence Cleary, and in 1955, she and her husband had twins, Marianne, now a cellist, and Malcolm, now a banker. As with so much of her life, Cleary drew on her experiences as a mother in writing her books. She had her children later in life, and she had no idea just how demanding motherhood could be. "You will notice," she says dryly, "how weary the mothers are in the later books." Her children proved to be the inspiration for several works of fiction, including the *Mitch and Amy* books and a perenniel favorite, *The Mouse and the Motorcycle*, which was also her first attempt at fantasy. She remembers its beginnings this way: "I probably would not have written fantasy if I had not had a fourth-grade son who was disgusted with reading, who wanted to read about motorcycles but found all the books too hard, and who happened to run a high fever in the middle of the night when we were staying in a strange hotel. *The Mouse and the Motorcycle* was the result."

HOW SHE WRITES HER BOOKS

Young people write Cleary lots of letters: she sometimes receives over 100 in a day! Many of these children want to know how she gets her ideas and how she writes her books. She responds that many of the ideas come from her own life, and especially her memories of her own childhood.

She starts each new book on the same day each year—January 2—the day she started her first book, *Henry Huggins*. She writes the book out longhand and never works from an outline. She doesn't start at the begininng, but more often in the middle of the story, and is sometimes not sure how the story will end.

THE NATURE OF HER SUCCESS AND HER LEGACY

Cleary has sold over 30 millions books worldwide. Her books have been translated into over 14 languages, and TV versions of *Henry and Ribsy* have enjoyed success in Japan and Europe. In the words of fellow writer Katherine Paterson, "She is, and I do not exaggerate, wildly popular with children." How does Cleary account for her success? "Children find what they need in books. I write stories I enjoy telling and let children decide on their social values. What they find touches me deeply. I have had children write that they wished they could live at my house or that they would like to live on Klickitat Street. They often write that they read my books when they are feeling sad."

It is very important to Cleary that children experience the pleasure of reading: "That the written word has something to say that is worth discovering, and most of all, the feeling that *now* the reader is free to go on as far as he wants to go."

In 1975, Cleary was awarded the Laura Ingalls Wilder Award, an honor that is presented once every five years to an author who has made a "substantial and lasting contribution to literature for children." In giving that award, Caroline Feller Bauer of the awarding committee said this: "Who is Beverly Cleary? She is the woman who knows the importance of losing a first tooth and of having brand-new boots. She understands how frightening it can be to sleep alone in your own room at night, even if you had wanted the room more than anything in the world. She writes about girls and boys with equal ease. She writes naturally and charmingly of the problems and pleasures of growing up, of going to school, and of getting along with friends and family. . . . She writes memorably."

HOBBIES AND OTHER INTERESTS

Cleary and her husband live in Carmel, California, near the ocean. In addition to writing, she loves to sew and travel.

SELECTED WRITINGS

FOR YOUNG READERS

Henry Huggins, 1950
Ellen Tebbits, 1951
Henry and Beezus, 1952
Otis Spofford, 1953
Henry and Ribsy, 1954
Beezus and Ramona, 1955
Fifteen, 1956
Henry and the Paper Route, 1957
Emily's Runaway Imagination, 1961

The Mouse and the Motorcycle, 1964
Ribsy, 1964
Mitch and Amy, 1967
Ramona the Pest, 1968
Runaway Ralph, 1970
Socks, 1973
Ramona the Brave, 1975
Ramona and Her Father, 1977
Ramona and Her Mother, 1979
Ramona Quimby, Age 8, 1981
Ralph S. Mouse, 1982
Dear Mr. Henshaw, 1983
Lucky Chuck, 1984
Ramona Forever, 1984
The Growing-Up Feet, 1987
Janet's Thingamajig, 1987
Strider, 1991

FOR ADULTS

A Girl from Yamhill, 1988

HONORS AND AWARDS

Dorothy Canfield Fisher Memorial Children's Book Award: 1958, for *Fifteen*; 1961, for *Ribsy*; 1985, for *Dear Mr. Henshaw*
Notable Book Citation (American Library Association): 1961, for *Jean and Johnny*; 1966, for *The Mouse and the Motorcycle*; 1978, for *Ramona and Her Father*; 1984, for *Dear Mr. Henshaw*
Laura Ingalls Wilder Award (American Library Association): 1975, "for substantial and lasting contributions to literature for children"
Catholic Library Association Regina Medal: 1980, for "contiuned distinguished contributions to literature"
American Book Award: 1981, for *Ramona and Her Mother*
School Library Journal Best Books: 1981, for *Ramona Quimby, Age 8*; 1982, for *Ralph S. Mouse*; 1983, for *Dear Mr. Henshaw*
George G. Stone Center for Children's Books Award: 1983
Society of Children's Writers Golden Kite Award: 1983, for *Ralph S. Mouse*
Christopher Award: 1984
Newbery Medal (American Library Association): 1984, for *Dear Mr. Henshaw*
Everychild Honor Citation: 1985, for 35-year contribution to children's literature

FURTHER READING

BOOKS

Cleary, Beverly. *A Girl from Yamhill,* 1988

Contemporary Authors New Revision Series, Vol. 36
Hopkins, Lee Burnett. *More Books by More People*, 1974
Something about the Author, Vol. 43
Twentieth-Century Children's Writers, 1989

PERIODICALS

Booklist, Oct. 15, 1990, p.448
Christian Science Monitor, May 14, 1982, p.B6
Horn Book, Aug. 1975, p.359; Aug. 1984, p.429
People, Oct. 3, 1988, p.59
Publishers Weekly, Feb. 23, 1976, p.54
Top of the News, Winter 1977, p.171
Wilson Library Bulletin, Oct. 1961, p.179

ADDRESS

William Morrow, Inc.
105 Madison Avenue
New York, NY 10016

OBITUARY

Kurt Cobain 1967-1994
American Musician and Songwriter
Lead Singer and Guitarist for Nirvana

BIRTH

Kurt Donald Cobain was born in Aberdeen, Washington, on February 20, 1967. He was the first of two children of Donald Cobain, an auto mechanic at the local service station, and Wendy Fradenburg Cobain, a homemaker who later worked as a secretary. Cobain had one sister, Kim, three years younger.

YOUTH

Aberdeen is a small town in the big forests along the Pacific coast, about 100 miles southwest of Seattle. The climate there can be pretty miserable: it is usually gray, overcast, and very wet. Logging towns are often first to feel any downturn in the economy. When money gets tight, the construction industry grinds to a halt. Unfortunately, Aberdeen was no exception. The logging camps weren't hiring, the mills had closed, and there were few jobs. The only businesses doing well were the bars and the pawnshop. Life there could be pretty grim and gritty.

Yet Cobain was happy when he was young. As his mother, now Wendy O'Connor, recalls, "He got up every day with such joy that there was another day to be had. When we'd go downtown to the stores, he would sing to people. He was focused on the world." By the age of two he started showing an interest in music, which his family fostered. They gave him records by the Beatles and the Monkees, and also a bass drum. Kurt would march around the neighborhood, pounding on the drum and singing Beatles songs. He eventually got a whole Mickey Mouse drum set and took drum lessons. People started noticing his artistic skill when Cobain was in early grade school, encouraging his talent for drawing and painting.

But life turned sour when Cobain was still very young. He was diagnosed as hyperactive and given Ritalin, a drug that calms children who are hyperactive. In Cobain, though, it kept him awake until 4:00 a.m., and he needed sedatives to fall asleep. But by far the worst trauma was his parents' divorce in 1975, when he was about eight. As Kurt described it, "I had a really good childhood up until I was nine years old. Then a classic case of divorce really affected me and I moved back and forth between relatives all the time. And I just became really depressed and withdrawn." His mother agrees. "It just destroyed his life," she said a few years back. "He changed completely. I think he was ashamed. And he became very inward—he just held everything back. He became real shy. I think he's still suffering."

For about a year he stayed with his mother, sister, and his mother's new boyfriend. But he didn't like the boyfriend's abusive behavior, so Kurt went to live with his father in Montesano, a small logging town about 20 miles from Aberdeen. They didn't seem to have much in common. Don urged his son to try hunting and sports and ridiculed his interest in art and music. Pushed by his father, Kurt joined the wrestling team. On the day of a big match, with his father watching in the audience, he passively allowed his opponent to pin him—four times. His father walked out in disgust. His dad had also remarried, and Kurt didn't get along very well with his new stepmother and her two kids. He was shuffled among the relatives, living at different times with three sets of aunts and uncles and grandparents, changing schools every six months or so.

EARLY MEMORIES

There were some good experiences along the way. At one point he lived with his uncle Chuck, a musician. For Kurt's 14th birthday, Chuck bought him a used electric guitar with a little 10-watt amp. He quit playing drums, took guitar lessons for about a week, and started writing his own songs. "It was definitely a good release. I thought of it as a job. It was my mission. I knew I had to practice. As soon as I got my guitar, I just became so obsessed with it."

EDUCATION

School was hard for Cobain. He always felt like a misfit. He was small, sensitive, artistic, nonathletic, and sickly (with chronic bronchitis, mild scoliosis, and, later, acute, undiagnosed stomach pain). He never fit in with the macho culture of a logging town. "If he would have been anywhere else," his mother says, "he would have been fine—there would have been enough of his kind not to stick out so much. But this town is just exactly like Peyton Place. Everybody is watching everyone and judging, and they have their little slots they like everyone to stay in—and he didn't." He was an outcast, taunted, beaten up routinely. Some of the kids thought he was gay, and that increased the level of hostility and violence. "Every day after school," he recalls, "this one kid would hold me down in the snow and sit on my head." Mostly he was a loner, but he met a few other kids like him—including Chris (now Krist) Novoselic, later the bass player for Nirvana. He started hanging out with a local rock group, the Melvins. He also started drinking and smoking marijuana.

Between doing drugs, skipping school, and moving around so much, his schoolwork suffered. About six months before he was due to graduate from high school, Cobain realized that he first needed to make up about two years worth of high school credits. He had won two college scholarships for his artwork, but he couldn't use them without finishing high school. He dropped out instead, in May 1985, determined to make a career in music.

FIRST JOBS

For a while Cobain worked at a series of day jobs, making music at night. He worked at a restaurant, then got a job as a janitor at his old school, Aberdeen High. Sometimes he had his own apartment, sometimes he crashed with friends, and at one point he ended up sleeping under a bridge. He started spray painting graffiti all over town. One night, he and two friends painted "Homo Sex Rules" on the side of a bank, hoping to shake people up a bit. When a police car appeared, his friends ran and hid in a dumpster, but Kurt got caught. He received a $180 fine and a 30-day suspended sentence.

Throughout this time, music was his passion. His taste in music had evolved greatly since he was a kid. From his early love for the Beatles and the Monkees, he turned to harder rock as a young teen, '70s bands like

Led Zeppelin, Kiss, and Black Sabbath. He started reading music magazines and became interested in punk music, following the rise and crash of the Sex Pistols. The only problem, though, was that he had never *heard* punk music—the record store in Aberdeen didn't carry any. But soon he started to go to shows in Seattle and Olympia, a college town, and got ahold of a record by the LA punk band Black Flag. "The intensity, the aggression, the *hatred*," Cobain once said, explaining the appeal. "You could hear a lead singer just scream at the top of his lungs. I felt that way. I wanted to die. I wanted to kill. I wanted to smash things."

As Jon Pareles explains in the *New York Times*, "Punk offered an outlet for frustration and created a kind of community of outcasts; it provided a refuge, one Mr. Cobain compared to the Buddhist concept of nirvana. And to its truest devotees, punk is not simply a musical style awaiting its chance at the big time. It is a culture of refusal, turning away in disgust from a mainstream that fawns over material success and chases thoughtless pleasure."

CAREER HIGHLIGHTS

THE EARLY YEARS

In 1986, Cobain and Novoselic formed a band; they went through several musicians and names before hooking up with Dave Grohl and settling on Nirvana. They started out playing around Aberdeen and soon moved on to clubs in Olympia, Tacoma, and Seattle, supporting themselves with food stamps and odd jobs.

In 1988 they recorded their first single, "Love Buzz"/"Big Cheese," on the independent label Sub Pop, the original home of what became known as the Seattle sound, or grunge. The music combined the hard driving sound of heavy metal with the sound and attitudes of punk music, the loud abrasiveness, uncensored, raw lyrics, and feelings of anger, despair, alienation, and hopelessness. The group went on to record their first album, *Bleach*, on Sub Pop as well. Selling 35,000 copies, an impressive total for an independent release, *Bleach* earned them new fans, more club dates, critical raves, and a contract with a major label, Geffen Records.

NEVERMIND

Despite that success, nothing prepared the group for the uproar that greeted the 1991 release of *Nevermind*. Critics hailed the band for what *Guitar Player* magazine called its "tight hybrid of punk rock energy, grinding metallic riffs, and catchy pop songcraft," which many likened to that of the Beatles. The songs, which Cobain wrote, derive their power from several sources. One is the searing, sarcastic, furious, and self-deprecating lyrics ("I feel stupid/And contagious/Here we are now/Entertain us"). Another is the sound—Cobain's corrosive guitar playing, using distortion and feedback, combined with his dramatic and powerful singing, his voice wailing in primal screams.

The response from listeners was overwhelming. The group, and its recording company, had hoped the album might sell about 100,000 copies, very respectable numbers for an alternative group. To date, *Nevermind* has sold nearly 10 million copies. It pushed Michael Jackson's *Dangerous* off the number one spot on the pop music chart, thrust alternative music, and particularly grunge and the Seattle sound, into the commercial mainstream, and forever changed Nirvana—and their listeners. Many felt that the album, particularly the song "Smells Like Teen Spirit," articulated their feelings of rage, frustration, and alienation. As Anthony DeCurtis described it in *Rolling Stone*, "'Smells Like Teen Spirit' proved a defining moment in rock history. A political song that never mentions politics, an anthem whose lyrics can't be understood, a hugely popular hit that denounces commercialism, a collective shout of alienation, it was '(I Can't Get No) Satisfaction' for a new time and a new tribe of disaffected youth."

THE AFTERMATH

For Cobain, the backlash was immediate. A loner, he was ill-equipped to deal with the fame, adulation, pressure, and constant media attention that came with becoming a rock superstar overnight. Despite their obvious broad appeal, his songs were intended to be deeply personal and individualistic. He had no intention of being a role model or a spokesperson for his generation, he often complained. He worried that he'd sold out.

Despite his musical success, his personal life was about to blow up. He'd been involved with Courtney Love, the talented and flamboyant lead singer of the punk band Hole. In early 1992, shortly after the album's release, they got married and announced that Love was pregnant. Within a few months, rumors of Cobain's drug use began to leak out, first in the Seattle music press and then in the national media. Reviews of his performances began to describe erratic and lethargic behavior. In September 1992, *Vanity Fair* magazine ran a cover story on Love. Quoting unnamed sources, the article said that both Cobain and Love had been using heroin, and that Love had continued to use it even after she knew that she was pregnant. Cobain and Love issued a statement saying that they had both used heroin, that they had sought treatment for their addictions, and that Love had immediately stopped using drugs when she learned that she was pregnant.

Allegations, rumors, and denials have swirled around in the national press to this day, but several points are clear. Cobain had used heroin (he says it was the only drug that controlled the unrelenting stomach pain he had suffered for years); he would return to using heroin later. And Cobain and Love temporarily lost custody of their newborn baby, Frances Bean Cobain, after the *Vanity Fair* piece appeared. The social services department removed her from the home while investigating the couple, but later dropped all charges. Although Frances Bean was returned to their custody, the experience deeply affected Cobain.

The band went on to release two more albums: *Incesticide* (1992), a collection of outtakes and rarities, and *In Utero* (1993), considered inspired but less commercial than their previous album. Like *Nevermind*, both recordings contained powerful lyrics, dynamic guitar work, and powerful rhythms. While neither sold in stratospheric numbers—the group was trying for something a bit more raw than their previous record—both were considered strong follow-up albums. *In Utero*, in fact, debuted at number one on the pop charts.

COBAIN'S DEATH

In retrospect, there seems to have been a pattern of serious, self-destructive events in the weeks leading up to Cobain's suicide. On March 4, 1994, he took an overdose of sedatives combined with champagne in Rome, and ended up in a coma. At the time, it was said to be an accident. Two weeks later, on March 18 at their Seattle home, Cobain locked himself in a room with a gun. Love called the police, who talked him into coming out. That episode was described as part of an argument with his wife. Reports indicate that his heroin use had escalated, and Love staged an intervention on March 25, bringing together his friends and bandmates to force Cobain to confront what drugs were doing to him. He checked into a drug rehabilitation center within a few days, but walked out on March 31. Over the next few days, his family, friends, and even private detectives started searching for him. He was found dead of a self-inflicted gunshot wound on April 8 in a room over the garage of his Seattle home. He is believed to have died on April 5, 1994.

As Jon Pareles wrote in the *New York Times*, "Mr. Cobain had had the whole package: wealth, fame, credibility, a wife and child. But like the fans who heard their own feelings in his weary, desperate, infuriated voice, Mr. Cobain didn't have what satisfied him, and he never found out exactly what that might have been."

COBAIN'S LEGACY

In a special issue devoted to Cobain after his death, *Rolling Stone* magazine said this: "Kurt Cobain never wanted to be the spokesman for a generation, though that doesn't mean much: Anybody who did would never have become one. It's not a role you campaign for. It is thrust upon you, and you live with it. Or don't.

"People looked to Kurt Cobain because his songs captured what they felt before they knew they felt it. Even his struggles—with fame, with drugs, with his identity—caught the generational drama of our time. Seeing himself since his boyhood as an outcast, he was stunned—and confused, and frightened, and repulsed, and, truth be told, not entirely disappointed (no one forms a band to remain anonymous)—to find himself a star. If Cobain staggered across the stage of rock stardom, seemed more willing to play the fool than the hero and took drugs more for relief than pleasure, that was fine with his contemporaries. For people who came of age amid the greed, the designer-drug indulgence and the image-driven celebrity of the '80s, anyone who could make an easy peace with success was fatally suspect.

"Whatever importance Cobain assumed as a symbol, however, one thing is certain: He and his band Nirvana announced the end of one rock & roll era and the start of another. In essence, Nirvana transformed the '80s into the '90s."

MARRIAGE AND FAMILY

Kurt Cobain and Courtney Love were married on February 24, 1992, in Waikiki, Hawaii. Their daughter, Frances Bean Cobain, was born on August 19, 1992.

RECORDINGS

"Love Buzz"/"Big Cheese," 1988 (debut single)
Bleach, 1989
Nevermind, 1991
Incesticide, 1992
In Utero, 1993

HONORS AND AWARDS

MTV Music Video Awards: 1992 (2 awards), for Best New Artist and Best Alternative Video, both for "Smells Like Teen Spirit"; 1993, for Best Alternative Video, for "In Bloom"

FURTHER READING

BOOKS

Azerrad, Michael. *Come as You Are: The Story of Nirvana*, 1993
Morrell, Brad. *Nirvana and the Sound of Seattle*, 1993

PERIODICALS

Details, Nov. 1993, p.102; June 1994, p.130

Entertainment Weekly, Apr. 22, 1994, p.16
Esquire, July 1994, p.55
Los Angeles Times, Sep. 21, 1992, p.F1; Aug. 29, 1993, Calendar section p.8; Apr. 9, 1994, p.A10
New Yorker, Apr. 25, 1994, p.102
New York Times, Apr. 9, 1994, p.A1; Apr. 11, 1994, p.B1
People, Mar. 21, 1994, p.55; Apr. 25, 1994, p.38
Rolling Stone, Jan. 23, 1992, p.38; Apr. 16, 1992, p.36; Jan. 27, 1994, p.34; May 19, 1994, p.17; June 2, 1994, pp.30-67, Special Issue devoted to Kurt Cobain
Us, June 1994, p.38
Vanity Fair, Sep. 1992, p.230

F.W. de Klerk 1936-
Former South African State President
Winner of the 1993 Nobel Peace Prize,
Shared with Nelson Mandela

BIRTH

Frederik Willem (F.W.) de Klerk, the Afrikaner leader who boldly initiated reforms to free his country from its racially violent past, was born on March 18, 1936, in the Mayfair suburb of Johannesburg, South Africa. He was the second son of Jan and Corrie (Coetzer) de Klerk, and younger by eight years than his only sibling, Willem. Young Frederick Willem was called F.W. to distinguish him from the grandfather whose name he bore. Also, it is a common Afrikaner custom for men to use initials instead of their full name. In Afrikaans, the language developed from 17th-century Dutch that was spoken in the de Klerk household, the initials are pronounced "eff-veer"—and *no* periods are used.

The de Klerk family was deeply rooted in South African politics: F. W.'s father was a teacher, a cabinet minister, and one-time president of the Senate; his paternal grandfather, for whom he was named, was a prominent and politically active clergyman in the Transvaal (Province) and a Cape rebel during the Boer War at the turn of this century; his paternal great-grandfather was Senator Jan van Rooy; and his maternal grandfather, F. W. Coetzer, was a member of the Free State Provincial Council. An uncle by marriage, J. G. (Hans) Strijdom, was leader of the National Party (NP) in the Transvaal and prime minister of South Africa in the 1950s.

SOUTH AFRICAN POLITICS—AN HISTORICAL REVIEW

To truly understand de Klerk's historic role in transforming South Africa, one must first understand its history. This lush, fertile, mineral-rich region at the southern tip of the African continent has been inhabited by native African tribal groups since about 100 A.D. White settlers, primarily of Dutch, German, and French Huguenot descent, began moving there in the seventeenth and eighteenth centuries. These settlers, then called Boers (the Dutch word for farmers), formed the basis for the modern-day Afrikaners. After driving off the native Africans, they gradually occupied much of the workable farmland. They were later joined by many British settlers.

The Dutch colony was taken over in the early 1800s by British troops, who made English the official language in 1828. During the latter part of the nineteenth century, Britain stepped in and annexed additional Boer territory, particularly after diamonds and gold were discovered. Fighting broke out between the Boers and the British in the Boer War, as it came to be known. The British were victorious, and all of the Boer territory became British colonies. While whites battled over who would govern the territories, the black Africans gradually lost their independence and came under white rule. In 1910, several white colonies joined together to form the Union of South Africa, as part of the British Empire, with a constitution that gave power to the whites.

This history between the British and the Boers contributed greatly to the country's political development. The Boers, or Afrikaners as they are known today, were suspicious and distrustful of the British and fearful of the Africans. Afrikaner leaders promoted a feeling of nationalism, claiming that they had a God-given mission to rule South Africa. The National Party, an Afrikaner nationalist group, was formed to promote these ideas. Prior to World War II, it accomplished many Afrikaner goals. Afrikaans became a second, official language, in addition to English, and South Africa achieved complete political independence from Britain.

When the National Party took power in 1948, apartheid (uh-PAHR-tayt) became the official government policy. Since its inception, this cruel and repressive racist practice, which mandates the separation of the races, has been the dominant political issue in South Africa. It denies civil, social, and economic equality to non-whites, and is responsible for the upheaval and continuing struggle in a nation where blacks are the overwhelming majority. Based on the doctrine of white supremacy, apartheid classified all South Africans by race and restricted the lives of blacks by holding them in political and economic subservience. Blacks were forced to live in miserable conditions of poverty in all-black homelands, with grossly inadequate food, housing, medical care, and education. Forbidden to own land and barred from many occupations, they were required to carry permits at all times to travel to white areas to find work. Blacks had no political rights in South Africa, no right to vote and no legal means to effect change.

This separatist, nationalistic environment was the political, economic, and cultural milieu in which de Klerk was raised.

YOUTH

De Klerk's early years were described in the 1991 biography *F W de Klerk: A Man in His Time*, written by his brother, Willem. He tells of their constant exposure to the inner circles of National Party politics, both as children and young men. "Public figures were regular guests; even as children and students we, and particularly he, were involved in the organization of election campaigns; . . . he attended dozens of political meetings with our father; and he was involved in many a late night political argument, when I confronted father and brother with enlightened politics, which led to some spirited debates." (Willem was then, and still is, considered an ultrazealous liberal by the standards of the family and the National Party that formed their political lineage. He is a former Dutch Reformed pastor and was an editor and columnist for the newspapers *Transvaler* and *Rapport* for 15 years, but was forced to resign because of his progressive opinions. He now teaches journalism at Rand Afrikaans University.)

Despite their eight-year age difference, the de Klerk boys shared enough time at home to forge a bond that the political philosophies of later years have not broken. Much has been made of their differences (Afrikaners call it *broedertwis*, or brotherly falling out), but their affection for one another is as real now as it was when they were young. F. W. may have adopted his father's establishment doctrines, and Willem, according to *Time*, "the less strident beliefs of his mother's family," yet both brothers have memories of a happy and secure childhood. Their parents gave them a loving, comfortable home, where there was fun and laughter and where "a sense of proportion was inculcated into us," recalls Willem. "Excesses had to be avoided. . . . 'Doe gewoon, das gek genoeg' (act normally—

that's quite mad enough) was our father's Dutch maxim. And F W [has become] exactly that: an ordinary balanced person who avoids one-sidedness."

EDUCATION

Jan de Klerk was a school headmaster at the time of his younger son's birth, but his ever-widening political activities necessitated a number of family moves. F. W. attended seven primary schools in as many years, and then graduated in 1953 as a boarding student from Monument Höerskool (High School) in Krugersdorp, about twenty miles from Johannesburg. He was given what is called a first-class matric pass, but his teachers were disappointed with the quality of his work. Brother Willem has said that F. W. was probably bored with his school work and distracted by tennis and girls during those school years.

De Klerk then attended Potchefstroom University for Higher Christian Education, a school in the southern Transvaal. This time, he excelled academically while assuming a leading role in student movements as well. He was an executive member of the political-cultural Afrikaanse Studentebond and also served on the National Party's Youth Council. Friends from those days have told stories to Willem, however, about another side to F. W.'s university life. He was, they say, "the soul of every party . . . something of a ladies' man, and a jovial ringleader in student merry-making." He also continued to be an avid tennis player, but his activity on the hockey field proved less successful when his nose was broken and required reconstructive surgery. De Klerk was awarded his bachelor of arts and bachelor of law degrees from Potchefstroom University in 1958.

After leaving the university, de Klerk went to England on a six-week scholarship. He returned to the Transvaal to join a firm of English-speaking lawyers so that he could polish his language skills. "I'm still not very proud of my English," he has said, but he seems to express himself with ease in his second language.

FIRST JOBS

De Klerk entered the legal profession in Klerksdorp, the same town where he had attended high school. While clerking for the Pelser firm, de Klerk recalls, he and Peet Pelser, who later became a cabinet member, spent more time discussing politics than they did law. Later he joined the MacRobert firm in Pretoria (South Africa's administrative capital) to further his law apprenticeship. De Klerk went into partnership in 1962 at Vereeniging, the industrial city near Johannesburg where the treaty was signed ending the Boer War. He maintained a successful practice for ten years until he was tempted by the offer of a law professorship at Potchefstroom, his alma mater. "We had just returned from a trip abroad," he remembers. "I was able to look at my work from a distance, and I realized I did not want to be restricted to a lawyer's office. . . . I jumped at the offer to become an academic, because I wanted to expand my horizons. . . ." His plans soon changed, however, when a vacancy for a seat in Parliament arose unexpectedly in his district.

CAREER HIGHLIGHTS

Putting aside his plans to teach, de Klerk made a quick decision to accept the backing of the National Party (NP), and won a seat in the South African parliament in a by-election on November 29, 1972. He formally entered politics as the new year began, soon joining parliamentary study groups and building a reputation as a well-briefed debater on topics that ranged from labor, home affairs, and justice, to new policies and more liberal censorship laws. He frequently traveled abroad during this period, specifically to develop an international perspective. A 1976 trip sponsored by the United States Information Agency (USIA) brought him to the U.S. for a brief study of the American democratic system of government.

In 1978, shortly before his forty-second birthday, de Klerk was appointed to the Cabinet of President Pieter W. Botha. Like his father before him, de Klerk moved into a succession of ministries—Posts and Telecommunications, Social Welfare and Pensions, Environmental Planning, and Internal Affairs among them. He became the leader of the National Party in Transvaal Province in 1982, replacing the ultraconservative Andries Treurnicht. De Klerk was named chairman of the Ministers' Council of the House of Assembly in 1985, an appointment that was a significant move toward his eventual election as head of state. He was chosen leader of the House at the end of the following year and national leader of his party in February 1989, when Botha was forced to step down from that NP post after suffering a minor stroke. Botha retained the presidency for another half-year, but his failing effectiveness, as well as his uncertain health, made way for a general election and a new president—F. W. de Klerk.

THE FIRST STEPS TOWARD A NEW SOUTH AFRICA

From September 20, 1989, the day he was sworn into office as president of the Republic of South Africa, the pragmatic de Klerk set out to break the cycle of conflict, accepting the certainty that the white power structure would have to be dismantled. He came to power at a time of tremendous civil unrest. There were ongoing violent conflicts in the townships, the segregated areas where blacks were forced to live, between black residents and South African security forces, and also between blacks of different political groups. De Klerk developed a policy of racial reconciliation: he lifted the state of emergency imposed by Botha, repealed many apartheid laws, and freed political prisoners, most notable among them the heroic African leader Nelson Mandela, who was released after 27 years in prison. He also legalized Mandela's African National Congress (ANC), which had been outlawed since 1960.

Negotiations began on what would eventually lead to a new South African constitution. The Pretoria Minute, a document outlining preliminary agreements, was co-signed in mid-1990 by de Klerk and Mandela. De Klerk acquiesced in principle throughout subsequent talks to a peaceful transition to one-man, one-vote representation. And in March 1992 his fellow white South Africans agreed: they voted to continue talks aimed toward writing a new Constitution that would end apartheid, creating a new political system and allowing full participation by the black majority. Yet de Klerk continued to be criticized by the black opposition, wrote Larry Olmstead in the *New York Times*, for "hard bargaining on behalf of white interests, for failing to curb factional violence in black areas, and for failing to move decisively against white militants."

In June 1993, announcement was made of the long-awaited giant step toward victory in the black South Africans' struggle for freedom. Black and white political leaders together decided on the country's first-ever free elections, set for April 27, 1994. Finally, *all* South Africans will have the right to vote, the right to fully participate in electing their national and local leaders. And as a result, Nelson Mandela will almost certainly succeed the man who set the wheels of reform in motion.

While there is much cause for celebration, there is concern for the future as well. As Scott MacLeod wrote in *Time*, "it will still take years of patient reconstruction to undo the damage of the apartheid era and break the cycle of violence." The transition clearly will not be easy. There has been open and often violent animosity among competing factions, both black and white. Militant separatists have waged a campaign of terror in opposition to their more moderate leaders, including Afrikaner groups that oppose de Klerk and ANC factions that oppose Mandela. There has also been fighting between Mandela's supporters in the ANC and members of the Zulu-based Inkatha Freedom Party, led by Mangosuthu G. Buthelezi. Some 11,000 people have been killed during the past three years in ANC-Inkatha violence. Currently, the Inkatha party led by Buthelezi is boycotting the elections, but his authority seems to be weakening, and many members of the Zulu nation are calling for free elections. [See Appendix for Update on de Klerk.]

NOBEL PEACE PRIZE

In October 1993, F. W. de Klerk and Nelson Mandela jointly won the Nobel Peace Prize for their efforts to end apartheid and create a new, nonracial democracy. According to the Nobel committee, de Klerk and Mandela had shown "personal integrity and great political courage." In accepting the prize, de Klerk spoke of his hopes for the future. The election, he said, will "not be about blacks or whites, or Afrikaners and Xhosas, . . . or apartheid or armed struggle. It will be about future peace and stability, about progress and prosperity, about nation building." Peace, stability, progress, prosperity—these are de Klerk's hopes for the nation.

MARRIAGE AND FAMILY

De Klerk has been married for 35 years to Marike Willemse, whom he met at college. F. W.'s brother, still a practicing clergyman at that time, performed the wedding ceremony on April 11, 1959. The de Klerks have three grown children. Jan, the eldest son, is a farmer in the Western Transvaal; Willem is in public relations; and Susan is a teacher. There are also two grandchildren. "My wife and children are like a fortress around me," confides de Klerk. "Without their love and consideration I would have been in a muddle. Since early times I have been very busy and often away from home. But I was determined not to become the absent husband and father. So I spend a lot of quality time with my family. . . . We share each other's burdens and joys. The closeness of our relationship is very important to me."

HOBBIES AND OTHER INTERESTS

Although earnestly dedicated to the responsibilities of his political office, F. W. de Klerk is a man who can relax easily. He has a wide circle of friends with whom he socializes, plays golf, and enjoys an occasional game of tennis. The family owns a beach house at Hermanus, a seaside resort in the far southwestern reaches of Cape Province, and it is there that he finds quiet hours for reading or for the brisk walks that his brother says "stimulate his circulation and calm his mind." F. W. is a chain smoker, much to the concern of those close to him, but he continues to rationalize his nicotine habit with an illogical quote from his late father: "A happy smoker is never a troublemaker."

The de Klerks are regular churchgoers, and belong to the Gereformeerde Kerk (Reformed Church), known colloquially as the "Dopperkirk." The smallest of the three Afrikaans congregations, it is less rigid in its tenets than the Dutch Reformed denomination, from which it evolved.

HONORS AND AWARDS

Decoration for Meritorious Service: 1981, in recognition of exceptional service to the Republic of South Africa
Liberty Medal (awarded by the United States): 1993, shared with Nelson Mandela
Nobel Peace Prize: 1993, shared with Nelson Mandela
Man of the Year (*Time* magazine): 1993, shared with Nelson Mandela, Yasir Arafat, and Yitzhak Rabin

FURTHER READING

BOOKS

De Klerk, Willem. *F W de Klerk: The Man in His Time*, 1991 (translated by Henri Snijders)
Ottaway, David B. *Chained Together: Mandela, de Klerk, and the Struggle to Remake South Africa*, 1993
Who's Who, 1993

PERIODICALS

Current Biography Yearbook 1990
Africa Report, July-Aug. 1989, p.36
The Economist, Mar. 11, 1989, p.44; Oct. 17, 1992, p.52
Jet, July 8, 1991, p.13; Apr. 6, 1992, p.18
Maclean's, Mar. 30, 1992, p.22
Newsweek, Mar. 30, 1992, p.40; Sep. 28, 1992, p.30
New York Times, July 4, 1993, p.A10; July 5, 1993, p.A3
New York Times Biographical Service, Feb. 1990, p.153
New York Times Magazine, Nov. 19, 1989, p.42; Jan. 31, 1993, p.36
Orbis, Summer 1990, p.323, p.337
Time, Sep. 11, 1989, p.42; Oct. 9, 1989, p.49; Feb. 5, 1990, p.32; Feb. 11, 1991, p.56; Mar. 30, 1992, p.34; June 14, 1993, p.34

ADDRESS

State President's Office
Private Bag X-1000
Cape Town 8000
South Africa

BRIEF ENTRY

Rita Dove 1952-
American Poet, Novelist, and Short Story Writer
Poet Laureate of the United States

EARLY LIFE AND CAREER

Rita Dove was born in Akron, Ohio, August 28, 1952. She was an excellent student throughout her school years. In 1970, she was selected as a Presidential Scholar, one of the 100 best high school graduates in the U.S. She attended Miami University of Ohio, where she graduated with highest honors. She later attended the University of Tubingen in Germany as the recipient of a Fulbright fellowship. She also earned a master's degree from the University of Iowa in 1977. Dove has received numerous awards and fellowships from such groups as the Guggenheim Foundation, the Andrew W. Mellon Foundation, and the National Endowment for the Arts. She currently teaches creative writing at the University of Virginia, where she holds the Commonwealth Chair in English. She is married to a German writer, Fred Viebahn, and they have a daughter, Aviva.

MAJOR ACCOMPLISHMENTS

Dove's collections of poetry include *The Yellow House on the Corner* (1980), *Museum* (1983), and the Pulitzer-Prize winning *Thomas and Beulah* (1986). In the words of critic Helen Vendler, "Pure shapes, her poems exhibit the thrift that Yeats called the sign of a perfected manner."

POET LAUREATE

Dove was named Poet Laureate in May of 1993 and began her duties in October. She is the seventh Poet Laureate Consultant in Poetry and the second woman to be named to the position since the "Poet Laureate" title was added to the "Consultant in Poetry" post in 1985. As Poet Laureate, Dove is responsible for advising the Library of Congress's programs in poetry and literature and also for helping develop the literature collection. She will also organize the Library's series of free readings and lectures. In naming her to the position, Dr. James H. Billington, the Librarian of Congress, noted: "I take much pleasure in announcing the selection of a younger poet of distinction and versatility. . . . We will be pleased to have an outstanding representative of a new and richly variegated generation of American poets."

Dove will continue in her post for the 1993-94 session, which runs from October to May. She is now dividing her time between the Library of Congress in Washington and her continuing duties at the University of Virginia.

FURTHER READING

Contemporary Authors New Revision Series, Vol. 27
New York Times, May 19, 1993, p.C15
Who's Who in America, 1990-91

ADDRESS

Poetry Office
Library of Congress
Washington, D.C. 20540-8910

Linda Ellerbee 1944-
American Broadcast Journalist
Producer, Writer, and Host of Nickelodeon's "Nick News"

BIRTH

Linda Ellerbee was born Linda Jane Smith on August 15, 1944, in Bryan, Texas. She was the only child of Hallie (Mainer) Smith and Lonnie Ray Smith, a vice-president of an insurance company. When Linda was four, the family moved to Houston, Texas.

YOUTH

Growing up, Linda split her time between Houston, where her dad worked and where she eventually attended school, and

Trinity, a small town where her parents had grown up. They went back to visit family most weekends and much of the summer, and Linda, an only child, enjoyed spending time with her grandparents, aunts, uncles, and cousins. The comfort and security of life in a small town, she wrote, gave her the confidence and self-assurance that she carries today. She loved to play outside there, riding bikes, climbing trees, splashing in the creek, and exploring the town. It was also in Trinity that she developed a passion for reading, which all of her family encouraged—she read comics, romance novels, anything she could get her hands on. It was only years later that her relatives admitted that they encouraged her to read "not to broaden my horizons, not because they especially believed in reading, although they did, but because it was the only way they knew to shut me up. I was crushed."

EARLY MEMORIES

Although Ellerbee grew up to be a successful TV newscaster, she hated TV as a child. In her autobiography *Move On: Adventures in the Real World*, she writes entertainingly but poignantly of the summer she was eight when, in her words, "a television ate my best friend." Her friend Lucy got a television set, the first in their neighborhood to do so, and she disappeared inside the house, after school and all day Saturday, to sit and watch TV. As Ellerbee tells it, "Maybe the TV hadn't actually eaten her. But she may as well have been dead; once they pointed her in the direction of that box, she never looked up and she never looked back. . . . I'm not kidding when I say I lost my best friend. I really did. I had no interest in sitting still when I could be climbing trees or riding bikes or annoying the neighbors. . . . And Lucy had no interest in any of those things."

Television had a similar effect on her family. They quit playing cards, reading, and just about anything except watching TV all the time—even while eating dinner. "Television changed my family forever. We stopped eating dinner at the dining-room table after my mother found out about TV trays. . . . Dinner was served in time for one program and finished in time for another. During dinner, we used to talk to one another. Now television talked to us. If you had something you absolutely had to say, you waited until the commercial, which is, I suspect, where I learned to speak in thirty-second bursts. As a future writer, it was good practice in editing my thoughts. As a little girl, it was lonely as hell."

EDUCATION

Attending school in Houston, Ellerbee felt like an outsider. "I just didn't fit into any particular group, and I think I wanted to. I was the kind of kid who'd bad-mouth the idea of homecoming and then be really hurt when no one asked me." In fact, Ellerbee says, "I wasn't very likable. I never learned to keep my mouth shut. I wasn't very nice to people."

As a high school student she demonstrated a talent for art. She won several awards for her paintings, including a scholarship to college. But she decided not to become an artist when she made two discoveries: "One was that I wasn't good enough, and two was that it was a lot of hard work. Writing had always been easy for me."

After graduating from Mirabeau Beauregard Lamar Senior High School, Ellerbee enrolled at Vanderbilt University in Nashville, Tennessee, in the fall of 1962. She planned to study history. While not a great student, she was a talented writer, as she soon proved. She entered a contest sponsored by the United Methodist Church for which the prize was a summer studying in Bolivia. Ellerbee, who hadn't attended church in over five years, submitted an essay suggesting that if she were selected, she might be converted to Methodism. Her essay won, and she spent the summer in Bolivia. "I learned a lot that summer," she mentions in *"And So It Goes"*: *Adventures in Television*, "but when it was over I still wrote better than I prayed." Ellerbee never completed college, dropping out after only two years.

MARRIAGE AND FAMILY

Ellerbee left Vanderbilt in 1964 when she married fellow student Mac Smith, the first of her four husbands. They were divorced in 1966. In 1968 she married Van Veselka, with whom she had two children: Vanessa, born in 1969, and Joshua, born in 1970. That marriage ended by 1971. In 1973, she married Tom Ellerbee, an architect, whose name she continues to use professionally; that marriage ended within a year. Finally she was married to John David Klein, a journalist, from about 1976 to 1978.

FIRST JOBS

Ellerbee has had an eventful life, with many adventures in both her personal and professional life. Her first "real" job as an adult came after she dropped out of college to get married. She and her husband, Mac Smith, moved to Chicago, where he attended graduate school and she worked as a bookkeeper, trade magazine writer, and disc jockey on radio station WVON. When the marriage broke up in 1966, she left Chicago for a brief stint in California as a program director on radio station KSJO before returning to Houston, in 1968, to take care of her sick mother.

In Houston she met and married her second husband, Van Veselka, the son of one of her mother's friends. Linda and Van lived first on the Texas-Mexico border, where their daughter was born in 1969. When Veselka got a job soon afterward in Juneau, Alaska, they moved north. In Juneau they had a second baby and moved into a commune with about thirteen others. Ellerbee found another job in radio, on KJNO, and later worked as a speech writer for a state senator.

That period in American history, the late 1960s and early 1970s, was, for many, an exhilarating time of great expectations. For Ellerbee, though, it was also a time of great revelations and disappointments. She was soon disillusioned with communal life, where it seemed that just a few people, including her, did all the work. When her husband lost his job and then left her for another woman, Ellerbee made a commitment to herself, her children, and her career: with two kids to support, "I swore I would never allow myself to become helpless again." She got a job back in Houston writing radio news for the Associated Press (AP), a wire service that distributes reports on breaking news around the country, and she and her two kids moved back home to Texas in mid-1972.

CHOOSING A CAREER

Ellerbee found her way into TV news really by accident. One slow night less than six months after she started with AP, she sat at her computer writing a letter to a friend. In it she criticized her boss, two local newspapers, the city of Dallas, and the Vietnam War. When she was done, she accidentally hit the wrong key and sent the letter out on the wire to radio and television stations in Texas and three other states. It was read on the air, she became an instant celebrity, and she was promptly fired. Amazingly, though, the news director at a Houston TV station liked the way she wrote and hired her on the spot—with a big increase in salary.

Ellerbee made her debut on television in January 1973 on KHOU, the CBS affiliate station in Houston. She worked there for nine months, during which time she met and married her third husband, Tom Ellerbee. In late 1973, she was offered a job as a general assignment reporter at WCBS, the affiliate station in New York City. She took the job, but her marriage didn't survive the move. She spent two years in New York working the 3:00 p.m. to midnight shift, and then left local news in late 1975 to take a job at the network level with NBC News.

CAREER HIGHLIGHTS

For almost 20 years now, Ellerbee has been writing, reporting, anchoring, and producing national news for television. She spent the first 12 years as a correspondent and anchor with NBC, starting out as a reporter with the Washington bureau covering the House of Representatives. During that time she married and divorced her fourth and last husband, John David Klein. In 1978 she was tapped to co-anchor a weekly prime-time news show, "Weekend." While the show was not a ratings success, it was a tremendous experience for Ellerbee. She solidified her writing skills, learned how to create a story by matching words to pictures, and began to develop the dry, acerbic style for which she has become known. When "Weekend" was canceled in the spring of 1979, Ellerbee returned to New York as a correspondent for the "NBC Nightly News."

"NBC NEWS OVERNIGHT"

In 1982, Ellerbee was picked to co-anchor "NBC News Overnight," an hour-long news show that aired weeknights at 1:30 a.m. Despite the late hour, the show was a hit: it won almost universal praise from critics and drew an average of two million viewers each night, quickly developing a cult following. "Overnight" was the show that solidified Ellerbee's reputation. Several factors contributed to the show's success, as explained here by *Rolling Stone* magazine: "It was the first network program to offer news without the grim self-importance of the nightly news anchormen and without the glammed-up look of big-city local news; it was news that emphasized the reporting and interpreting skills of its anchors and correspondents instead of flashy graphics or stagy on-camera confrontations." Unlike most news anchors, Ellerbee and her co-anchor (first Lloyd Dobyns and later Bill Schechner) wrote the material themselves, and they were frequently praised for their literate, distinctive style, wry, direct delivery, dry, irreverent wit, intellectual honesty, and rare intelligence. Indeed, the show was cited by the Alfred I. duPont—Columbia University Awards, the most prestigious award in broadcast journalism, as possibly "the best written and most intelligent TV news anywhere." Despite all the praise, there simply weren't enough viewers at that late hour to allow the show to make a profit, and it was canceled in late 1983.

Ellerbee continued to work for NBC for three more years. She briefly hosted an ill-conceived, short-lived news program called "Summer Sunday" that traveled around the U.S. broadcasting live from different locations. She also worked as a correspondent for the "Today Show." She left NBC in June 1986 after unsuccessful contract negotiations and was immediately hired by ABC, where she worked for just over a year. Her primary project there was writing and anchoring "Our World," a prime-time historical series that devoted each episode to recreating a different period in recent American history, using newsreel footage, TV and movie clips, and contemporary music. It, too, was canceled. For that show, she and her co-writers won an Emmy for best writing.

But in late 1987, Ellerbee left ABC and network news. She had approached the summit in the TV news business, and decided to get out. As Ellerbee later explained, "it seemed that the major networks were going to do fewer of the experimental news shows that I like doing. Also you don't see a lot of older women on the networks, and I didn't want to wait and find out if they would allow me to grow old on the air. So I quit."

Ellerbee went on to several different projects. For a while she provided commentary on political issues for CNN. She wrote two autobiographies, funny books that deal with serious issues about her life and career in television news. She also started a weekly syndicated newspaper column that continues to this day. But the biggest project was starting her own TV news company, Lucky Duck Productions, with her partner and steady companion, Rolfe Tessem. Lucky Duck produces programs for all parts of the television market: the networks, syndication, cable, and public stations. The company is named after Ellerbee's good-luck charm, the stuffed duck that finds its way on to the set wherever she is working. The independent company has produced a variety of news programs, including "The Other Epidemic," a special on breast cancer; "Ms. Smith Goes to Washington," an award-winning report on the first 100 days in office of the group of women elected to Congress in 1992; "The Verdict," a live report on a Supreme Court decision on abortion; and "Contraception, the Stalled Revolution," a special on birth control.

"NICK NEWS"

Lucky Duck's greatest emphasis, though, has been in the area of news programs for children for the cable station Nickelodeon. These include a series of specials on such topics as the Gulf War, television itself, the environment, the Los Angeles riots, and AIDS. The AIDS program, "A Conversation with Magic," featured frank talk about the disease with Magic Johnson. Her best known current work, though, is the prime-time series "Nick News." Ellerbee is the executive producer, writer, and host for this weekly half-hour TV news magazine show for kids. The show was originally called "Nick News W/5" for the basic five questions of journalism—who, what, when, where, and why—and it continues to ask those questions about true stories from today's world.

Above all, Ellerbee says, she wants to treat her audience with respect, as intelligent people. "We started from the notion that we would never talk down to our audience. These kids are smart. We cover the behavior of nations, not how crayons are made. When we first started the show, our motto was 'Question authority.' Then one day we looked around and said that's not broad enough. It ought to be 'Question everything.'" Ellerbee's approach apparently worked: the show has been a huge success with critics, parents, and most importantly, kids. The show has won numerous awards, including the duPont—Columbia Award, the Parents' Choice Foundation Gold Television Award, and the Television Critics Association Award.

While her professional life has flourished in the past few years, Ellerbee has faced adversity in her personal life. In the late 1980s she realized that she was an alcoholic and entered the Betty Ford Center to dry out, which she discusses in her book *Move On.* She has remained sober since then. In 1993 she learned that she had breast cancer and had a double mastectomy. The cancer was caught early, and between the surgery and chemotherapy the doctors believe they got it all. Her latest checkups confirm that as well. These tragedies have forced her to rethink her goals about what is important in life. In reflecting on her experience with cancer, Ellerbee says, "If this is the worst thing that happens to me in my life, I will be *so* grateful. I do work that I love, I'm in a stable relationship with a wonderful man, my kids are healthy, and we *get along*. So in many ways," Ellerbee says, "this has been the best year of my life."

LOOKS AND TV NEWS

It's impossible to read about Linda Ellerbee for long without coming upon the issue of appearance. Television news is a field in which appearance has sometimes been more important than intelligence or competence, particularly for women. As Tony Kornheiser reported in the *Washington Post*, "In the TV news business the cute ones are called 'Twinkies.' This is not a term of endearment; it is used to describe anchors whose most discernible talent is a pretty face. Linda Ellerbee, one pistol-packing mama of an anchor, has been called many things—from smart to smug, from sharp to snide—but never a twinkie."

In her typically forthright way, Ellerbee herself criticizes the emphasis on looks: "The issue is how pretty versus how smart. There have been women—and men—on television who could not write, could not report, and could not produce, but you wouldn't know it by watching them because they're propped up by very good people. What bothered me . . . was how much attention was paid to how pretty someone should be to anchor. Forget pretty. Let's talk about stupidity. How *smart* should you have to be?" Ellerbee has outright refused to conform to the stereotypical image expected of those in TV news, insisting instead to be judged by her ability. "I want to be perceived as someone who thinks a lot before she sits down and writes this stuff. I want to be perceived as someone who is not here because she won a Miss America contest or because she would devour anything in her way to get to anchor the nightly news. I want to be perceived as a responsible reporter and a smart one."

HOBBIES AND OTHER INTERESTS

Ellerbee enjoys watching baseball on TV and reading, "anything except romances, gothic horrors, and Stephen King." She shares a recently remodeled brownstone in Greenwich Village, New York, with Rolfe Tessem and assorted pets. She also enjoys spending time with her now-grown children, Vanessa, a musician in Seattle, and Josh, an aspiring writer who works as a bartender in New York City.

WRITINGS

"And So It Goes": *Adventures in Television*, 1986
Move On: Adventures in the Real World, 1991

HONORS AND AWARDS

Emmy Award: 1986, for Outstanding Individual Achievement in News
 and Documentary Programming for Writing, for "Our World"

George Foster Peabody Broadcasting Award (University of Georgia): 1992, as Executive Producer of the Nickelodeon Special, "It's Only Television"
Television Critics Association Award: 1993, for outstanding achievement in children's programming

FURTHER READING

BOOKS

Ellerbee, Linda. *"And So It Goes": Adventures in Television,* 1986
Ellerbee, Linda. *Move On: Adventures in the Real World,* 1991
Who's Who in America, 1994

PERIODICALS

Current Biography Yearbook 1986
Glamour, Nov. 1988, p.84
National Geographic World, Apr. 1993, p.7
People, June 27, 1983, p. 51; July 28, 1986, p.32; Sep. 20, 1993, p.59
Rolling Stone, Jan. 19, 1984, p.76
Us, June 1986, p.39
Washington Post, Oct. 18, 1983, p.D1

ADDRESS

Lucky Duck Productions
96 Morton Street
6th Floor
New York, NY 10014

Sergei Fedorov 1969-
Russian Professional Hockey Player
Star Center of the Detroit Red Wings

BIRTH

Sergei Viktorovich Fedorov was born December 13, 1969, in Pskov, Russia, just north of the capital city of Moscow. The eldest child of Natasha and Viktor Fedorov, a professional athlete who played soccer and hockey, he has one brother, Fodor, who is soon to be thirteen years old. When Sergei was born, Russia was still a republic of what was then the Soviet Union (U.S.S.R.) and has now become the Federation of Independent States.

YOUTH

Fedorov's birthplace was Pskov, but he grew up 20 miles from the Barents sea in Apatiti, a suburb of Murmansk, the largest city in the world north of the Arctic Circle. Since there are almost a dozen years in age between him and his kid brother, his companions at school and at play were friends and relatives. Fedorov was an active, robust youngster. He lived a normal life within an affectionate family circle, trying his hand at a variety of sports during those years, with hockey quickly becoming his consuming passion.

EDUCATION

Fedorov attended high school in his native country before moving on to the career for which he is exceptionally well suited. Since he had no plans to further his education at a university, or even at an advanced preparatory level, he left school to join a specialized army program that would allow him to concentrate on professional hockey.

CHOOSING A CAREER

When a boy is a prodigy at hockey and has been encouraged and guided since childhood by his own father—a professional athlete and hockey coach himself—chances are good that the career chooses the boy rather than the reverse. With Fedorov's skill and enthusiasm for the game, he willingly abandoned other interests to get a chance to skate in the Red Army. Technically, he was a soldier, but his only military exercises were performed on hockey blades. He was of such star quality that he started coming to the United States with the Soviet team at the age of 15, and he vividly recalls his early impressions of American life: "I saw a lot. How people lived—not exactly everything, of course. But I just thought . . . Oh! there is something very different here." At the same time, Fedorov began to attract the attention of NHL scouts.

CAREER HIGHLIGHTS

While still living in the Soviet Union and playing on the Soviet Red Army team, Fedorov was drafted by the Detroit Red Wings in June 1989, following his most successful season with his team. Chosen in the fourth round, the rising star was selected over Pavel Bure, whom most scouts had rated considerably higher. Praise for Fedorov was not lacking, however, as evidenced by the prideful endorsement of [then] Wings general manager Jimmy Devellano, who proclaimed, "We got the best player in the world!" At the time, most people thought that such comparisons were moot—the Soviets were considered unlikely to part with a nineteen-year-old superstar.

Fedorov and the Detroit club seized their opportunity and shocked the hockey world just over a year later. While the Soviet team was playing at the Goodwill Games in Portland, Oregon, Fedorov disappeared from the team hotel. With a private plane standing by, the Red Wings spirited him back to Detroit and signed him to a five-year contract that would give him about a quarter of a million dollars a year—an incredible fortune by Soviet team standards. Fedorov refused, though, to officially defect and request asylum, asking only for a work visa as a foreigner with special talents, under the same process U.S. and Canadian players use to work in each other's countries. The Soviets were furious enough to consider canceling two exhibition series with the NHL, and even threatened an international lawsuit. Fedorov had, after all, been a major factor in his national team's gold-medal wins in the 1989 and 1990 World Championships. Viktor Tiknov, the Red Army coach, was baffled. "He betrayed me," he said simply.

Expectations were mixed in Detroit. Wings star Steve Yzerman, thought to be a major influence in the decision to draft Fedorov, repeated enthusiastically, "He's great!" Bryan Murray, then team coach and now general manager, was more studied and subdued in his assessment. "He's a hard-working, talented young man. He checks well, he's very versatile. And he doesn't mind the physical stuff. He's a very willing participant. . . . He goes to the front of the net, and he's not afraid of the traffic. . . . But to put the label of superstar on him would be unfair."

That, however, was before Fedorov's 1990-91 rookie season. Playing offense, usually center, the young Russian lit up Detroit with 31 goals and 48 assists. He finished second in the balloting for the Calder Trophy, the NHL rookie-of-the-year award. Murray's opinion was far more eloquent after the season when he declared without qualification, "His potential is unlimited." *Hockey Digest* went so far as to label him "the best of all Russians playing in this hemisphere." Fedorov had surprised players and fans with a new, aggressive approach to the game, unusual for a European trained to employ finesse on the ice. He had quickly learned to adapt to a tougher style after being upended and knocked into the boards a few times. Fedorov would shrug his shoulders and insist (through an interpreter at that early stage) that he had "always played that way" but, in reality, he knew he had shifted to a different game. He admits as much now when he describes the Russian technique. "It's more speed," he says, "more a passing game. More controlling the puck and more technical stuff—skills, big time." Free-lance writer Jack Lessenberry, who contributed a lively feature story on Fedorov to the Red Wings publication, *Inside Line*, explains that "Russian hockey is, in a way, more like a ballet on ice."

A DIFFERENT CULTURE

Fedorov worked diligently to improve his sketchy English and to adjust to life in the States. He studied with a language tutor two hours a day, three days a week but, in his eagerness to use new words, he sometimes created difficult situations. One such episode happened early in his first season, when he repeated one of his new words at an inappropriate time.

Passing through security at Montreal's Dorval Airport, he innocently remarked, "Oh, bomb," when teammate Per Djoos set off a metal detector. Djoos and Fedorov were both frisked and their luggage was searched before Coach Murray stepped in to clear his players. A more amusing story, which has made the rounds many times, tells of how the Russian, struggling with his new language, shook up a trainer by asking for "love." He meant "glove."

Fedorov came on "gangbusters" (a slang expression he'd enjoy using) in the 1991-92 season, scoring 32 goals. For his outstanding skill and efforts, he was named to the all-star team. Fedorov was praised especially for his remarkable ability to change speed and shake through defensive lines while streaking towards the goal. His play that year made him runner-up to Montreal's center, Guy Carboneau, for the Selke Trophy, given to the league's best defensive forward.

Fedorov's success has continued in an upward spiral. He netted 34 goals and 53 assists in 1992-93, a record that earned him a new four-year contract worth $11.7 million early in 1993. "The Red Wings won't regret this," he said. "I'll earn every dollar of it." Good to his promise, he started racking up points with a torrid pace that consistently brought home-game crowds out of their seats. By the time he joined other top NHL players for the forty-fifth All-Star Game in January 1994, he was only four points behind the great Wayne Gretzky of the Los Angeles Kings in the year's scoring race. Fedorov also was ahead of the field for the award for all-around best player of the season.

THE HAT TRICK, AND THE FIRST 100-POINT SEASON

On March 1, 1994, a sellout crowd at Detroit's Joe Louis Arena stood and cheered for Fedorov and scattered their hats across the ice when he scored a rare "hat trick" (a three-goal game) on a night that also saw him achieve his first 100-point season. Fedorov's only other hat trick had been in the Soviet Union when he was a fifteen-year-old kid, but he handled the thrill with characteristic modesty. "A long time ago," he said. "It was great, but the most important thing is that we played pretty solid defense." The Wings had done just that with their 5-2 win over the Calgary Flames, a victory that gave them a first-place tie in the Central Division with the Toronto Maple Leafs.

Accolades pour in for Fedorov, who is not only likely to win the Hart MVP Trophy (most valuable player), but also the Art Ross Trophy (scoring title), and the Selke, all in the same season. Sportswriters suggest that, with his low-count penalty minutes, he also is a strong candidate for the Lady Byng Trophy for gentlemanly play. Fedorov had not been ranked among the game's top few players until this season. His chance to prove himself came when Steve Yzerman was sidelined with a back injury, giving Fedorov more ice time to prove his skills at both scoring and solid defense. And he has used the opportunity well, winning praise from observers. Defenseman and teammate Mark Howe, son of the famed Gordie and himself in his twenty-first hockey season, says, "I've told a lot of people that he's the best skater I've ever played with." And Chicago Blackhawks coach Darryl Sutter, a man rarely given to superlatives, recently admitted to reporters that, "Right now, Fedorov is the best in the league." His current coach, Scotty Bowman, who has led some of the greats in previous stints with Montreal, Buffalo, and Pittsburgh, told Les Bowen of Knight-Ridder Newspapers in December 1993 that he would rank the flashy young center "right at the top." Fedorov has lived up to his coach's assessment.

The combination of Detroit's top scoring lines—anchored by Fedorov and Yzerman—gives the Wings considerable punch. As of mid-March, the team led the league in goals and possessed its second-best-ever record. Fedorov's personal goal count for the 1993-94 season had already reached 47, and he continued to run a close second to Gretzky in total points for the season. Those who watch him and write about him agree that Fedorov has the potential for a long and exciting career.

MAJOR INFLUENCES

The thoroughly Americanized young man from halfway around the world recalls his roots when talking about those who have inspired him in his career. His father is mentioned first of all for the early advice and sound training, and then his boyhood hero, Igo Larinov, former outstanding center with the Soviet Central Army team. He also is quick to credit Sergei Makarov, Vladimir Krutov, and Viacheslav Fetisov, Red Army teammates, for their positive influence on his developing game. And Fedorov also shows his appreciation for Detroit left-wing Shawn Burr, the man who befriended him and helped him to absorb and understand a new culture.

MARRIAGE AND FAMILY

Fedorov is unmarried, and there seems to be no evidence, so far, of any serious romantic relationship in his life. He has bought a house in the metropolitan Detroit area, where he was joined by his parents and young brother. When he first moved to Detroit, Fedorov lived in a riverfront apartment with his extended family, *Pravda* journalist Valeri Maleev, his wife Inesa, and their son Dennis; he had once before been billeted with the Maleevs when he was playing in the Soviet league and was a two-hour drive from his own home near Murmansk.

Viktor, Natasha, and Fodor Fedorov probably will return to their native country some time soon, but Sergei has decided to apply for U.S. citizenship when he becomes eligible in about a year and a half. By then, he will have fulfilled the five-year residency requirement. "This is my home now," he says. "I may return to Russia to visit . . . my relatives, take a vacation, maybe even stay a long time. But I would like to live in the States. I like this country, and I love Detroit." That's good news for Coach Bowman, and for the fans who howl their approval every time the popular young center glides onto the ice at Joe Louis.

HOBBIES AND OTHER INTERESTS

Sergei Fedorov enjoys other things besides hockey. He played tennis in high school, but his current interests extend to golf, heavy-metal music (often to the annoyance of his teammates on road trips, where they share close quarters), and corn flakes. "He *loves* corn flakes," says a friend, but he also still craves Russian food. Of late, with his mother in residence, he is able to indulge in homemade borscht (a rich beet soup) and other delicacies that he remembers from his boyhood.

Some of Fedorov's spare time is spent on remodeling the 34-foot motorboat that is his most recent major purchase. His land transportation usually is a flashy red Corvette; some time ago, he sent home his Chevy Blazer when he realized how useful the four-wheel-drive vehicle would be for his family on Russia's winter roads.

AWARDS AND HONORS

NHL All-Star Team: 1991-92, 1992-93, 1993-94

FURTHER READING

PERIODICALS

Detroit Free Press, June 18, 1989, p.15E; Sep. 12, 1990, p.1D; Dec. 14, 1993, p.1C; Feb. 12, 1994, p.2D; Mar. 2, 1994, p.2D

Detroit News, July 25, 1990, pp. A1, C1; Dec. 24, 1990, p.D2; Feb. 16, 1992, p.E8; March 2, 1994, p.C1
Inside Line (Red Wings publication), Dec. 1993, p.28
Los Angeles Times, Dec. 27, 1993, Sports section, p.1A
Maclean's, Apr. 13, 1992, p.21
Newsday, Dec. 26, 1993, Sports section, p.20
Seattle Post-Intelligencer, July 27, 1990, p.C7
The Sporting News, Aug. 20, 1990, p.35
USA Today, Nov. 2, 1990, p.9C; Mar. 21, 1994, p.2C

ADDRESS

Detroit Red Wings
Joe Louis Arena
600 Civic Center Drive
Detroit, MI 48226

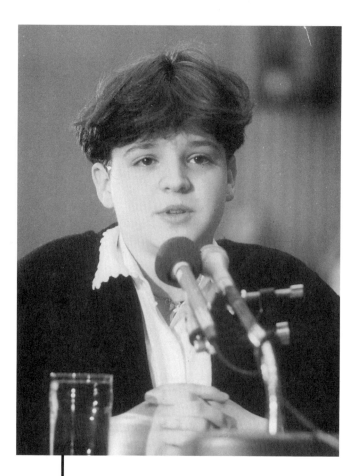

Zlata Filipovic 1980-
Bosnian Diarist
Author of *Zlata's Diary*, a Journal About War in Her Homeland

BIRTH

Zlata Filipovic (Fi-LEE-po-vich) is a young Bosnian girl who became a celebrity with the publication of her personal diary about war in her native land. She was born in Sarajevo, in the Yugoslav republic of Bosnia-Herzogovina, on December 3, 1980, the only child of Malik and Alica Filipovic. Her ethnic and religious backgrounds are a mixture of Slavic identities—Muslim and Christian, Serb and Croat. Mainly, she is Croat, but without religious connection. Zlata's father is a lawyer and her mother is a biochemist, but neither has been able to concentrate on their professional lives since 1992, when Bosnia-Herzogovina was plunged into war after declaring independence from its Serbian neighbors.

A BRIEF OVERVIEW OF EVENTS LEADING TO CONFLICT

Zlata's story is best understood within the context of central European history. Until the collapse of communism throughout Europe in the late 1980s and early 1990s, Yugoslavia was a union of six republics (Serbia, Croatia, Bosnia-Herzogovina, Slovenia, Montenegro, and Macedonia). The country, as a unit, had come about after the First World War. The provinces of Croatia, Slovenia, and Bosnia-Herzogovina, all component parts of the defeated Austro-Hungarian Empire, joined with Serbia and the other Balkan states of Dalmatia, Montenegro, and Macedonia to form the Kingdom of the Serbs, Croats, and Slovenes. From the beginning, it was an uneasy alliance of ethnic cultures that struggled through a decade of strained relations within its own borders, and disputes and nullified treaties with neighboring countries. It was an absolute monarchy from 1929, when its name was officially changed to Yugoslavia, until 1931. Further geographical divisions were made in the ensuing years until, in 1941, the country was invaded by Germany and occupied for four years by Axis troops (Germans, Italians, Hungarians, and Bulgarians).

After World War II, Yugoslavia established a decentralized socialist state that flourished under a self-managed economy independent of the Soviet Union. Nevertheless, centuries-old hatreds and rivalries began to ferment again with the disintegration of communism and the end of authoritarian control. Clashes broke out between multiculturalists and nationalists. Then, beginning in 1992, rebel Serb aggression battered Bosnia with such horrors of bombardment that Sarajevo, the capital city, existed under siege and in a state of terror—little food, no running water or plumbing, no electricity or heat, and constant fear of snipers and bombings. An international peace accord eventually was brokered by the United Nations although, as late as August 1994, the fragile truce was being eroded by continued fighting between Muslim and Serb forces in north-central Bosnia. Sarajevo, under the cease-fire agreement since February, has returned to what George Jahn of the Associated Press calls "an illusion of normalcy," adding that "appearances deceive [and it is a city] still grappling with the losses of family and friends in a war that has left 200,000 dead or missing."

LIFE IN PREWAR SARAJEVO

Before war tore her world apart, Zlata Filipovic lived a normal, middle-class existence. She had a happy, mundane childhood in prewar Sarajevo, the city that had so spectacularly hosted the 1984 Winter Olympics. Her father's law office was next door to the family apartment in the

Skenderija district of the city, and there was a country house in Dobrosevici. In the diary that she began keeping in September 1991, just before she turned eleven and entered fifth grade, she wrote innocently about a life that was comfortable and filled with ordinary happenings. Her childhood musings were about vacations in the mountains, tennis and piano lessons, pizza, Madonna, MTV, and supermodels. Any problems of her pampered existence centered around the complaints of the average child—school work and minor inconveniences. "Oh, why did this have to happen on my birthday," she wrote when a sinus infection kept her confined to bed. "Oh, I am so unlucky!"

THE CHRONICLES OF HORROR

Zlata's recountings of the ups and downs of a growing girl's life dramatically changed in tone as her city descended into war. Stripped of a normal existence, she grew sadder and wiser in her writings as she depicted the chaos and unspeakable atrocities and lamented the loss of a childhood interrupted by war. William Drodziak of the *Washington Post* foreign bureau describes her "anguished accounts of the perilous foraging for food, the long days without water, gas, or electricity, and the fearful nights spent in dark, freezing bunkers that became Sarajevo under siege." Tragically, Zlata wrote of the death of her friend, Nina, in an artillery barrage: "a bomb or shell fell on the park. A lot of people were hurt. Selma lost a kidney and NINA DIED. A piece of shell stopped in her brain and she died. Oh, she was so cute and a nice girl. We were together in kindergarten and often we played in the park. I will draw a flower vase [in the diary] for Nina WHO WAS KILLED IN THIS DISGUSTING WAR!" Months later, in recording the death of a boy from her school literary group, she despaired, "Oh, God . . . what is happening here?"

In heartbreaking detail, Zlata confided in the diary she named "Mimmy" (after her goldfish), admittedly borrowing from World War II's famous diarist, Anne Frank, the teenage Jewish girl who hid from German troops in the attic of an Amsterdam warehouse and wrote daily observations to an imaginary friend called "Kitty." As the months progressed and the war in Bosnia escalated, Zlata's writings took on a more mature and political stance, although the entries continued in simple prose.

Zlata's journal was submitted during the summer of 1993 to a teacher at an improvised school. The teacher, with the help of UNICEF (United Nations International Emergency Children's Fund), arranged for its publication in paperback by a small antiwar press in Sarajevo. The diary quickly attracted the attention of journalists and television crews from around the world, whose glowing accounts of this precocious young girl made her an instant celebrity. Zlata's connections with UNICEF provided an escape from Sarajevo two days before Christmas 1993, when she and her parents were escorted through government and Serb checkpoints by a French contingent to board a UN plane for Paris. The slim book, reproducing Zlata's handwriting and sketches, had already been translated into French and English and, since that time, has gone on to be published in more than twelve countries. Zlata was in the United States in the spring of 1994 on a promotional tour for her published diary—she met President Clinton, sat for TV interviews, and was featured in major newspapers and magazines from coast to coast. Even movie rights were discussed in the frenzy of activity over a book that agents heralded as "a riveting story."

Not all reviewers of *Zlata's Diary* were so generous. There were those who saw it as contrived, and as striking a false note in its swift transformation from a childlike, innocent beginning to a sophisticalted, politically focused conclusion. David Rieff, writing in a late March issue of the *New Republic*, believed that the diary may have been altered in its translations. He noted that "her references to various political events are nowhere to be found in the original edition," adding, "the problem is that so much has been added. What might have been a moving tale simply told reads instead like propaganda, whether or not the text has been tampered with; and crude propaganda at that." The publishers deny any tampering with the original Croat edition, which they say was abridged and did not contain the full text. Reiff wondered also about Zlata comparing herself to the martyred Anne Frank: "It is more than a little surprising to find her invoking Anne Frank after confessing on January 14, 1992, that 'every night I dream that I'm asking Michael Jackson for his autograph,' and then breaking off to watch a Bugs Bunny cartoon' . . . and nowhere giving any sign of a precocious interest in history and literature."

ZLATA'S FAMILY

Malik, Alica, and Zlata make up the immediate Filipovic family, but there are other close relatives whom they were anguished to leave when they went to Paris. Zlata has maternal grandparents in the Sarajevo area, and an uncle and aunt whose children were her playmates. Malik's sister, Melica, also lived nearby.

Zlata and her parents have returned home after their stay in France and their whirlwind promotional tour in the United States. Sadly, their weekend house in Dobrosevici was destroyed in the bombings.

FURTHER READING

BOOKS

Zlata's Diary: A Child's Life in Sarajevo, 1994 (this translation from the Croat appeared in Great Britain in 1993; the diary originally had been published in France that same year as *La Journal de Zlata*)

PERIODICALS

Los Angeles Times, Mar. 15, 1994, p.1; Mar. 23, 1994, p.1
Maclean's, Mar. 28, 1994, p.37
New Republic, Mar. 28, 1994
Newsday, Mar. 18, 1994, p.15
New Yorker, Mar. 28, 1994, p.43
New York Times, Jan. 6, 1994, p.A1; Feb. 28, 1994, p.C15
New York Times Book Review, Mar. 6, 1994, p.7
People, Mar. 21, 1994, p.66
Philadelphia Inquirer, Mar. 19, 1994, p.F1; Apr. 3, 1994, p.F1
Washington Post, Jan. 13, 1994, p.C1; Mar. 12, 1994, p.D1; Mar. 20, 1994, Book section, p.2

ADDRESS

c/o Guilia Melucci
Viking Senior Publicist
Penguin USA
375 Hudson Street
New York, NY 10014

BRIEF ENTRY

Daisy Fuentes 1966-
Cuban-Born American VJ on MTV

EARLY LIFE AND CAREER

Daisy Fuentes was born on November 17, 1966, in Havana, Cuba. Her father is a real estate investor, and her mother is a painter. Because her mother was a Spanish citizen, they were able to emigrate from Cuba when Daisy was three. The family lived in Spain for four years before settling in New Jersey, where Fuentes grew up. She soon became fluent in both Spanish and English.

While attending Bergen Community College, Fuentes started modeling. She met the wife of a TV executive, who encouraged her to try for a job with a Spanish TV station in New York City. As Fuentes relates, "She was really impressed with my Spanish. She said we needed more young people who knew how to speak both languages properly." And Fuentes fit the bill. She got the job at the TV station, starting out as the weather anchor. It helped her get the experience she needed on the air, she says, but it was "extremely boring."

MAJOR ACCOMPLISHMENTS

So boring, in fact, that in 1987 she sent off an unsolicited audition tape to MTV. Executives at the music video network loved it, and they picked her to host the new cable series "MTV Internacional," an hourlong Spanish-language music show that is syndicated in the U.S. and in 17 Latin American countries. The series debuted in July 1988, and response to Fuentes was so positive that she became a regular VJ on MTV. During the summer, she also hosts the popular "Beach MTV," and her sunny smile and bubbly personality light up the show. In addition, Fuentes has been studying acting, appearing on the soap opera "Loving" and on the season opener of the PBS mystery series "Ghostwriter." She also recently signed a multi-year modeling contract with Revlon, to represent that company's cosmetic and beauty lines.

In October 1993, the video network started a new 24-hour-per-day channel, MTV Latino, broadcast in Latin America and in key markets in the U.S. Fuentes will work on that channel as well, hosting features about Latin musicians. She has long been a pop idol in Latin America—with love letters from fans and adoring hordes at all her appearances—and this move is sure to increase her popularity, both in the U.S. and abroad.

FURTHER READING

Boston Globe, Aug. 2, 1990, Arts and Film Section, p.25
People, Sept. 13, 1993, p.15
Philadelphia Daily News, Aug. 8, 1990, Features, p.38
Vogue, Aug. 1991, p.110

ADDRESS

MTV
1515 Broadway
New York, NY 10036

Ruth Bader Ginsburg 1933-
American Jurist and Legal Scholar
Associate Justice, United States
Supreme Court

BIRTH

Ruth Bader Ginsburg, the second woman ever to sit on the United States Supreme Court, was born on March 15, 1933, in the Flatbush section of Brooklyn, New York. She was the second daughter of Nathan and Celia (Amster) Bader, whose only other child, Marilyn, died of meningitis at the age of six. It was Marilyn who first called her little sister "Kiki," a pet name still used by relatives and old friends.

YOUTH

Reared as an only child, Ruth benefitted from the intellectual ambition of her mother, whose own hopes for education beyond high school were denied when she had to go to work in New York's garment district to help send an older brother to college. In the early decades of this century, this sexual double standard was a way of life, and it was commonplace for boys to be given first consideration for higher education. But as David Margolis explained in the *New York Times*, Celia Bader, "a voracious reader herself, hooked [her little girl] on reading through trips to a public library atop a Chinese restaurant off King's Highway in Brooklyn. Ever since, Judge Ginsburg has said, she has associated the aroma of Chinese food with the pleasures of reading."

This early introduction to books made a deep impression on Ruth, a thoughtful child by nature, and set her on a path to eventual academic achievement. In her Rose Garden speech after President Clinton named her to the Supreme Court in June 1993, Ginsburg paid tender tribute to the mother who had instilled in her the love of learning. Exhibiting rare emotion, she said, "I pray that I may be all that she would have been had she lived in an age when women could aspire and achieve, and daughters are cherished as much as sons."

Friends from Ginsburg's childhood and adolescence say that her brilliance as a student and her quiet demeanor did not keep her from having a host of friends. She was active and immensely popular, even though, as one former classmate put it, "scary smart."

EDUCATION

Ginsburg's introduction to formal education came at Public School 238 in her Flatbush neighborhood. It was there that she first demonstrated an interest in the law by writing editorials for the school paper about the Magna Carta and the Bill of Rights. Later, at Brooklyn's highly regarded James Madison High School, she won scholastic honors while also participating in a number of extracurricular activities—among them, baton twirling. Sadly, the day before graduation in June 1950, her mother died of cancer, and Ruth did not attend the commencement ceremony; her numerous awards were delivered to her at home.

She won further recognition at Cornell University in upstate New York, where she was elected to Phi Beta Kappa and Phi Kappa Phi, honorary scholastic societies. She graduated summa cum laude in 1954 with a bachelor's degree in government and also distinguished herself in all subjects.

Ginsburg then took a short break from her education. She had recently married Martin Ginsburg, then a law student. The newlyweds spent the next two years at Fort Sill, Oklahoma, where Martin did army service and where their first child, Jane, was born in 1955. They then moved to Cambridge, Massachusetts, where Ginsburg and her husband attended Harvard Law School for two years (1956-58). She transferred to Columbia Law for her senior year when her husband, newly graduated, took a position with a New York City law firm. At both universities, she was elected to the prestigious Law Review and, upon graduation from Columbia with a J.D. (juris doctor), she tied for first place in the Class of 1959.

CHOOSING A CAREER

The workings of government had fascinated young Ruth Bader throughout her school years, and she settled on the law as a career while still in undergraduate school. She has said, however, that she does not recall any one particular event that influenced her decision. Her widowed father had reservations and tried to direct her toward teaching, which he considered a more sensible choice. The pervading attitudes of the 1950s did not lend themselves easily to women in the legal profession and Nathan Bader, a man of modest means, worried about his daughter's financial security. Ruth, however, was inspired by her government studies and could not be forced to change her mind. She went ahead with her law school plans.

CAREER HIGHLIGHTS

Even with an enviable academic record, Ginsburg faced discrimination in trying to find a job as a lawyer. None of the firms to which she applied offered her a job, and a clerkship also seemed out of reach. She had worked impossible hours in an effort to study, to help her husband through a bout with cancer, and to care for their little daughter. Some years later, Ginsburg would write about her difficulty in finding work: "In the Fifties, the traditional law firms were just beginning to turn around on hiring Jews. But to be a woman, a Jew and a mother to boot—that combination was a bit much." When she was recommended for a clerkship with then-Supreme Court Justice Felix Frankfurter, a man celebrated for his marked liberal tendencies, he too declined to interview her. Finally, in spite of the rampant discrimination against women in those times, Ginsburg was hired to clerk (1959-61) for the Honorable Edmund L. Palmieri of the U.S. District Court in Manhattan. She has often said that she found that experience both valuable and stimulating.

Ginsburg worked next on an international civil procedures project at Columbia and, as part of that program, spent two summers in Sweden. That assignment resulted in a book, *Civil Procedures in Sweden*, written with Anders Bruzelius—but more, it was the beginning of the feminist consciousness that eventually led her to become a champion of women's rights.

From 1963 to 1972, Ginsburg taught at Rutgers University Law School, commuting to Newark, New Jersey, each day while juggling her expanding family responsibilities at home in New York. A second child, James, was born in 1965, and Ginsburg's seriously ill father had become part of the household. Nevertheless, the Ginsburgs remained dedicated to their professional goals, with Ruth never considering a leave of absence.

While at Rutgers, Ginsburg began litigating sex-discrimination cases. She became a pioneer in the field, successfully arguing five cases before the U.S. Supreme Court for the American Civil Liberties Union (ACLU), an organization she served as general counsel and national board member. She was the director of the Women's Rights Project for the ACLU, and in that position she "adopted a strategy intended to convince the Justices that laws that discriminated between men and women—even those laws that were meant to help women—were based on unfair and harmful stereotypes and were in most cases unconstitutional," according to Neil A. Lewis of *The New York Times*. For the Supreme Court cases, she organized the briefs, found plaintiffs, and gave the oral arguments. One such case, *Craig v. Boren*, which Ginsburg argued before the court in 1976, resulted in a standard still used in cases of sex discrimination. The Oklahoma law, struck down after Ginsburg's Supreme Court challenge, allowed women aged 19 to buy 3.2 percent beer, while men had to be 21 to do so.

Harvard invited her to teach a one-semester course in 1971 but, says the *Wall Street Journal*, "dawdled in offering her a job. In swooped Columbia Law School, which quickly hired [her] as its first tenured female faculty member." Ginsburg taught at Columbia from 1971 to 1980. During those years, she was also a visiting lecturer on a number of prestigious faculties, among them the New York University School of Law, University of Amsterdam (Netherlands), University of Strasbourg (France), the Salzburg (Austria) Seminar in American Studies, and the Aspen (Colorado) Institute. In addition, she was honored with a year's fellowship (1977-78) at the Center for Advanced Study in the Behavioral Sciences at Stanford in California.

A FEDERAL JUDGESHIP

The national acclaim Ginsburg had gained as counsel to the ACLU led to her 1980 appointment by then-President Carter to the U.S. Court of Appeals for the District of Columbia. Long a heroine to liberals as a strong advocate for women's equality, she assumed a surprisingly moderate and unpredictable judicial role, "showing little of the passion that so fueled her earlier work," said *Newsweek* in June 1993. The crusader for gender equality proved to be a cautious, centrist judge during her thirteen years on the federal bench. Her frequent criticism of the broad scope of *Roe v. Wade*, the Supreme Court's landmark 1973 ruling that guaranteed women's right to an abortion, has been condemned by some women's advocacy groups. Yet according to Ginsburg's defenders, she objects not to the outcome of the *Roe* decision—the legality of abortion—but instead to the judicial reasoning that underlies it. In the *Roe* decision, the justices concluded that an individual's constitutional right to privacy guarantees the right to an abortion. Ginsburg believes that the right to an abortion should be based instead on the legal right to equal protection.

ELEVATION TO THE HIGHEST COURT

In early 1993, when Justice Byron White announced his imminent retirement from the Supreme Court, President Clinton began a frustrating and uncommonly public search for White's replacement. He was looking for "a bold politician who could muster a bloc to counter the court's conservatives," suggested *Business Week*, but in nominating Ruth Bader Ginsburg on June 14, he "got a detail-oriented professional whose rulings . . . reveal neither a conservative ideologue nor a wild-eyed radical."

Ginsburg's Senate confirmation was swift and without obstruction, and she took her oath of office on August 1, 1993—publicly at the White House and privately at the Supreme Court. A formal ceremony was held in chambers October 1, three days before the start of the new term.

Justice Ginsburg is the second woman ever to serve on the nation's highest court, joining Sandra Day O'Connor, a Ronald Reagan appointee who was seated in 1981. Ginsburg also is the first Jew to serve since the late Abe Fortas resigned in 1969.

MARRIAGE AND FAMILY

Ruth Bader and Martin D. Ginsburg were introduced by mutual friends during Ruth's first semester at Cornell, and they remained sweethearts throughout their college years. They were married on June 23, 1954, shortly after her graduation. The Ginsburgs have two children, now grown. Their daughter, Jane Carol, is a tenured professor at Columbia Law School where her mother, who taught there from 1963 to 1972, was the first woman ever granted that status. Their son, James Steven, is a University of Chicago law student currently on leave to work as a classical record producer.

A co-op apartment in Washington's Watergate complex is home to Ruth and Martin Ginsburg. Martin is a noted tax attorney in his own right, but also fills another role, that of family cook. Ruth makes no claims to culinary expertise. "In certain respects," says *People* magazine, "the Ginsburgs' domestic life resembles the gender-blend ideal that Ruth has fought for."

MAJOR INFLUENCES

In a role reversal that is rare even by today's standards, Martin Ginsburg has been the bedrock upon which the new justice's remarkable career was established and has flourished. He, more than any other person in her life, has advised and supported her—in the beginning by sharing household and child-care responsibilities so that she could attend law school, and later, by arranging his own professional activities to coincide with her growing opportunities. In 1980, when she was appointed to a federal judgeship, he left behind a successful career as a tenured law professor at Columbia to be with her in Washington. Justice Ginsburg readily concedes that, without her husband's unqualified support, she might never have reached the chambers of the Supreme Court.

Two others, in particular, have inspired Ginsburg: her mother, a woman of "tremendous intellect," she says, who urged her to develop her abilities to the fullest; and Robert E. Cushman, her government professor at Cornell, a man she describes as "a defender of our deep-seated national values—freedom of thought, speech, and press." Ginsburg worked as Cushman's student assistant in the mid-1950s, in the midst of the McCarthy era. This was a time named for the late U.S. Senator Joseph P. McCarthy, a demagogue who hysterically exploited people's fears of communism, and who eventually was censured by Congress for his irresponsible and damaging tactics.

HOBBIES AND OTHER INTERESTS

Beyond her love of family and the law, opera is Justice Ginsburg's great passion—so much so that she had made plans to be an extra at the Washington Opera during the 1993-94 season until, as the *New York Times* reports wryly, "a more tempting part came her way."

A lifetime given to prodigious study, self-discipline, and meticulous scheduling has only intensified a public image of cautious reserve, but Ginsburg is open and friendly in the company of those close to her. She is a competent horsewoman who also enjoys golf, sailing, and waterskiing. Her quieter pursuits include watching old movies and settling down with mystery stories.

WRITINGS

Civil Procedure in Sweden (with Andrew Bruzelius), 1965

Text, Cases and Materials on Sex-Based Discrimination (with Herma Hill Kay and Kenneth M. Davidson), 1974

In addition, Justice Ginsburg has contributed numerous articles to law reviews and other periodicals on civil procedure, conflict of laws, and constitutional and comparative law.

FURTHER READING

BOOKS

Gilbert, Lynn, and Gaylen Moore. *Particular Passions: Talks With Women Who Have Shaped Our Times*, 1981
Swiger, Elinor Porter. *Women Lawyers at Work*, 1978
Who's Who in America, 1992-93

PERIODICALS

Business Week, June 28, 1993, p.30
Detroit Free Press, June 15, 1993, p. A1; July 11, 1993, p.F1; Oct. 4, 1993, p.A1
Newsweek, June 28, 1993, p.29
New York Times, June 15, 1993, pp.A1, A13; June 16, 1993, pp. A1, B1; June 25, 1993, p.A1; July 22, 1993, pp. A1, A10; July 23, 1993, p.A1
People, June 28, 1993, p.49
Time, June 28, 1993, p.38
U.S. News & World Report, June 28, 1993, p.26
Wall Street Journal, June 15, 1993, pp. A1, A14

ADDRESS

U.S. Supreme Court
Supreme Court Building
1 First Street NE
Washington, DC 20543

Whoopi Goldberg 1949?-
American Actress and Comedienne
Co-Star of *Sister Act*, *Ghost*, and "Star Trek: The Next Generation"

BIRTH

The multi-award winning actress known as Whoopi Goldberg was born Caryn Johnson in New York City on November 13, 1949, to Robert and Emma (Harris) Johnson. Caryn's only sibling was an older brother, Clyde. When Robert Johnson deserted his family, Caryn's mother, a practical nurse and later a Head Start teacher, raised her children alone in Manhattan's racially mixed Chelsea district.

Many inconsistencies have been noted in the various dates given for Goldberg's birth—as there are for other events in her life—but 1949 is generally believed to be the accurate year.

YOUTH

The girl who grew up as Caryn Johnson, and who traveled a rugged path from housing project to Hollywood stardom, insists that she had a "good childhood," although her interests were quite different from those of the other neighborhood kids. "I was a very quiet and very dull child," she recalls. "I liked things that other kids weren't into at the time—movies, theater, ballet. When you grow up in Manhattan, all things are accessible."

She always believed that she would be a performer, and the vivid imagination of her early years was stimulated even further, she says, as she watched old dramas and "screwball comedies of the 1930s" on the family's black-and-white television set. She learned to imitate a wide range of voices and attitudes, a talent that comes from the contrast of life at home and life in the street during her girlhood. She recalls that most of the children in her neighborhood spoke in rough "city talk," but she and Clyde grew up exposed also to the mannerly and precise diction of their mother. She quickly learned what she calls "doublespeak." Switching from one voice to the other, whether out with the gang or in the more restrained atmosphere at home, is certain to have given Goldberg the edge that later marked the dramatic and inventive characterizations in her one-woman shows.

When Goldberg was eight years old, she started performing with the Helena Rubinstein Children's Theatre at the Hudson Guild, a neighborhood community center that offered children a safe place to play and to learn. She spent hours there every week and remembers how much she loved acting even then, explaining with a chuckle, "I liked the idea that you could pretend to be somebody else, and nobody would cart you off to a hospital." Caryn and the others in her group reaped additional benefits when they were taken on summer day trips away from the hot city streets and out to Hudson Guild's farm and petting zoo in suburban New Jersey.

EDUCATION

Goldberg, as Caryn Johnson, attended elementary classes at St. Columba's, a Catholic school in Manhattan. About two weeks into ninth grade, she dropped out of high school. She blames her loss of focus on dyslexia, a reading affliction that distorts the appearance of the written word. It was about that time, she says, that she started using drugs, "because they were there," and because nearly everyone around her was doing them. She spent her days wandering around Central Park, listening to people play drums and doing drugs. Before long, she was hooked. "To this day," writes Laura Randolph in *Ebony*, "she doesn't know what made her realize she had to stop, but she knows that if she hadn't stopped, she'd probably be six feet under instead of on top of the world."

GETTING CLEAN—AND GETTING MARRIED

Goldberg ended up at Horizon House, a drug treatment center in New York. Getting clean took many tries, the actress says now. "You fall a lot because it's *hard*." The whole experience, including rehabilitation, is a searing memory that has made Goldberg an especially frank anti-drugs spokesperson.

At the same time, Goldberg became involved with her counselor at Horizon House. She and Martin (she refuses to divulge his full name) were married in 1971. She is evasive about further details, except that they were married briefly and had one child, Alexandrea Martin, born in 1974.

FIRST JOBS

Once she was free of drugs and able to take control of her life, Whoopi Goldberg embarked seriously on her chosen profession. First, she found work singing in the choruses of Broadway shows. After her brief marriage and the birth of her daughter, she moved to California in 1974 to pursue an acting career. There, she honed her comedic skills in a San Diego improvisational troupe, but had to take a series of supplemental jobs that ranged from bricklaying to doing the hair and makeup of corpses in a funeral parlor. She also reluctantly relied on occasional public assistance. After five years, she was able to support herself and her child, and says with pride, "The greatest thing I was ever able to do was give a welfare check back and [tell the department], 'Here, I don't need this anymore.'"

CAREER HIGHLIGHTS

CARYN JOHNSON TO WHOOPI GOLDBERG

She changed her name about this time, too. At first, Caryn had decided on "Whoopi Cushion" (a reference to the joke store item), but Emma Johnson was not amused, urging her unconventional daughter to choose a more respectable surname. "Goldberg" was a name allegedly plucked out of her family background. "In the early years," writes the publication *Let's Talk*, "the shock of discovering [that] the German-Jewish sounding Whoopi Goldberg was actually born a black American Catholic had its own special effect on audiences."

Goldberg went north to the San Francisco area, where she joined the Blake Street Hawkeyes Theatre in Berkeley, partnering in the beginning with comedian David Schein. After she moved into solo performances, she created "The Spook Show," a series of tragicomic portrayals that played to local standing-room-only crowds before Goldberg took the show on a national and European tour. As she described it, the show was "a blend of straight theatre, stand-up comedy, Greek comedy, political satire, and world assessment through characters." And critics were impressed—Mel Gussow of the *New York Times* called Goldberg a cross between Lily Tomlin and Richard Pryor, "not simply a stand-up comedian but a satirist with a cutting edge and an actress with a wry attitude toward life and public performance."

When the director and producer Mike Nichols caught her act in New York in 1983, he was so impressed that he quickly signed her to create an evening of original material. *Whoopi Goldberg on Broadway* opened to rave reviews the following season. While many critics mentioned the often coarse and colorful language, which she continues to use to this day, they also applauded her solo characterizations as perceptive, compassionate, moving, and funny. The program was later taped as a special for HBO, and the album from the stage production won a Grammy as best comedy recording of the year in 1985.

THE COLOR PURPLE

Goldberg's film career was launched in 1985 with the film adaptation of Alice Walker's Pulitzer Prize-winning novel, *The Color Purple*. Director Steven Spielberg cast her in the demanding role of Celie, the central character, and her performance earned her an Oscar nomination as well as the 1985 Golden Globe and Image awards for best actress in a dramatic motion picture. That same year she had won her Grammy, and the next year an Emmy for a guest appearance on TV's "Moonlighting." In 1986, she did the first "Comic Relief" with Billy Crystal and Robin Williams, now an annual fundraiser to benefit the homeless. The dreadlocked, sassy Goldberg was everywhere, and everyone was talking about her. However, a string of critically panned films followed closely on the heels of her success, and Goldberg's new-found movie career was in serious trouble. "She quickly discovered," says *Ebony*, "the only thing Hollywood loves more than a rising star is a falling one."

Goldberg kept busy in other forums while criticism of her questionable career choices swirled around her. She appeared live on stage, did Gap commercials, co-hosted the AIDS television show, "That's What Friends Are For," and took her one-woman production on the road. From 1988 through 1993 she appeared in a series of guest appearances on "Star Trek: The Next Generation" as Guinan, a part she actively campaigned for when the show was first being cast. She remembered the original "Star Trek," which also featured a diverse crew, including Nichelle Nichols as Uhura, the ship's communication's officer. "Not only was Uhura proof that black folks would make it into the future, she was beautiful, smart, and had power." In 1990 she appeared in *Ghost*, which proved to be the major box-office hit of the year. Her performance as the funky psychic, Oda Mae Brown, won a string of honors, topped by the Academy Award for best supporting actress. In the eyes of Hollywood, Whoopi was back on track.

SISTER ACT

Other roles followed: *Serafina!* (1992), made on location in South Africa, in which Goldberg played the teacher of a young girl fighting apartheid; *The Player* (1992), in which she played a detective in the acclaimed Robert Altman satire on Hollywood; *Made in America* (1993), a romantic comedy in which she starred with Ted Danson; and *Sister Act*, the surprise hit of 1992, which featured Goldberg hiding out in a convent in a nun's habit. For the latter film, she won acclaim, but also a reputation in the film community for being testy, opinionated, and difficult to work with. "I've thrown tantrums," she admits, "but it's always about work. Incompetence makes me mad." Disputes with management over the direction of the movie and the characterization of her role led Goldberg to grouse, "Working for Disney, I do feel like a nigger again, and I'm not afraid to say it." Things were finally smoothed out, however, and the success of the film brought her an offer to star in its 1993 sequel, *Sister Act 2: Back in the Habit*—an offer she accepted only after negotiating a reported $6.5 million salary. The sequel failed to attain the same level of success as the earlier hit. Recently, Goldberg has completed a movie, *Corrina, Corrina*, scheduled for release in 1994, and is currently working on another production, *Boys on the Side*.

MARRIAGE AND FAMILY

Goldberg has been married twice. Her first marriage, in 1971 to Martin, the father of her child, ended in divorce. In September 1986, Goldberg was married again, this time to a Dutch cinematographer and filmmaker, David Edward Claessen. That union ended within three years, and the actress pointedly remarks that she probably will remain single.

Whoopi has had several male companions over the past two decades, but her relationship with Ted Danson, the "Cheers" actor with whom she appeared in *Made in America*, stirred up more public controversy than either of the pair was prepared to deflect. Danson separated from his wife of 15 years, and the affair became a matter of widespread gossip. At a Friars Club roast in the fall of 1993, Danson's appearance in blackface and his comedy routine (which Goldberg purportedly wrote and staunchly defended) was deemed tasteless and racist by some and produced an even greater ruckus. When the actress was asked by a reporter if the Friars incident had provoked their abrupt breakup, her sharp answer was, "It's [personal] questions like you've been asking, *that's* what did in my relationship with Ted."

Goldberg has a granddaughter, Amarah Skye, born four years ago to Alexandrea, then fifteen years old and unmarried. There were rumors at the time of a rift between mother and daughter, but Whoopi, whose stardom has not always been easy on her family, supported the girl's decision to go ahead with her pregnancy. "Fortunately, she had a choice," says Whoopi, who for years has been a strong and vocal supporter of women's right to choose on the issue of abortion. "She chose to be a parent, it wasn't forced on her. And I said, 'If that's what you want, I'll be there for you.'"

At home, she insists, she is "Caryn Johnson, parent, Caryn Johnson, grandmother. It's a whole different gig. . . . I turn into a real person . . . there's no room for Whoopi Goldberg in that." Her principal residence is her farm in Connecticut, where she keeps a few horses, and where she goes when she needs privacy. She also has property in Montana and keeps a penthouse apartment in Los Angeles for when she is working in films or television. Until 1992, she lived part of every year in a beachfront house in Malibu.

Alexandrea and Amarah, as well as Goldberg's mother and brother, live in the San Francisco area.

HOBBIES AND OTHER INTERESTS

In addition to the time she devotes to doing comedy shows for charities, Goldberg is an avid reader who devours biographies. She collects art, which she learned to appreciate as a young girl visiting museums in her native New York. She also collects first editions of books, especially those trimmed in gold and children's books, which she claims stir her imagination for writing and performing. She is the author of a children's story, *Alice*, published in 1992, and the producer of widely acclaimed, stimulating programs for young people on the Nickelodeon channel.

SELECTED WORKS

BOOKS

Alice, 1992 (juvenile)

FEATURE FILMS

The Color Purple, 1985
Jumpin' Jack Flash, 1986
Burglar, 1987
Fatal Beauty, 1987
Clara's Heart, 1988
The Telephone, 1988
Homer and Eddie, 1989
Ghost, 1990
The Long Walk Home, 1990
Soapdish, 1991
The Player, 1992
Sarafina!, 1992
Sister Act, 1992
Wisecracks, 1992
Made in America, 1993
National Lampoon's Loaded Weapon, 1993
Sister Act 2: Back in the Habit, 1993

TV AND CABLE

"Whoopi Goldberg: Direct From Broadway," 1984
"Comic Relief," 1986-1994
"Whoopi Goldberg's Fontaine . . . Why Am I Straight?" 1988
"Star Trek: The Next Generation," 1988-1993
"That's What Friends Are For," 1990
"Bagdad Cafe," 1990-1991
"Tales from the Whoop" (Nickelodeon specials)
"Whoopi Goldberg: Chez Whoopi," 1991
"The Whoopi Goldberg Show," 1992 (talk show)

THEATER

The Spook Show (Dance Theater Workshop, Chelsea), 1983
Whoopi Goldberg on Broadway, 1984-85
Love Letters, 1992

RECORDINGS

Whoopi Goldberg, Direct From Broadway, 1985
Comic Relief, 1986 (album and videocassette)
Fontaine . . . Why Am I Straight? 1988

HONORS AND AWARDS

Image Award, NAACP (National Association for the Advancement of Colored People): 1985, and two in 1990

Grammy Award: 1985, for *Whoopi Goldberg, Direct From Broadway*
Golden Globe: 1985, for *The Color Purple*
Hans Christian Anderson Award: 1987, for outstanding achievement by a dyslexic
Humanitarian of the Year (Starlight Foundation): 1989
Academy Award: 1990, for *Ghost*, for best supporting actress
Golden Globe and British Academy Award: 1990, for *Ghost*
Golden Apple Award (Hollywood Women's Press Club): 1991
Norma Zarky Humanitarian Award (Women in Film): 1991, shared with Robin Williams and Billy Crystal
Bella Rackoff Humanitarian Award (Women in Show Business): 1991
American Cinema Award: 1992
American Comedy Award: 1992, for *Sister Act*
Woman of the Year Award (Hasty Pudding Society, Harvard University): 1993

FURTHER READING

BOOKS

Adams, Mary Agnes. *Whoopi Goldberg: From Street to Stardom*, 1993
Blue, Rose. *Whoopi Goldberg: Entertainer* (Black Americans of Achievement series), Fall 1994
Notable Black American Women, 1992
Who's Who, 1993-94

PERIODICALS

Current Biography Yearbook 1985
Cosmopolitan, Mar. 1991, p.185; Dec. 1991, p.194; Nov. 1992, p.208
Ebony, Mar. 1991, p.110
Gentlemen's Quarterly, July 1993, p.88
Jet, Aug. 13, 1990, p.58
Ladies Home Journal, Oct. 1992, p.56
McCall's, Nov. 1990, p.110; June 1993, p.18
Newsweek, Jan. 20, 1992, p.58
People, Dec. 28, 1992, p.96; June 7, 1993, p.90
Time, Sep.. 21, 1992, p.58
Us, Apr. 1994, p.58
Vogue, Jan. 1991, p.178

ADDRESS

c/o Addis & Wechsler Associates
955 South Carillo Drive, Third Floor
Los Angeles, CA 90048

Tonya Harding 1970-
American Figure Skater

BIRTH

Tonya Harding was born November 12, 1970, in Portland, Oregon. She was the only child of Albert Harding and LaVona Harding, although LaVona, who has been married seven times, had four children from earlier marriages. They were all much older than Tonya, and she never considered them family.

EARLY LIFE

The Hardings were poor and money was always tight. Al was often out of work, and the jobs he did have were low paying. LaVona was a waitress, and after her daughter started skating, she often worked nights to cover the ever-increasing costs.

Tonya remembers living in eight different houses: when the rent was raised, they'd often have to move. One time, the three of them lived in a 17-foot trailer. She also remembers being lonely, but enjoying the time she spent with her dad. He taught her to hunt and fish and bought her her first gun when she was five; she killed her first deer when she was 13.

BEGINNING TO SKATE

Harding started skating at three, at Lloyd Center in Portland. She was a natural. The family approached Diane Rawlinson, a former professional skater who had begun coaching in Portland, for lessons for the little girl. Rawlinson thought she was too small, but Tonya wouldn't take "no" for an answer. For several days, she skated in circles around Diane while she was teaching other kids. When Rawlinson saw the determination and ability of the little girl, she finally agreed to take her on.

Harding won her first competition at the age of five in Sun Valley, Idaho, and she had won more than 50 trophies by the time she was 14. But no matter how hard she worked, she couldn't seem to please her mother. One of Tonya's fellow skaters from her youth, Antje Spethman, remembers that Tonya "was great, a natural. The only problem was that horrible mother of hers." When Harding made a mistake, her mother abused her verbally and physically, shouting obscenities at the little girl and beating her with a hairbrush in front of her fellow skaters and their parents. LaVona denies these accusations, but when Tonya was raising money for skating through sponsorships, a group of businessmen in Portland dropped her because of her mother's abusive attitude and behavior.

EDUCATION

Because the family moved so often, Tonya never made many friends in school. When she was a sophomore at Portland's Milwaukie High School, she dropped out. She says that she resented her teachers' attitude that she should spend more time on her school work than on her skating. She did, however, complete a high school equivalency course in 1987 at Portland Community College to satisfy the requirement of one of her sponsors at the time, Blue Cross and Blue Shield Insurance Company.

FAMILY LIFE

Harding's mother left the family the same year that Tonya dropped out of high school. Tonya lived with her dad until he got a job in another state; then she moved in with her mother and her mother's new husband. That same year, one of LaVona's sons from an earlier marriage, Chris Davison, came by the house when Tonya was alone. According to Harding, he was drunk and he tried to molest her. When she pushed him away and locked him out of the house, he threatened to kill her. He was later arrested and spent time in jail. LaVona maintained that her son was innocent, and that Tonya just had a "vivid imagination."

Harding met Jeff Gillooly in 1985. They dated for several years, lived together, and were married in 1990. Harding filed for divorce 15 months later, citing physical abuse. Several times in their on-again-off-again relationship Tonya has filed abuse charges against Gillooly and obtained restraining orders against him, claiming that she feared for her safety. They were divorced in 1993, but continued to live together until February 1994.

CAREER HIGHLIGHTS

Throughout the stormy periods in her personal life, Harding continued to skate. But there were problems with her performance on the ice. Harding's outstanding physical ability as a skater—her strength and jumping ability—was never matched with an equal determination to spend the hours practicing necessary to make a skating champion. Her first coach, Diane Rawlinson, considered her undisciplined and unwilling to put in the hours to develop a career as a competitive figure skater.

Money was always a problem, too. Many figure skaters spend up to $40,000 a year to train, and Tonya had to do the best she could on about half that. Rawlinson often offered her coaching services for free, and Tonya's mother made all her costumes in her early years. Tonya worked at odd jobs—as a delivery girl and at a fast food restaurant—to pay the bills.

Tonya's relationship with her mother was also a problem. Tonya appears to have taken her mother's verbal and physical abuse as a child, but she rebelled as an adolescent, turning her back on her mother—and often other figures of authority—and making her own decisions.

Despite all the personal and professional obstacles, Harding's rise in the skating world was swift. In 1984, at only 14 years old, she became the first woman to land a triple-lutz jump, which she did at the junior national championships. It helped her to reach sixth place in the competition. In 1985, Harding qualified for the senior division of women's skating, but she failed to make the Nationals. In 1986, she placed sixth in the Nationals. Despite a serious car accident in which she injured her back, she came back strong the next year, placing fifth. In 1988 she competed in her first Olympic trials, where she placed a respectable fifth; it was a good showing, but she didn't make the team. In her attempt at the 1989 Nationals, she placed third. 1990 was a better year for Harding, as she skated to a first place in the Skate America competition and second in the U.S. Olympic Festival. She also made a coaching change, from Rawlinson to Dody Teachman. But while coming down with pneumonia, she skated to a dismal seventh place in the Nationals.

In 1991, Harding finally appeared to be coming into her own. At the Nationals that year, Harding stunned the skating world by becoming the first American woman to land a triple axel in competition, an extremely difficult three-and one-half rotation jump that had been landed by only one other woman in the world, Midori Ito of Japan. The National Championship was hers. At the World Championships that year, Harding finished second, behind Kristi Yamaguchi and in front of Nancy Kerrigan, making them the strongest U.S. women's team in years. Harding took the summer of 1991 off to relax and then set her sights on the 1992 Olympics. After all the years of struggle and hardship, she was looking forward to a win and to the lucrative endorsements that often go hand-in-hand with a medal.

1992 OLYMPICS

In 1992, she won a berth on the U.S. Olympic team by placing third in the Nationals, but her lack of discipline caught up with her when it was time to compete for an Olympic medal. She didn't appear in the opening ceremonies in Albertville, France, arrived just 72 hours before her first skating event, then slept for 16 hours, missing valuable practice time. When it was time to skate, Harding did poorly, ending in fourth after missing her major jumps and falling, which put her out of medal contention. Later that year, she placed sixth at the World Championships.

Also in 1992, Harding was involved in an altercation after a minor car accident, when she allegedly swung a baseball bat at the driver of the other car involved in the incident. By now, Harding had developed the image of a hard-headed, tough little girl from Portland, so unlike the "ice queens" thought to dominate figure skating. She was no privileged girl from a wealthy family. Her body was tightly muscled from pumping iron, and she lacked the long, graceful limbs of other skaters. She had lived a hard life; she liked to play pool and drag race, and she could take apart a car engine. The media picked up on this persona, and many stories on Harding dealt less with her skating than with her tough and turbulent personal life and with her unladylike image.

She also seemed hindered by mishaps on the ice. Once, during a competition, her costume broke and she had to stop and get herself back together again. Another time she stopped a competition complaining of a loose skating blade. The asthma that had plagued her for many years seemed to become more of a problem now, although she was also seen smoking, which would typically worsen an asthmatic condition.

At the Nationals in 1993, Harding placed fourth, thereby missing her chance to compete in the World Championships. With the decline in her skating fortunes came a parallel slide in her financial support. Top skaters such as Harding receive money to cover the cost of their training from the national skating associations, but the amount of money given out is based on the skater's ranking, and Harding was slipping in the standings.

In October 1993, Harding made headlines again as she and Gillooly were brought into police custody after a gun went off in the parking lot of their apartment building. Harding insisted it was an accident; neighbors claimed that they had heard arguing. In November of 1993, Harding withdrew from a regional competition in Portland where she was to qualify for the World Championships. She claimed that she had received a death threat; although some in the skating organizations and the press did not believe her, the incident led to Harding being allowed to bypass the regional competition and move on to the Nationals, to be held in Detroit.

THE ATTACK ON KERRIGAN

Then on January 6, 1994, on the eve of the 1994 National Championships, Harding became part of one of the biggest scandals in sports history. Nancy Kerrigan, favored to win the Nationals and the Olympic gold medal, was brutally attacked as she came off the ice after a practice session just prior to the competition. An unknown assailant had struck her on the knee with a metal baton.

With Kerrigan in the hospital, Harding went on to win the 1994 World Championships. But it was a tainted win. As the investigation developed, the prosecution uncovered the shocking story that rocked the country: Harding's ex-husband, Jeff Gillooly, with three accomplices, including Shawn Eckardt, Harding's bodyguard, had organized and paid for the crime. Gillooly named Harding as a partner in the plan. Harding denied any involvement.

On January 13, 1994, Shawn Eckardt confessed to the FBI, and named Harding, Gillooly, Shane Stant, and Derrick Smith as his accomplices in planning and executing the crime. Eckardt and Smith were arrested, Stant surrendered to the FBI, Gillooly confessed to the FBI and was later taken into custody. (It also came to light that Eckardt had been behind the death threat to the Portland ice rink in November 1993 that had allowed Harding to skate in the Nationals without competing on the regional level.)

The story held the front pages of newspapers all over the world as the press and the public feasted on the sordid details of the attack and those involved. The U.S. Olympic Committee (USOC) ruled that Harding could not skate in the Olympics, because she was under investigation for a crime. But Harding sued to be able to compete, and the USOC backed down and allowed her to skate after she agreed to drop her lawsuit. Many in the sports community were outraged at what they thought was a lack of courage on the part of the USOC.

In the words of *Sports Illustrated* writer E.M. Swift: "In athletics, fair play and sportsmanship are bedrock principles that should not be sacrificed—at any price."

1994 OLYMPICS

The women's figure skating events at the 1994 Olympics were a media circus. Television and press crews from around the world descended on the little town of Lillehammer, Norway, and aimed their lenses at Harding and Kerrigan. Harding had by this time sold the rights to her Olympic story to the TV tabloid "Inside Edition," and she was followed everywhere. But the constant attention proved a distraction to her skating. She looked tired and undertrained, and she did poorly. She was in tenth place after the short program, effectively out of medal contention.

Then in the long program, Harding disrupted the proceedings when she almost missed her chance to skate by showing up late. Just a few minutes into her routine, she burst into tears after missing a jump. She skated over to the referee and claimed that she had broken a lace in her skating boot and that she needed time to get a proper lace. She was granted a reskate, but it wasn't enough to overcome her earlier mistakes, and she placed eighth overall in the competition.

THE INVESTIGATION

Even while she was skating in the Olympics, Harding was under investigation for her part in the attack on Kerrigan. A grand jury in Portland was hearing evidence to determine if there was enough proof to indict Harding for her part in the crime. Before she had left for Norway, she had been interviewed by the FBI for ten hours.

The public may never know what really happened, because on March 16, 1994, Harding made a plea bargain in the case. She pled guilty to a single charge—conspiring to hinder the prosecution. That is, she admitted she was guilty of trying to cover up the crime, but not of being involved in planning it. Her conviction carries a maximum prison sentence of five years and a fine of $100,000. Because Oregon has certain rules about sentencing offenders, though, Harding received probation, meaning she would not serve time in prison. But under the terms of her probation, she cannot leave the area without informing her probation officer. She also must pay a fine of $100,000 and spend 500 hours doing community service. Further terms of the agreement state that she will give $50,000 to a Special Olympics fund, pay $10,000 in legal fees, and take a psychiatric examination. She was also forced to resign from the U.S. Figure Skating Association.

Then, on June 30, 1994, the U.S. Figure Skating Association stripped Harding of her national title and banned her from the association for life. They claimed that: "By a preponderance of the evidence, the panel did conclude that she had prior knowledge and was involved prior to the incident" to injure Kerrigan. Now Harding cannot skate in any U.S. Figure Skating Association sanctioned event, either amateur or professional, and it appears that her career in skating is over. Harding and her attorney did not attend the hearing, nor do they plan to appeal the decision.

FUTURE PLANS

Without question, Harding's hopes for the sponsorships that come with an Olympic medal are gone for now, although she has signed with a Los Angeles agency to look into appearing in films, TV, and endorsements. She has agreed to write a book about her life, with California writer Tristine Rainer. She has also decided to work as a celebrity manager for a group of professional wrestlers.

In June of 1994, Harding announced that she would appear as a waitress in an upcoming film, *Breakaway*, about a woman who runs from the mob. "I've looked at several movie offers and parts, but I liked the script of *Breakaway* and the role they've offered me," she said.

HOBBIES AND OTHER INTERESTS

Harding's hobbies include playing pool, drag racing, roller blading, boating, frisbee football, and working on cars.

HONORS AND AWARDS

U.S. Skating Championships: 1991, First Place; 1992, Second Place; 1994, First Place (removed June 1994)
World Figure Skating Championships: 1991, Second Place

FURTHER READING

BOOKS

Coffey, Frank, and Joe Layden. *Thin Ice: The Complete, Uncensored Story of Tonya Harding*, 1994

Haight, Abby, and J.E. Vader. *Fire on Ice: The Exclusive Inside Story of Tonya Harding*, 1994

PERIODICALS

Boston Globe, Jan. 13, 1994, p.35
New York Times, Mar. 17, 1991, Section VIII, p.1; Feb. 15, 1994, p.A7; Feb. 24, 1994, p.B9; Mar. 17, 1994, p.A1; June 30, 1994, p.B7
Newsweek, Mar. 2, 1992, p.50
The Oregonian, Jan. 4, 1989, p.E1; Oct. 19, 1989, p.E3; Mar. 10, 1991, p.F1, F7; Jan. 5, 1992, p.E1; Feb. 21, 1993, p.L1; Nov. 6, 1993, p.D1; Jan. 23, 1994, p.A1; May 17, 1994, p.B6
Sports Illustrated, Jan. 13, 1992, p.54; Feb. 21, 1994, p.21; Feb. 28, 1994, p.33
Time, Feb. 10, 1992, p.55; Jan. 24, 1994, p.48; Feb. 21, 1994, p.53

ADDRESS

P.O. Box 3255
Gresham, OR 97030

Melissa Joan Hart 1976-
American Actress
Star of the Hit Nickelodeon Series
"Clarissa Explains It All"

BIRTH

Melissa Joan Hart was born on April 18, 1976, in Smithtown, New York. Her parents are William Hart, a lobster wholesaler, and Paula Hart, a show business manager; together, they handle their own children's professional careers. Melissa is the oldest of their six children, with four sisters and one brother, Trisha, Elizabeth, Brian, Emily, and Alexandra, just born in November 1993. All the children except the new baby are active in show business.

YOUTH

When Melissa was three, the family moved to Sayville, on the South Shore of Long Island, just outside New York City. Her childhood was dominated by her acting career, which she began in earnest at the age of four.

EDUCATION

According to Melissa, her first memory of school was "walking into kindergarten and seeing a doll in a cradle. I walked over to pick it up and a little girl yelled at me. Later that day we became best friends." Melissa attended Cherry Avenue Elementary School and Sayville Junior High, both in her home town. She then transferred to the Professional Children's High School in New York City, a school designed to accommodate the needs of children pursuing careers in the performing arts.

While filming "Clarissa," Hart splits her time between attending high school and being tutored three hours a day on the set, as required by law. "It's easier in some ways and harder in some ways," Hart once confided. "It's only 15 hours a week, not a lot. But it's with one tutor for the whole 15 hours, one on one." During this final year of high school, she is also doing an internship at Nickelodeon in TV and film production. By studying the technical aspects of filmmaking, she is preparing someday to direct or produce. First, though, she hopes to be accepted by New York University for fall 1994.

FIRST JOBS

Melissa started in show business early. Her first job was an audition at age four for a Splashy doll commercial. She got that part, and since that time has been working nonstop. By the age of five she had appeared in 22 commercials, and over 150 to date, including those for Rice Krispies, Arnold Bread, Fritos, General Electric, and Tylenol.

From commercials, Hart went on to appear on TV and on stage. On TV, she starred in the Emmy-award winning movie "Christmas Snow" and guest starred on "The Equalizer," "The Luci Arnaz Show," "The Adventures of Con Sawyer and Hucklemary Finn," "Another World," and "Saturday Night Live." In the theater, she made her off-Broadway debut with the Circle Repertory Company in 1989 in Joseph Pintauro's play *Beside Herself*, co-starring William Hurt. The following year, she appeared in the Circle Rep's production of Peter Hedges's *Imagining Brad*. In 1992, she appeared in a Broadway production of Arthur Miller's *The Crucible*.

CAREER HIGHLIGHTS

"CLARISSA EXPLAINS IT ALL"

Meanwhile, Hart's big break came in 1991. The cable channel Nickelodeon, still in its early days with little original programming, was auditioning hundreds of young women across the country for a part in a new weekly series. Already a veteran performer, Hart won the role. "Clarissa Explains It All" debuted in March 1991. The series was originally shown on Sundays at 6:30 p.m. before moving to its current slot on Saturdays at 8:00 p.m., leading off the popular SNICK lineup.

"Clarissa" is a situation comedy about the Darling family: Clarissa, her parents, Marshall, an architect, and Janet, "a regular mom pretty much," and her younger brother, Ferguson, or Ferg-Face. Offering Clarissa's unique view of family life, the series has won acclaim for its pioneering format and techniques. Clarissa often speaks directly to the camera "explaining it all," providing commentary and advice on parents, siblings, fashion, and dating. Episodes mix live action with a wide variety of special effects, including dream sequences, monologues, quick scenes, computer animation, and instant replay.

Yet the highlight of the show is definitely Clarissa. A computer whiz, Clarissa is an individual—funny, observant, creative, unaffected, outspoken, down-to-earth, and smart. She is also opinionated, and she is not the least bit reluctant to share her views with others. Central to the success of the series is Hart's portrayal of Clarissa. Critics have applauded her intelligence, low-key charm, and natural performing style—qualities shared by both the character and the actress that portrays her. Yet Hart is quick to point out their differences, highlighting the character's

individualism and creativity. "Clarissa is cool because she doesn't worry about peer pressure. She sets her own trends and doesn't care what anyone says. I'd like to be like that."

"Clarissa is a lot more outgoing and always has a plan for everything, whereas I'm shy to people I don't know well and I do things spur of the moment. Now that I've found Clarissa I really like what she is, who she is, and I'm starting to become more like her. She helps kids deal with peer pressure because she doesn't care what anyone thinks. She dresses really different. Her thing is: just be yourself, be original. Don't be afraid of what people think. Live your own life."

Since its debut, "Clarissa Explains It All" has become tremendously popular with the Nickelodeon audience—so popular, in fact, that Hart was astounded at the screaming mobs at recent public appearances. Staffers have been overwhelmed by the quantity of fan mail the series generates. And television commentators have been surprised by the show's appeal to a broad audience. The series draws roughly equal numbers of male and female viewers, disproving the traditional view that teenage boys won't watch a series about girls. The success of "Clarissa Explains It All" has led Hart and the network, Nickelodeon, to want to continue the series for as long as possible. The only problem, of course, is that teenage girls grow up. The cast and crew is currently working at a steady pace—three weeks on, two weeks off—trying to film as many episodes as possible before Hart looks too old for the part.

HOME AND FAMILY

Hart splits her time among three homes: the family home on Long Island's South Shore, a rambling, 11-room house where her father still has his business; a townhouse in Greenwich Village, in Manhattan, where she spends time with her mother and siblings so that she can attend high school in the city; and a condominium owned by Nickelodeon near its studios in Orlando, Florida, where she stays while taping "Clarissa."

MAJOR INFLUENCES

Once, when an interviewer asked about role models, Hart talked about her admiration for Shirley Temple. "I have a lot of her movies. I would like to meet her. She has inspired me. She is a tap dancer, singer, and actress. She was also a U.S. Ambassador." In addition, Hart has said that her idols include Wynona Ryder and Julia Roberts.

HOBBIES AND OTHER INTERESTS

In interviews, Hart has revealed several of her favorite things, like baked clams, sleeping late, dancing, "The Simpsons," "Roseanne," skiing, going to the beach, and chocolate ice cream. She also collects Shirley Temple memorabilia. Hart listens to progressive music, especially the Ramones, R.E.M., and They Might Be Giants, and enjoyed hanging out at the Lollapalooza concert last summer. She likes to read, particularly plays. Some of her favorite books include the play *Romeo and Juliet* by William Shakespeare and the novel *Of Mice and Men* by John Steinbeck.

HONORS AND AWARDS

Youth in Film Awards: 1992 and 1993 (2 awards), Best Actress in a Cable Show

FURTHER READING

BOOKS

Kriegerman, Mitchell, and Mollie Fermaglich. *Clarissa's All-in-One Perfect Complete Book of Everything Important (Until I Change My Mind!)*, 1993

PERIODICALS

New York Newsday, Apr. 4, 1991, p.71; June 12, 1991, p.95; Oct. 2, 1991, p.53
New York Times, Aug. 25, 1991, Section II, p.21
Orlando Sentinel, June 22, 1991, p.E1; Jan. 3, 1993, p.D1
People, June 10, 1991, p.101
USA Today, Aug. 13, 1993, p.D3
Washington Post, Aug. 8, 1993, TV Section, p.6

ADDRESS

Nickelodeon
1515 Broadway
New York, NY 10036

BRIEF ENTRY

Geoff Hooper 1979-
American Winner of the 1993 National Spelling Bee

EARLY LIFE

Geoffrey Hooper was born on March 3, 1979, in Salem, Oregon. His parents are Gary and Annette Hooper, and he has an older sister, Lisa. Lisa was sure of her brother's spelling skills early in his life. "When I was a senior in high school, Geoff was proofreading my term papers. He was in the third grade," she recalls. The family now lives in Bartlett, Tennessee, where Geoff is a ninth-grader at White Station High School in Memphis.

MAJOR ACCOMPLISHMENTS

THE NATIONAL SPELLING BEE

The National Spelling Bee is sponsored by the Scripps Howard media organization. Spellers can compete through their eighth grade year. More than nine million students take part in regional contests each year, and competitors come from the U.S., Mexico, Guam, Puerto Rico, the Virgin Islands, and Defense Department Schools in Germany. Geoff was one of 235 regional winners from 47 states. He beat out the previous winner from his region, 12-year-old Srinivas Ayyagari, for the chance to compete on the national level in Washington, where the finals were held in June of 1993. Going into the championship, Geoff felt good. He said he was "ready to have fun and meet the other spellers. I like spelling bees because I like seeing how I match up with everybody."

The national finalists receive advance copies of all words to be spelled in the first two rounds. Then they're on their own. On Thursday, June 3, after successfully spelling slalom, tragedia, oleander, ankh, anorak, neutercame, empyrean, isopleth, pharisaical, caparison, stupefacient, and enchilada, Geoff faced the last round of competition. It was down to him and the only other speller left, David Urban of Texas. David misspelled renascent. Then Geoff got his final word—kamikaze. As related in Geoff's local paper, the Memphis *Commercial Appeal*, "A groan went up from the crowd, but Geoff just smiled as he coolly spelled it for the championship."

As his prize, Geoff received $5,000, the Heritage Edition of the New Encyclopedia, a Franklin electronic dictionary, a loving cup, and a day of fame. He appeared on "Good Morning America" and got to meet Vice President Al Gore. Geoff remembers the occasion as a special series of "firsts" for him. He rode on a plane, visited Washington and New York, rode on a subway, stayed in a hotel suite, and rode in a limousine—all for the first time. "And your last," joked his dad. "Next week you'll be back to normal, asking if you can go down the street and shoot some baskets."

In addition to his spelling ability, Geoff plays soccer and basketball, and he reads twice as much as he watches television.

FURTHER READING

New York Times, June 4, 1993, p.A14
Washington Post, June 4, 1993, p.C2

ADDRESS

Scripps Howard National Spelling Bee
P.O. Box 5380
Cincinnati, OH 45201

Whitney Houston 1963-
American Singer
Top Female Recording Artist

BIRTH

Whitney Elizabeth Houston was born in Newark, New Jersey, on August 9, 1963, to John R. and Emily Drinkard (Cissy) Houston. Cissy is a rhythm & blues/gospel vocalist who sang backup for her niece, Dionne Warwick, as well as Elvis Presley, Aretha Franklin, Wilson Pickett, and others. It was an ideal environment for a future singer. Their home was always filled with musicians, and Whitney has been surrounded by music since infancy. Franklin, whom she calls Auntie Ree, is a strong presence in her life and a longtime close friend of the Houston family.

Whitney is the youngest of three children. Her brothers are Gary Garland, who now sings in her act, and Michael Houston, her road manager. Gary, a former Denver Nuggets basketball player, is Whitney's half-brother from her mother's first marriage.

YOUTH

The Houstons moved from Newark to East Orange, a nearby New Jersey community, after the major race riots of 1967. There, for the most part, they lived an ordinary, middle-class life. John tended house and children whenever Cissy worked as lead singer with the Sweet Inspirations, considered one of the best backup groups in pop music. There was strict and loving discipline in the home, and a strong association, both in music and worship, with the New Hope Baptist Church. David Hinckley, writing in *New Jersey Monthly* soon after Whitney's first blazing rise to the top of the charts, states simply: "What Whitney came from was a traditional home, anchored by the family and sheltered by the church."

By the time she was seven, young Whitney had joined her mother in the church choir, but it was not until she was about eleven, on the day of her debut as a soloist in the church choir, that she began to recognize the possibilities in her developing voice. She still remembers being terrified as she raised her voice before the congregation to sing "Guide Me, O Thou Great Jehovah." "No one moved," she recalls. "They seemed almost in a trance.... When I finished, everyone clapped and started crying. From then on, I knew God had blessed me."

She was also blessed with the active involvement of both parents in her life. If John Houston was, as his daughter calls him, "Mom's support network," Cissy played no small role in her children's upbringing. She was a conscientious mother who took her responsibilities seriously enough to sacrifice the best interests of her own career. She was the one who doled out the punishments, including spankings in the early years, and who drew the line at Whitney's dating too young, or at cruising around and staying out late during her rebellious teen years. As one family friend says, "She was tough. That's why Whitney's a class act."

Tensions arose in the Houston household as careers and household duties were juggled. When Whitney was in high school, her parents separated, although they were never divorced and they remain supportive of one another. An added sustaining presence came into Whitney's life in those transitional years—that of Robyn Crawford, a friend the budding young singer met at summer camp. According to *Life* magazine, Robyn served "as bulwark and reality check" while Whitney's career began its fast upward spiral. Crawford is now a personal assistant in Houston's corporate entity.

EARLY MEMORIES

The gifted vocalist of today spent a lot of time as a young girl dreaming of a singing career. "I remember when I was about twelve," Houston says, "I would go into our basement where my mother kept her recording equipment, and I'd take the mike and put on Aretha and we'd go at it for hours. I'd just close my eyes and sing all by myself, and imagine I was on stage singing to a packed house."

EDUCATION

Houston is a 1981 graduate of Mount St. Dominic Academy, a Catholic high school in Caldwell, New Jersey. Her parents felt that she would be held to stricter standards there than in a large, impersonal public school. Her academic record was good, but she was already venturing into the music world, singing backup for her mother, Chaka Khan, and Lou Rawls, and she had little time to become involved in extracurricular activities. There was no chance, either, that John and Cissy would allow their daughter to drop out of high school.

FIRST JOBS

Even though she waited until after graduation to sign with a record company, Houston started modeling when she was only sixteen. Her work with Click, a trendy new Manhattan operation at the time, showcased such poise and youthful beauty that it drew the attention of the prestigious Wilhelmina agency. Whitney switched to Wilhelmina and soon was being featured in *Glamour, Seventeen*, and several other publications. At the same time, she was making frequent club appearances with her mother and training for a recording career.

CAREER HIGHLIGHTS

In 1983, after considering bids from most of the major recording companies, Houston signed with Arista and its shrewd and successful producer, Clive Davis, who earlier had helped to launch the careers of Janis Joplin, Barry Manilow, and Billy Joel. Davis's skillful packaging of Houston's talent resulted in her 1985 debut album, *Whitney Houston*, which boasted an incredible string of hits. Among these were "The Greatest Love of All" and "Saving All My Love For You," two songs that became—and have remained—a conspicuous part of the singer's identity. The album sold nine million copies in this country, and several million more overseas. While completing the album, Houston had already been introduced to an enthusiastic listening public in duets with established recording artists such as Teddy Pendergrass and Jermaine Jackson.

The staggering success of the *Whitney Houston* album led to club dates, music videos, and a concert tour that lasted for two years. Occasionally, during her seemingly endless months on the road, she would return to her gospel roots in impromptu appearances with CeCe and BeBe Winans. She told friends that these unscheduled meetings "fed her soul."

A follow-up album, titled simply, *Whitney*, was released in 1987, taking Houston to an even higher level of recognition with more chart-topping hits—"I Wanna Dance With Somebody (Who Loves Me)," "So Emotional," "Love Will Save the Day," and "Where Do Broken Hearts Go." By now, the young singer, just 24 years old, was the only artist to accumulate seven consecutive No.1 pop hits, surpassing records set previously by The Beatles and The Bee Gees. Her musical dexterity prompted observers to note how smoothly she had made the transition from gospel/soul/rhythm & blues to pop ballads and up-tempo dance tracks. Nicholas Jennings, writing for *Maclean's*, dramatically described the impact of Houston's stirring three-octave range: "She swoops from thrilling heights to a whisper. Electrified, the audience rises to its feet."

Soon after the second album's release, Houston began to tour again. She was away for the better part of two more years, filling concert dates in this country and in Australia and Japan. Everywhere she went, she was celebrated for her powerful voice, charisma, sensuality, and stunning beauty. She came home to work on a third album, *I'm Your Baby Tonight*, one that would deliver two more hot singles, the title track and a ballad called "All The Man That I Need," bringing her total of No. 1 hits to nine. While the newest album was successful, selling more than three million copies, it fell far short of the numbers produced by her first two powerhouse offerings. The artist was defensive, though, about her work, saying, "Three million people buying records? That doesn't sound like a bad number to me."

THE BODYGUARD

Houston continued to appear in concert and to tour on an exhausting schedule that took her to major spots around the globe. Then, in 1992, Hollywood actor-director Kevin Costner cast her to play the lead in a romantic film about a singer who hires a bodyguard when her life is threatened by an obsessed fan. Screen acting added still another dimension to Houston's widening career, but it was her magical voice that sent box-office receipts zooming to $267 million worldwide. The movie's soundtrack album sold 28 million copies, mainly because of its hit single, "I Will Always Love You," which dominated the charts for months and made the album the most popular of the year. The song, called a "soaring romantic ballad" by the *New York Times*, had been written and recorded in the 1970s by country singer Dolly Parton, but it claimed a vigorous new life with Houston's provocative rendition. It also created some love/hate listener emotions as it saturated the airwaves and was repeatedly flashed across television screens in ads and on its music video. With the song's fabulous success has come a string of pop music awards, making Whitney Houston one of the most-honored female recording artists of all time.

Houston is back in the studio, working on a new recording that is expected to be issued by the end of 1994. She says that someday she would like to concentrate on an all-gospel album.

MAJOR INFLUENCES

Houston's most powerful influence has been her mother, who not only "blessed her with the right genes," says *Essence*, but who patiently trained her to develop and strengthen her voice. In the first several years that Whitney sang in the choir at New Hope, Cissy would not allow her to perform solo, wisely advising her young daughter to bring her voice along slowly and to learn control through choral harmonizing. "She was always encouraging me to sing [and to use] my God-given talent," says Whitney. "She gave me birth, love, confidence, and constant direction."

Looking back now, after years of her own celebrated success and her exposure to the elite of the popular music industry, Houston still credits her mother with being her greatest inspiration. She recalls being taken to Cissy's studio recording sessions in New York when she was just a little girl. "I remember when I was six or seven, crawling up to the window to watch my mother sing. And I'd be talking to Aunt Ree. I had no idea that Aretha Franklin was famous—just that I liked to hear *her* sing, too."

MARRIAGE AND FAMILY

Whitney Houston was married to rhythm & blues idol Bobby Brown on July 18, 1992, in a lavish ceremony on her New Jersey estate. The vows were witnessed by family and close friends, and 800 guests, including some of the biggest names in show business, partied at the reception that followed. There was some controversy in the media at the time regarding their marriage. Houston "was accused of making matrimony a career move," writes *TV Guide*, adding, "it was said that Brown's street credibility [his rough background and bad-boy image] would bolster Houston's stature with young African-Americans." This, and other unsubstantiated rumors, have made the couple frequent media targets, but both spouses repeatedly deny allegations of Brown's infidelity or the imminent breakup of their marriage. Houston and Brown have a baby daughter, Bobbi Kristina Houston Brown (B.K. for short), born in the spring of 1993. Until a recent miscarriage, they had been expecting a second child next year.

The Mendham Township estate in New Jersey is Houston's principal residence, but she and her husband also spend time at their condominium on Williams Island, off Miami Beach, and Houston recently bought another Florida home at Boca Raton. The New Jersey property has tennis courts, a playground, a new basketball court, and a high-tech music studio.

HOBBIES AND OTHER INTERESTS

Other than caring for her little daughter and spending time with her husband, parents, brothers, and extended family, Houston enjoys swimming and playing tennis. She has worked hard to maintain a normal home life, despite her celebrity.

Houston also lends time and energy to worthwhile causes, among them the United Negro College Fund, the Children's Diabetes Foundation, and the Warwick Foundation (for charitable works). She has sung at numerous benefits, too, the most memorable of which was the 1991 HBO television special, "Welcome Home, Heroes," honoring the troops who served in the Persian Gulf War.

CREDITS

RECORD DEBUT

"Hold Me" (duet with Teddy Pendergrass), 1984

RECORDINGS

Whitney Houston, 1985
Whitney, 1987
I'm Your Baby Tonight, 1990
The Bodyguard, 1993 (adapted from the movie soundtrack)

HIT SINGLES

"You Give Good Love," 1985
"Saving All My Love For You," 1985
"The Greatest Love of All," 1985
"How Will I Know," 1985
"I Wanna Dance With Somebody (Who Loves Me)," 1987
"So Emotional," 1987
"Love Will Save the Day," 1987
"Where Do Broken Hearts Go," 1987
"I'm Your Baby Tonight," 1990
"All The Man That I Need," 1990
"I Will Always Love You," 1992
"Run To You," 1992

FILMS

The Bodyguard, 1993

HONORS AND AWARDS

American Music Awards: 1986 (two), 1987 (five), 1988 (two), 1989 (two), 1994 (five)
Billboard Magazine Awards: 1986, Artist of the Year; 1994, specific performance awards (eleven)
Grammy Awards: 1985, 1987, and 1993 (three)
Emmy Awards: 1986
People's Choice Awards: 1987, 1988, and 1989
Soul Train Awards: 1994 (two: the Sammy Davis, Jr. Special Award and Song of the Year)

FURTHER READING

PERIODICALS

Ebony, June 1990, p.132; May 1991, p.110; Sep. 1992, p.124; Jan. 1993, p.119
Essence, Dec. 1990, p.55; Feb. 1994, p.62
Jet, Nov. 1, 1993, p.61; Feb. 28, 1994, p.56
Ladies Home Journal, Apr. 1993, p.40
Life, Nov. 1990, p.78
McCall's, May 1989, p.151
New York Times, Mar. 6, 1994, Section 4, p.2
People, May 3, 1993, p.141
Rolling Stone, June 10, 1993, p.44
TV Guide, Mar. 30, 1991, p.12; Feb. 26, 1994, p.10
Vanity Fair, Nov. 1992, p.242

ADDRESS

Arista Records, Inc.
Arista Building
6 West 57th Street,
New York, NY 10019

Dan Jansen 1965-
American Speed Skater
Olympic Gold Medalist in 1994

BIRTH

Dan Ervin Jansen was born June 17, 1965, in Milwaukee, Wisconsin, to Harry and Geraldine Jansen. Dan, or D.J. as his family calls him, was the youngest of nine children—Mary, Janet, Jane, Joanne, Diane, Jim, Dick, and Mike—all, it seems, born to skate. Harry was a policeman before his retirement, and Geraldine was a nurse. Most of the children, now grown, followed in their parent's footsteps: two of the boys are now policeman, one is a fireman, and all the girls became nurses.

YOUTH

The Jansens have always been a warm and close-knit family. One of their shared passions is skating. Mary, Janet, Jim, and Dick were state champion speed skaters, and Mike was on the U.S. national team five times. When he was only four, D.J. began to skate. "It was either that or stay home by myself," he recalls. He was "no better than anyone else in the family," his father remembers. "He had real wobbly ankles and had to work very hard on them." By the time he was eight, he was winning regional competitions, and by the age of 12, he was a national champion. "He was brought up in a family where if you don't try, you can't possibly succeed unless you put one foot forward," says his mother. The family still lives where the kids grew up, in the Milwaukee suburb of West Allis, and D.J. skated at the local rink where his idol, Olympic champion speed skater Eric Heiden, had trained.

EDUCATION

Dan attended the local public schools and continued to do well in sports. At West Allis Central High he was the starting tailback and co-captain of the football team and an all-county second baseman. But after graduating in 1983, he devoted himself to skating and set his sights on the Olympics.

CAREER HIGHLIGHTS

1984 OLYMPICS

In 1984, at the age of 18, Jansen competed in his first Olympics, held in Sarajevo, in what was then Yugoslavia. He skated in what were to become his two main events, the 500-meter and the 1,000-meter races. He placed very well—he was fourth in the 500, missing a bronze medal by only .16 seconds. In the 1,000, he placed sixteenth. All in all, it was a fine showing for a young and talented athlete.

In 1985, Jansen won a silver medal at the world sprint championships, and in 1986, at the World Cup competition, he placed first in both the 500 and 1,000 meters. In 1987 he was sidelined with a torn tendon and mononucleosis. Despite his medical problems, he managed to place third in both the 500 and 1,000 at the World Cup that year.

But then personal tragedy struck the Jansen family. In 1987, his sister Jane, then 26, was diagnosed with leukemia. Jane received the news just 24 hours after the birth of her third daughter. A bone marrow transplant offered the only hope. The family was tested to determine the best donor. (When a cancer patient requires a bone marrow transplant, doctors need to determine which relative's marrow most closely matches the patient to prevent the body from rejecting the transplant.)

Doctors determined that Dan and his sister Joanne would be the best candidates. Dan knew that if he were the donor, his chances for competing in the 1988 Olympics would be jeopardized. But that made absolutely no difference to Dan, for whom family has always come first. "When they told me about Jane and the transplant, I didn't have to think twice. Skating is great, the Olympics are great, but it's nothing compared to your sister's life. It's not even close." In the end, the doctors chose Joanne; further tests showed that her marrow was closest to Jane's, and because Dan had recently had mono, there was a chance he might infect his sister. The operation appeared successful, and Jane's cancer went into remission.

Dan trained and competed in the 1988 World Cup, placing third in the 500 and 1,000. He also placed first in the world sprint championship, a competition determined by a combined total of points scored in two 500 and two 1,000 meter races. He was ready to go to Calgary, in Alberta, Canada, for his second try at an Olympic medal, and this year he was competing as the favorite.

1988 OLYMPICS

Dan Jansen will probably be forever remembered by what happened at the 1988 Olympics in Calgary, Alberta, Canada. Jane's cancer had recurred in December 1987, and by the following February she was gravely ill. The Jansen family insisted that Dan compete, and most of the family accompanied him to Calgary. But the day before his first race, his mother and father returned to Wisconsin; Jane had taken a decided turn for the worse. The morning of his first race, Dan got a phone call at 6 in the morning from his brother Mike; Jane was dying. Dan talked with his sister, who could hear him but couldn't speak. He told Mike to give her a kiss for him. She died hours later. Dan got the news just before he was to skate in the 500. Wobbly, not able to concentrate, Dan slid out of control and was unable to finish the race. When he stood up, his face in his hands, the world wept with him.

Four days later, Jansen skated again, this time in the 1,000. The media had turned out in full force; Dan and the U.S. team had dedicated the Olympics to Jane, and everyone wanted to see him bring home a medal. But it was not to be. He fell again. The stunned fans wept for their would-be hero. Mike Pearl, an executive of CBS sports, recalls his most vivid memory of that Olympics: "When Dan Jansen fell a second time, people in our studios, men and women, . . .[were] walking down the halls crying."

Jansen returned to Wisconsin for his sister's funeral. The outpouring of sympathy for the young skater and his family was enormous: Jansen received over 10,000 cards and letters, from people as diverse as President Ronald Reagan to Mark Arrowood, a 30-year-old Special Olympian. He sent Jansen his own gold medal from the Special Olympics, with a letter

saying: "Dear Dan, I watched you on TV. I'm sorry you fell two times
.... I want to share one of my gold medals with you because I don't
like to see you not get one. Try again in four more years."

In the latter portion of 1988, Jansen was back racing, winning the World
Cup title in the 1,000 and placing second in the 500. That fall, he returned
to Calgary, this time as a student at the University, and spent one semester
studying and training.

The 1989 and 1990 seasons were difficult ones for Jansen. He was unable
to place better than fourth in his events in the World Cup, and he had
to endure endless reminders of his sister's death and its aftermath by the
media. Some members of the press asked him questions that were incredibly rude and insensitive, such as if he felt he had "let his sister down"
by not winning a medal. He also remembers getting heckled by a group
of men in a bar who laughed at him and asked him if was going to fall.

In 1990, he thought it was time for a coaching change, and he began to
train under former U.S. Olympic gold medalist Peter Mueller. Mueller also
became the coach of Jansen's friend and fellow speed skating champ
Bonnie Blair, and the improvement showed in both skaters. In the 1991
World Cup Jansen placed first in the 500 and 1,000. He now had his eyes
on Albertville, France, site of the 1992 Winter Olympics.

1992 OLYMPICS

Jansen went into Albertville as the favorite in both his events, having just
won the 500 in record time in a World Cup race. He had also been
working with sport psychologist Jim Loehr to help him prepare mentally.
"I think I'm a better skater," said Jansen at the time. "I'm stronger and
better mentally than I was." But he disliked the media preoccupation with
winning a gold medal. "My biggest gripe is the emphasis put on medals.
The medals are terrific, but people should respect the athletes who work
hard to get there and not look at them as if they failed or they choked
if they didn't win a medal."

He held a special press conference prior to the competition to deal with
the inevitable questions about his last Olympics, and then he tried to concentrate on winning. But this wasn't to be Dan Jansen's Olympics, either.
The rink at Albertville was outdoors, and the weather conditions were
less than ideal. The ice was mushy and slow. Although he thought he
had skated well in his first event, the 500, he wound up in fourth place,
and finished an abysmal twenty-sixth in the 1,000. "I can't say I'm disappointed," he said. "I'm surprised more than anything." Even his archrival, Germany's Uwe-Jens Mey, was puzzled: "I feel very sorry for him.
I value him greatly as an athlete. But the Olympics don't obey normal
rules."

Dan was determined to try again, and to win. Immediately after the competition, he met with his coach. "I said 'Pete, do you want to do this again?' And he said, 'If you want to do it, I want to do it,' and that was about it," Jansen recalled. With two years to go until the next Olympics, Jansen set out to do his best, and Mueller kept the pressure on. His training was rigorous: in addition to skating, Jansen's workout included running, bike riding, and weight-lifting for six hours a day, every day. At 6 feet and 190 pounds, Jansen is big for his sport, and he has always tried to use his size and strength to their best advantage. He now looked forward to Lillehammer, Norway, as his next and last chance to show the world that he could compete, and win, in the Olympics.

1994 OLYMPICS

Once again Jansen was the gold medal favorite. In December 1993, he had become the first man to skate the 500 meters under 36 seconds. He had to put up with the media's obsessive concern about his past performance—as well as taunts by the Japanese speed skaters, who thought Jansen just didn't have the stuff to finish in first. He had determined that this Olympics would be his last, and he was going to give it his all.

But there was agony in the Jansen camp again as Dan fell in the 500, placing eighth. The fastest speed skater in history seemed cursed when it came to Olympic competition. Then came the final race of Jansen's Olympic career, the 1,000 meters. In front of 12,000 roaring fans, Dan Jansen broke the ten-year jinx. He finished in 1 minute, 12.43 seconds, breaking the world record and winning his first gold medal. People all over the Olympic community—other speed skaters at the rink, the crowd at the figure skating arena, throughout the Olympic village—and throughout the world, shared the joy of the Jansen clan for what had been such a long time coming. "I'm so happy," said Jansen. "I waited so long. It's an unbelievable relief. It's over. We

finally got a happy ending. There are so many people I'm happy for now, more than myself. We've waited so long. Now we can go home and not know that I was the best without a medal. I am the best, and I have a medal."

On the medal stand, Jansen wept as the National Anthem was played. He lifted his eyes to the sky, and gave a small salute, a tribute to his sister Jane. Then he took a victory lap around the ice, with his infant daughter, Jane, in his arms. "Our saga started back in Calgary, when Dan lost his sister Jane," said Jansen's wife, Robin. "The saga ended today and we wanted it to end with the new Jane in our lives."

Jansen has always been a popular sports figure. In addition to his All-American good looks, he is a quiet and self-effacing young man, who is every bit as down to earth as he appears. John Teaford, coach of the U.S. speed skating team in 1992, said this about Jansen: "With someone like Dan, it's a comfort to see that there really are heroes; that America's family members are out there winning. No drugs, no big salaries, no scandals." And Jansen genuinely loves his sport. "I like the individuality of this sport. I'm sort of shy and introverted. Skating has been a way for me to express myself. I like the fact that when you succeed, you can feel proud of yourself. That's what I want to be, proud of myself." Jansen has always been amused that he is the object of fanatical admirers in places like Holland, where speed skaters are worshiped, but relatively unknown in his own country. With his final Olympics over, Jansen now looks forward to a different way of life—one that will probably make him very well known.

FUTURE PLANS

Despite his early Olympic losses, Jansen has been successful in picking up endorsements. He began working for Miller Brewing Company in Milwaukee in 1988 in the sports marketing department—a job that basically funded his training and travel for several years. In addition, his face has appeared on Kellogg's Corn Flakes boxes around the country, and he has toured as a motivational speaker paid by the Olympic committee. Now that he has won a gold medal, the speculation is that many more endorsement contracts will come his way. As he makes the transition from athlete to spokesman, Jansen has these plans in mind: "to raise my family. And hopefully be successful in the business world."

MARRIAGE AND FAMILY

While on a tour as a speaker for the Olympics in 1988, Jansen met Robin Wicker, a personnel recruiter for Interstate Hotel Corporation. Both were involved with other people at the time of their first meeting—Dan was engaged to Canadian speed skater Natalia Greiner. They broke off their previous relationships and were married in April of 1990. Robin, who is an identical twin, was hoping that she and Dan would also have twins, but when their first child, Jane, was born May 27, 1993, they were absolutely delighted. For many fans, the memory of Dan taking his victory lap around the ice in Norway with Jane in his arms is their fondest, and most apt, memory of the 1994 Olympics.

HOBBIES AND OTHER INTERESTS

In addition to skating, Jansen loves to play golf, tennis and softball. He also gives time to charity, including the Special Olympics.

HONORS AND AWARDS

Olympic Speed Skating, 1,000 meters: 1994, gold medal
World Cup Speed Skating, 500 meters: 1986, first place; 1991, first place
World Cup Speed Skating, 1,000 meters: 1986, first place; 1988, first place; 1991, first place

FURTHER READING

BOOKS

Kindred, Dave. *Heroes, Fools, and Other Dreamers*, 1988

PERIODICALS

Boston Globe, Feb. 19, 1988, p.29
Chicago Tribune, Feb. 2, 1992, Sports, p.1; Dec. 26, 1993, Sports, p.3
Houston Post, Dec. 29, 1990, p.C8
Los Angeles Times, Dec. 26, 1991, p.D1; Feb. 19, 1994, p.A1
Newsday, Feb. 2, 1992, p.18
New York Times, Feb. 20, 1994, p.A24
People, Jan. 13, 1992, p.32
Philadelphia Daily News, Feb. 2, 1988, p. 78; Jan. 29, 1992, p.66
Philadelphia Inquirer, Feb. 15, 1994, p.A1
San Francisco Chronicle, Dec. 24, 1991, p.C5; Feb. 19, 1994, p.D1
Sports Illustrated, Feb. 22, 1988, p.32; Feb. 14, 1994, p.28; Feb. 21, 1994, p.20
Wisconsin State Journal, Feb. 16, 1992, p.E1

ADDRESS

Integrated Sports International
1 Meadowlands Plaza
Suite 1501
East Rutherford, NJ 07073

Nancy Kerrigan 1969-
American Figure Skater
Olympic Silver Medalist in 1994, Bronze Medalist in 1992

BIRTH

Nancy Kerrigan was born October 13, 1969, in Woburn, Massachusetts. She is the daughter of Daniel and Brenda Kerrigan. Daniel is a welder who has also worked additional jobs to finance his daughter's figure skating, and Brenda is a homemaker. Nancy has two older brothers, Mark, now a plumber, and Michael, who works at the rink in nearby Stoneham where Nancy spent so many hours in her youth.

YOUTH

Nancy grew up in the Boston suburb of Stoneham in the house where her family still lives. She comes from a very close family: her grandparents live just two houses away, and her grandmother still cooks huge Sunday breakfasts for the clan.

Nancy is particularly close to her mother. Brenda Kerrigan contracted an eye virus when Nancy was just a baby; it left her totally blind in one eye and with only limited vision in the other. "My mother's strength has given me so much inspiration," says Nancy. "What I do is nothing compared to dealing with something like she has had to do."

STARTING TO SKATE

The Kerrigans lived two blocks from the local ice rink, and Nancy started to skate at the age of six, one of 100 children in a class. When she first took to the ice, she wanted to be a hockey player like her brothers, but her mother was firm. "No way," she said. "You're going into figure skating." "I only have one girl," Brenda Kerrigan said recently. "I told her she had to do girl things."

Nancy's talent was noticed by her first coach, Theresa Martin. She recommended smaller classes, then private lessons, then daily instruction. Nancy started to compete early, and she had won local and regional championships by the time she was a teenager. But that success came at a price: she got up at 4 A.M. every day to practice before school. And some traditions of growing up, such as slumber parties, took a different twist in Nancy Kerrigan's young life. One of her childhood friends, Tricia Halpin, remembers waking up at Nancy's house in the morning and finding her hostess already gone to the rink for practice.

The Kerrigans made great financial sacrifices so that Nancy could skate. Her father worked all kinds of odd jobs, even running the Zamboni machine at the rink where Nancy skated, to cover the costs of her training. Nancy dished up ice cream at the local Friendly's as a teenager to help out. The Kerrigans remortgaged their house several times to cover the bills, which ran up to $40,000 a year.

Her father told *People* magazine: "Since Nancy started skating, the family hasn't been on a real vacation. We go to skating events." Nancy feels guilty about her parents' sacrifices: "I feel like everything they did was for me. It's scary when they are spending so much money and you don't know what you will get for it."

EDUCATION

Nancy attended Emerson Elementary School in Stoneham and graduated from Stoneham High. She was an average student, and she is remembered as a young person determined to make it as a skater. Her parents had to arrange with her high school principal for her to arrive late and leave early, so she could get in the hours of practice her sport requires. "It was clear that she was totally committed to skating, that she wanted to take the minimum course load," says her former principal, Thomas Ryan. "I suggested she might want to think about taking an extra course or two, in case skating didn't work out. But she'd have none of it. I was amazed. Most people aren't that sure at age 14. But she was."

She didn't have many friends throughout her youth, which she considered another sacrifice to be made for her sport. "I lost a lot of friends when I started skating because I just wasn't around. And some of them thought I was getting special treatment because I would arrive at school late and leave early. But I really didn't care what they thought. I just wanted to skate."

Kerrigan recently received her associate degree in business from Emmanuel College in Boston, a degree she worked on from 1988 to 1993 while she was concentrating on her skating.

CAREER HIGHLIGHTS

Kerrigan's first major win was in the National Collegiate competition in 1988. From there, she advanced to the major national and international events, usually placing in the top five. In 1990, she took first place in the U.S. Olympic Festival championships. After that win, she was asked to compete in the Goodwill Games. Figure skating titles are determined by the combination of marks a skater receives on the short and long programs. Kerrigan has always been a strong performer on the short program, but her long program has frequently proved to be her undoing. After a solid showing in the short program in the Goodwill Games, Kerrigan skated one of the worst long programs in her life. She left the ice in tears. But she didn't give up. Her coaches, Mary and Evy Scotvold, urged her to get beyond the feeling of failure that overwhelmed her every time she missed a series of jumps in competitions. Kerrigan worked with a sport psychologist on her problems with nerves and low self-esteem. By 1991, she was back on track.

At the World Championships in 1991, she was part of a team that swept the first three place medals, the first time in 73 years that three women from the same country had achieved that dominance. Her fellow skaters on the team were athletes who would be prominent in her career: Kristi Yamaguchi and Tonya Harding. It was the first time that Kerrigan had competed in an international event, and she was already a standout for her elegance and delicacy of expression.

In 1992, Kerrigan placed second at the National championships, and she, Yamaguchi, and Harding readied themselves for the 1992 Olympics in Albertville, as the strongest U.S. team in years.

1992 OLYMPICS

Kerrigan did extremely well at the Olympics in 1992. She was in second place after the short program. And the television audience loved her. She seemed a throwback to a previous age, when an elegant line and graceful, balletic movements, rather than athleticism, were the signature of women's figure skating. Kerrigan's grace on the ice seemed enhanced by her glamorous costumes, provided by famed designer Vera Wang. The television audience also loved her family story. For many, one of the most moving memories of that Olympics was of Brenda Kerrigan sitting in front of a special television monitor provided by CBS so that she could see her daughter skate.

Kerrigan was also exhilarated by the silver medal performance of her friend and fellow team member Paul Wylie. Wylie, who has trained with Kerrigan and occasionally been her pairs partner, has always been one of her greatest supporters.

Kristi Yamaguchi, Kerrigan's roommate at the Olympics, went on to win the gold medal, and Kerrigan, after a poor showing in the long program, won the bronze. Harding, plagued with health and personal problems and unable to land her signature triple axel, placed fifth in the competition.

After the Olympics, Kerrigan received numerous endorsement offers, and she embarked on an exhausting nationwide tour of personal appearances and exhibitions. Although she won the Nationals in 1993, the hectic schedule took its toll on her skating, as was evident in her dismal showing at the 1993 World Championships. After a series of missed jumps in her long program, she lost her composure and the lead. She placed ninth in her long program and fifth overall. Kerrigan knew she had to rededicate herself to skating.

A BRUTAL ATTACK

With a year of hard work behind her and her eyes on the 1994 Olympics, Kerrigan went to the Nationals in January 1994 and became a part of sports history—but not for her skating. On the eve of the competition, as she was leaving the ice, an assailant with a metal baton clubbed Kerrigan just above her right knee, then fled the arena. Kerrigan fell to the floor, screaming "Why? Why? Why?" The brutal attacked stunned the sports world. But the ensuing investigation and what it uncovered brought an even greater shock. Within days of the attack, Jeff Gillooly, the ex-husband of Tonya Harding, and three accomplices confessed to planning and paying for the crime. Gillooly later implicated Harding. As of this writing, Harding has pled guilty to a single charge in the assault—conspiring to hinder the prosecution of the case. As a result she has been fined, given a three-year probation, banned from the United States Figure Skating Association, and forbidden to compete as an amateur.

What followed was a media circus. Kerrigan, who luckily was not seriously injured, was virtually a hostage in her own home as reporters followed her every move. There was a flurry of activity in the media, as networks and production companies vied for the rights to market and exploit the event. "Drama of Skating Attack Spawns Marketing Free-For-All—From Muffins to Movie Rights, the Competition Is Fierce," read a headline from the *Philadelphia Inquirer*. At one extreme, a Chicago company offered five million dollars to the two for a winner-take-all skate-off. Meanwhile, Kerrigan undertook physical therapy and tried to prepare for the Olympics. She hosted an exhibition one month after the attack in which she skated very well, in part to prove that she was able to compete.

1994 OLYMPICS

Kerrigan and her family left early for Lillehammer, Norway, site of the 1994 Olympics. While there, they were kept aware of the continuing investigation into the attack and were told by the FBI that Harding's arrest was imminent. It came as a great shock to the Kerrigans, and to many others, when Harding was allowed to skate in the Olympics. It was assumed by many in the skating world that, because she was under investigation for her role in the crime, she would not be allowed to skate. But Harding sued the U.S. Olympic committee for $25 million, demanding the right to skate. The U.S.O.C. backed down, and the eyes of the world were on Lillehammer for the first encounter of the two rivals.

Their first meeting, indeed all their moves at Lillehammer, were subjected to the glare of publicity that surrounded every aspect of the case. It seemed to affect Harding more than Kerrigan; she did poorly in practice and in the competition.

Kerrigan seemed serene the night of the short program, and she skated beautifully. Her performance landed her in first place. The day before the long program, Kerrigan's chief challenger for the gold medal, Oksana Baiul of Ukraine, had a collision on the ice that required stitches and resulted in a seriously bruised back. It looked as if it was Kerrigan's turn to win the gold.

Kerrigan had planned a triple flip as the first jump in her long program. But she did a double instead—perhaps because of nerves, or perhaps because it just didn't feel right. It was a move that might have sent her into a tailspin in previous competitions. But she went on to skate an otherwise flawless program, in the words of *Sports Illustrated* writer E.M. Swift, "strong and fast and angular and increasingly animated as it became clear to her and everyone else that this was the best long program she had ever skated in competition."

To everyone's surprise, it wasn't enough. Baiul was given two painkilling injections just before she skated—with drugs on the Olympic Committee's "approved list." She performed a beautiful program, even throwing in a few unplanned triple jumps. The resulting scores showed one of the closest margins of victory in Olympic figure skating history as Baiul edged Kerrigan for the gold. Kerrigan had to settle for silver.

Kerrigan was visibly and vocally unhappy with the outcome. When she thought that the medal ceremony had been delayed to allow the sobbing Baiul to fix her makeup, she was overheard saying "Oh, come on. So she's going to get out here and cry again. What's the difference." After the Olympics, other cracks in her rather wholesome image began to appear. Kerrigan had signed a deal with Disney studios for a reported $650,000. In an appearance at Disney World shortly after Lillehammer, microphones picked up Kerrigan voicing similarly negative things during a parade: "This is so corny, this is so dumb. I hate it. This is the most corny thing I've ever done." This caused some concern to Kerrigan's public relations staff, who want to make sure she presents an untarnished image to the public. "If she continues, it will be very bad for her image," said David Burns, who is head of the Burns Sports Celebrity Service. He added that he thinks the people who manage Kerrigan will make sure she stops "expressing negatives in interviews."

All this points to a certain inexperience and discomfort with the fame and the glare of life in the spotlight that is now part of Kerrigan's life as she makes the transition from Olympic athlete to a superstar on the celebrity endorsement circuit.

BECOMING A PROFESSIONAL

Kerrigan announced in March 1994 that she would no longer compete in national or international amateur championships. Her plans now are to concentrate on her lucrative career as a spokesperson for a variety of products; her current sponsorship programs are said to be worth four million dollars. And she plans to perform with a professional touring ice show, scheduled to stop in 62 cities in 1994. Kerrigan's agent, Jerry Solomon, is also working on sponsorships, speaking tours, and movie and television deals. Whether she will be able to translate her elegance and poise on the ice remains to be seen. She knows she is very shy, and that can be a problem. "I've had to learn to not be so shy because it makes it very hard on people who are trying to meet me," she said recently. She can appear awkward in her public appearances, but a recent stint as a guest host on "Saturday Night Live" did show a Kerrigan who was able to laugh at herself.

HOME AND FAMILY

Kerrigan currently lives in a condominium in Plymouth, Massachusetts. Her previous engagement to Boston accountant Bill Chase ended in 1993. She has recently been linked romantically to Michael Collins, the son of figure skating promoter Tom Collins.

HONORS AND AWARDS

National Collegiate Championships: 1988, first place
Olympic Figure Skating: 1992, bronze medal; 1994, silver medal
U.S. Olympic Festival: 1990, first place
World Championships: 1991, third place; 1992, second place; 1993, fifth place

FURTHER READING

BOOKS

Morrissette, Mikki. *Nancy Kerrigan: Heart of a Champion*, 1994 (juvenile)
Reisfeld, Randi. *The Kerrigan Courage: Nancy's Story*, 1994 (juvenile)

PERIODICALS

Boston Globe, Mar. 13, 1991, p.47; Jan. 25, 1993; p.37; Jan. 13, 1994, p.35
Philadelphia Inquirer, Feb. 4, 1994, p.A1
New York Times, Mar. 17, 1991, Section 8, p.1; Feb. 15, 1994, p.A7; Feb. 24, 1994, p.B7; Mar 10, 1994, p.63; Mar. 13, 1994, p.10
Newsweek, Mar. 2, 1992, p.50; Jan. 17, 1994, p.41
People, Feb. 3, 1992, p.34; May 3, 1993, p.138
Sports Illustrated, Mar, 2, 1992, p.16; Feb. 22, 1993, p.22; Feb. 21, 1994, p.33; Feb. 28, 1994, p.21
Time, Feb. 10, 1992, p.55; Jan. 24, 1994, p.50; Feb. 21, 1994, p.53
Variety, Feb. 7-13, 1994, p.1

ADDRESS

ProServ
1101 Wilson Blvd.
Suite 1800
Arlington, VA 22209

BRIEF ENTRY

Alexi Lalas 1970-
American Professional Soccer Player
Member of the 1994 U.S. World Cup
Soccer Team

EARLY LIFE

Alexander Lalas was born June 1, 1970, in Royal Oak, Michigan, to Demetrius and Anne Lalas. He has one brother, Greg, who is younger. When Alexi was eight, his family moved to Athens, Greece, the land of his father's family, where Alexi began to play soccer. When the family returned to the U.S. four years later, Alexi still loved to play soccer and also began to play ice hockey. He attended the Cranbrook Academy, a prestigious private school in Bloomfield Hills, Michigan, where he played on both the soccer team and on the ice hockey team that won the 1988 state title.

When it came time for college, Alexi tried to find a school where he could play soccer, but faced rejection at every turn. "I was getting rejected by everybody. It was a total nightmare," Lalas remembers. He decided to go to Rutgers University in New Jersey. He still played hockey, but in soccer he really made his mark. The team made it to the finals in 1989 and 1990, and in 1991 Lalas won the Hermann Trophy, given annually to the best player in college soccer. He also started a rock band, the Gypsies, still together today. "Music's a big part of my life," Lalas said recently. "It's cathartic, something that enables me to do well on the soccer field."

The U.S. won a gold medal in 1991 at the Pan American Games, and Alexi was on the team. In 1992, he left Rutgers to play with the U.S. Olympic team, which lost its first games in the 1992 Olympics in Barcelona, Spain. He then tried to make it in the European soccer leagues, trying out for the Arsenal, an English team. He didn't make it and went home to the States. Wondering what he was going to do with his life, he got a call from the U.S. national team asking if he'd like to try out.

MAJOR ACCOMPLISHMENTS

Soccer is the most popular game in the world, but it has never really caught on in the U.S. When the U.S. was chosen as the site for the 1994 World Cup, the U.S. team began to receive a lot of exposure in the press, and Lalas—with his long red hair, skinny goatee, and funny, provocative comments—became a favorite with the fans. In several pre-World Cup matches, Lalas was mobbed by admirers, which took the outgoing player by surprise. "I have a hard time understanding it," he said. "I never had that kind of person that I looked up to when I was growing up." When his love of 7-Eleven's Slurpees became known—"Without Slurpees, there is no humankind," according to Lalas—fans sent addresses of their favorite stores. And when you've got an athlete, who, in the words of sports writer Don Bosley, "uses the words 'cool' and 'surreal' in the same sentence," coupled with his profile as the first "soccer rocker," you've got the makings of a genuine cult hero.

Lalas was delighted to be part of the Cup. He remembered his earlier experience with World Cup, watching a game in Italy in 1990: "I painted my face and went to see the U.S. play Austria. It never occurred to me that I could be out there. Just stepping on the field in the World Cup is the highlight of my career, when you consider where I came from."

The 1994 U.S. team did better in the competition than anyone expected, becoming the first U.S. team to advance to the second round of the Cup since 1930. And the media hype didn't hurt Lalas one bit, as he played some of the best soccer of his life. In his position as a defender, he was up against the best soccer players in the world, and he did his job brilliantly.

Lalas loves music, and when he's not playing soccer he likes to write songs and play with his band, the Gypsies. He sings lead and plays guitar, and the band has a recording, *Woodland*. But his musical career will probably have to be put on hold for now, because in August 1994, Lalas signed on with the Italian League to play soccer in Europe for one year. It is one of the best soccer teams in the world. Lalas's many fans look forward to following his continuing professional career, first in Europe, then in the U.S., where Lalas hopes to return to play on one of the U.S. Major League Soccer professional teams in 1995.

HONORS AND AWARDS

Hermann Trophy: 1991
Pan American Games: 1991, Gold Medal

FURTHER READING

Chicago Tribune, June 4, 1994, p.C5
Detroit Free Press, Aug. 4, 1994, p.C2
Sports Illustrated for Kids, June 1994, p.36
Wall Street Journal, June 24, 1994, p.A8

ADDRESS

U.S. Soccer
1801 S. Prairie Ave.
Chicago, IL 60616

Charlotte Lopez 1976-
Puerto Rican-Born American
Miss Teen USA 1993

BIRTH

Charlotte Ann Lopez was born in Puerto Rico on September 25, 1976. While this much is certain, further information about her early life is sketchy, at best. Charlotte was put into foster care when she was about three, and many of the details about her family background are either unknown or are in confidential files held by the social services department in Vermont. She does know, though, that her mother's maiden name was Emma Lopez, and that she has an older brother, Duane, and a younger sister, Diana. While Charlotte doesn't know who her father is, all three children are believed to have different fathers.

YOUTH

Charlotte Lopez's life story is an amazing one, filled with heartache and sadness and laughter and triumph—and over all her amazing ability, at so young an age, to rely only on herself. Even for information about her early life she has no one to turn to, no one who can tell her stories about her family history, her mom and dad, her life as a baby. She has to rely on an impersonal social services case file and her own sketchy memories, which she calls impressions, from those early years.

Charlotte moved from Puerto Rico to Vermont in 1977, when she was about a year old, with her mother, Emma (who was then pregnant with Diana), and her brother, Duane. She doesn't know why they moved to Vermont. "I remember sitting on her [Emma's] lap and eating macaroni and cheese out of a Wendy's cup," Charlotte says. "Food wasn't around much, so when it was that was a big memory." According to what Charlotte has been able to read in her file, her mother was having severe personal problems and was unable to care for her children. She repeatedly left the young girls in the care of their ten-year-old brother for several hours or more. Neighbors reported the situation to social workers, who found the children to be neglected and malnourished. They were removed from the home and placed into foster care when Charlotte was three years old. That was the last time she saw her mother.

FOSTER CARE

The foster care system, run in each state by their social services department, cares for children who have been separated from their families, often during a crisis—perhaps because of a death in the family, a serious financial problem, or a suspected abuse situation. Adults who volunteer to become foster parents undergo a screening and training process, then open their hearts and their homes to children who need help.

According to one expert, there are probably 500,000 children in foster care across the U.S. in any one day, and about five million children pass in and out of the system each year. Foster care is designed to be temporary; children stay with a foster family only while their situation is being investigated and stabilized. The goal is to return the child to his or her own family, if at all possible; or, if not, to prepare the child to be adopted.

LOST IN THE SYSTEM

For Charlotte Lopez, the system failed. She and Diana were, in her own words, "lost in the system. It's a really rare situation that my sister and I weren't adopted. After a while, I came to terms and said, 'Charlotte, you've just got to love yourself and cherish the life you have.'" Altogether, Charlotte was stuck in foster care for thirteen years, in six different homes.

Although she and her sister were able to stay together for most of that time, they were separated from their brother very early, and only reunited quite recently.

Starting out at age three, Charlotte was in two different homes during that first year, then she and Diana moved in with the Wensley family in their comfortable, middle-class home in Shaftsbury, Vermont. She remained there for eleven years. It was very hard at first. "When they came to us, they were in pretty tough shape," Bill Wensley reveals. His wife, Cari, adds, "For several years they had terrible nightmares. There were nights when I would get up eight times."

Fortunately, all that changed. Described now as sunny, laughing, and exuberant, Charlotte and her sister were soon busy with school and other activities. They studied hard at school and got good grades, took ballet and piano lessons, went on ski trips and other vacations with the Wensleys and their two children, sang in the church youth choir, were active in sports, and watched "Star Search" and beauty pageants on TV. They were popular, hardworking kids. "It was great growing up," Charlotte now says. "We lived out in the middle of nowhere and . . . we had the woods and we'd be outside playing all day. We had a big house, and every Sunday we got all dressed up and went to Sunday school. . . . We were sheltered from everything."

But there was something missing. Charlotte, understandably, wanted to be adopted, to have her own family: "I wanted to be adopted," she explains, "because I needed someone to be a permanent part of my life." As she grew older, tensions developed with the Wensley family about this issue and about their strict rules. She began to wonder why, after all those years, she had never been adopted: perhaps her birth mother had refused to allow it, or perhaps there was something the matter with her. When Charlotte was fourteen, she asked to be moved to a different foster home. Her sister, Diana, decided to stay with the Wensleys and has since been adopted by them.

There was only one foster home available at that time that was near Charlotte's school. That was with Janet Henry, who runs a shelter in Bennington for teenagers in crisis, mostly runaways and kids who have been physically or sexually abused. The teens often require close supervision and Henry has devised strict rules, which presented a striking change from the Wensley's family situation. "The first time I saw the police bring in a girl in shackles and handcuffs who had run away from home, my chin just dropped," Charlotte recalls. It was tough, but she learned to follow the rules and decided to stick with it. She continued to excel in other areas of her life, with good grades, good friends, a job at a Tastee-Freez, a new boyfriend, and election to Homecoming Queen and Prom Queen.

It was at this point that she and her sister started searching for their brother, with the help of the social services system. They learned that he was currently a musician living in Colorado, but were dismayed to discover that he had grown up in foster care just 20 minutes away from them in Vermont—and they had never known it. They were reunited at Christmas 1992.

But Charlotte still felt that something was missing in her life: she wanted to live with a family and be adopted by them. As she recalls, "One night I was dreaming that I went to college and it was Christmas break and everyone left and I didn't have anywhere to go. . . . I decided then that I really wanted to move into a permanent family situation." After two years with Janet Henry, she asked social services to try to find a family to adopt her.

ADOPTION—A FAMILY AT LAST

Meanwhile, in nearby Dorset, Vermont, Jill Charles, the artistic director of the Dorset Theater Festival, was caring for foster children. She started out as a single parent but then continued after her marriage to Al Scheps, owner of an Italian delicatessen. Together they cared for several children, each of whom eventually left their home. After a while, though, they started thinking about adopting a child.

Although Charles and Scheps had been planning to adopt a younger child, they met Charlotte and immediately hit it off. As Charles explains with sensitivity and compassion, "She was at a foster home for teenagers for two years. She was looking for a more traditional family that would give her some stability for the rest of her life. She wanted a place to come home to, where her children would have grandparents." Charlotte's long-time wish came true when Charles and Scheps decided to adopt her. During the lengthy legal process, she is living with them and attending her senior year of high school at Burr and Burton Seminary. Finally, Charlotte will have real parents and a place she can always call home.

MISS TEEN USA

Charlotte started out on the state beauty pageant circuit in November 1992. The judges, impressed with her poise, spontaneity, and speaking ability, voted her Miss Vermont Teen USA.

In August 1993, Charlotte traveled to Biloxi, Mississippi, for the national pageant. Unlike many of the other girls, who had spent years preparing for it, she had had no classes, modeling experience, or other training— except for years spent watching beauty pageants on TV. She appeared in an evening gown that cost just $37.99, which she had bought on sale— she had plenty of money, she explains, "but I wanted to get an inexpensive dress to prove the point that it's not the dress, it's what is inside the dress." She proved her point. Charlotte quickly won the hearts of the judges and the media by talking frankly about her experiences as a foster child, and she was crowned Miss Teen USA for 1993. Her prizes included $40,000 in cash plus a salary of $30,000 for the year, a Pontiac Sunbird convertible, trips to the Caribbean, Hawaii, and Disney World, a camcorder, $12,000 worth of fur and leather coats, and other merchandise including clothing, shoes, and cosmetics.

As Miss Teen USA, Charlotte will make numerous public and media appearances throughout her year-long reign. Perhaps the most thrilling event was her chance to make a guest appearance on "Star Search" and meet her hero, host Ed McMahon, after years of imitating the show with her sister. Yet more importantly, Charlotte plans to use her reign to inspire other foster children and to educate the general public. "Some people think that foster children are delinquents and have nothing going for them," she explains. "My sister and brother and I couldn't help our situation. We were put in foster care because our mother wasn't able to take care of us, not because we were terrible kids."

FUTURE PLANS

Charlotte's immediate plans include finishing high school. Then she and her sister will hit the road next summer in her new Sunbird (black with a white top and tinted glass). They plan to head out West, with a first stop in Colorado to visit their brother Duane. Then Charlotte plans to attend college and study broadcasting, although she also talks about becoming an entertainer. She has also started work on a book about her experiences in foster care, already titled *Lost in the System*. And TV producers have expressed interest in filming a movie version of her life, with Charlotte in the starring role. Whatever develops, it is clear that Charlotte Lopez has the drive, motivation, and parental support to succeed at whatever she tries.

HONORS AND AWARDS

Miss Vermont Teen USA: 1992
Miss Teen USA: 1993

FURTHER READING

PERIODICALS

Boston Globe, Aug. 29, 1993, New England section, p.
Chicago Tribune, Sep. 28, 1993, Kidsnews section, p.1
Glamour, Jan. 1994, p.130
People, Aug. 30, 1993, p.110
Philadelphia Daily News, Jan. 25, 1994, p.I5
USA Today, Aug. 13, 1993, p.D8

ADDRESS

Miss Teen USA
5750 Wilshire Boulevard
Suite 225
Los Angeles, CA 90036

Wilma Mankiller 1945-
Native American Principal Chief of the Cherokee Nation of Oklahoma
First Female Chief of a Major Indian Tribe

BIRTH

Wilma Pearl Mankiller was born on November 18, 1945, in Tahlequah, Oklahoma. Her father, Charley Mankiller, was a full Cherokee Indian; her mother, Clara Irene (Sitton), was white, of mixed Dutch-Irish ancestry. Wilma was the sixth of their 11 children, with six brothers and four sisters: Louis (Don), Frieda, Robert, Frances, John, Linda, Richard, Vanessa, James, and William. The family name, Mankiller, is a Cherokee military rank, similar to "general," that a long-ago ancestor took as his surname. It intrigues people, and inspires questions. "Some people are

215

startled when I am introduced to them as Wilma Mankiller," she explains. "They think it's a fierce-sounding name. Many find it amusing and make nervous jokes, and there are still those times when people display their ignorance. . . . When someone unknowingly or out of ignorance makes a snide comment about my name, I often resort to humor. I look the person in the eye and say with a straight face that Mankiller is actually a well-earned nickname. That usually shuts the person up."

CHEROKEE HISTORY

According to Mankiller, her life story cannot be understood without the surrounding context of Cherokee history. As she starts to describe her childhood in her compelling autobiography, *Mankiller: A Chief and Her People*, she stops and says, "But I have started my story far too early. Especially in the context of a tribal people, no individual's life stands apart and alone from the rest. My own story has meaning only as long as it is a part of the overall story of my people. For above all else, I am a Cherokee woman."

The Cherokee people, along with many other Indian tribes, lived for centuries in the southeastern part of what later became the United States, in parts of Kentucky, Tennessee, Alabama, Georgia, South Carolina, North Carolina, and Virginia. In recounting tribal history, Mankiller says that "Even today there are people who believe that this vast domain called America was nothing but a wild and virgin land just waiting for the advent of the wise and superior Europeans to tame and domesticate it. In 1492, there were *more than seventy-five million native people* in the Western Hemisphere, with six million of those residing in what is now the United States. They spoke two thousand languages, and had been part of thriving civilizations long before the coming of Columbus. This rich culture of the native people nonetheless was demolished methodically and ruthlessly within a historically short period. The time for suffering had begun."

One of the largest and most powerful Indian tribes, the Cherokees had developed a sophisticated society, with farms and plantations, businesses and schools. As more and more white settlers moved westward in the eighteenth and early nineteenth centuries, though, they gradually encroached on the traditional Cherokee lands. In 1828, gold was discovered in the heart of Cherokee country, near the modern-day town of Dahlonega in what is now northern Georgia. This discovery brought more than 10,000 gold seekers to the area, and the Cherokees' fate was sealed. In 1838, President Andrew Jackson ordered the Cherokees to leave their homes and move to "Indian Territory" in the western United States, in what is now Oklahoma. U.S. Army troops were sent to enforce the order. During 1838-39, some 16,000 Cherokees, including even old people and children, set out on the 1,200-mile march. There were some wagons and horses for the neediest, but most walked the entire way to Oklahoma. The harsh conditions, hunger, disease, and abusive U.S. soldiers killed about 4,000 along the way, on what the Cherokees called "the trail where we cried"; it English it has become known as the "Trail of Tears."

The U.S. government gave the Cherokees a tract of land in northeastern Oklahoma and a treaty promising protection and ownership of their lands "as long as grass shall grow and rivers run." But the government didn't offer much in the way of practical assistance. Life was hard at first. Over time, though, the Cherokees rebuilt their society, creating a government, clearing land for farms, and building homes, schools, and churches. This "Golden Age," as historians call it today, ended with the Civil War and subsequent western land rush, as white settlers again moved onto Indian lands. The federal government continued to intervene in Cherokee affairs: in 1907, when Oklahoma became a state, the United States abolished the Cherokees' right to self-government, dismantling their tribal government and reapportioning their lands; and in the 1950s, it relocated many families, taking them away from the tribe and resettling them in cities. It wasn't until 1975 that the U.S. gave the Cherokee Indians the right to self-determination.

YOUTH

In many ways, Mankiller's personal experiences echo the historical struggles of her tribe. During her early years, she grew up on Mankiller Flats, a 160-acre tract of land in Adair County, a rural part of northeastern Oklahoma. The land had been deeded to her grandfather by the U.S. government in 1907, when it took all the land held communally by the Cherokees and divided it into individual plots. The Mankiller family was extremely poor. They had no electricity, indoor toilets, or running water, and many of their clothes were made from flour sacks. There were no school buses, so the children had to walk three miles each way to the Rocky Mountain School, even in extreme heat or cold.

Still, they were happy. They rode horses to the nearby spring for cool water, enjoyed life on the rolling, wooded hills, and worked on their family's farm, growing strawberries, green beans, peanuts, and other crops. Despite their poverty, they always had plenty to eat—food they grew, or bartered with their neighbors, or hunted themselves. And the family took part in all the local Cherokee social and cultural activities, developing a real bond and sense of kinship with their community.

All that changed in 1956. With two consecutive years of drought, their crops failed, and the land could no longer support their family. Charley Mankiller went to ask for help from the federal Bureau of Indian Affairs. They suggested relocating to San Francisco, California, as part of a program designed to "mainstream" rural Indians into urban areas to sever their ties to their land and culture. They "mainstreamed" the Mankillers right into a housing project in a desperately poor and dangerous neighborhood—the notorious "Tenderloin" district of San Francisco. Years later, Wilma would compare the experience to the 1838 Trail of Tears. "Relocation was yet another answer from the federal government to the continuing dilemma of what to do with us," Mankiller said. "We are a people with . . . an awful lot of problems, so in the fifties they decided to mainstream us, to try to take us away from the tribal land base and the tribal culture, get us into the cities. It was supposed to be a better life."

It wasn't. It was dirty, ugly, crowded, and loud. They had never seen such traffic, or television, or neon lights, or listened to sirens wail all night long—they thought it was wolves, howling somewhere outside. The elevator was another mystery. People would get on, but when the doors next opened, different people would come out. Wilma decided to take the stairs. Some of her stories are amusing now, but at the time it was very painful. Everything was so different, and the family felt very isolated and alone, separated from their land and their Cherokee friends and neighbors. It was the first time that Wilma felt different from other people, and the first time she experienced prejudice.

With time, their situation improved, and they adjusted. Charley Mankiller got a job as a warehouse worker and union organizer—"the only full-blooded Indian union organizer I ever ran into," Wilma once said—and they moved to a better neighborhood. During the next few years the family lived in several different areas as their financial situation fluctuated, but none was nearly as bad as their first experience in the housing project.

EDUCATION

After they moved to California, school was a real struggle for Wilma. She did well in reading, but poorly in other subjects, and the other kids teased and humiliated her mercilessly because of her academic troubles, Oklahoma accent, distinctive name, poor clothes, and Indian features. She later discovered that this was a common experience for Native Americans relocated during the 1950s. As a teenager, though, she was miserable. She even ran away from home several times, each time going to see her maternal grandmother in Riverbank, a small town about 100 miles east of San Francisco. But her grandmother would always call her parents to take her back home. Finally she did get to stay with her grandmother, who had moved to a ranch in the country with Wilma's uncle and his family. The year she spent there served to boost her self-confidence and to improve her attitude about others.

After that, things improved a bit for Wilma, particularly after she discovered the Indian Center in San Francisco. There were social activities for Native American children and adults, as well as political discussions. For Wilma, it was a safe place to hang out and share her frustrations with kids who could understand her. It was a lifesaver during her teen years, giving her the self-confidence to stay in school through her high school graduation in 1963.

Years later she did return to school, and despite repeated interruptions she successfully completed college. She received her bachelor's degree in social science in 1979 from Flaming Rainbow University in Stilwell, Oklahoma; later she took graduate courses in community planning from the University of Arkansas.

MARRIAGE AND FAMILY

Like many young women in the early 1960s, Mankiller had no plans for her life after high school. She got a job as a clerk, and soon met Hector Hugo Olaya de Bardi, a charming and handsome student from a wealthy Ecuadorean family. They married in Reno, Nevada, on November 13, 1963. Wilma soon settled into her life as wife and mother of two daughters: Felicia, born in 1964, and Gina, born in 1966, both of whom are now grown with children of their own.

All of that soon changed, though. Living in San Francisco in the late 1960s, Mankiller was soon touched by the social upheaval and unrest taking place in American society, like the movements for civil rights, black power, an end to the Vietnam War, and women's rights. Unrest was also brewing in the Native American community. In 1969, a group of demonstrators took over the former prison on Alcatraz island, in San Francisco Bay, to call attention to the mistreatment of Indians. Mankiller joined their group, the American Native Rights Movement, and began to reexamine her experiences as a Native American. "Those college students who participated in Alcatraz articulated a lot of feelings I had that I'd never been able to express. I was a mother, so I couldn't join them, but I did fund-raising and got involved in the activist movement."

The experience refocused her life. Feeling stifled at home, she began attending college classes at night, starting out at a local community college and then building up the courage to transfer to San Francisco State University. She also worked as the Native American program coordinator for the public school system in Oakland, California, and traveled whenever possible to Indian tribal events throughout the state. In 1974 she and her husband divorced, their marriage torn apart by his desire for a traditional housewife and her desire to be active in community affairs. Two years later, Mankiller decided to return with her children to the land of her tribe. She first visited Oklahoma in 1976 and settled there permanently the following year, building a house on Mankiller Flats, her family's land.

FIRST JOBS

Since she began working for the Cherokee Nation in 1977, Mankiller has focused on supporting traditional Cherokee values and culture while also encouraging ongoing economic development. She started out as Economic

Stimulus Coordinator, encouraging native people to be trained in environmental sciences, while simultaneously finishing up her college coursework for her bachelor's degree. Two years later, she enrolled in the master's program in community planning at the University of Arkansas and took on the job of Program Development Specialist, writing grants that raised money for tribal projects. That same year she had a dreadful car accident. Driving on a back road, her car was hit head on. By a devastating coincidence, the other driver, who was killed, was one of Mankiller's best friends. Wilma's legs and ribs were broken and her face was crushed. She spent about a year recuperating and had to undergo 17 operations, mostly rebuilding her right leg and reconstructing her face. In 1980, while still recovering from the accident, Mankiller discovered she has myasthenia gravis, a form of muscular dystrophy that weakens and gradually destroys the muscular system, sometimes to the point of paralysis. She had to undergo surgery and chemotherapy, as well as medication that has caused her to gain weight.

CAREER HIGHLIGHTS

Mankiller returned to work in 1981, just one month after surgery. She soon helped to found the Cherokee Nation Community Development Department and was named its first director. As such she began many community programs, including the first tribal program for the elderly, a children's nutrition program, and a nursery and garden business. She also developed her philosophy of tribal management, which involved working on the grass-roots level to create change. She had long believed that the best way to help tribe members was not by government handouts; instead, she wanted to help Cherokees increase their feelings of self-esteem, giving people the confidence that they could help themselves. As she explains, "We operate from a bubble-up theory that's a little bit different from that of most tribes. We [tribal government] simply act as a resource; our people define and resolve many of their problems at the community level. They plan a project, such as a community building, and then erect it. That puts them in a position of assuming responsibility for change, and it builds pride. People develop a sense that they can indeed alter their lives and community."

The best example of this, and still one of her finest achievements, is the Bell Community Revitalization Project. In this small, poor, predominately Cherokee community of about 100 families, over 25% had no indoor plumbing, over 50% lived in inadequate housing, and over 60% were unemployed. Mankiller told them that the tribal government would provide technical assistance and money, but that the people of Bell would have to plan what they wanted and do the work. Other officials were convinced that the local people couldn't do it. They were soon proved wrong: every Indian family in Bell got involved, rehabilitating existing houses, constructing new ones, rebuilding the water system, and in the process gaining a feeling of control over their lives. The experience in Bell has been taken as a model for self-sufficiency in other Cherokee community projects. "Working with local people in their communities," according to Mankiller, is the key to her approach. "If you trust people, if you believe in people, and you involve people in trying to resolve the problems in their communities, you can be successful. . . . What seems impossible is entirely possible."

Mankiller's approach to and success with economic revitalization so impressed Ross Swimmer, Principal Chief of the Cherokee Nation, that he urged her to run for Deputy Chief. Many community members strongly objected to a woman holding that position—in fact, she even received death threats. In responding to their concerns, Mankiller referred back to tribal history, explaining that the belief that women should be subservient to men was one that Cherokees had adopted fairly recently from whites; before that, Cherokee women had been very active in tribal affairs. Mankiller narrowly won that election in 1983. Two years later, when President Ronald Reagan appointed Swimmer head of the federal Bureau of Indian Affairs, Mankiller was appointed Principal Chief of the Cherokee Nation of Oklahoma, the first woman ever in tribal history to hold that job. Mankiller tried to downplay the issue of gender; as she claimed at the time, the Cherokees were more concerned "about jobs and education, not whether the tribe is run by a woman or not." And experience bears that out: she was elected Principal Chief in 1987. Voters who were uncertain about electing a woman may have been reassured by her marriage the previous year to Charlie Soap, a full-blooded Cherokee community activist who speaks the Cherokee language (Mankiller doesn't). Mankiller was reelected in 1991, with a resounding 83% of the vote.

As Principal Chief of the 156,000-member Cherokee Nation of Oklahoma, Mankiller has managed an annual budget of over $86 million and has directed a staff of 1,200 employees spread out over 7,000 square miles. She and her staff have overseen a vast network of social services, community services, and economic development programs. According to Mankiller, her priorities have included "a new education plan, Cherokee language and literacy projects, developing Sequoyah High School into a magnet school, developing a comprehensive health-care system, an extensive array of services for children and youths, settlement of old land claims, taxation, housing initiatives, safeguarding the environment, and economic development."

In addition to her official responsibilities as Principal Chief, Mankiller has also affected how people think—how Cherokee people think about themselves and their abilities, and how white people think about Cherokees in the modern world. For Mankiller, life requires a constant balancing between traditional and contemporary cultures, between

Cherokee heritage and modern society—and she has worked hard to maintain that balance, for herself and all her people. "Today, we are helping to erase the stereotypes created by media and by western films of the drunken Indian on a horse, chasing wagon trains across the prairie. I suppose some people still think that all native people live in tepees and wear tribal garb every day. They do not realize that many of us wear business suits and drive station wagons. The beauty of society today is that young Cherokee men and women can pursue any professional fields they want and remain true to traditional values. It all comes back to our heritage and our roots. It is so vital that we retain that sense of culture, history, and tribal identity."

On April 5, 1994, Mankiller announced before about 500 tribal employees that she would not seek reelection in 1995. During her almost ten years as Principal Chief, she has "established herself," according to the *New York Times,* "as one of the premier authorities on Indian affairs." She is widely credited with expanding tribal membership by 100,000; increasing the annual budget by $40 million; earning the respect of three U.S. presidents and dozens of Congressional committees; and revitalizing the Cherokee Nation. Her health, Mankiller reported, did not affect her decision to retire. "Almost all of my life I've been blessed with the ability to know when it's time to make a change," Mankiller said. "I've come to the point where I feel certain that it's time for another change for myself and the Cherokee Nation." She went on to cite the biblical passage "To every thing there is a season," and then added, "My season here is coming to an end." Cherokees first wept at her announcement—and then they stood and cheered for her.

MEMORABLE EXPERIENCES

Mankiller has endured a tremendous amount of physical suffering during the past fifteen years. When asked to identify a turning point in her life, she recalled the day of her dreadful car accident in 1979. "That accident changed my life. I had experienced death, felt its presence, touched it, and then let it go. It was a very spiritual thing, a rare natural gift. From that point on, I have always thought of myself as the woman who lived before and the woman who lives afterward." She suffered further in 1980, when she developed the debilitating symptoms of myasthenia gravis that made her so weak that she couldn't get out of bed. And in 1990 recurrent kidney infections became so severe that her kidneys failed. Her oldest brother, Don, volunteered to donate one of his kidneys. Mankiller had a kidney transplant, which saved her life.

WRITINGS

Mankiller: A Chief and Her People, 1993 (with Michael Wallis)

HONORS AND AWARDS

American Indian Woman of the Year (Oklahoma Federation of Indian Women): 1986
Harvard Foundation Citation for Outstanding Contributions to American Leadership and Native American Culture (Harvard University): 1986
Oklahoma Women's Hall of Fame: 1986
Woman of the Year (*Ms.* magazine): 1987
100 Most Important Women in America (*Ladies Home Journal* magazine): 1988
John W. Gardner Leadership Award (U.S. Public Health Service): 1988
Indian Health Service Award (U.S. Public Health Service): 1989
International Women's Forum Hall of Fame: 1992
National Racial Justice Award: 1992
National Women's Hall of Fame: 1993

FURTHER READING

BOOKS

Glassman, Bruce. *Wilma Mankiller: Chief of the Cherokee Nation*, 1992 (juvenile)
Mankiller, Wilma, and Michael Wallis. *Mankiller: A Chief and Her People*, 1993
Rand, Jacki Thompson. *Wilma Mankiller*, 1993 (juvenile)
Simon, Charnan. *Wilma P. Mankiller: Chief of the Cherokee*, 1991 (juvenile)
Who's Who of American Women, 1993-94

PERIODICALS

Chicago Tribune, May 14, 1986, Tempo Section, p.1
Current Biography Yearbook 1988
Los Angeles Times, Sep. 18, 1986, Part 5, p.26
Ms., Jan. 1988, p.68
New York Times, Nov. 4, 1993, p.C1
Parade, Aug. 18, 1991, p.4
People, Dec. 2, 1985, p.91
Philadelphia Inquirer, Feb. 9, 1988, p.A2

ADDRESS

Office of the Cherokee Principal Chief
P.O. Box 948
Tahlequah, OK 74465-0948

Shannon Miller 1977-
American Gymnast
1993 and 1994 World Champion
1992 Olympic Silver and Bronze Medalist

BIRTH

Shannon Lee Miller, who has won more Olympic and World Championship medals than any other American gymnast, was born March 10, 1977, in Rolla, Missouri. Her father, Ron, is a professor of physics at Oklahoma Central University, and her mother, Claudia, is a bank vice president. Shannon has a sister, Tessa, who is older, and a brother, Troy, who is younger. The family moved to Edmond, Oklahoma, when Shannon was an infant.

EARLY LIFE OF A GYMNAST

Shannon started tumbling around the family living room when she was five, after her parents had bought her and her sister a trampoline. "We started doing tricks on the trampoline and learning stuff by ourselves," Miller says. "So my mother decided to start us in gymnastics before we either wrecked the furniture or hurt ourselves." When she was six, she began to take lessons, and by the time she was eight, she made her first trip overseas, to the former Soviet Union, to take part in a training exhibition. While she was there, she met her future coach, Steve Nunno. Nunno, a former gymnast himself, had begun coaching with the famous Bela Karolyi, the coach of such world champions as Nadia Comaneci, Mary Lou Retton, and Kim Zmeskal. Nunno had opened a training gym, Dynamo Gymnastics, in Edmond, Oklahoma, and Shannon was eager and determined to learn as much as she could. Her parents signed her up.

Nunno remembers his young protege as being full of talent, and extremely hard on herself. Shannon would often cry out of frustration when she couldn't do a particular move. "I thought it was because she didn't want to do gymnastics," recalls Nunno. "She doesn't talk too much—you've probably heard—so it took a year for me to figure out she was discouraged in herself because she hadn't done something well." Many commentators note that Shannon's shy, soft-spoken demeanor contrasts with her determination to be the best gymnast she can be.

CAREER HIGHLIGHTS

TRAINING TO BE A CHAMPION

Shannon devoted herself to her sport at a very young age, and she has kept to a schedule of working out six hours a day, six days a week, for years. She often kept a pillow, blanket, food, and homework in the back seat of the family car so she could catch up on her studies—and on sleep—as her parents drove her to and from practice each day.

In gymnastic competition, there are four different types of events: the balance beam, the uneven bars, the vault, and floor exercise, as well as the all-around, an event that combines all the apparatus as well as floor exercise. Miller excels in all areas. She has a small, compact body, the "munchkin model" that is the preferred body type for world gymnastic champions. Today, at the age of 17, she is 4'11" and 86 pounds; at the time of her first Olympics, she was only 4'8" and 72 pounds. While Shannon has the small, powerful frame of a modern gymnast, she also has a grace and technical brilliance that defines her championship style.

Miller's hard work and dedication paid off, as she became the top-ranked junior gymnast in the U.S. by the time she was 11, in 1988. In 1989, she placed third at the Olympic Festival competition. By 1990, she had garnered a first place win at the Catania Cup in Italy, a second place in the American Classic, and a sixth in the American Cup. In 1991, Miller placed second at the World Championships. It was a remarkable performance: she was the top U.S. scorer, and she was the first U.S. gymnast ever to qualify in all four apparatus events.

INJURY AND A STUNNING COMEBACK

In 1992, while preparing for the World Championships and the Olympics, Shannon fell during a practice session and dislocated her elbow, chipping a bone in the process. The injury required immediate surgery, with doctors reattaching the chip with a microscrew. Shannon, determined as ever, made a speedy recovery. She took only one day off, then began to train again. "I did one-arm vaults," she recalls. "I had to keep the rest of my body in shape while my arm got better." Within five weeks, she was back on the apparatus and ready to compete. But she had to miss both the World Championships and the U.S. Championships. She went on to the Olympic trials, which she won. She was one of the top two picks for the U.S. Olympic team, along with Kim Zmeskal, then the reigning World Champ. With Zmeskal clearly the focus and the favorite, the media began to cover the two, and to try to create a rivalry between them. But Miller didn't feel any sense of competition with her famous U.S. teammate. "There is no rivalry with Kim," she said. "I compete for the best scores against all gymnasts, not just Kim."

1992 OLYMPICS

At the 1992 Olympics in Barcelona, Spain, the glare of the media didn't seem to affect Shannon, and she performed beautifully, winning two silver and three bronze medals, more than any other American that year. She won a silver medal in the balance beam competition, missing the gold medal by only 0.012 points. She won another silver in the individual all-around, and in both the uneven bars and the floor exercise she placed third, for two bronze medals. When the U.S. team won a bronze in the team competition, Miller's individual score was the highest. At the conclusion of the '92 Olympics, Miller had come into her own as a champion: she was the first U.S. woman to win five Olympic gymnastics medals since Mary Lou Retton in 1984.

For Zmeskal, the Olympics were a great disappointment. Favored to win several medals, she did not do well, and ended up with only a team bronze. After her loss, the U.S. team and the sport of gymnastics itself came under close scrutiny as coaches were accused of putting too much pressure on, and requiring too intense training from, girls who were too young to cope with the stress. Charges appeared, claiming harsh treatment at the hands of coaches and of fitness regimes that stressed slimness to the point of eating disorders. The focus was mainly on Karolyi, but

Nunno and his athletes were also closely examined. Nunno's assistant Peggy Liddick said that the gym establishes rules for healthy eating, not strict or fad diets. "No ice cream. No junk food. You're an athlete and that's basic," Liddick said. Shannon occasionally has a taste for fast food, and she does indulge once in awhile. Also, Nunno stresses to his gymnasts that it's important to do well in school and to keep life in balance. "If you have a bad day at the gym, but a great day at school, you can come in feeling good because there are other things in your life. If the gym is the only thing in you life, it's hard to break out of the slump."

Miller had this to say about how she and the other athletes deal with the pressure and training: "We just do it because we like to do it. If we didn't want to do it, we wouldn't. No one is forcing us."

After the Olympics, Miller took part in the 30-city Tour of the Olympic and World Champion Gymnasts. Back in Oklahoma, her hometown gave her a parade, and a local dealer gave her a car (even though she couldn't drive yet). She appeared in an ad for Trivial Pursuit, agreed to promote Elite sportswear, and signed with an agent. But Shannon seemed pretty much the same person. She went back to her local public school, back to the gym to continue training with Nunno, and back to her former routine: out of bed at 6:30 a.m.; 7 a.m. to 8:30 a.m. in the gym; 8:30 a.m. to 10:30 a.m. breakfast and morning study period; 10:30 a.m. to 2:20 p.m. school; 2:30 p.m. to 3:30 p.m. lunch break; 4 p.m. to 9 p.m. in the gym; 9:30 p.m. dinner; 9:45 p.m. to 11:15 p.m. homework.

Her strict regimen continued to pay off in 1993, when Miller topped all other competitors to win the all-around title at the World Championships. Her response was typical for the soft-spoken, composed Miller: "I didn't worry about the score. I had done my job, and wherever I finished I would be happy." She led the entire field in the event, with the highest scores in each category. She won by a hair's breadth—.007—but she was the champion. That same year,

Miller won three gold medals and one silver at the Olympic festival, a competition that also saw her lead her team to first place.

In 1994, Miller became the first American to win two consecutive World Championship all-around titles. At 17, she is the best in the world, but at an age when most women gymnasts retire. And what about the 1996 Olympics? "I've thought about it," she says. "Hopefully, I will be able to compete in Atlanta. I think that's going to be great and I think it's going to be very exciting being in the U.S." Right now, Miller is looking forward to competing in the Goodwill Games in St. Petersburg, Russia, and as of this writing, she plans to take part in the Olympic trials in 1996. "My long-term goal would be to win a gold in the Olympics in 1996. I would love it, and that's what I'm shooting for. But the most important thing would be to lead the U.S. team to the gold medal."

EDUCATION

Shannon attends public schools in Edmond, where she is now about to start her senior year. She maintains a straight-A average at Edmond North High School, despite the demands of her training. In fact, Miller believes that the discipline of gymnastics has helped her with her schoolwork. "I don't think I would do as well in school if I didn't have gymnastics," says Miller. "I might not use my time as wisely—I would say I could do things later. Now I have to get them done." She admits that she has missed out on alot of the typical experiences of most teenagers in the U.S., but she believes it has been worth it. "The whole experience has been great. I get to travel, and it's really neat to meet other athletes from other sports."

HOME AND FAMILY

Because Steve Nunno's gym is in the town where the Millers live, Shannon never had to live away from home to train, a real advantage for a young athlete. The Millers are a very close family, and they are very involved with gymnastics. Tessa is a coach at Nunno's gym, and Troy is an up-and-coming young tumbler. Claudia is a judge on the national circuit, and Ron uses films of Shannon to illustrate theories of physics to his college classes. As Claudia recalls, "He loves to use the reverse Hecht on bars, which is a move where Shannon swings down, releases, and goes back over the bar and catches it. He shows a video of her missing the bar, and the students have to calculate the force with which she hits the ground."

Shannon still answers all of her own fan mail, even when the questions from her fans are outside her realm of experience. She received one letter from a fan asking for advice about a boyfriend. "Shannon said to me, 'Mom, how would I know?'" recalls Claudia Miller. Shannon wrote her back to say she "didn't have any experience in that area, but when she does get a boyfriend, she will write to *her* for advice."

HOBBIES AND OTHER INTERESTS

Shannon's hobbies include swimming, skiing, shopping, sewing, reading mysteries, and watching TV. She loves animals, and she has a horse, a cat, a dog, some gerbils, and a fish. She's also involved with a number of charities, including the Children's Miracle Network, Muscular Dystrophy, Feed the Children, U.S. Army's Stay in School program, the American Cancer Society, the American Lung Association, and the American Red Cross.

HONORS AND AWARDS

U.S. Gymnastics Championships: 1991, Gold Medal (balance beam), Bronze Medal (vault)
World Gymnastics Championships: 1991, Silver Medal (uneven bars); 1993, 3 Gold Medals (all-around, uneven bars, floor exercise); 1994, 2 Gold Medals (all-around and balance beam)
Olympic Gymnastics: 1992, 2 Silver Medals (balance beam and all-around), 3 Bronze Medals (floor exercise, uneven bars, and U.S. Team)
U.S. Olympic Festival: 1993, 4 Gold Medals (all-around, vault, balance beam, and Team)

FURTHER READING

PERIODICALS

Chicago Tribune, Sep. 13, 1991, p.C1; Aug. 2, 1992, p.C1
Dallas Morning News, July 31, 1992, p.A6; Sep. 30, 1993, p.D13
Houston Post, Apr. 11, 1993, p.B11
International Gymnast, Aug./Sep. 1991, p.49; Mar. 1992, p.25; May 1992, p.17; Oct. 1992, p.25; May 1993, p.10; June/July 1993, p.8
Los Angeles Times, July 15, 1992, p.A9
Newsweek, Aug. 10, 1992, p.20, p.22
San Jose Mercury News, July 11, 1993, p. D5
Sports Illustrated, Aug. 10, 1992, p.76; Dec. 14, 1992, p.76; Apr. 26, 1993, p.46
Sports Illustrated for Kids, July 1993, p.34
Sporting News, July 20, 1992, p.12
Time, July 27, 1992, p.56; Aug. 10, 1992, p.57

ADDRESS

USA Gymnastics
201 S. Capitol Ave.
Indianapolis, IN 46225

Toni Morrison 1931-
American Writer and Author of *Song of Solomon, Beloved,* and *Jazz*
Winner of the 1993 Nobel Prize in Literature

BIRTH

Toni Morrison was born Chloe Anthony Wofford on February 18, 1931, in Lorain, Ohio. Her parents were George Wofford and Ramah (Willis) Wofford. Morrison was the second of their four children.

The first African-American woman to win the Nobel Prize in Literature, Morrison grew up listening to the music, history, and folklore of her black family and community. Many of these stories were about her family heritage—stories whose people, places, and themes echo in her mature writings.

Morrison never knew her father's parents. George Wofford headed north from Georgia at age 16 and eventually found work in Lorain. Morrison hasn't disclosed much about his background, except to say that he endured racist treatment that left him bitter toward whites. But she has discussed her mother's family. Morrison's great-grandmother was born a slave, as was her son, John Solomon Willis. Willis, Morrison's grandfather, was five when the Emancipation Proclamation freed the slaves. The family received 88 acres of Alabama land from the U.S. government during Reconstruction, after the Civil War. But Willis eventually lost the family land because of debts he owed, and he and his wife, Ardelia, became poor sharecroppers. Sharecroppers are farmers who don't own their own land, but instead work on someone else's land, usually for very little money. According to Morrison, "They had lost their land, like a lot of black people at the turn of the century, and they were sharecroppers, which meant they were never able to get out of debt." In about 1912, they decided to head north, first to Kentucky, where her grandfather worked in a coal mine, and then to Lorain, Ohio, a steel mill town on Lake Erie, outside of Cleveland.

YOUTH

Morrison grew up in Lorain, and her memories of that era have been crucial to her writing. "I use so much of my recollections about childhood as a starting point when I work, as a kind of matrix or well-spring; even if I'm not writing *about* it, it's a place where I start—mostly for a kind of gaze. Our family was large and close and very much dependent on one another. Everything I did as a child was extremely important. If I didn't mind the food on the stove and it burned, there was no second thing to do—food was not all around in refrigerators the way it is now. If you weeded the garden, if you earned any money—everything you did made a difference to the well-being of somebody else."

Morrison grew up during the Great Depression, and times were very tough. Her father held down three jobs for 17 years, welding in the shipyards, working road construction, and washing cars. He deserves credit, according to Morrison, for helping her develop her strong sense of self-esteem. Her mother looked after the home and children, chased away the bill collectors, and sang. Ramah Wofford sang in the church choir and all day long while doing her chores—opera, jazz, blues, even Victorian music. The love of music was a tradition in her family. Ramah's father was a violinist—even when he lost his land, he managed to keep his violin—and he passed this love of music down to Ramah, who shared it with her daughter.

THE IMPORTANCE OF COMMUNITY

The family didn't have much money, but they did have a strong sense of community, something that Morrison often incorporates in her work. Their neighborhood was somewhat integrated, according to Morrison: "I never lived in a black neighborhood. Poor neighborhoods, yes, black neighborhoods, no . . . . There were Germans, Irish, Afro-Americans, Eastern Europeans, Italians, Greeks. In a sense we were integrated. We all went to the same school. However, uncrossed ethnic and religious lines existed." Those uncrossed lines contributed to the unity and cohesiveness of the small black community in Lorain. It was an era when black people couldn't expect much help from the government or the rest of society, and instead looked to their neighbors for help with the sick, the elderly, and the children. "All sorts of people cared about me in terms of what I was doing—not just my parents and my aunts and my uncles, but everybody on the street. If I was misbehaving somewhere, put on lipstick too soon, they felt not only free but obliged to tell me not to do it, and I knew I had better, because they were like surrogate parents—this layer upon layer of adults that participated in our lives."

EARLY MEMORIES

The issue of race was of great importance while Morrison was growing up. As she now says, "I grew up in a basically racist household with more than a child's share of contempt for white people." Her father, she relates, distrusted every word or gesture made by whites, while her mother was a bit more optimistic: "They differed about whether the moral fiber of white people would ever improve."

And they had good reason to feel that way. The Wofford family experienced daily the prejudice toward African-Americans that was so common at that time. Morrison has told about one particularly horrifying experience with that prejudice. When she was about two years old, her parents fell behind in paying their rent, then about $4 per month. The landlord set the house on fire—while they were in it. As she describes it, "It was this hysterical, out-of-the-ordinary, bizarre form of evil. If you internalized it you'd be truly and thoroughly depressed because that's how much your life meant. For $4 a month somebody would just burn you to a crisp.

"So what you did instead was laugh at him, at the absurdity, at the monumental crudeness of it. That way you gave back yourself to yourself. You know what I mean? You distanced yourself from the implications of the act.

"That's what laughter does. You take it back. You take your life back. You take your integrity back."

EDUCATION

Little Chloe Wofford, as she was called then, was a good student, the first child in her first-grade class to be able to read. She always loved to read;

she soon discovered it was the thing she did best. When she was a teenager, her teachers began introducing her to many of the classics: the great Russian novels, Gustave Flaubert, Jane Austen. "Those books were not written for a little black girl in Lorain, Ohio, but they were so magnificently done that I got them—they spoke directly to me out of their own specificity. . . . [When] I wrote my first novel years later, I wanted to capture that same specificity about the nature and feeling of the culture I grew up in." She took four years of Latin, was inducted into the National Honor Society, and graduated from Lorain High School in 1949. And because her father had worked three jobs for so many years, she was able to leave Lorain and go on to college.

Morrison went to Washington, D.C., to attend Howard University, then an all-black school. She started using the name Toni when other students had trouble pronouncing Chloe. Morrison was unimpressed by the shallow life at Howard: "It was about getting married, buying clothes, and going to parties. It was also about being cool, loving Sarah Vaughn (who only moved her hand a little when she sang) and MJQ [the Modern Jazz Quartet]." She did develop one passion there, though. She joined the Howard University Players, a theater group, and in the summer toured the South with a repertory group composed of students and professors. After hearing her parents' and grandparents' stories, the South was a revelation; she explored her reaction to the area in *Song of Solomon*. Morrison received her bachelor's degree in English from Howard University in 1953.

Morrison then attended Cornell University, earning her master's degree in English in 1955. For her thesis, she wrote on the theme of suicide in the works of Virginia Woolf and William Faulkner.

CAREER HIGHLIGHTS

ACADEMIC CAREER

The next ten years brought a host of changes: starting a career as a college teacher; getting married, having children, and getting divorced; and beginning to write.

After leaving Cornell in 1955, Morrison spent the next two years teaching English at Texas Southern University in Houston. She then took a position at Howard, where she had received her bachelor's degree, and taught there from 1957 to 1964. It was during the years at Howard that she first started to write. She also met and married her husband, Harold Morrison, an architect from Jamaica, and gave birth to her first child, Harold Ford.

In 1964, after leaving Howard, Morrison and her husband and young son went to Europe for the summer. While there, the couple separated; they later divorced. Since that time, she has refused to discuss her former husband or their marriage. Morrison returned to the U.S. with her three-year-old son and another baby on the way. She went back to the family home in Lorain and gave birth there to her second son, Slade Kevin.

EDITORIAL CAREER

Morrison stayed with her family for a little over a year before moving in 1965 to Syracuse, New York, to take a job as a textbook editor with Random House. Life in Syracuse, with two young children, no friends, and no community support, was difficult for Morrison. It was there that she began seriously to write.

In 1967 she moved from Syracuse to New York City. She was soon transferred from textbooks to the trade division of Random House, an assignment that suited her well. "I look very hard for black fiction because I want to participate in developing a canon of black work," she explained at that time. "We've had the first rush on black entertainment, where blacks were writing for whites, and whites were encouraging this kind of self-flagellation. Now we can get down to the craft of writing, where black people are talking to black people." At Random House she edited the autobiographies of Muhammed Ali and Angela Davis and the fiction of Toni Cade Bambara and Gayl Jones. She also edited *The Black Book* (1974), an eclectic collection of memorabilia that contains family photographs, slave quilts, newspaper clippings, excerpts from slave narratives, advertisements, and other pieces of black history, including the story that inspired her to write *Beloved*.

In the 1970s Morrison resumed teaching, combining part-time university appointments with her editorial responsibilities. Since that time, she has held posts at the State University of New York at Purchase, Yale University, Bard College, the State University at Albany, Bowdoin College, University of California at Berkeley, San Jose State University, Syracuse University, the University of Michigan, and Princeton University, where she currently holds the Robert F. Goheen Professorship in the Humanities Council. She continued to work at Random House until 1983, when she left to write full time.

Throughout the years, many have expressed surprise at Morrison's ability to juggle several different roles, combining single parenthood with teaching, editing, and writing. "People used to say, how come you do so many things? It never appeared to me that I was doing very much of anything; really, everything I did was always about one thing, which is books. I was either editing them or writing them or reading them or teaching them, so it was very coherent." Of course, Morrison is able to put it into perspective. Remembering the serious and even life-threatening troubles her family had suffered, particularly their landlord's attempt to burn the house down, Morrison says, "it was clear that the problems I faced couldn't compare to that."

BECOMING A WRITER

Morrison had first started to write in 1962, while teaching at Howard. She joined a group of about ten writers who met monthly to offer each other support and to critique each other's work. The only requirement was that each member had to bring a writing sample to every meeting. Morrison kept bringing material that she had written earlier, while in school. One day she ran out of the old stuff and had to sit down and write something new—a story about a young black girl who wishes she had blue eyes. That story later became *The Bluest Eye*, Morrison's first published novel.

Morrison returned to working on that story in the mid 1960s, while living in Syracuse. She was new in town, and by that time a single parent. As she tells it, "I had two small children in a strange place and I was very lonely. Writing was something for me to do in the evenings, after the children were asleep." It may have started out as a way to pass the time, but writing soon changed her life. "After I had written that book, I began to order my experience in that form. I thought of myself as a writer, even when I took the job of editor here [in New York]. I wasn't able to stop. It was for me the most extraordinary way of thinking and feeling—it became the one thing I was doing that I had absolutely no intention of living without. I just wanted to do it better and better."

WRITING CAREER

In fact, "better and better" is how critics describe the development of Morrison's writing in the six novels she has published over the last 24 years. She is considered a master storyteller with an impressive command of literary technique. Her use of language is praised above all: lyrical, eloquent, and powerful, it evokes the spoken voice of black America. Her works are filled with wit, passion, exoticism, magic, a sense of place, and deep sympathy for her characters. For Morrison, the experience of being black in America is still, to this day, deeply rooted in slavery. Throughout her writing, one feels its horrifying consequences on the lives of black individuals and their communities. Using what she calls "literary archeology," blending historical fact with her own autobiography and imagination, Morrison has crafted eloquent and powerful depictions of American black life and history. As Michiko Kakutani explained in the *New York Times*, her achievement lies "in creating a body of work that stands radiantly on its own as an American epic. She has taken the specific and often terrible history of black people in America and lofted it into the timeless realm of myth."

In her first work, *The Bluest Eye* (1970), Morrison tells the story of Pecola Breedlove, a young black girl growing up in white society. Ignored by her mother and raped by her father, Pecola believes everything would be better if she had blue eyes. This impressive first novel was followed up by the equally impressive *Sula* (1974), a story of a lifelong friendship between two very different women, one of whom is some kind of evil. The novel was nominated for the National Book Award, a prestigious honor. In *Song of Solomon* (1977), her next work, Macon Dead, called Milkman, takes an epic journey of self-discovery. Searching for gold, he finds instead his family heritage, rooted in the painful history of slavery. This powerful novel was published to immediate critical and popular acclaim: it won the National Book Critics Circle Award and was chosen as a main selection by the Book of the Month Club, their first selection by a black writer since *Native Son* in 1940. With *Song of Solomon*, Morrison was established as one of America's greatest writers. Her next novel, *Tar Baby* (1981), is a highly symbolic story, a contemporary reworking of the African American folk tale about the Tar Baby and B'rer Rabbit; it is generally considered her least distinguished work.

Morrison next began a trilogy of novels, including two published to date, *Beloved* (1987) and *Jazz* (1992), that are connected not by characters and events, but by theme. "The conceptual connection," Morrison explains, "is the search for the beloved—the part of the self that is you, and loves you, and is always there for you." *Beloved* is based on a true event in the life of Margaret Garner, a slave who escaped from Kentucky in 1855. In the novel, Morrison tells the life story of Sethe, a runaway slave. The central incident occurs when Sethe, believing she is about to be captured, slits the throat of her baby daughter rather than doom her to a life of slavery. This brutal scene is both horrifying and utterly compelling. "For me, Morrison explains, "it was the ultimate gesture of the loving mother. It wa also the outrageous claim of a slave. The *last* thing a slave women owns is her children." Yet the novelist also says, "It was absolutely the right thing to do, but she had no right to do it." *Beloved* generated a great deal of controversy. When the novel failed to win the National Book Award, a group of 48 black writers mounted a protest, writing a tribute to Morrison in the *New York Times Book Review*. Shortly afterward, the book won the Pulitzer Prize for fiction.

Morrison followed that book up with *Jazz*, the second novel in her three-part series. On the first page of this haunting, passionate love story set in Harlem in the 1920s, Morrison introduces Joe Trace, a cosmetics salesman who shoots his teenage love, Dorcas, and his wife, Violet, who attempts to cut Dorcas's body at the funeral parlor. This lyrical novel takes its inspiration from that unexpected element in jazz music, according to Morrison, "when you don't know what's going to happen"—even though the word "jazz" never appears in the story. "Novel by novel," as John Leonard says in *The Nation*, "Toni Morrison reimagines the lost history of her people, their love and work and nightmare passage and redemptive music. It's a brilliant project, a ghostly chorale, a constellation of humming spheres with its own gravity and now this brand-new star [*Jazz*], which is even trickier than usual."

THE NOBEL PRIZE

On October 7, 1993, Morrison won the Nobel Prize in Literature. It came as a surprise to the author, who was not believed to be one of the candidates for this year's prize. In announcing the award, the Nobel committee cited, in particular, *Song of Solomon, Beloved,* and *Jazz*. Morrison was honored for work "characterized by visionary force and poetic import [that] gives life to an essential aspect of American reality."

The announcement quickly drew a wide range of responses. The novelist Alice Walker articulated the views of many, saying "No one writes more beautifully than Toni Morrison. She has consistently explored issues of true complexity and terror and love in the lives of African Americans. Harsh criticism has not dissuaded her. Prizes have not trapped her. She is a writer who well deserves this honor." Yet some objected to the choice, calling Morrison's work racist, melodramatic, bombastic, and unfairly hostile to black men and labelling the award "a triumph of political correctness." Others, though, reject such criticism, instead seeing the award as simple recognition of her remarkable literary achievements. As summarized by novelist Nadine Gordimer, the last woman to win the prize, "The Nobel Prize in Literature is not awarded for gender or race. If it were, many thousands of mediocre writers might qualify. The significance of Toni Morrison's winning the prize is simply that she is recognized internationally as an outstandingly fine writer."

HOME AND FAMILY

Toni Wofford Morrison was married to Harold Morrison for seven years, from 1958 to about 1965. They had two children, both now grown: Harold Ford, a musician and sound engineer, and Slade Kevin, an architect. Morrison divides her time among several homes, one in New York City, one on the banks of the Hudson River, north of the City, and one near Princeton, where she is currently teaching.

HOBBIES AND OTHER INTERESTS

Although she reads widely, Morrison has often said that, in fact, she has no real hobbies. Explaining that raising children, running a house, teaching, and writing had left her little time, Morrison revealed: "I don't go anywhere. I don't have any elaborate social life. I don't go anywhere to be happy, I don't go on vacations, I don't ski. I don't do any of the so-called fun things in life. Writing is what I do, for me that is where it is—where the vacation is, the fun is, the danger, the excitement—all of that is in my work."

WRITINGS

FICTION

The Bluest Eye, 1970
Sula, 1973
Song of Solomon, 1977
Tar Baby, 1981
Beloved, 1987
Jazz, 1992

OTHER

The Black Book, 1974 (collection; editor)
Dreaming Emmett, 1986 (play; first production)
Playing In the Dark: Whiteness and the Literary Imagination, 1992 (criticism)
Race-ing Justice, En-gendering Power: Essays on Anita Hill, Clarence Thomas, and the Social Construction of Reality, 1993 (essays; editor)

HONORS AND AWARDS

National Book Critics Circle Award for Fiction: 1977, for *Song of Solomon*
American Academy and Institute of Arts and Letters Award for Literature: 1978
Anisfield—Wolf Book Award in Race Relations: 1987, for *Beloved*
American Book Awards: 1988, for *Beloved*
Robert F. Kennedy Memorial Book Award: 1988, for *Beloved*
Frederic G. Melcher Award: 1988, for *Beloved*
Pulitzer Prize for Fiction: 1988, for *Beloved*
Commonwealth Award in Literature (Modern Language Association): 1989
Nobel Prize in Literature: 1993

FURTHER READING

BOOKS

Contemporary Literary Criticism Yearbook 1988
Contemporary Novelists, 5th Edition, 1986
Dictionary of Literary Biography, Vol. 33
Samuels, Wilfred D., and Clenora Hudson-Weems. *Toni Morrison*, 1990
Something about the Author, Vol. 57
Who's Who in America, 1992-1993

PERIODICALS

Current Biography Yearbook 1979
Ebony, July 1988, p.100
Lear's, Oct. 1992, p.68
New York Times, Oct. 8, 1993, pp.A1, B10
New York Times Biographical Service, Sept. 1977, p.1293; May 1979, p.665; Apr. 1988, p.375
New York Times Book Review, Jan 24, 1988, p.36
New York Times Magazine, Aug. 11, 1974, p.14; July 4, 1976, p.104
Newsweek, Mar. 30, 1981, p.52; Oct. 18, 1993, p.89
Publishers Weekly, Aug. 21, 1987, p.50
Washington Post, Oct. 8, 1993, pp.A1, D1; Oct. 10, 1993, p.B1; Oct. 15, 1993, p.A25

VIDEOS

Profile of a Writer: Toni Morrison, 1987

ADDRESS

Alfred A. Knopf, Inc.
201 East 50th Street
New York, NY 10022

OBITUARY

Richard Nixon 1913-1994
American Political Leader, Author, and Lawyer
Thirty-Seventh President of the United States

BIRTH

Richard Milhous Nixon, who resigned in disgrace from the U.S. presidency in 1974 in the wake of the shattering political scandal known as Watergate, was born on January 9, 1913, in Yorba Linda, California. The second of five sons of Francis Anthony (Frank) and Hannah Milhous Nixon, he was born on his father's lemon farm in a California Quaker community. Both parents had come from the Midwest, but had moved to southern California under vastly different circumstances—Hannah, as a young girl, with her modestly affluent family, and Frank, at 28, as a proud but uneducated man who had left a life of struggle and aimlessness behind him.

Of Nixon's four brothers, two died young. Harold Samuel, the eldest, died at 23 after a long bout with tuberculosis; Arthur Burdg, the frail little brother upon whom Richard had doted, was only seven when he succumbed to meningitis. (Francis) Donald, however, lived to the age of 72. Now, since the former president's death on April 22, 1994, the only surviving Nixon is Edward Calvert, who was born in 1930 when his two elder brothers were already young adults.

YOUTH

Nixon spent the early part of his boyhood in Yorba Linda, in the humble home that his father had built near a lemon grove that ultimately failed to provide a living. The Nixon family lived in a community of Quakers, the religious Society of Friends, who are committed to simplicity in worship and daily life, and to pacifism. There were few extravagances in their modest environment, and except for the normal play of small children, there were no activities other than those connected with church. In *Nixon: The Education of a Politician, 1913-1962*, author Stephen Ambrose tells that young Richard had "no hobbies, not even [the usual] forms of recreation for rural boys." He loved books, however, and could read well enough to enjoy stories by the time he was five—dog stories, and tales of heroism, loyalty, and persistence. The works of Clarence Buddington Kelland were among his favorites.

Before he was seven, Richard could play the piano reasonably well, and he eventually took both violin and piano lessons, choosing the latter as his favorite. While he was still in grammar school, he stayed with relatives in a nearby town for part of one year so that he could concentrate on his piano music. His interests were in things far beyond his age. His mother often was quoted in later years as saying, "He always carried such a weight," referring to the seriousness with which he took responsibilities.

Whittier became home for the Nixon family after they gave up on citrus farming in 1922. Frank had a short-term job with Union Oil Company, then opened a gas station and general store. Hannah worked for a time at a lemon packinghouse, but she and the boys soon became regular helpers at the store. Richard put in long, hard hours, often rising before dawn when he was in high school to drive into the Los Angeles markets for fresh produce. In his late teens, his mother helped to care for Harold and other patients in a small TB clinic in Arizona. Richard found odd jobs in the summer months (one time as a carnival barker) so that he could be near them and help with expenses. Pinching pennies was a way of life. Recalling the poverty of those early years, Nixon would say, "We had very little ... I wore my brother's shoes and my brother below me wore mine. We never ate out—never. We certainly had to learn the value of money."

EARLY MEMORIES

Nearly every story of Richard Nixon's childhood mentions his vivid memory of being thrown from a buggy and having its rear wheel run over his head. The scar that remained on his scalp throughout his lifetime was merely the visible reminder of such a close call; his enduring mental image was of falling and then running—a panicky little three-year-old boy afraid of being left behind. "I must have been in shock, but I managed to get up and run after the buggy while my mother tried to make the horse stop," he recalled later. Otto Friedrich, writing in *Time* soon after the former president's death, would point to that early episode as symbolic of the heights and depths of Nixon's career, saying that "In a sense, [he] spent his whole life falling and running and falling again."

EDUCATION

Nixon's earliest school years were spent in Yorba Linda. He was, from the beginning, a solemn child who applied himself to his lessons with an earnestness that set him apart from his contemporaries. The family moved to East Whittier when Richard was nine, and there he continued his education. He attended nearby Fullerton High School for two years instead of Whittier High, mainly because his parents had been disappointed with Harold's experience in what they felt was too free an atmosphere. Richard returned to Whittier High for his junior and senior years, graduating in 1930.

Public speaking had become a passion with Nixon by this time. He was a skilled debater, although his approach troubled his high school debate coach, who told author Roger Morris, "there was something mean in the way he argued his points. . . . He cared too much about winning." Still, Nixon excelled as a debater and class leader throughout both high school and four years at Whittier College, where he was elected student body president in his senior year. He would speak later of having to forgo the prospect of partial scholarships to Harvard and Yale because of the dearth of family finances, but it is just as likely that he remained in Whittier because he was needed at home to help in his father's general store and gas station. Harold's health was failing by this time, and a new baby (Edward) had been born the same year as Richard's high school graduation, adding greatly to family responsibilities.

Nixon ranked second in his 1934 Whittier graduating class, earning a B.A. with honors and winning a full-tuition scholarship to law school at Duke University. There, as a competitive speaker and campaigner, he was again elected president of the student body. He received his LL.B. with honors in 1937, graduated third in his class, and was admitted to the California bar later that year.

CHOOSING A CAREER

Home again in Whittier, Nixon joined the law firm of Wingert & Bewley (soon to be Bewley, Knoop & Nixon) and became active in community affairs. He belonged to a number of clubs and a theater group (where he would meet his future wife, Pat), and also began to make public speeches on current issues. Politics had been a consuming interest throughout his school years—almost from the time he learned to read—and now, as World War II loomed closer, he shifted his energies toward government service. In January 1942, about a month after the Japanese attack on Pearl Harbor, Nixon went to Washington as an attorney for the Office of Price Administration. Despite the Quakers' traditional commitment to pacifism, he soon won a Navy commission and served as a ground officer for the Combat Air Transport Command in the South Pacific. An amusing note from a *Time* profile on the former president tells of his card-playing activities during those Navy years and of his remarkable prowess at bluffing in stud poker. "By the end of the war," claims the article, "he had won and saved a stake estimated at as much as $10,000 [substantially more than an average year's salary for a young lawyer in the 1940s]. He invested half of it the following year in launching his political career."

CAREER HIGHLIGHTS

Newly discharged from the Navy in 1946, Nixon embarked upon a political journey that would span nearly a half-century. He unseated a popular five-term Democratic representative from California's Twelfth Congressional District in a hard-hitting campaign, insinuating that his opponent had communist sympathies. At that time strong anticommunist feelings were common throughout the United States. To be branded a communist was the kiss of death for a politician. Nixon later admitted using deceptive tactics, saying, "Of course I knew Jerry Voorhis wasn't a communist, but I had to win. That's the thing you don't understand. The important thing is to win." Years before, that same craftiness had troubled Nixon's high school debate coach.

Nixon served two terms in the U.S. House of Representatives. He was on the subcommittee that drafted the 1947 Taft-Hartley Act (a major law reversing pro-labor policies and restricting political activities of labor unions), but his support of foreign aid and a number of civil rights issues often contradicted his otherwise conservative stance. The work that Nixon contributed to the initial preparation of the renowned Marshall Plan, a program of economic aid to re-build war-devastated Europe, marked his emergence into the sphere of international affairs, the eventual stage for his most noteworthy accomplishments.

Richard Nixon made his leap to national attention in 1948 with his service on the House Committee on Un-American Activities and its investigation of Alger Hiss. Hiss was a respected former State Department official accused of having been a secret Soviet agent during the 1930s. Nixon forced a confrontation between Hiss and his accuser, magazine editor Whittaker Chambers. Claiming that he and the defendant had once belonged to the same communist cell (unit), Chambers was able to produce evidence strongly suggesting the validity of his charges. Hiss vehemently denied guilt, but was convicted of perjury and imprisoned in a highly controversial judgment that is contested to this day. Since then, many have argued that the proceedings were a frightening example of the anticommunist hysteria of the times. Nixon later would point to the Hiss case as the source of hostility toward him by "substantial segments of the press and the intellectual community."

In 1950, Nixon was elected to the Senate by a huge plurality. In that campaign, both candidates stooped to mud-slinging, and Nixon once again struck out with a barrage of communist innuendos. Congresswoman Helen Gahagan Douglas, a vocal supporter of the New Deal (an economic recovery and social reform policy begun in the 1930s by President Franklin D. Roosevelt), was no match for her Republican opponent. It was Douglas who characterized him as "Tricky Dick," a name that would stick to him throughout his political life.

Nixon served two years in the Senate before becoming the running mate of Dwight D. Eisenhower, the immensely popular wartime general chosen in 1952 as Republican nominee for president. Vigorously campaigning against corruption and communism, the vice-presidential candidate was dealt a severe blow when he was accused of improperly benefiting from an $18,000 "slush" fund set up by his California backers. His defense was quick and desperate in the now-famous and emotional "Checkers" speech. He insisted that he had received no personal gifts except that of a little black and white dog, Checkers, and that his wife Pat rejected luxury items in favor of a "good Republican cloth coat." The televised defense saved Nixon's candidacy, and the Eisenhower-Nixon ticket went on to victory.

His two terms as vice president showcased Richard Nixon's considerable political savvy and his growing mastery of foreign affairs as he traveled around the globe on diplomatic missions and goodwill tours. Only 40 at the time of his inauguration, and with a mere six years of experience in government service, he took on his role with eagerness and skill—and with a visibility seldom before noted in that post. At the end of Eisenhower's term in 1960, Nixon won his party's nomination for the presidency, but narrowly lost the election to the Democratic candidate,

Sen. John F. Kennedy of Massachusetts. The crushing defeat sent Nixon home to California, where he became counsel for a brief period to a Los Angeles law firm. In 1962, he reentered public life, running for governor of California against the incumbent, Edmund G. (Pat) Brown, but failed in his bid. Nixon bitterly blamed both that loss and his 1960 defeat on the media. He moved to New York and into corporate law with a Wall Street firm.

THE WHITE HOUSE—AND THE WATERGATE CRISIS

Nixon spent the next six years carefully rebuilding his political prestige. In 1968, he entered the presidential race against Hubert H. Humphrey, the candidate of a seriously divided Democratic Party. This time success was his. On January 20, 1969, Richard Milhous Nixon was sworn in as the 37th president of the United States.

His first term produced a number of positive elements, among them the establishment of the Environmental Protection Agency, the lowering of the voting age to 18, proposed reforms of the welfare system, and the launching of the war on cancer. However, Nixon's most striking accomplishments were two shrewd foreign-policy maneuvers: his visit to Beijing, where he reopened relations between mainland China and the United States; and his successful strategic-arms bargaining in Moscow, with its ensuing détente (relaxation of tensions between the U.S. and the

Soviet Union). However, America's continuing involvement in Vietnam cast a pall over these achievements. A major campaign promise had been to end the controversial war in Southeast Asia. But as negotiations floundered abroad and antiwar demonstrations escalated at home, Nixon grew furious with a balky Democratic Congress and what he had long perceived as a hostile liberal press.

In 1971, the Supreme Court upheld the right of news organizations to publish the Pentagon Papers, a collection of classified documents on the Vietnam War. In response, Nixon angrily and recklessly took action to keep his initiatives secret and to circumvent leaks of information: he authorized the acceleration of an already established pattern of illegal conduct—phone taps, tape recordings, falsified records, and surveillance in search of damaging information to sabotage his political "enemies." Disclosure of these tactics would not come to light for nearly two years, in spite of the notorious 1972 break-in at Democratic National Headquarters in Washington's Watergate office complex. At the time, there was nothing to connect the aborted burglary with the president, although subpoenaed tapes eventually revealed that this and a whole series of misdeeds were perpetrated by the White House or its operatives. But at that point in 1972, Nixon was in the midst of a vigorous reelection campaign that would carry him to a landslide victory that autumn. He effected a Vietnam peace accord (after unsanctioned bombing in North Vietnam and Cambodia) as he took his second oath of office but, says *Newsweek*, "the Watergate conspiracy was steadily unraveling, and so was his presidency."

The next 18 months saw the nation in a constitutional crisis. The investigation of the break-in at Watergate led to a complex trail of crimes and misdemeanors implicating the president. Nineteen of his associates and advisers eventually were imprisoned for their involvement, and Nixon engineered a frantic cover-up to protect his presidency. The nation was shocked again when tapes of conversations taken in the Oval Office revealed not only his complicity in the Watergate affair, but his vulgarity and malice, his obsession with silencing his enemies, and his ruthlessness. He was fighting for what he termed "executive privilege" on constitutional grounds, but it turned out that he was using the power of his office to cover up his own misdeeds. Ultimately, after the House Judiciary Committee had recommended his impeachment, Richard Nixon resigned, leaving Washington in disgrace on August 9, 1974. He was the only U.S. president ever to be driven from office. His successor, Gerald Ford, saved him from prosecution with a presidential pardon, and the acceptance of that pardon was his sole, and unspoken, confession of guilt. Columnist Michael Gartner, writing in *USA Today* soon after Nixon's recent death, recalled the crisis as "a frightening moment for democracy."

THE ROAD BACK

Depression and physical illness kept Nixon out of the public eye for the first few years. In 1978, he moved east with his wife from their California home, first to New York and then to New Jersey. He renewed his contacts and quietly tried to rebuild his reputation. He began to offer his views on global policy, and his perspective and wealth of experience brought him growing prominence as an international authority and elder statesman. By the time of his death, he was seen by some as he wished to be seen. Some came to regard him as "an inspiring example of dogged determination in the face of adversity," wrote *U.S. News & World Report*. In that article, Nixon's opponent in the 1972 presidential race, George McGovern, was quoted as saying, "I developed a kind of grudging respect for him. Not too many people could psychologically withstand being thrown out of the White House. It takes an enormous amount of self-discipline that I had to recognize was remarkable."

Five living presidents—Gerald Ford, Jimmy Carter, Ronald Reagan, George Bush, and Bill Clinton—attended Richard Nixon's funeral April 27, 1994, on the lawn in front of his Yorba Linda birthplace. "He would be so proud," said Henry Kissinger, once Nixon's secretary of state, "that President Clinton [and the former chief executives] are here, symbolizing that his long and sometimes bitter journey had concluded in reconciliation."

NIXON'S LEGACY

The Nixon era marked an end to the so-called "Imperial Presidency" in the U.S., as the balance of power began to shift away from the executive branch and toward Congress. The power of the press also began to rise in the wake of Watergate, as public oficials were subjected to the glare of scrutiny in unprecedented fashion. Since Nixon's time, every major investigation into the abuse of power has include the tagline "-gate," such as "Irangate," the investigation into the diversion of funds during the presidency of Ronald Reagan, or the current "Whitewatergate," the investigation into a failed savings and loan and alleged misuse of power involving Bill and Hillary Clinton. A wariness of political power and a watchdog stance against its abuse may be Nixon's unwitting legacy to the country he longed to serve, and the office he lost in disgrace.

MARRIAGE AND FAMILY

Richard Nixon was married for 53 years to the former Thelma Catherine Ryan, a high school business subjects teacher whom he had met during tryouts for a local theater production in Whittier. Mrs. Nixon, born in the frontier town of Ely, Nevada, March 16, 1912—the day before St. Patrick's Day—was appropriately nicknamed Pat by her Irish father; she formally changed her middle name to Patricia in her father's memory after his death in 1930. Although she projected an air of restraint and "aloof friendliness," as once described by a friend, Pat was a woman who had built a strong sense of self in spite of years of poverty and self-sacrificing family responsibilities. She did not respond enthusiastically at first to Nixon's romantic pursuit but, after two years of courtship, the couple married on June 21, 1940, at the Mission Inn in Riverside, California.

Roger Morris, in *Richard Milhous Nixon*, his biography of the former president, noted that Nixon's life "took a new direction [the day of his marriage]. He had wed a woman of matching resolve, of comparable if not larger ambition, of perhaps greater strength, and he had won her in a supplicant's courtship that gave her substance all the more force in their early relationship." Pat Nixon's image to the world was that of a wife who retired to the background of her husband's burgeoning career yet, in her subtle way, she became his goodwill ambassador during the presidential years. It was clear to those who knew her well that she remained a source of unwavering strength to him in his most tragic moments. Mrs. Nixon died of cancer in June 1993.

Two daughters were born to the Nixons—Patricia (Tricia), on February 21, 1946, in Whittier, and Julie, on July 5, 1948, in Washington, D.C. Tricia is married to Edward Finch Cox, and Julie is married to Dwight David Eisenhower II, the grandson of the man whom her father served twice as vice president.

There are four Nixon grandchildren: Christopher Cox, and Jennie, Alex, and Melanie Eisenhower.

HOBBIES AND OTHER INTERESTS

Nixon was an avid sports fan. Most of all, he loved to watch football, the game that he doggedly had tried to play both in high school and at tiny Whittier College. Friends from his youth would tell biographer Morris in later years about Nixon's ineptness and lack of coordination on the field, but they never failed to mention, as well, his bulldog tenacity—"he'd get knocked down and come right back" . . . "he was always there for every practice" . . . "I don't know a guy that ever tried so hard, really."

In his middle years, the former president played a respectable game of golf and held a 175 bowling average. Music and reading, both more suited to his solitary nature, were among his other interests. He listened to symphonic music and continued to play the piano for relaxation, and was said to have spent long hours with his books.

WRITINGS

Six Crises, 1962
RN: The Memoirs of Richard Nixon, 1978
The Real War, 1980

Leaders, 1982
Real Peace: A Strategy for the West, 1984
No More Vietnams, 1985
1999: Victory Without War, 1988
In The Arena: A Memoir of Victory, Defeat and Renewal, 1990
Seize the Moment: America's Challenge in a One-Superpower World, 1992
Beyond Peace, 1994 (completed a few days before Nixon's death, and published on the day of his funeral, April 27, 1994)

Nixon also was the author of official reports, policy statements, speeches, tributes, and numerous other published texts.

FURTHER READING

BOOKS

Aiken, Jonathan. *Nixon: A Life*, 1994 (first published in England, 1992)
Ambrose, Stephen E. *Nixon: The Education of a Politician, 1913-1962*, 1987
─────. *Nixon: Ruin and Recovery, 1973-1990*, 1991
Bernstein, Carl, and Bob Woodward. *All the President's Men*, 1974
Eisenhower, Julie Nixon. *Pat Nixon: The Untold Story*, 1986
Haldeman, H.R. *The Haldeman Diaries: Inside the Nixon White House*, 1994
Woodward, Bob, and Carl Bernstein. *The Final Days*, 1976

PERIODICALS

Detroit Free Press, Apr. 23, 1994, p.1A; Apr. 28, 1994, p.1A; May 17, 1994, p.5A; May 20, 1994, p. 11A
Insight, Dec. 28, 1992, p.23
Newsweek, May 2, 1994, p.20
New Yorker, Dec. 14, 1992, p.76
New York Times, Dec. 16, 1993, p.A17; Mar. 25, 1994, p.A29; Apr. 23, 1994; p.A1; Apr. 24, p.A1; Apr. 28, 1994, p.A1
Time, May 2, 1994, p.26; May 9, 1994, p.48
U.S. News & World Report, Oct. 25, 1993, p.46; May 2, 1994, pp.24, 34, 37
USA Today, Apr. 25, 1994, p.10A; Apr. 27, 1994, p.11A

Greg Norman 1955-
Australian Professional Golfer Known as the "Great White Shark"
Two-Time Winner of the British Open Championship

BIRTH

Gregory John Norman was born February 10, 1955, in the rural town of Mt. Isa in Queensland, Australia, to Mervyn and Toini (Hovi) Norman. His father worked for the large Mt. Isa Mining Company in the first months of Greg's life, but soon moved the family away to the coast to establish his own professional engineering business. Toini Norman, the daughter of Finnish immigrants, was an accomplished amateur golfer who played with a handicap of 3 for 18 holes of golf. (In golf, a "handicap" is the number of strokes a player shoots above "par," or the standard number of strokes for each hole). It was through Toini that Greg eventually became interested in the game that would shape his life.

The only other child in the Norman family was Greg's sister, Janis, two years his senior.

YOUTH

Greg was still a baby when his family left the outback (Australia's bush country), so his memories begin in the northeastern port city of Townsville on Halifax Bay, an inlet of the Pacific Ocean. There, Greg grew up in a tropical setting—skindiving, sailing competitively, fishing, riding and, like most Australian boys, playing rugby. "Life," he says, "rolled on easily and comfortably, with the need to study occasionally punctuating an otherwise perfect outdoors existence."

The childhood adventures related in his autobiography, *Greg Norman: My Story*, read like a storybook. He tells of lengthy trips with school friends Peter and David Hay on their father's cruiser, spearfishing among the coral islands in the Great Barrier Reef and anchoring in sheltered coves at night to build campfires and sleep under the stars. Tales of sailing in the *Peter Pan*, a small boat built for Janis and Greg by their father, and of horseback riding for miles along Queensland's sandy beaches add still other colorful elements to his fond memories of a boyhood spent outdoors. Those years in the sun and the surf have intensified Greg Norman's startlingly Nordic coloring, but he explains that the blond—almost white—hair, which he calls his "fair thatch," is basically inherited from his Finnish mother and his father's mixed Scandinavian, German, and English heritage.

EARLY MEMORIES

Among the youthful times Greg remembers best is a several-week stay on a cattle station (ranch) when he was barely into his teen years. Merv Norman had arranged the adventure because his young son was so keen on horses and outdoor life. At the station, Greg rode along with the seasoned cowboys (called jackeroos in Australia), rounding up the strays and separating cattle from the herd for slaughter. "It was hard bush work," he remembers, "and I loved the chase," but he confesses that some of the gorier tasks involved were distasteful enough to dissuade him from any thoughts of life as a range herder.

EDUCATION

Greg attended the local schools in Townsville, but didn't enjoy it at all. "To say I disliked school would about sum up my approach to the world of learning," he says in his autobiography. He managed to pass all his subjects and remembers being relatively good at geography and technical drawing, but hating French.

FIRST JOBS

Greg's first paychecks were earned with backbreaking work during his high school years. He and a friend found jobs at the Australian Match Manufacturing Company where, during school holidays, they sawed huge logs into smaller sections, soaked them in boiling water, then scraped bark from the almost unmanageable billets in preparation for further processing. "It did not take me long to realize that there were easier ways of making a dollar," he said later.

By the time he finished high school, Norman had abandoned thoughts of either a university degree or an air force career, mainly because of his mediocre grades, but also because he was put off by the long years of required study. By his own admission, he drifted for 12 months, "mostly doing nothing," until the sheer boredom of being a beach bum—and a near-drowning experience in the ocean—made him think about pursuing a professional golf career. Norman needed to earn his own money to finance his plans, since his parents had little reason to believe that he would stay focused. He took a part-time packing job at Precision Golf Forgings company warehouse in Brisbane, arranging his hours so that he could hurry off every afternoon to practice, often until darkness fell.

CHOOSING A CAREER

It was almost by chance that Greg Norman became a golfer at all. One day when he was about sixteen, he offered to caddy for his mother. When she finished her round, he borrowed her clubs, headed straight for the fairways, and started swinging. His natural athleticism helped him to make enough good shots to tempt him back to the course again and again. Soon he was, in his own words, "hooked." He practiced diligently, and lowered his handicap from 27 to zero within two years, making a name for himself in amateur play. But it was not until he had left his surfing days behind him that he finally devoted himself exclusively to golf.

By the time he was 20, Norman was already a dominant amateur player who had captured the Queensland Junior Tournament and earned an entry into the Australian Open. He turned pro. He had convinced his parents of his determination to play professional golf, and they were solidly behind the decision. His first job at a club was at the Beverley Park Golf Club in Sydney, New South Wales (NSW), 500 miles from home. There, he rose each morning at daybreak to practice before working long hours in the pro shop and again late every evening retrieving balls on the driving range.

Frustrated less by the rigorous work than by restrictive NSW rules, Norman returned to Brisbane after a few months, hoping for a better chance to round out his training schedule with tournament play. In 1975 he was taken on at Royal Queensland, his home course, by Charlie Earp, the teaching professional who is largely credited with developing Norman's aggressive game.

CAREER HIGHLIGHTS

Norman was winning trainee championships much of the time during his early years on the Australian pro tour, but his important breakthrough came in the third pro tournament he ever played. He won the West Lakes Classic in Adelaide (South Australia) in 1976, beating out his country's greats as well as a number of well-known international players. The young prodigy from the north was on his way, and in his pocket was $7,000 in first-prize money—"more money than I had ever seen," he says. His trip to the tournament had been financed through an award offered by a Queensland golf shoe manufacturer, but in those early days on the tour he was also supplementing his meager income by wagering on his matches at his home course. Norman reveals that his parents "would have been horrified" at the extent of his golf-course gambling, yet he defends the practice, saying that his wins helped pay for his later trips. Gambling also taught him something about pressure, since he refused sponsorship and counted on his betting wins to pay his own way.

Between 1979 and 1984, the year he became a regular on the American PGA (Professional Golf Association) circuit, Norman had racked up 28 tour victories at home and abroad. Among these were the Hong Kong Open, the Suntory World Match Play, and the Dunlop Masters (twice each), as well as the 1980 Australian Open.

The PGA Tour includes many of the most prestigious tournaments in golf, including the Masters, the PGA Championship, and the U.S. Open. Norman first came to the attention of American fans with his fourth-place finish at the 1981 Masters Tournament in Augusta, Georgia, and in 1983 he finished well enough to collect prize money in nine PGA events. The 1984 Kemper Open was Norman's first victory on the PGA tour. Just two weeks later, he lost to Fuzzy Zoeller in a playoff at the U.S. Open, but went on later that season to beat his longtime hero, Jack Nicklaus, in the Canadian Open. By this time, his following was growing steadily and, in reference to his appearance and background, he had already acquired the nickname, "Great White Shark."

Norman's formidable swing (clocked at 130 miles per hour) and his cheerful personality made him a popular figure in the golfing world. One well-remembered incident from those days is his good-humored acceptance of loss in the 1984 U.S. Open, when he playfully flipped his white towel in surrender to Zoeller—he had come from behind for a good chance at the title but, in losing, was gracious enough to hide his frustration. For a young man who had displayed fits of temper on the golf course during his teen years, he had taught himself to be a good loser, and the fans loved it.

THE BEST YEARS AND THE WORST

The span between the middle of 1986 and the middle of 1987 saw Norman riding a high wave. He won the coveted British Open in 1986 with an even-par 280, including "a second-round 63," wrote Jaime Diaz in the *New York Times*, "that many considered the finest round ever played in a major championship." That year he led going into the finals of all four major tournaments—the Masters, U.S. Open, PGA, and British Open—but suffered back-to-back heartbreaks in the final strokes of each. Norman captured ten individual championships during that 1986-87 period, however, and was a second-time team winner of the Dunhill Cup.

The next few years brought 15 more victories, but also more than a fair share of disappointments. Rumors abounded that Norman was overrated, too aggressive, short on strategy, and showing strain. Then came a 27-month winless drought, with 1991 admittedly the most dismal year in his career to date. He fell to fifty-third place on the money list after being first in two of the previous five seasons. He seriously considered quitting, but his basic competitive nature kept him focused, and he went to work on refining his game.

The efforts paid off the next year with eight top-ten finishes in 16 starts, capped by victory over Bruce Lietzke in the Canadian Open. Greg Norman was back on his game, and up to fourth place in the world. The Doral Ryder Open was his in 1993, when he broke the tournament record by four points with a 23-under par total.

Then, in July 1993 at Royal St. George's in Sandwich, England, he claimed the British Open title for the second time in his career. When he edged out No. 1 Nick Faldo, it was with a 64—the lowest winning final round in British Open history. This is only the latest chapter in the celebrated career of Greg Norman. The years of hard work and perseverance have paid off: in 17 years in the fiercely competitive world of international golf, he has achieved 65 victories to date.

THE GREAT WHITE SHARK

The nickname, "Great White Shark," which has followed Greg Norman throughout his career, came about almost by chance, but it is so appropriate to his blond, swashbuckling, Crocodile Dundee image that he is easily identifiable even to those who are not golf enthusiasts. More than a dozen years ago, when he was new to the U.S. scene and high on the leader board at the 1981 Masters tournament, he brashly answered a reporter's inquiries about his pastimes, saying that he loved to scuba dive and to fish for sharks (not totally accurate, he admits—actually, he mainly took pot shots at sharks who interfered with his catch on fishing expeditions). The parallel fit, however, and a newspaper headline claimed, "Great White Shark Near Masters Lead." The name stuck. "I don't know who wrote it," says Norman. "Some guy in Augusta. I'd [like to] thank him, because the guy made a hell of a lot of money for me . . . . I love the image all the way through. It suits me. I do live on the edge. I do love to fish. I dive with the sharks. The blond hair, the aggressive style, it all fits together well."

MARRIAGE AND FAMILY

Norman met his future wife, American Airlines flight attendant Laura Andrassy, en route from Detroit to New York after the 1979 Open at Inverness in Toledo, Ohio. She was impressed by his gentlemanly manners and quick smile, and their infatuation soon bloomed into a real romance. They were married July 1, 1981, at St. Mary's Church in Springfield, Virginia.

The Normans have two children. Daughter Morgan Leigh was born in 1982, and son Gregory three years later. The family lives on a multi-acre spread at Hobe Sound, Florida, where the main house overlooks the Indian River and a beach house sits at the edge of the Atlantic Ocean. "I've got the best of every world I could ever imagine," he says, "as a kid growing up and as an adult being able to afford it." Friends seeing the family together are warmed by the closeness of their relationships. Morgan Leigh, who alternately calls her father "Dad" and "Sharkie," was affectionately dubbed "Little White Shark" herself when, as a toddler, she often romped in front of television cameras at golf tournaments. Both she and her brother hold dual Australian/U.S. citizenship, and they can make a choice of the two when they reach adulthood. Greg Norman enjoys and appreciates his life in this country, but takes great pride in being Australian. He plans to retire someday to his homeland, where he and Laura hope to buy and operate a cattle station either in Queensland or New South Wales. "I love my country so much," he says. . . . I'm very patriotic. I guess I want to die there."

MAJOR INFLUENCES

Several people have had a positive impact on Norman's professional life, but no one more so than Charlie Earp, the head pro who trained him in Brisbane. It was Earp who wisely used the unorthodox approach of encouraging Greg's rough and powerful game before helping him to fine-tune it for control. "Norman became so determined to improve," his mentor laughingly recalled several years later, "I had to bar him from the bloody course. He practiced so much, it looked like bloody pigs had been rooting up the fairway." To this day, though, Greg Norman practices with the same discipline that he imposed upon himself in his early days under Earp's tutelage. He keeps a written record of his practice sessions and his progress.

Jack Nicklaus, already a famous golfer when Norman was still a teenager surfing and snorkeling in Australian waters, also became a strong influence—years before the two met. Toini Norman had given her son two of Nicklaus's books, *Golf My Way* and *55 Ways to Lower Your Golf Score,* when she noticed his first spark of real interest in the sport. Reading the American pro's advice (sometimes under the desk at school) helped Greg to develop his fledgling game. "Jack Nicklaus has always been my idol," he says. Later, on the pro tour, the two men became friends and competitors whose similarities in play and courteous demeanor, and even in appearance at comparative ages, have often been noted.

Others have played important roles in shaping Greg Norman's career, among them his mother, whose enthusiasm for golf was the key, and his strong-willed father, whose sense of discipline was the engine that drove him to excel. Norman concedes that he is "basically the same" as his father, who has always believed in doing things "right now" and "doing them *right.*"

HOBBIES AND OTHER INTERESTS

Golf, with its prize money and the millions more it brings in endorsements, has made it easy for Greg Norman to indulge his other passions—boating, deep-sea fishing, hunting, and fast, pricey automobiles. He owns

Ferraris, an Aston Martin, and a Rolls Royce, as well as the more commonplace wheels needed for family transport.

But sports and fast cars are only part of Norman's life. He is a major sponsor of Ronald McDonald Children's Charities and hosts an annual golf tournament to benefit its activities. He also donates all profits from a book that tells the touchingly human story of his friendship with Jamie Hutton, a young Wisconsin leukemia victim whose wish to meet Norman was granted by the Thursday's Child Foundation. Hutton's dream came true when he bravely walked along with his hero on the last two rounds of the 1988 MCI Heritage Golf Classic, inspiring the Great White Shark to win his first American victory in nearly two years.

WRITINGS

Greg Norman: My Story (with Don Lawrence), 1983
Shark Attack! Greg Norman's Guide to Aggressive Golf (with George Peper), 1989
Greg Norman's Instant Lessons (with George Peper and Jim McQueen), 1993

HONORS AND AWARDS

Canadian Open: 1984, 1992
Kemper Open: 1984, 1986
British Open: 1986, 1993
Arnold Palmer Award (Professional Golfers Association): 1986
Player of the Year (Golf Writers Association of America): 1986
Mary Bea Porter Award for Humanitarianism (Metro Golf Writers Association): 1988
Vardon Trophy (Professional Golfers Association): 1989, 1990

FURTHER READING

BOOKS

Creighton, Susan. *Greg Norman*, 1988 (juvenile)
Hobbs, Michael. *Fifty Masters of Golf*, 1983
Levy, Lawrence, and Gordon White, Jr. *A Victory for Jamie: The Story of Greg Norman and Jamie Hutton*, 1989
Norman, Greg, with Don Lawrence. *Greg Norman: My Story*, 1983
Norman, Greg, and George Peper. *Shark Attack! Greg Norman's Guide to Aggressive Golf*, 1989
Norman, Greg, and George Peper, with Jim McQueen, illustrator. *Greg Norman's Instant Lessons*, 1993
Who's Who in America, 1992-93

PERIODICALS

Current Biography Yearbook 1989
Golf, June 1990, p.47; Apr. 1991, p.68; Feb. 1992, p.58; Aug. 1993, p.12
Golf Digest, Oct. 1989, p.95; Nov. 1989, p.57; Dec. 1992, p.158
New York Times, July 20, 1993, p.B10
People, Apr. 13, 1987, p.149
Sport, Sep. 1987, p.23
Sporting News, July 9, 1990, p.44
Sports Illustrated, July 28, 1986, p.14; Apr. 20, 1987, p.36; June 22, 1987, p.32; Oct. 28, 1991, p.6; July 26, 1993, p.12; Aug. 23, 1993, p.14
Time, Nov. 21, 1988, p.118

ADDRESS

Great White Shark Enterprises
P.O. Box 1189
Hobe Sound, FL 33475

BRIEF ENTRY—OBITUARY

Severo Ochoa   1905-1993
Spanish-Born American Biochemist
Winner of the 1959 Nobel Prize in Physiology and Medicine

EARLY LIFE AND CAREER

Severo Ochoa (say-VAY-roh oh-CHOH-ah) was born on September 24, 1905, in the Spanish coastal town of Luarca. He excelled in school, particularly in chemistry, and he attended the University of Madrid Medical School at 17. He was always more interested in conducting medical research than in treating patients, so when he received his degree in 1929 he began working in the physiology lab of Dr. Otto Meyorhoff in Germany. There he concentrated on how enzymes—complex proteins—function. He returned to Spain in the 1930s and taught at the University of Madrid Medical School, but when the Spanish Civil War broke out, Ochoa decided to return to Germany and to Dr. Meyerhoff's lab.

From Germany he moved first to Oxford University in England and then to the U.S., where he became a citizen in 1956. He taught at Washington University in St. Louis, then at New York University, eventually becoming the chairman of the department of biochemistry.

MAJOR ACCOMPLISHMENTS

THE NOBEL PRIZE

Ochoa received the Nobel Prize in Physiology and Medicine in 1959 for his discovery of an enzyme that could synthesize RNA (ribonucleic acid). RNA is the acid that takes the instructions of DNA (deoxyribonucleic acid) and transforms them into information used by genes for making protein. Ochoa's research led to the making of RNA in a test tube. Until that was possible, scientists were unable to determine how the information contained in RNA was decoded and translated into a protein. Ochoa shared the Nobel with his colleague Dr. Arthur Kornberg, who had been a former student. Of Ochoa's importance to science, Kornberg had this to say: "His contribution to biochemistry is gigantic and easily accounts for the wide recognition he has had."

Ochoa returned to Spain in 1986, and he died in Madrid on November 1, 1993, of pneumonia. His wife, Carmen, had died in 1986. They had no children.

FURTHER READING

New York Times, Nov. 3, 1993, p.C23
Who's Who in America, 1990-91

OBITUARY

River Phoenix   1970-1993
American Film Star
Actor Acclaimed for His Work in *Stand By Me* and *My Own Private Idaho*

BIRTH

River Jude Phoenix was born in a log cabin in Madras, Oregon, on August 23, 1970. His parents, John and Arlyn "Heart" Phoenix, were itinerant fruit pickers living a bohemian lifestyle in the nation's northwest at the time of his birth. He was the eldest of their five children, all but one of whom were given ethereal names to harmonize in spirit with the surname the couple would eventually borrow from the phoenix, the mythical bird who burned itself on a pyre and rose again from the ashes as a symbol of regeneration and hope.

John and Arlyn chose for their firstborn a symbolic name, after the river of life in the Hermann Hesse novel, *Siddhartha*, then a cult classic. Their daughters were named in the same fashion: Rainbow Joan of Arc, called Rain; Libertad Mariposa, translated into Liberty Butterfly and shortened to Libby; and Summer Joy. The family's only other boy, Joaquin Rafael, asked at the age of four to change his name so that he could be like the others. Given permission by his father (who was raking leaves at the time), he chose Leaf. Several years ago, Arlyn explained their unusual names in *Interview* magazine: "Those are all such beautiful things. We just wanted to remind people of the beauty around them." John Phoenix's daughter from his first marriage, Jo Dean, is now called Trust, and her young daughter is named Victory.

YOUTH

The first seven years of River Phoenix's life were rather unconventional. After his birth, he traveled with his parents around the West in an old Volkswagen bus, stopping where John and Arlyn could find odd jobs and where their vision of a natural, spiritual life could be nurtured. Their background was average enough by the standards of the time. Arlyn Dunetz, or Heart, as she prefers, was a Manhattan secretary who left husband and job in the late 1960s to seek a different kind of life. John, who refuses to divulge his true surname, was a furniture refinisher anxious to sever ties with a rough and unhappy past. Arlyn and John met as kindred souls in California—she was hitchhiking when he picked her up. As River said years later, "they decided to drop out and find themselves. They're still looking."

In Colorado, the young couple chose religion as their alternative to the psychedelic drugs they had been using. They joined a Christian commune and began a strange and uncharted journey as missionaries for a sect called Children of God. After Rain, their second child, was born in Texas, they took off for Mexico, Puerto Rico, and Venezuela. At the time, River was only two. The family grew, and so, eventually, did the parents' disillusionment with the Children of God and what they deemed its unseemly practices. They sneaked away from the cult, with no money, four little kids, and no immediate means of support. In Venezuela, River and Rainbow sang on Caracas street corners and in front of tourist hotels for whatever *centimos* they could get to buy food for their family. "A lot of the songs were religious and positive," remembered River. "[Songs] like 'You Gotta Be a Baby to Go to Heaven.' That's what we were into."

The Phoenix family endured abject poverty after their defection from the Children of God. They scratched for sustenance and prayed for guidance while living in a hut on the beach at Caracas. River, the eldest, remembered it well: "We had nothing at all. [The hut] was infested with rats and the ceiling had flying cockroaches, but there were banana trees outside and that was my reality. I wasn't unhappy. . . . I was just living."

HOME AGAIN

River's nomadic, counter-culture childhood continued when the family returned to the United States in 1978. Freighter passage had been arranged to Florida by a priest acquaintance, but lean times continued and a sort of hand-to-mouth existence became the norm. John, who had been working as a gardener, injured his back, and Arlyn had to fill in with odd jobs in addition to caring for the children, who now numbered five. The parents, although jaded by their religious experience, hung on to their off-beat lifestyle, and their children flourished, nourished by the environment of love and caring that Arlyn and John created and by their shared sense of purpose. "The family set a goal," Phoenix once said, "through any talents that we might develop, to better the world, to have a positive influence. Think globally, act locally, that sort of thing . . . . Just doing our part. We didn't want to be selfish and into material things and [just] make money." It was at this difficult time that Arlyn and John chose the surname Phoenix as their symbol of new hope.

Encouraged by River and Rain's developing talent, the family finally set out for California in a dilapidated station wagon, this time pinning their dreams on the two little performers—now nine and seven years old. "I figured I'd play guitar and sing with my sister," recalled River, "and we would be on television the next day. We were really naive." They repeated their Caracas street-corner performances in Los Angeles while Arlyn looked for work. After she found a secretarial job with NBC in Los Angeles, she quickly lined up an agent to promote her children's talent.

EDUCATION

One of the most startling facts about the knowledgeable and articulate River Phoenix was his lack of formal education. He dropped out of school by the fourth grade, saying later, "I didn't have the time once I was working, or the energy. I do miss it, and a part of me knows that I could really have been influenced by it."

Although he didn't attend school, River was far from uneducated. Details are sketchy about this facet of his short life, but River Phoenix is said to have been instructed at home by a tutor, Ed Squires, who obviously exposed the boy (and his siblings) to books and music and other stimulating educational experiences.

CHOOSING A CAREER

Television commercials were River's first foray into show business. However, since he had been raised, as he said, "in an atmosphere of purity and truth," he was turned off by being paid to be phony. He wanted to be a serious actor and, at age 11, began his rise to stardom with 22 appearances in the CBS television series, *Seven Brides for Seven Brothers*. He also played guitar and sang with sister Rain on the daytime series *Fantasy*.

CAREER HIGHLIGHTS

River made his film debut in 1985 in the science-fiction adventure *Explorers*, but it was his evocative role as the tough-but-tender teenage ringleader in the sleeper hit *Stand By Me* (1986) that brought him into media focus. Even wider attention came that same year when he co-starred with Harrison Ford in *The Mosquito Coast*, an adaptation of the novel by Paul Theroux. "Much of the plot—the South American odyssey of an American dreamer's family—mirrored Phoenix's actual upbringing," noted Dan Yorkin in an *Us* feature soon afterward.

The roles kept coming. Even as the public became more aware of him as an exciting new actor, he seemed to maintain an unspoiled attitude about his meteoric rise. He was quoted as saying he wanted to stay away from the bad influences and superficial values of Hollywood, and when his parents and siblings moved back to Florida (their fortieth move in 20 years), he counted their home as his own, joining them after each shoot. "The Phoenixes are a team, a tribe, and a set of beliefs," said *Premiere* magazine in 1988. "River can lose himself in a role because his family provides him with a physical, emotional, and spiritual center. Somebody's home in his eyes because somebody's home at home, too." Phoenix, unlike some young actors, seemed sure to avoid the excesses of Hollywood.

In the late 1980s, Phoenix took on, for the first time, a lighter role when he starred in a romantic comedy, *A Night in the Life of Jimmy Reardon* (1988). In his first leading role, he played a hard-drinking teenager who loses his virginity to an older woman. The movie did not draw kudos. The money from his films, though, was giving the members of his family a more financially stable existence than they had ever known. His siblings started finding TV movies or guest spots on established series. John and Arlyn took over the management of their talented children's careers.

After River's *Jimmy Reardon* role came *Little Nikita*, then *Running on Empty* (1988). In this Sidney Lumet film, he played the son of fugitive 1960s political activists on the run. For this moving performance, which in many ways mirrored his own life, he received an Oscar nomination as best supporting actor. *Indiana Jones and the Last Crusade*, a big-budget movie, followed in 1989, and Phoenix was fast making his mark. He worked for some of the movie industry's best directors and shared billing with well-established stars. Considered one of the most gifted actors of his generation, he was widely praised for his sensitive, poignant, emotionally intense performances: "You saw this purity, this incandescence," director Sidney Lumet explained. No one could have imagined that Phoenix would make only a few more films, including the widely acclaimed *My Own Private Idaho* (1991), in which the actor played a narcoleptic teenage hustler living on the streets. For that intense performance, he won the prestigious Venice Film Festival Award and the National Society of Film Critics Award. *Dark Blood*, Phoenix's next project, was never completed.

A TRAGIC END

Colleagues and fans were stunned when filmdom's model of health and clean living fell victim to the excesses of a life that he had purportedly disdained. The 23-year-old Phoenix collapsed and died of a drug overdose on October 31, 1993, outside a trendy West Hollywood nightclub where he had hung out with the regulars and sometimes played guitar. The actor lay thrashing in convulsions on the sidewalk while his frantic brother called for help, and his sister threw herself on his body in a futile attempt to calm the seizures. Passersby, none of whom recognized him, "treated the crisis," said one news report, "as nonchalantly as a Hollywood Halloween freak show."

The image that many shared of River Phoenix—as an idealist, a preserver of the earth, a dedicated vegetarian, a well grounded person—was shattered with the coroner's report. Autopsy results showed that the actor had died of acute multiple drug intoxication, involving lethal levels of cocaine and heroin, the same mix that had snuffed out the life of comedian John Belushi 11 years earlier. Toxicological tests also detected marijuana, Valium, and an over-the-counter cold medication. "Sadly," wrote Matthew Gilbert in the *Boston Globe*, a generation has found its own James Dean in River Phoenix."

"Every generation faces moments when the myth of its own immortality is shattered. Somebody young and beautiful dies, somebody who, like them, was going to live forever. In the 50s it was James Dean. In the acid-mad 60s it was Jimi Hendrix, and Jim Morrison, and Janis Joplin. For today's teenagers death claimed its first victim this week, an intense actor named River Phoenix," wrote the *New York Times* shortly after his death. "Doubtless there will be other such deaths; and no one knows whether this young man's life will turn into legend. But his passing is particularly sad because, to many in his generation, River Phoenix had something beyond the bratty appeal of a Christian Slater or a Johnny Depp; something thoughtful, caught in the same conundrums. They had looked forward to growing up with him. Now that's not going to happen."

HONORS AND AWARDS

National Society of Film Critics Award: 1988, for Best Supporting Actor in *Running on Empty*; 1991, for Best Actor in *My Own Private Idaho*
Venice Film Festival Award: 1992, for Best Actor in *My Own Private Idaho*

ACTING CREDITS

FILMS

Explorers, 1985
The Mosquito Coast, 1986
Stand By Me, 1986
Little Nikita, 1988
A Night in the Life of Jimmy Reardon, 1988
Running on Empty, 1988
Indiana Jones and the Last Crusade, 1989
I Love You to Death, 1990
Dogfight, 1991
My Own Private Idaho, 1991
Sneakers, 1992
The Thing Called Love, 1993
Silent Tongue, 1994

TV

"Seven Brides for Seven Brothers," 1982-83
"Robert Kennedy and His Times" (Part 3), 1985
"Surviving," 1985

FURTHER READING

BOOKS

Catalano, Grace. *River Phoenix: Hero & Heartthrob,* 1988 (juvenile)
Who's Who in America, 1994

PERIODICALS

Interview, Mar. 1987, p.114; Nov. 1991, p.84
Life, Aug. 1987, p.47
Los Angeles Times, Nov. 24, 1993, p.A1 and Calendar section, p.1
New York Times, Nov. 1, 1993, p.B11; Nov. 2, 1993, p.A7
New York Times Biographical Service, Sep. 1991, p.1010
Newsweek, Nov. 15, 1993, p.85
People, Sep. 29, 1986, p.73; Nov. 15, 1993, p.126; Jan. 17, 1994, p.37
Seventeen, Mar. 1987, p.163; Apr. 1990, p.221
Time, Nov. 15, 1993, p.111
Us, Oct. 17, 1988, p.48; Sep. 1991, p.58; Jan. 1994, p.77
Washington Post, Mar. 18, 1988, p.D1

BRIEF ENTRY

Elizabeth Michele Pine 1975-
American Science Student
Winner of the 1993 Westinghouse Science
Talent Search

EARLY LIFE

Elizabeth Michele Pine was born on November 26, 1975, in Boston, Massachusetts. Her parents are Dr. Michael Pine and Joan Pine. Elizabeth has a brother, Gregory, who is a college student. She attended Illinois Mathematics and Science Academy in Aurora, Illinois, a public high school that offers advanced academic courses. She graduated from the academy in 1993. In addition to winning awards in science and math, Elizabeth won honors in literature and French, and, in 1992, she was named Chicagoland Outstanding Young Scientist of the Year. Part of the prize was the opportunity to attend the Nobel Prize ceremony in Sweden.

MAJOR ACCOMPLISHMENTS

During her high school years, Elizabeth studied the classification of two types of fungi: mushrooms and false-truffles. The typing of these two groups of organisms had been a source of controversy until Elizabeth's research resolved the debate. She conducted her research at the Field Museum of Natural History in Chicago. Using DNA sequencing—a method that determines the order of chemical elements in an organism—Elizabeth showed that while some groups of mushrooms and false-truffles look very different, they are really very similar on the molecular level. She even developed her own modifications to DNA sequencing in coming up with her discovery, which she entered in the 1993 Science Talent Search.

THE SCIENCE TALENT SEARCH

The Science Talent Search is an annual contest for high school seniors. It is sponsored by Westinghouse Electric Corporation and Science Service, a nonprofit organization that encourages the study of science. The Science Talent Search is the oldest high school competition in the country, and it offers the largest unrestricted science scholarships. From a group of 1,662 seniors, Elizabeth was one of 40 finalists in the final competition, and she was declared the winner on March 8, 1993. Her award includes a college scholarship worth $40,000.

Her response on learning that she had won is typical of this outgoing young student: "This is past exciting, this is shock!" Her parents and friends claim that she is a normal teenager who enjoys playing soccer and making jewelry. She also loves the rock group Enigma. "Quiet she is not," says her dad.

Now a freshman at Harvard/Radcliffe, Pine hopes to complete her doctorate in biology and plans to become a research scientist. She has this advice for young women going into science: "If you're going to be a geek, you're going to be a geek. Be yourself. Don't let anyone else's doubts scare you away from your goals."

FURTHER READING

Chicago Tribune, Jan. 31, 1993, p.C1; Mar. 9, 1993, p.L1
USA Today, June 1, 1993, p.A13

ADDRESS

Science Talent Search—Science Service
1719 N Street NW
Washington, D.C. 20036

Jonas Salk 1914-
American Physician and Scientist
Creator of the First Polio Vaccine

BIRTH

Jonas Edward Salk was born on October 28, 1914, in New York City. He was the oldest of three boys born to Dora (Press) and Daniel Salk. Daniel worked in the garment district of New York City, where clothing is made.

EDUCATION

The family moved to the Bronx section of New York soon after Jonas's birth. He attended the local public schools and proved to be an excellent student, although he was thin and small, and not too good at games. His parents, particularly his mother, encouraged him, and he knew he was somehow destined to make a difference. "Someday I shall grow up and do something in my own way, without anyone telling me how," he remembers thinking. He thought of his childhood as "a period of patient waiting."

At 14, he was sent to Townsend Harris High School for gifted boys. After high school, Salk attended City College in New York, where at first he thought he would study to become a lawyer. To earn extra money, he worked in a lab on campus, and also as a camp counselor. After receiving his B.S. (Bachelor of Science) degree in 1934, Salk went on to medical school at New York University (NYU). From the very beginning of his career in medicine, Salk was interested in research, rather than treating patients. His area of specialty also developed early: research into the human immune system, particularly the way that viruses cause illness.

After receiving his medical degree in 1939, Salk spent a year studying bacteriology at NYU, and he also completed his internship at Mt. Sinai Hospital in New York. At Sinai he was known as someone who handled the pressures of internship with ease. "Nobody ever saw Jonas ruffled," recalls a doctor, "You told him to do something and he got it done. It got done and so did a dozen things you hadn't thought of."

VIRUSES AND VACCINES

Most diseases are passed on by bacteria or viruses. In the late eighteenth century the scientist Edward Jenner developed the first vaccine to fight a viral disease. A vaccine is a form of bacteria or virus that can no longer *cause* illness, but can help the body to create antibodies to fight a disease. Vaccines come in two forms: "killed," in which the bacteria or virus is already dead, or "live," in which it has only been weakened. Jenner discovered that cowpox, which affected cows, could, if injected into humans, create immunity to smallpox. Although he didn't know it, he was working with a virus, a minuscule, parasitic microorganism that carries disease.

In 1936, Salk was sitting in a medical school class when his own destiny dealing with viruses and vaccines came to him like a bolt of lightening. He was told that the way to immunize against a bacterial infection was to give the person a vaccine in which the bacteria had been killed, thus causing immunity. In his next class, he was told that viruses worked differently, and that immunization was not possible. Salk recalls that it was "like an epiphany. I remember exactly where I was sitting, exactly how I felt at the time—as if a light went on. I said, 'Both statements can't be true.'"

FIRST JOBS

In 1942, Salk and his wife moved to Ann Arbor, Michigan, where he worked in the School of Public Health at the University of Michigan and concentrated on the influenza, or flu, virus.

Flu epidemics had ravaged the populations of the world for years when Salk began his research, particularly after World War I (1914- 1918), when hundreds of thousands of soldiers and civilians had died. Salk's assignment in the early 1940s was to develop a flu shot to protect soldiers fighting in World War II (1939-1945). He did just that, discovering along the way that just one flu vaccine could contain many different virus types, thus enabling the body to create antibodies for a number of different strains of flu.

CAREER HIGHLIGHTS

In 1947, Salk decided to move to the University of Pittsburgh Medical School, where a former professor had offered him the job as director of the Virus Research Laboratory and the chance to work on one of the most important projects of the century—the search for a polio vaccine.

POLIO

Poliomyelitis, or polio as it is called, is an ancient viral disease; Egyptian skeletons from 1700 B.C. show signs of its crippling effects. In the 1940s when Salk began his research into polio, the disease was a cause of terror in the population. The effects were devastating, causing crippling, paralysis, and death, especially in the young, which is why it was also known as "infantile paralysis."

The disease seemed particularly deadly in the summer months, when it would sweep through the population in epidemic proportions. In 1916, the first great epidemic broke out, killing thousands and leaving thousands more crippled for life. Parents were afraid to allow their children to play outside during the summer, attend camps, or visit local pools. Some city dwellers fled their homes for the country, but they were refused shelter by hotel owners who were just as terrified of the disease.

It is hard for young people today to imagine the fear and dread that parents and their children lived with in those times. One polio victim, Charles L. Mee, Jr., remembered it this way: "The rules were: Don't play with new friends, stick with your old friends whose germs you already have; stay away from crowded beaches and pools, especially in August; wash hands before eating; never use another person's eating utensil or toothbrush or drink out of the same Coke bottle or glass; don't bite another person's hands or fingers while playing or (for small children) put another child's toys in your mouth; don't pick up anything from the ground, especially around a beach or pool, or swallow any of the water in the pool; don't have any tooth extractions during the summer; don't get overtired or strained; if you get a headache, tell your mother."

Polio is caused by a virus that gets into the body through the intestines. Once there, it produces the familiar aches and pains of the flus we know today. In the majority of cases, that is the extent of the disease, and the body develops an immunity because the system has built up antibodies to fight the infection. But sometimes polio travels through veins or nerves to the spinal cord, where it attacks the nervous system and the brain. Polio destroys the muscles and paralyzes arms and legs, and often within 24 hours of the onset of the disease the patient is unable to walk.

Sometimes the muscles around the chest are affected, and the polio victim loses the ability to breathe. In the late 1940s and early 1950s, polio victims such as these were placed in iron lungs. These great iron cylinders performed the job of the wasted lungs, pressing and releasing the chest to force air into the body. It was the photos of hospital wards full of children as young as four or five encased in iron lungs that forms one of the most devastating memories for members of an earlier generation.

In 1950, Salk applied to the National Foundation for Infantile Paralysis (the group that founded the March of Dimes) for a grant to conduct research into the types of polio, with the idea of making a vaccine. In the late 1940s, researchers at Harvard and Yale had discovered that there were several types of polio: you could catch and recover from one strain, only to catch and be crippled by another. Polio afflicts humans and monkeys, so Salk and his fellow researchers used monkeys to test their theories and early vaccines. After two years of intensive research, Salk isolated three strains of polio and developed a "killed-virus" vaccine to treat all three forms of polio. He killed the viruses in formaldehyde and then mixed them with mineral oil. Injecting the killed-virus vaccine in a series of four shots enabled the body to develop immunity to all three strains of polio.

During this phase of his research, Salk worked round the clock, having little time for his family. Even when he was at home, his mind was on other things. "Why Jonas," his wife would say, "you're not listening to me at all." Salk replied, "My dear, I'm giving you my undevoted attention."

Salk tested the vaccine on animals, then on humans, including himself and his own family. Of this aspect of his research, Salk said, "I look upon it as ritual and symbolic. You wouldn't do unto others that which you wouldn't do unto yourself." In 1952 Salk oversaw a small test with children who had already contracted one strain of polio, and the vaccine proved effective in stimulating the growth of antibodies for the other strains. That same year was the worst year of the polio epidemic, with more than 57,000 cases in the U.S. alone. In April 1954, in the first large-scale trial of the Salk vaccine, 650,000 children were immunized. Records were kept and analyzed. The results, announced in 1955, were cause for joyous celebration. The vaccine worked, and it was safe.

But then something went wrong. Despite Salk's scrupulous instructions, one of the manufacturers of the vaccine had not followed the directions, and live polio viruses had been injected into some children. As a result, 204 children came down with polio; of them, 150 were paralyzed and 11 died. Salk was devastated. Vaccinations were halted, temporarily, but after the public was reassured that the vaccine was once again safe, inoculation began again. The success rate was stunning, and Salk became a hero. By 1960, polio had been reduced by 95 percent; it is estimated that the Salk vaccine had prevented 300,000 cases of polio in just six years.

Salk was a reluctant hero. Of his sudden fame, he said this: "To a scientist, fame is neither an end nor even a means to an end. Do you recall what Emerson said? 'The reward of a thing well done is to have done it.'" Although he received no money on the sale of the vaccine, he received an abundance of adulation, awards, and honorary degrees. He was offered but refused a ticker tape parade in New York City, declined to have Marlon Brando star in the story of his life, and would not endorse a line of children's pajamas that read "Thank you, Dr. Salk."

CONTROVERSY ARISES

Salk wasn't the only scientist searching for a polio vaccine. Many other scientists had been researching the disease to find the cause and cure. Three doctors at Harvard University had been the first researchers to grow the virus in primate tissue. This was crucial to making the vaccine, because it was the first time the virus could be grown in a lab. So when Salk's vaccine became so successful and he became such a media star, he had to face bitter colleagues who felt his contribution was less important than others' achievements. Some argued that Salk had made no real scientific discovery, that his work was simply applied science derived from the discoveries of other. In the words of his arch-rival and fellow vaccine creator Albert Sabin, Salk's contribution to science was simply "kitchen chemistry." Other scientists accused him of enjoying the publicity and fame. "The worst tragedy that could have befallen me was my success," Salk recalled. "I knew right away that I was through—cast out." Although he was nominated for a Nobel prize, he never won. The Nobel prizes in the area of polio research went to the Harvard researchers. He was not elected to the prestigious National Academy of Science until 1983. And his vaccine was replaced in the 1960s by the "live virus" type created by his rival, Albert Sabin, who until his death in 1993 remained a harsh critic of Salk.

There were two schools of thought on the polio vaccine. Some scientists favored Sabin's "live" virus that could stimulate the immune system to create the necessary antibodies to prevent a full-blown case of the disease. One of the advantages of the live virus vaccine was that it was cheaper and easier to give: people took it in the form of a sugar cube. But the Sabin vaccine also carried a greater risk of contracting polio. In a "live" vaccine, there is always a small chance—in the case of the Sabin vaccine, it is one in six or seven million—that the vaccine will cause the disease. Nonetheless, the Salk and Sabin vaccines together were responsible for eliminating polio in almost every area of the world. Today, Salk's vaccine is still used in Third World countries that lack the refrigeration necessary for the Sabin vaccine.

THE SALK INSTITUTE FOR BIOLOGICAL STUDIES

Salk continued his studies on disease and the immune system, concentrating on cancer during the late fifties and early sixties. In 1963, using funding provided by the March of Dimes, Salk founded the Salk Institute in La Jolla, California. He wanted to bring together scientists and scholars from different fields to devote themselves to research in the biological sciences. Such famous scientists as Leo Szilard, one of the most innovative researchers in physics, and Francis Crick, the co-discoverer of DNA (deoxyribonucleic acid), are former fellows of the institute. The institute is particularly devoted to exploring cancer, the immune system, the function of the brain, and genetics. Salk was the Institute's director from 1963 to 1975, and he conducted research in his own lab there from 1963 to 1984, concentrating on the immune system and its role in cancer and multiple sclerosis.

RESEARCH INTO AIDS

In 1986, Salk began research into the greatest virus mystery of our time, the AIDS (acquired immune deficiency syndrome) virus, or HIV (human immunodeficiency virus). He co-founded the Immune Response Corporation, a joint venture between scientists and a pharmaceutical company. After several years of research, he developed a vaccine, based on the killed virus model he had used in his polio vaccine. But this time, he used the vaccine on people already infected with HIV to try to stimulate the antibodies in the system to fight the disease. The vaccine is still being tested, and as before, Salk is a figure of controversy. In the opinion of one of his biographers, Richard Carter, "Salk is his own worst enemy. He seems to invite opposition. He is unnecessarily secretive and not overburdened with humility. He antagonizes individuals and institutions."

But the controversy doesn't bother Salk. "At the time I was working on polio, they said I was a 'young upstart.' Now I'm working on AIDS, and they're calling me an old 'has-been.'" Early results indicate that the vaccine does slow the course of the disease and prevents most HIV-positive patients from developing full-blown cases of AIDS. Salk is now at work on a vaccine that could prevent AIDS in those not yet infected. His approach is different from that used by other scientists, but that is fine with him. "I'm going to continue to do different things, differently. Life is not a popularity contest."

In addition to his research, Salk is a writer. His recent publications have been philosophical in nature, and in them he examines the relationship between intuition and reason. Salk argues that humans need to use both to live in harmony with nature and to solve the problems of our society and our world. "There's no distinction between social and medical problems for me. All solutions lead to improving the human condition. We're all called on to heal ourselves. Well, we can't without healing others, and that mutual interdependency is what makes community."

MARRIAGE AND FAMILY

Salk married Donna Lindsay, a psychologist, in 1939. They had three children, Peter, Darrell, and Jonathan, all of whom are now physicians. Salk's first marriage ended in divorce in 1968. He married Francoise Gilot, an artist, in 1970. They live in a home overlooking the Pacific Ocean in California, not far from the Salk Institute.

HOBBIES

Salk leads a fully active life, enjoying walking and other forms of exercise to keep fit.

HONORS AND AWARDS

Legion of Honor (France): 1955
Criss Award: 1955
Congressional Gold Medal: 1955
Presidential Citation: 1955
Albert Lasker Award: 1956
Howard Ricketts Award: 1957
Robert Koch Medal: 1963
Mellon Institute Award: 1969
Presidential Medal of Freedom: 1977

WRITINGS

Man Unfolding, 1963
The Survival of the Wisest, 1973

World Population and Human Values: A New Reality, 1981
Anatomy of Reality: The Merging of Intuition and Reason, 1983

FURTHER READING

BOOKS

Curson, Marjorie. *Jonas Salk,* 1990 (juvenile)
Curtis, Robert H., M.D. *Medicine Great Lives,* 1993
Hargrove, Jim. *The Story of Jonas Salk and the Discovery of the Polio Vaccine,* 1990 (juvenile)
Who's Who in America, 1992-93

PERIODICALS

Business Week, June 21, 1993, p.42
Current Biography Yearbook 1954
Esquire, Dec. 1983, p.40
50 Plus, July 1985, p.48
Life, Apr. 1990, p.36
Modern Maturity, Dec. 1984-Jan. 1985, p.92
New York Times Magazine, May 31, 1953, p.11; Jan. 10, 1954, p.7; July 17, 1955, p.9; Nov. 25, 1990, p.57
Newsweek, Apr. 25, 1955, p.64; May 19, 1980, p.19
Psychology Today, Mar. 1983, p.50
Science Digest, June 1984, p.51
U.S. News and World Report, July 9, 1990, p.52

ADDRESS

Salk Institute for Biological Studies
P.O. Box 85800
San Diego, CA 92186

OBITUARY

Richard Scarry 1919-1994
American Writer for Children
Author of More Than 250 Children's Books,
Including *Cars and Trucks and Things That Go,
Richard Scarry's Best Word Book Ever,* and
What Do People Do All Day?

BIRTH

Richard McClure Scarry (rhymes with "carry") was born June 5, 1919, in Boston, Massachusetts, to John James Scarry and Mary Louise Barbara Scarry. He had three brothers, John James, Jr.,

Edward, and Leo, and one sister, Barbara. His father owned several small department stores and made a comfortable income.

EARLY LIFE

Because of his father's business success, Scarry was sheltered from the painful deprivation many Americans suffered during the Depression, a period in the 1930s when up to one-third of the labor force was out of work. He said he "didn't even know there was a Depression," remembering instead the enjoyment of painting classes his mother took him to each Saturday at the Museum of Fine Arts in Boston. He also liked the animal books of Thornton Burgess, including *The Adventures of Buster Bear* and *The Adventures of Jerry Muskrat*.

EDUCATION

Scarry remembers not liking school and not doing very well. It took him five years to get through high school. When he finally graduated, he remembers, "I couldn't get into college because I didn't have enough credits."

After a brief stint at a Boston business college—at his father's request—Scarry entered the Boston Museum School of Fine Arts, where he studied drawing and painting from 1939 to 1942. He also attended the Archipenko Art School in New York and the Water Color School in Maine.

During World War II (1939-1945), Scarry served in North Africa, Italy, and France as an art director for Troop Information in the Morale Service Division, drawing maps and graphics. Then, after his war service ended in 1945, he returned to the U.S. and moved to New York, hoping to become a free lance artist.

MARRIAGE AND FAMILY

Scarry met Patricia Murphy, an author and actress, at a party in New York in 1949. Just a few days after their first meeting, he sent her a telegram that said only: "Must move grand piano. Heavy. Come immediately." "I knew a proposal when I saw one," Patricia Scarry remembers. They were married two weeks later, on September 11, 1949. Patricia is a children's author as well, and their one child, Richard (known as Huck), also writes books for kids.

CAREER HIGHLIGHTS

Scarry was able to make a decent living illustrating magazine articles and drawing illustrations for other authors' children's books. His first children's illustrations appeared in *The Boss of the Barnyard*, which was published in 1949 by Golden Books, for whom Scarry did many titles over the years.

RICHARD SCARRY

He continued to illustrate other authors' works, but in 1951 he decided to try his hand at writing and illustrating a book of his own, *The Great Big Car and Truck Book*. His first big success came in 1963 with *Richard Scarry's Best Word Book Ever*, and Scarry was on his way to becoming one of the most beloved and productive children's authors of all time.

Scarry's books are full of busy, active little animals, who take his delighted readers through all sorts of different scenes from daily life. Why animals? "I have this feeling—and it may not be very scientific—that children find it easier to relate to animals at that age. If you have a picture of a little girl with long blonde hair, then a dark-haired girl isn't going to relate to it as well as she might to a picture of a bunny rabbit."

The little pigs, cats, bears, birds, and other creatures are, to their creator, "not animals. They're real people living normal lives." These busy folks are shown doing all sorts of everyday tasks—from cleaning house and going to the store to building a house or a road. In most Scarry books, every space is crammed with detail: illustrations of kitchen gadgets or the parts of trucks, drawn and named for eager young readers. But more than just young readers love his books. "The experts tell me I reach an age group of 2 to 10," Scarry once said. "But I see babies looking at the pictures even if they're holding the book upside down. And plenty of teenagers, too, sneak back to my books when they think no one is looking."

Scarry's books are a delightful blend of education and entertainment. "Children learn from a story," he said, "and they grow attached to it. That's why they usually want it read to them night after night—and I think it's important that parents enjoy it as well." And Scarry remembered to entertain the adults who read—and reread—his books to their young children. In one memorable scene from *What Do People Do All Day?* Father Rabbit brings a huge bag of money to pay the builders of his family's new house. Afterwards, he's left with one penny, drawing an amused smile from many homeowning parents.

Scarry wrote many different kinds of children's books—ABC books, counting books, early readers—and certain characters, like Huckle Cat and Lowly Worm, are featured in numerous Scarry stories. Scarry said that Lowly was his favorite character, and he believed that young readers like to see familiar characters recur in books, just like they "like to see their familiar friends again and again—like in real life." Lowly and his animal companions are often depicted driving wildly imaginative vehicles, from pickle trucks to pencil cars to bananamobiles.

The Scarry family lived in New York and Connecticut for almost 20 years, from 1949 to 1968, when they decided to move to Switzerland after a skiing trip. "It was the usual 21-day excursion. But coming home, we had to pass through Lausanne in order to catch our plane from Geneva. From the train window I caught a glimpse of a child throwing a snowball—just that, nothing more—and I thought, 'Now is the time to move to Switzerland.'"

Scarry was a very prolific writer, and he was always at work on a new book. Even though he was a millionaire many times over, he was constantly on the lookout for new topics to cover, and he enjoyed the sometimes extensive research his detailed books required. His longtime editor, Ole Risom, said, "He works all the time, even when he isn't at his drawing board. Once we were sitting in Venice and this wild street musician came by, with a violin, a drum strapped on the back of his head and carrying a whistle. Dick started sketching him, then went chasing after him so he could make more sketches."

Scarry was not without his critics, who sometimes labelled his books violent and sexist. He disagreed strongly with the charge of violence in his works, but did try to modify any stereotypical gender roles. He noted with amusement that once, when he had a female telephone worker named Tina in a story, "Tina had a hard hat on, but I also added a ribbon with a bow to give it a feminine touch. The editor, thinking it was a mistake, changed the text to read, 'Tom, the telephone man.'" And, if you look carefully at the page, from *Richard Scarry's Postman Pig and His Busy Neighbors*, you'll see Tom with a pink bow.

Scarry's books have been adapted for several other media, including computer games, videos, and a television series for the Showtime cable channel.

After being in poor health for some time, Scarry died of a heart attack on April 30, 1994, in Gstaad, Switzerland, at the age of 74. At the time of his death, he was one of the most popular and successful children's authors of all time. More than 100 million copies of his more than 250 titles have been sold, and these well-loved works have been translated into over thirty languages. Eight of his books are among the best-selling hardcover children's books of all time.

THE NATURE OF HIS POPULARITY

"The greatest compliment I can receive is to be told that some of my books are held together with more Scotch tape than there is paper in the original book," Scarry once said." "They've been used so much, they've been torn to pieces."

Scarry had a deep respect for his young readers. "It is a precious thing to be communicating to children, helping them discover the gift of language and thought," said Scarry before his death. "I'm happy to be doing it."

HOBBIES AND OTHER INTERESTS

Scarry loved to ski and hike in the mountains of his adopted country of Switzerland. He also loved traveling and boating. The Scarry family had a house and a studio in the mountains outside of Lausanne, and an apartment in town that he said was "an expensive warehouse," full of papers and book. He also had a home on the French Riviera.

HONORS AND AWARDS

Edgar Allen Poe Special Award (Mystery Writers of America): 1976

SELECTED WRITINGS

The Great Big Car and Truck Book, 1951
Rabbit and His Friends, 1953
Tinker and Tanker, 1960
What Animals Do, 1963
Richard Scarry's Best Word Book Ever, 1963
Busy, Busy World, 1965
The Bunny Book, 1965
Storybook Dictionary, 1966
Is This the House of Mistress Mouse? 1966
Planes, 1967
Trains, 1967
Boats, 1967
Cars, 1967
Best Storybook Ever, 1968
What Do People Do All Day? 1968
The Adventures of Tinker and Tanker, 1968
Richard Scarry's Teeny Tiny Tales, 1969
Richard Scarry's Great Big Schoolhouse, 1969
ABC Word Book, 1971
Richard Scarry's Best Stories Ever, 1971
Richard Scarry's Great Air Book, 1971

Nicky Goes to the Doctor, 1972
Find Your ABC's, 1973
Richard Scarry's Please and Thank You Book, 1973
Richard Scarry's Best Rainy Day Book Ever, 1974
Cars and Trucks and Things That Go, 1974
Richard Scarry's Great Steamboat Mystery, 1975
Richard Scarry's Best Counting Book Ever, 1975
Richard Scarry's Animal Nursery Tales, 1975
Richard Scarry's All Day Long, 1976
Early Words, 1976
Richard Scarry's Busiest People Ever, 1976
Richard Scarry's Picture Dictionary, 1976
All Year Long, 1976
Richard Scarry's Lowly Worm Story Book, 1977
In My Town, 1978
Richard Scarry's Little Bedtime Book, 1978
Richard Scarry's Postman Pig and His Busy Neighbors, 1978
Richard Scarry's Best First Book Ever, 19790
Richard Scarry's Best Christmas Book Ever, 1981
Richard Scarry's Lowly Worm Word Book, 1981
Best Mistake Ever! 1984
Richard Scarry's Biggest Word Book Ever, 1985
Fun with Letters, 1986
Fun with Numbers, 1986
Fun with Words, 1986
Fun with Reading, 1986
Lowly Worm's Schoolbag, 1987
Welcome to Scarrytown, 1989
Richard Scarry's the Cat Family Takes a Trip, 1992
Huckle Cat's Busiest Day Ever, 1993

FURTHER READING

BOOKS

Contemporary Authors, New Revision Series, Vol. 39
Dictionary of Literary Biography, Vol. 61
Smaridge, Norah. *Famous Author-Illustrators for Young People,* 1973
Something about the Author, Vol. 75
Third Book of Junior Authors, 1972
Who's Who in America, 1994
Wintle, Justin, and Emma Fisher. *The Pied Pipers: Interviews with the Influential Creators of Children's Literature,* 1975
Writer's Directory, 1994-96

PERIODICALS

Boston Globe, May 4, 1994, p.77
Entertainment Weekly, May 13, 1994, p.54
New York Times, May 3, 1994, p.C19
New York Times Book Review, Apr. 27, 1986, p.38
Parents, Aug. 1980, p.62
People, Oct. 15, 1979, p.105; May 16, 1994, p.116
Publishers Weekly, Oct. 29, 1969, p.41; May 16, 1994, p.27

Emmitt Smith 1969-
American Professional Football Player
with the Dallas Cowboys
1994 MVP for the NFL and the Super Bowl

BIRTH

Emmitt James Smith III was born May 14, 1969, in Pensacola, Florida. He was the second of five children born to Emmitt Jr., a bus driver, and Mary Smith, a bank clerk. Sister Marsha is older and brothers Erik, Emory, and Emil are younger. Emmitt is called by the nickname "Scoey" in his family, after his mother's favorite comic, Scoey Mitchell.

EARLY YEARS

The Smith household was full of love, faith, and devotion to family. The Smiths, according to *Miami Herald* writer Dave Hyde, "possess all the best American graces—faith and humility, loyalty, humor, sacrifice and hard work." Emmitt's grandparents lived next door, and Emmitt and all his family contributed to the care of his invalid grandmother. The Smith home was a haven for the children in the neighborhood; all were welcome, but Mary Smith had strict rules: no fighting, no swearing, no drugs, no smoking. The kids in the neighborhood, some of them alone all day or neglected by their parents, flocked to the house, where whoever was over at dinnertime got fed, and whoever was still around at nighttime could sleep over. Both parents were active in every aspect of their children's upbringing: school, sports, church groups. After he had started in pro ball, a sports writer asked him how he managed to grow up and avoid the lure of drugs and gangs. "He gives you a strange look and says, 'It never occurred to me'," reports the writer.

YOUTH

Emmitt showed an early and avid interest in football. Mary Smith loves to tell how he would sit in his swing as an infant and watch football games on TV. He began to play two-on-two with his cousins when he was five, started in the midget leagues at seven, and by the time he was 11 and 145 pounds, his mom had to take his birth certificate to his games to prove his age.

Emmitt Jr. was a considerable athlete, too, and played semi-pro ball with the Pensacola Wings at age 40. "I just wanted to prove I had it in me," the dad says with a laugh. "I had to show to these kids that the old man could still play some ball."

When he was 13, Emmitt met his high school coach, Dwight Thomas, who vividly remembers meeting the only young man to show up in dress clothes. "It was like he was coming for an interview," says Thomas. "Coach Thomas," said the young man, "my name's Emmitt Smith and I want to play for you next year." The two of them turned around one of the poorest football programs in the state in a matter of years. Emmitt was such a powerhouse that once the defense of a competing football team wore his number—24—taped to their helmets.

"He was a coach's dream on the field and off it," says Thomas. "All he cared about was the team. He was never late for a practice or a meeting. He never brought attention to himself—and he could have every practice. If I pulled him from a game because we were winning, he'd just come to the sideline and root everyone on." This quiet confidence, selflessness, and devotion to the good of the team has been Emmitt Smith's style through high school, college, and pro ball.

EDUCATION

Smith attended public schools in Pensacola, including Pensacola Escambia High School, where he did well academically and displayed the talents that made him a sports legend even as a high school player. He was picked for the All-Southern team in 1985 and led Pensacola Escambia to two state championships. As the team's tailback, he set national career records with 45 100-yard rushing games and 109 touchdowns, placed third in the nation for total career rushing with an incredible 8,900 yards, and became the leading rusher in the history of Florida high school football.

In 1986, he was voted the most-wanted high school player by sports writers across the country, and in 1987 *Parade Magazine* named him the All-American High school Football Team Player of the Year. When he graduated in 1987, every major college invited him to play. His choice was considered so important that TV crews from CBS and ESPN followed him around before his announcement. He decided on the University of Florida, close enough to home that his folks could come and see him play.

CAREER HIGHLIGHTS

COLLEGE—FLORIDA GATORS

As a freshman for the UF Gators, Smith became the first back in NCAA history to rush for 1,000 yards in just seven games. He established the school rushing record and had the third best season rush total, placing him after two of his idols, Tony Dorsett and Herschel Walker. In that year's voting for the Heisman trophy, the most coveted award in college ball, he placed ninth, a rare honor for a freshman player. Smith really wanted to win the Heisman—with characteristic confidence, he said he'd like to "win it three times in a row." Smith's parents still had their say about their son's actions, though. Once, after scoring a touchdown, Emmitt did a little dance in the end zone. "We'll have no more of that," said Emmitt Jr. It never happened again.

In his second year at Florida, a knee injury kept him out of two games, but he was still able to run for over 900 yards that season, and when the 1989 season began, he was ready to come roaring back.

But that fall scandal rocked the Florida campus as allegations of gambling, drugs, and payoffs to players arose. Coach Galen Hall was forced to resign for admitted NCAA (National Collegiate Athletic Association) violations, and the two top quarterbacks, Kyle Morris and Shane Matthews, were suspended for gambling. Smith was never implicated in any wrongdoing, but the taint affected the team and its star player. The press surrounded them at their games and only wanted to talk about the scandal. As Mike Bianchi wrote in *USA Today*, "Emmitt Smith leads the nation in rushing, but his program leads the nation in turmoil." Smith overcame the adversity, providing leadership for the team: he set records for total yards for a junior, set SEC (Southeastern Conference) records for yards per carry, and became the first Florida player to rush 900 yards in three seasons. Then, when it came time to vote for the Heisman, several sports writers said that, even though he'd had a great season and was undeniably clean, Smith would not receive their vote, because of the scandal. He placed seventh in what would be his last year of eligibility for the Heisman.

In February 1990, during his junior year, Smith announced that he would leave the University of Florida to become eligible for the NFL (National Football League) draft. With tears running down his face, he spoke to his teammates. "Everyone who plays football dreams about playing in the NFL. I'm not going to give you a sob story about my family needing the money, because I don't think we do. I hope everyone can understand my decision."

That spring, Smith was the 17th player selected in the draft, and by the team he'd loved as a boy—the Dallas Cowboys. Coach Jimmy Johnson was undeterred by the questions raised by some pro scouts about Smith's size and speed. At 5'9" and 205 pounds, Smith was considered by some to be too small to handle NFL defensive lines. But Johnson, after an abysmal 1-15 season the year before, knew he needed a runner, and he wanted Smith. So did Joe Brodsky, who was the backfield coach for the Cowboys: "He'll take your breath away, and you won't get it back until he scores," said Brodsky.

The coaches were impressed with Smith's skills and his incredible ability to read both the offensive and defensive lines, looking for the "hole" and then plowing right through it. Smith describes it this way: "When I line up I don't see the wide receivers or the cornerbacks, but I see everybody else on both teams. It's not a blur, but a clear picture. I probably see things other people don't see. I can see changes in coverage. I can usually look at a defense and predict where the hole will be, regardless of where the play is called. That part is more difficult now. In high school, sometimes I'd tell the fullback where the hole was going to be before the snap and the majority of the time I was right. And sometimes I'd mess around and run to the hole with my eyes closed."

THE PROS—DALLAS COWBOYS

Smith missed the training season with the Cowboys while negotiating his contract. He finally started with the team in September 1990, after signing a three-year, $2.175 million contract. In his first season as a pro, Smith racked up some impressive statistics: he rushed for 937 yards, was named NFC Offensive Rookie of the Year and NFL Rookie of the Year, and played in his first Pro Bowl game. Smith was happy to refute those scouts who thought he couldn't make it in the NFL. "That shows scouts and computers don't know everything. They think they know everything. They measure your size and speed and put down how you look on paper. But they never measure one thing—the size of your heart. Well, my heart's pumping."

In the 1991-92 season, Smith won the NFL rushing title with 1,563 yards, becoming the first Cowboy to win that honor. He also won the NFL scoring record, and shared all his honors with his teammates. He bought bottles of champagne for the entire team, and Rolex watches for his offensive line. "I didn't do it by myself," said Emmitt. "That's why I'm going to spend my playoff money before I get it."

The 1992-93 season saw Smith lead the Cowboys to their first Super Bowl in years, where they defeated the Buffalo Bills. Along the way, he garnered the 1992 rushing title with 1,713 yards in the regular season. His style was described by the admiring Texas sport writer Blackie Sherrod as "frantic hopscotching, barefoot, on a blistering sidewalk."

Smith didn't start the 1993 season, due to continuing contract negotiations. He felt he had worked hard for the club, had helped bring them a Super Bowl, and he wanted his due. "I've done everything I can—including two rushing titles, three straight Pro Bowls, Rookie of the Year, and helping with the Super Bowl. Business is business, and now it's my turn." After holding out for 64 days, during which Dallas lost their first two games, including a humiliating defeat at the hands of Buffalo, the Dallas owner reached an agreement with the star back: a four-year, $13.6 million contract, making him the highest paid runner in football history. Smith proceeded to run to his third straight rushing title, with 1,486 yards, and led the Cowboys to their second straight Super Bowl Championship, where they beat the Bills again, 30-13. Smith was named Most Valuable Player in both the NFL and the Super Bowl, and many thought that Dallas had gotten their money's worth.

In March 1994, Jimmy Johnson resigned as coach of the Cowboys, replaced by Barry Switzer, former coach of the University of Oklahoma. Smith was concerned about the change, but said, "There's no need for me to moan and groan. I have to make the best of the situation and keep moving."

Whoever the coach of the Cowboys is, the team's continued success seems closely linked to the success of Emmitt Smith, who still has the desire and drive to bring his club to an unprecedented third Super Bowl. In the words of *The New York Times*'s Thomas George, "Smith is a pivotal young leader. He inspires his teammates with his temperament, locker-room folly, preparation and results. The Cowboys rally around him."

But Smith has no illusions about how brief a pro football career can be. "It's just a matter of time until someone or some injury catches up to me. I have to be prepared for that day." But he has plans for what he wants to accomplish before he retires, and how he would like to be remembered. "I think about it all the time," he says. "I'm chasing after legends, after Walter Payton and Tony Dorsett and Jim Brown and Eric Dickerson, after guys who made history. When my career's over, I want to have the new kids, the new backs, say, 'Boy, we have to chase a legend to be the best.' And they'll mean Emmitt Smith."

FUTURE PLANS

After his first season in the NFL, Smith started his own company, Emmitt, Inc., in Pensacola. He sells trading cards, T-shirts, and other sports memorabilia, and it's truly a family enterprise, with his mom, dad, sister and brothers pitching in. Business is so good that they've already had to move to bigger quarters, and the weeks before the last two Super Bowls have been especially hectic.

HOME AND FAMILY

Smith lives in a two-bedroom apartment in suburban Dallas during the football season. In the off-season, he lives with his folks back in Pensacola. He plans to build his dream house down the street from his family, but not until he finishes his college degree, as he promised his father. "The records, the touchdowns, the accomplishments are only momentary," says his father, Emmitt Jr. "Someone will come along and break the records. Education is something you have until the day you die. Nobody can take it away from you. The proudest day of my life will have nothing to do with one of his runs. The proudest day will be when I see my son walking down the aisle to pick up his diploma." He has 13 credits to go to receive his bachelor's degree in physical recreation from Florida, and hopes to complete his courses soon.

MAJOR INFLUENCES

Smith names his family as his greatest influence. "There is nothing I am today that I would be without family. I inherited my athletic skills, and I learned all about life—how to love, how to act, how to treat people, how to expect to be treated—from my family. It's family, not football, that has been the greatest gift of all. I could get hurt tomorrow, and football would be over. Family will always be there."

HOBBIES AND OTHER INTERESTS

Smith enjoys playing video games and listening to music, especially rhythm and blues. He is actively involved with his local church and several charities, including his own, Emmitt Smith Charities. In addition, he holds football training camps for Dallas kids, where he is sometimes helped out by his fellow Cowboys.

HONORS AND AWARDS

National High School Player of the Year (Gatorade): 1986
All-American High School Football Team Player of the Year (*Parade Magazine*): 1987
All-American College Team (*Sporting News*): 1989
NFL Pro Bowl: 1991, 1992, 1993, 1994
NFL Rookie of the Year: 1991
NFL Rushing Record: 1991, 1992, 1993
NFL Scoring Record: 1992
NFL MVP: 1994
Super Bowl MVP: 1994

FURTHER READING

BOOKS

Who's Who in America, 1994

PERIODICALS

Houston Post, Nov. 9, 1991, p.C1; Dec. 23, 1991, p.C5; Dec. 25, 1991, p.B5; Aug. 30, 1992, p.M13
Miami Herald, Dec. 26, 1985, p.D6; Dec. 7, 1986, p.F3; Oct. 29, 1987, p.D1
New York Times, Jan. 25, 1993, p.C1; Nov. 3, 1993, p.B17; Jan. 26, 1994, p.B8
Parade Magazine, Jan. 11, 1987, p.16
Philadelphia Daily News, Dec. 20, 1990, p.81; Jan. 26, 1994, p.83
Senior Scholastic, Sep. 3, 1993, p.24

Sport, Aug. 1993, p.109; July 1994, p.52
Sporting News, Nov. 13, 1989, p.G10; Jan. 31, 1994, p.26
Sports Illustrated, Nov. 16, 1987, p.44; Oct. 21, 1991, p.71; Sep. 6, 1993, p.34; Sep. 27, 1993, p.30; Jan. 10, 1994, p.34; Jan. 31, 1994, p.22; Feb. 14, 1994, p.142
USA Today, Oct. 18, 1989, p.C1

ADDRESS

Dallas Cowboys
Cowboys Center
1 Cowboys Parkway
Irving, TX 75063-4727

Will Smith 1968-
American Rapper and Actor
Star of "The Fresh Prince of Bel-Air"

BIRTH

Willard Smith, Jr., known to his fans as The Fresh Prince, was born on September 25, 1968, in Philadelphia, Pennsylvania. His father, Willard Smith, was a refrigeration engineer, designing and installing refrigeration units in supermarkets. His mother, Carolyn Smith, was a secretary for the local school district until recently, when she moved out to California to be near her newly famous son. Smith is the second of four children, with an older sister, Pam, a younger brother, Harry, and a younger sister, Ellen.

YOUTH

In describing Smith's childhood, writers often comment on his strong family roots. While the media often portrays rap music as a product of the ghetto, that was not the case for Will Smith. Smith grew up in a stable, comfortably middle-class family in the Wynnefield section of West Philadelphia. They were all amateur musicians, and Will tried several different instruments, including piano and drums, "but I liked writing music better than playing," he now says.

Smith often acknowledges the important role his father has played in his life. Describing his childhood, he says, "My father had me under total control. It's very important for a boy to grow up having such a strong male figure around. I always felt loved, but I was also scared of my dad. Just to hear him call my name would strike fear in my heart." One time, his father took him for a ride in the skid-row section of Philadelphia. As Smith recalls, "He pointed to the bums sleeping in the doorways and said: 'This is what people look like when they do drugs'." The lesson worked. Growing up, Will was always able to resist peer pressure to try drugs, knowing his father would kill him if he did. "My father was the man with all the answers, the disciplinarian," he says. "He did his shaping up by taking little chunks out of your behind." He goes on to say, "Dad was tough but not tyrannical. He kept me in line. He'd get this look that said, 'One more step, Will, and it'll get ugly.' . . . He's a steady and positive figure in my life."

When Smith was about 13, his parents divorced. But he weathered that crisis well. "It really didn't bother me. I was extremely precocious and realized my parents were much better off being apart. It brought peace to the house and each parent. My mother moved in with her mother, and we spent weekends together. Our family remained close-knit, except my parents never talked to each other."

STARTING TO RAP

By this point, Smith had already gotten started as a rapper. He began rapping at parties when he was about 12 or 13. At first, he wasn't looking at music as a career; he was just out to have fun. In 1981, at one of the parties, he hooked up with Jeffrey Townes, or DJ Jazzy Jeff, a local DJ who had started mixing and scratching in his basement studio at the age of ten. Together, they started making the rounds. Smith says that rap was a natural next step from his early interest in stories, words, and rhymes: "Ever since I was a little kid I've been inventing stories where I made myself into superheroes. I also loved the books by Dr. Seuss. Words and rhymes got me going. So as a young teenager, I fell into rap. It was a natural progression. My fantasies fit the form perfectly."

It was at these house parties that Smith first developed the skills to make it as a rapper, according to Quincy Jones, the award-winning musician and executive producer of "The Fresh Prince of Bel-Air." "He has high self-esteem," Jones says. "I guess you have to if you're going to be a rapper. People pay $15 to go to a house party, and if you're no good, the crowd lets you know pretty quickly and not kindly. Those are the kind of parties where Will started. In its broadest sense, rapping can verge on slapstick. Will learned to entertain in that environment, and that certainly takes care of your inhibitions. I think that's why he's such a natural on television."

EDUCATION

Smith started out in Catholic schools, which his parents considered academically superior to the local public schools, and graduated in 1986 from Overbrook High School in Philadelphia. He got his nickname in eighth grade, when a teacher started to call him Prince—short for Prince Charming, because he was always able to charm his way out of trouble (Fresh, as in cool, was added later). He played around a bit in class, telling jokes and acting the clown. But he was also a good student, writing poetry and stories, studying math, and scoring 1260 (out of 1600) on the Scholastic Aptitude Test (SAT), a college entrance examination. With that score, he had offers from about 100 colleges and universities, including a scholarship to the pre-engineering program at the prestigious and tough Massachusetts Institute of Technology (MIT). In the meantime, though, DJ Jazzy Jeff and the Fresh Prince put out their first single two weeks before Smith's high school graduation. With tour dates booked, a lucrative contract, and the money pouring in, he decided to delay his college admission and try to make it in the music business.

FIRST JOBS

Their first single, "Girls Ain't Nothin' But Trouble," recorded on an independent label, was such an immediate hit that it earned for the duo a recording contract with Jive Records, which paid them $30,000 and bought out their original contract. The next year, they released the hit singles "Nightmare on My Street," a take-off on the Freddy Krueger film *Nightmare on Elm Street*, and "Parents Just Don't Understand," whose video quickly made it onto MTV. With the success of those two singles, DJ Jazzy Jeff and the Fresh Prince had arrived.

CAREER HIGHLIGHTS

SUCCESS AS A RAPPER

A multi-talented artist, Smith has gone on to earn fame in other areas, but it was his success as a rapper that provided the foundation for his continuing popularity. The duo's first LP, *Rock the House* (1987), did well, selling about half a million records, but their second release, *He's the DJ, I'm the Rapper* (1988), was an immediate smash, going double platinum with sales well over 2 million copies. The record earned the first ever Grammy Award for rap music and the first MTV rap video award as well.

With its widespread popularity today, it may be hard to remember that rap music is a fairly recent phenomena, achieving broad success only in the late 1980s. Some large part of the credit for that goes to DJ Jazzy Jeff and the Fresh Prince. Unlike many other rappers, they avoided the "gangsta" image and urban themes common to much of the genre. Instead, their approach reflected their own interests and experiences growing up, which were solidly middle class. Their music incorporates a range of influences, including hip hop, to be sure, but also funk, rhythm and blues, rock, and jazz—"danceable, ultra-funky, and extremely musical," according to the *Philadelphia Daily News*. As the front man for the duo, the Fresh Prince quickly became known for his charming manner, charisma, supreme self-confidence, funky humor, infectious energy, and mischievous wit. But above all, he was called a brilliant storyteller whose poetic raps appealed to all, cutting across racial and class lines.

Yet their approach has been condemned by some rap critics, who praise more militant and socially conscious forms of rap and dismiss their songs as fluffy and trivial. "Rap can be political, but it doesn't have to be," Jazzy Jeff once explained. "It can be jazz, it can be rhythm and blues, it can be classical, it can be political or comic." Some have argued that their ability to cross racial lines and to appeal to a broad mainstream audience means that they have turned their back on the black experience. Yet Smith denies these charges. "I do what makes me feel good. I also feel the pressure to be a good influence. I write lyrics my mother can listen to. When she goes to work, and people talk about my records, I want her to be proud of me. Rapping comes from your background, and mine was a regular working-class neighborhood. Those are the issues I deal with." His fans clearly agree with Fresh Prince, as sales of their records attest.

"THE FRESH PRINCE OF BEL-AIR"

Smith's move into acting had a lot to do with being in the right place at the right time. While asking for directions, he had a chance encounter with Benny Medina, an executive with Warner Brothers Records in Los Angeles. Medina had developed an idea for a TV series based on his own life. Growing up in the ghetto in East L.A., left an orphan when his mother died, raised in a series of foster homes and juvenile-detention centers, Medina had been informally adopted as a teenager by a wealthy white couple in Beverly Hills. Smith, Medina decided, would be the young actor to play himself. They sold the idea for the series to producer Quincy Jones, who sold it to NBC.

On "The Fresh Prince of Bel-Air," which debuted in Fall 1990, Smith plays Will, a teenager from Philadelphia whose mother sends him out to live with their rich relatives in California. The show has evolved with time, delving more deeply into the characters, their relationships, and social issues. As the 1993-94 season closed, Will met his father, who deserted the family years ago and leaves again; Will also returned to Philadelphia to visit his family and decided to stay there. An ongoing hit series, "Fresh Prince of Bel-Air" now ranks as the top-rated series among teens.

Using the same humor that characterizes his rap hits, Smith has used "Fresh Prince" to showcase some of the class distinctions within black culture. Yet his work on the TV show soon came under the same type of attack that his rap music has endured. "Look what the Fresh Prince represents," Smith says with pride of the character he plays. "He operates on several different levels—as a symbol of urban youth, a symbol of black youth and, most specifically, of black male youth. As a rapper, some people knocked him for being too middle-class, too clean-cut. Now, as a TV character, he's accused of being unreal. Well, my mission has been to make him more real, and I suppose that means more like me. The truth is that I know there are millions and millions of black youths like me—kids who have never touched a drug or a drink, kids whose parents stressed education, kids who are filled with self-esteem, kids who want to have fun, want to laugh, want to rap, want to party, but aren't afraid of responsibility. Those same kids—and include me among them—are tired of the white media, especially the white news media, portraying black youths as criminals to be feared, as opposed to progressive young people to be respected. Let's recognize the reality of a talented new generation, righteous in their thinking, pumped up on pride and ready to take on the world."

EXPANDING HIS ACTING REPERTOIRE

From TV, Smith's acting career has expanded into feature films. In his first, *Where the Day Takes You* (1992), he had a small part as a homeless man. He next appeared in *Made in America* (1993), a romantic comedy co-starring Whoopi Goldberg, Ted Danson, and Nia Long. But his greatest stretch as an actor, by far, has been his recent role in *Six Degrees of Separation* (1994). In this screen adaptation of the award-winning play by John Guare, Smith plays a gay con man and hustler named John. Passing himself off as a Harvard student, John gains the trust of a wealthy Manhattan couple (played by Stockard Channing and Donald Sutherland) by claiming to be a friend of their children—and the son of Sidney Poitier. For Smith, this dramatic role represented a real departure from his previous experience in rap and a TV sit-com, and critics were impressed with his convincing portrayal. In discussing his work, Smith made it clear that he chose this role to prove to others that he could handle a wide range of acting roles and to open up additional opportunities. As he says, "Television is the most fun. Music is the most rewarding. And film is the most interesting." With the success he's had in all three areas, Smith should be able to pick and choose his future projects for years to come.

MARRIAGE AND FAMILY

Smith married Sheree Zampino on May 9, 1992. It wasn't an easy courtship. They met when they both attended the taping of the TV show "A Different World," where a mutual friend worked. At first, Sheree wouldn't even date him for six months, and it took Will two years to convince her to marry him. They now have one son, Willard Smith III, whom they call "Trey." They make their home in southern California, where "The Fresh Prince of Bel-Air" is filmed, although Smith often returns to Philadelphia to visit family and friends there.

HOBBIES AND OTHER INTERESTS

Smith's hobbies include playing pool, Nintendo, basketball, football, bowling, and wall ball—it's like hand ball, where you hit a ball against a wall, but with 15 people playing at a time.

RECORDINGS

Rock the House, 1987 (reissued 1989)
He's the DJ, I'm the Rapper, 1988
And in This Corner . . . 1989
Homebase, 1991
Code Red, 1993

All recordings released by the duo D.J. Jazzy Jeff and the Fresh Prince.

TV AND FILM CREDITS

"The Fresh Prince of Bel-Air," 1990— (TV series)
Where the Day Takes You, 1992

Made in America, 1993
Six Degrees of Separation, 1994

HONORS AND AWARDS

American Music Awards: 1989 (2 awards), Favorite Rap Artist and Favorite Rap Album for *He's the DJ, I'm the Rapper*; 1992, Favorite Rap album for *Homebase* (with DJ Jazzy Jeff)
Grammy Awards: 1989, for Best Rap Single for "Parents Just Don't Understand"; 1991, for Best Rap Performance by a Duo or Group for "Summertime" (with DJ Jazzy Jeff)
MTV Music Awards: 1991, Best Rap Video for *Parents Just Don't Understand*
Soul Train Music Awards: 1989, for Best Rap Album for *He's the DJ, I'm the Rapper* (with DJ Jazzy Jeff)
NAACP Image Awards: 1992, for Best Rap Artist (with DJ Jazzy Jeff)

FURTHER READING

BOOKS

Who's Who in America, 1994
Who's Who among Black Americans, 1994-95

PERIODICALS

Essence, Feb. 1993, p.60
Parade Magazine, Feb. 2, 1992, p.14
People, Oct. 3, 1988, p.81; Sep. 24, 1990, p.83
Rolling Stone, Dec. 1, 1988, p.19; Sep. 20, 1990, p.45
Seventeen, May 1989, p.97
TV Guide, Oct. 13, 1990, p.8; Jan. 23, 1993, p.11
Us, Sep. 17, 1990, p.26
Vanity Fair, Oct. 1990, p.130

ADDRESS

"Fresh Prince of Bel-Air"
NBC
3000 West Alameda Avenue
Burbank, CA 91523

Steven Spielberg 1947-
American Filmmaker
Director of *Jaws*, *E.T.*, *Raiders of the Lost Ark*, and *Jurassic Park*, the Highest-Grossing Movie of All Time

BIRTH

Steven Spielberg was born on December 18, 1947, in Cincinnati, Ohio. His father, Arnold Spielberg, was a computer scientist and executive, and his mother, Leah (Posner) Spielberg, was a homemaker and retired concert pianist. Steven was their oldest child, with three sisters, Ann, Sue, and Nancy. The Spielbergs later divorced. Now remarried, Steven's mother, Leah Adler, owns a kosher restaurant called the Milky Way in Los Angeles, California.

YOUTH

Steven's father was an electrical engineer, one of those working on the first computers. He and the family moved often as he took a succession of jobs in the developing computer industry. The Spielbergs moved first to Haddenfield, New Jersey, when Steven was four, to Scottsdale, Arizona (a suburb of Phoenix), when he was nine, and to Saratoga, California (a suburb of San Jose), when he was 16—all middle-class, suburban neighborhoods like those he has recreated in many of his films. "You saw my house when you saw *Close Encounters, Poltergeist,* and *E.T.,*" Spielberg claims. "The house in *E.T.* is very much like the house I was raised in. That's my bedroom!"

As a child, Spielberg enjoyed the typical activities of suburban middle-class life, like Little League baseball, Boy Scouts, and playing pranks on others. But it was not always an easy childhood. "I was a loner and always lonely. I was the only Jewish kid in school, and I was very shy and uncertain." With the family's frequent moves, it was especially hard to adjust: "Just as I'd become accustomed to a school and a teacher and a best friend, the FOR SALE sign would dig into the front lawn and we'd be packing." Spielberg describes the fears that he had as a child—of monsters in the closet, of things falling out of a crack in his bedroom wall, of the dark and the trees and the wind outside his window at night. He became so frightened of the wicked queen in *Snow White and the Seven Dwarves* that his parents wouldn't let him watch much TV or movies—they worried about the violence, and wanted their children to develop more intellectual pursuits. To control his fears, he tried passing them on to his sisters, telling scary stories and playing practical jokes on them. He would stand outside their bedroom windows howling, he locked them in closets, and once he served his sister Nancy a salad—with the head of one of her dolls on a nice plate of lettuce. As his sister Ann said years later, "At the preview of *Jaws,* I remember thinking, 'For years he just scared us. Now he gets to scare the masses.'"

To add to Spielberg's troubles, there was constant friction between his parents. At first, it was just their different interests—his mother playing piano with her chamber group in one room, his father arguing about electronics with his colleagues in another. Over time, though, their differences became more obvious. As he recalls in a lengthy interview with Denise Worrell published in *Icons: Intimate Portraits,* "I was 17 when my parents divorced. They hung in there to protect us until we were a little older, but they knew they were going to separate years before they actually did it. I don't think they were aware of how acutely we were aware of their unhappiness—not violence, but just a pervading unhappiness you could cut with a fork, cut with a spoon, at dinner every night.

"For years, the word *divorce* for me was like a seven-letter word, the ugliest word in the English language. Sound traveled from bedroom to bedroom, and the word always came seeping through the heating ducts. My sisters and I would stay up at night, listening to our parents argue, hiding from that word. . . . I feared that word. I feared the imminent separation of my family. I knew it was coming; I just didn't know when. And when the separation finally came, we were no better off for having waited six years for it to occur." Yet Spielberg goes on to praise his parents' devotion to their children, despite their personal problems: "I have two wonderful parents. They raised me really well. Sometimes parents can work together to raise a wonderful family and not have anything in common with each other. This happens a lot in America."

SCHOOL MEMORIES

"I hated school," Spielberg now admits. "I just didn't think it applied to what I wanted to do. From age 12 or 13 I knew I wanted to be a movie director, and I didn't think that science or math or foreign languages were going to help me turn out the little eight-millimeter sagas I was making to avoid homework. . . . I did just enough homework to move to the next grade every year with my friends and not fall to the wrath of my academically minded father. I give my dad credit for singlehandedly keeping my math grades high enough so I wouldn't be held back. My worst subject was physical education; I failed that three years in a row in high school. I couldn't do a chin-up or a fraction. I can do a chin-up now, but I still can't do a fraction.

"At school I felt like a real nerd, the nerd of the block. The skinny, acne-faced, wimpy kind of kid who gets pushed around by big football jocks and picked on all the way home from school. I was always running to hide in my bedroom where I was safe. I would often get home and say 'Safe.' I would actually call out 'Safe' to myself."

EDUCATION

Spielberg was an indifferent student throughout his school career. He often skipped classes to stay home and work on his movies—in fact, he documented one of his childhood tricks in *E.T.*, when Elliott held the thermometer up to the light bulb to convince his mother that he was too sick to go to school. Spielberg spent most of his high school years in Arizona at Arcadia High School in Scottsdale. When the family moved to California, though, he finished up his senior year there, graduating from Saratoga High School in 1965.

He hoped to attend film school at the University of Southern California (USC) or the University of California at Los Angeles (UCLA), but his grades were too low. Instead, he enrolled at California State College at Long Beach in 1965, spending his time watching old movies instead of doing his schoolwork. He officially dropped out of college in 1968.

LEARNING TO MAKE MOVIES

By that time, Spielberg had been making movies for years. When he was 12, his mother bought a home movie camera as a gift for Father's Day. Arnold Spielberg was such a poor photographer, and Steven complained so much, that his father finally let him try. He was hooked. For his first movie, he set up his elaborate Lionel train set and filmed a giant crash. Since that time, his life has been dominated by making movies.

Spielberg made what he considers his first real movie at age 13 to earn a merit badge for Boy Scouts. Using his father's camera, he made a four-minute Western starring his fellow troop members, all wearing cowboy outfits and plastic guns from their Halloween costumes. "I screened the movie for the counselor and he insisted that I show it to the entire troop of 75 Boy Scouts before he would credit me and give me the merit badge. A lot of them were in the film, and when I started the picture and they saw themselves, they began whooping it up and cheering and having a great time. In that one moment I knew what I wanted to do for the rest of my life."

Spielberg has described these early movies as an attempt to create a new identity for himself—to convince his classmates that he wasn't a wimp. When he was 13, a school bully kept tormenting him, so Spielberg decided to try and enlist his help. As he recalls, "I figured, if you can't beat him, get him to join you. So one day I went over to him in school and said, 'I'm making this movie about all these soldiers fighting the Nazis and I want you to play the war hero.' At first he laughed in my face. . . . Then later he came back to me and said, 'Do you still make movies?' and I said yes. He said, 'I'll be in one of them.' I got him to come out on a weekend and I made a picture around him. I made him the squad leader, with helmet, fatigues, and backpack. He was this big 14-year-old who looked like John Wayne. After that he became my best friend."

Spielberg continued to make movies throughout high school, including a two-and-a-half hour 8-mm science fiction film, *Firelight* (1964), a precursor to *Close Encounters of the Third Kind* ("Eight-millimeter" refers to the size of the film used. Today, most movies are filmed on 70-mm film.) He even managed to convince a local theater to show it. "Nobody ever said no to Steven," his mother claims. "He always gets what he wants."

FIRST JOBS

Spielberg began pushing his way into the film industry when he was about 18. During summer vacation, he took the studio tour at Universal

Pictures. When the tourists' tram didn't stop at the sound stages, he snuck away during a bathroom stop. There he met Chuck Silvers, a film editor, who actually talked to him, asked to see some of his films, and wrote him a pass to return the next day. For the rest of that summer, Spielberg put on a business suit each morning, packed his lunch in one of his father's old briefcases, and fooled the guard at the studio gate into believing that he worked there. He set up shop in an unused office, added his name to the building directory, and hung out with filmmakers, trying to get them to watch his films. Even after he started college, he arranged his schedule so he could spend three days a week there. And over time, it worked.

He continued to make short films, and finally the breakthrough came with *Amblin'*, his first 35-mm movie, the format used by professional filmmakers. This love story about a boy and girl hitchhiking across the Mojave Desert to the Pacific Ocean was, according to Spielberg, "a slick, very professional-looking 35-mm film, although it had as much soul and content as a piece of driftwood." He has also called it "an attack of crass commercialism," and apparently he was right. After showing the film at Universal, their head of TV production, Sidney Sheinberg, offered him a seven-year contract to direct TV series. At age 20, according to Spielberg, "I quit college so fast I didn't even clean out my locker."

He did his first job, directing the legendary actress Joan Crawford in the pilot for "Night Gallery," and then quit. After a year, he came crawling back, "ready to eat crow and pay my dues." He went on to direct episodes on "Marcus Welby, M.D.," "The Psychiatrist," "Name of the Game," and "Columbo," as well as TV movies. On one of those, *Duel* (1971), he finally proved himself to the Hollywood establishment. A suspenseful story about an innocent man being pursued by a large and menacing truck with an unseen driver, *Duel* was so successful on American TV that it was released internationally as a feature film. From there, Spielberg went on to direct Goldie Hawn and Richard Atherton in *The Sugarland Express* (1974).

CAREER HIGHLIGHTS

JAWS

Until that point, Spielberg was just one more young director trying to make it to the big time. With his next film, *Jaws* (1975), he made it. This suspenseful and frightening story of a shark that terrorizes a New England beach community was a nightmare to film. Everything that could go wrong did, particularly the scenes filmed in the Atlantic Ocean with the mechanical shark (affectionately known as Bruce to cast and crew). Soon none of that mattered, though, as *Jaws* became the highest-grossing movie of its time, pulling in about $410 million in its first two years. It immediately made Spielberg's name as a successful director.

A STRING OF HITS

In the almost 20 years since then, he's had an amazing string of movies, most phenomenally successful, with just a few that flopped. As a filmmaker, he has juggled different roles on different pictures, sometimes developing story ideas, or writing screenplays, or serving as the director or producer. The director of a film is the person in charge of all the creative and technical aspects, including the actors, sets, costumes, and special effects, while the producer is the person responsible for all the business aspects of filmmaking, particularly the financial decisions. During the last ten years, he produced many films through the studio he set up on the Universal lot, Amblin Entertainment (named after his first successful short film), one of the largest independent production companies in Hollywood. Spielberg has used his clout and his position as a producer to help launch the careers of other talented young directors, just as Sydney Sheinberg at Universal once helped him. The list of films that he has produced is long and diverse: *I Wanna Hold Your Hand, Used Cars, Poltergeist, Continental Divide, Gremlins* and *Gremlins II, Innerspace,* all three *Back to the Future* movies, *The Goonies, An American Tail, The Money Pit, Batteries Not Included, The Land Before Time, Who Framed Roger Rabbit? Dad, Arachnophobia, Joe Versus the Volcano,* and *Cape Fear.*

Certainly his success as a producer has cemented his reputation in Hollywood, but it is the movies that he directed that have ensured his popularity among audiences nationwide. Dating back almost twenty years, to the release of *Jaws,* his films typically share certain settings and themes: an ordinary person, usually in a middle-class, suburban environment, dealing with an extraordinary situation. Added to this seemingly mundane concern, however, are an array of imaginative, and often spectacular, special effects.

Even a partial listing of films directed by Spielberg showcases his talent: *Close Encounters of the Third Kind* (1977), the experiences of several typical middle Americans dealing with the landing of an alien spacecraft; *Raiders of the Lost Ark* (1981) and its two sequels, *Indiana Jones and the Temple of Doom* (1984) and *Indiana Jones and the Last Crusade* (1989), the adventure series starring Harrison Ford as Indiana Jones; the beloved movie *E.T.: The Extra-Terrestrial* (1982), until recently the highest-grossing movie of all time, about a young boy, Elliott, and his encounter with a lovable alien trapped on Earth; *The Color Purple* (1985), Spielberg's retelling of Alice Walker's renowned novel about a poor and abused southern black woman; *Empire of the Sun* (1987), based on J.G. Ballard's autobiographical tale about a boy in Shanghai, China, during World War II who is separated from his parents and locked up in a Japanese prison camp; *Always* (1989), a nostalgic remake of the 1943 romantic movie *A Guy Named Joe,* about a heroic firefighter killed in action who comes back as a guardian angel; and *Hook* (1991), a new twist on J.M. Barrie's Peter Pan story in which Peter finally does grow up, headlining Robin Williams as Peter, Dustin Hoffman as Hook, and Julia Roberts as Tinker Bell.

JURASSIC PARK

Spielberg's most recent blockbuster is *Jurassic Park* (1993), based on the novel by Michael Crichton. In the film, a wealthy developer, John Hammond, has discovered a way to use biogenetics to clone dinosaurs from the DNA found in drops of ancient blood inside a mosquito preserved in amber. Hammond sets up a huge park on a tropical Caribbean island and invites several others, including his two grandchildren, two scientists, a mathematician, and a lawyer, to preview the park. "What's interesting to me about this particular project is there is as much science as there is adventure and thrills," Spielberg says. "Jurassic Park is a cross between a zoo and a theme park. It's about the idea that man has been able to bring dinosaurs back to earth millions and millions of years later, and what happens when we come together." And what happens is massive destruction, as the people in the park quickly discover that the dinosaurs are both much smarter and much more dangerous than they had ever dreamed—particularly the towering Tyrannosaurus and vicious Velociraptors. The action is so frightening, in fact, that experts generally agree that *Jurassic Park* is inappropriate for children under age nine.

Much of the film's success derives from the surprisingly believable dinosaurs. Four separate special effects units created their realistic moves on camera, using animation, miniature photography, animatronics (electronically controlled models), computer-generated graphics, as well as full-size, live-action models—including a Tyrannosaurus rex that was 20-feet tall and weighed over 3000 pounds! Equally awesome is the marketing campaign tied in with the film's huge stars. Over 1000 products have been licensed to carry the *Jurassic Park* logo, including those from Kenner, McDonalds, and Sega. Considering that the film is widely judged too scary for younger kids, many have questioned this promotional campaign. But apparently it worked: *Jurassic Park* was recently named the highest grossing movie of all time, earning a phenomenal $840 million in just five months, and the numbers are still climbing.

Spielberg's next film is *Schindler's List*, due out in late 1993. Based on a novel by Thomas Kenneally, this film tells the story of a German businessman during World War II who risks his life to save 1300 Jewish workers from the Nazi death camps. Spielberg grew up hearing stories of the Holocaust from his Jewish relatives, and this film is clearly important to him—he's been at work on it for ten years. "This has been the best experience I've had making a movie. I feel more connected with the material than I've ever felt before," he said during filming. "In a funny way, I'm more qualified to make this movie than any of the others I've made—other than *E.T.* and *Close Encounters*. At 45, I am more qualified. This is truly my roots, my *Color Purple*. Jokingly my mom will say it will be good for the Jews. I say it's good for all of us."

Perhaps with this film, Spielberg will finally please his critics. Despite his tremendous popular success, he has achieved little critical approval and has never won an Academy Award (an Oscar) for Best Director for any of his films. Reviewers have often argued that he has thrown away his talent on lightweight entertainment—"kid" stories—and have urged him to handle more serious, "adult" topics. Some have doubted his ability to handle intellectually and emotionally complex material. Clearly, though, audiences disagree. Despite critics' reservations, his films have been huge successes. To date, Spielberg has made six of the 20 highest-grossing movies of all time: after *Jurassic Park* at number 1, his box office hits include *E.T.: The Extra-Terrestrial* at #2, *Indiana Jones and the Last Crusade* at #6, *Jaws* at #9, *Back to the Future* at #17 (produced by Spielberg), and *Raiders of the Lost Ark* at #18. These successes have made him the second-highest paid entertainer (after Oprah Winfrey) on *Forbes* magazine's annual list, with $72 million earned in 1992-93. Audiences clearly love his films, and their devotion has made Spielberg the number one American filmmaker today. [See Appendix for Update on Spielberg.]

MARRIAGE AND FAMILY

On November 27, 1985, Spielberg was married to actress Amy Irving. They divorced in 1989 and now share custody of their son Max. Spielberg later got involved with the actress Kate Capshaw, who appeared in the second and third *Indiana Jones* movies. They were married on October 12, 1991, and they have three children: adopted son Theo, daughter Sasha, and son Sawyer. Spielberg is also stepfather to Capshaw's daughter, Jessica, from a previous marriage.

HOBBIES AND OTHER INTERESTS

A confirmed workaholic, Spielberg is not known to have a lot of hobbies, although he does enjoy spending time with his children.

DIRECTING CREDITS

Amblin', 1970 (short feature)
Something Evil, 1970 (TV movie)
Duel, 1971 (TV movie; re-edited and released as a feature film in 1973)
Savage, 1973 (TV movie)

The Sugarland Express, 1974 (director and co-author)
Jaws, 1975
Close Encounters of the Third Kind, 1977 (director and co-author)
1941, 1979
Raiders of the Lost Ark, 1981
E.T.: The Extra-Terrestrial, 1982 (director and co-producer)
Twilight Zone: The Movie, 1983 (segment director and co-producer)
Indiana Jones and the Temple of Doom, 1984
The Color Purple, 1985 (director and co-producer)
Steven Spielberg's Amazing Stories, 1985 (TV series; episode director and producer)
Empire of the Sun, 1987 (director and co-producer)
Always, 1989 (director and co-producer)
Indiana Jones and the Last Crusade, 1989 (director and producer)
Hook, 1991
Jurassic Park, 1993

HONORS AND AWARDS

Hasty Pudding Man of the Year (Hasty Pudding Theatricals, Harvard University): 1983
Outstanding Directorial Achievement Award for Feature Films (Directors Guild of America): 1985, for *The Color Purple*
British Academy of Film and Television Arts Awards—Film: 1986
Irving G. Thalberg Award (Academy of Motion Picture Arts and Sciences): 1986, in recognition of his consistent excellence in filmmaking
Golden Lion Award (Venice Film Festival): 1993, for Lifetime Achievement

FURTHER READING

BOOKS

Collins, Tom. *Steven Spielberg: Creator of E.T.*, 1983 (juvenile)
Conklin, Thomas. *Meet Steven Spielberg*, 1994 (juvenile)
Crawley, Tony. *The Steven Spielberg Story: The Man Behind the Movies*, 1983
Hargrove, Jim. *Steven Spielberg: Amazing Filmmaker*, 1988 (juvenile)
Leather, Michael C. *The Picture Life of Steven Spielberg*, 1988 (juvenile)
Mabery, D.L. *Steven Spielberg*, 1986 (juvenile)
Mott, Donald R., and Cheryl McAllister Saunders. *Steven Spielberg*, 1986
Who's Who in America, 1992-93
Worrell, Denise. *Icons: Intimate Portraits*, 1989

PERIODICALS

Current Biography 1978
Film Comment, Jan. 1978, p.49

New York Times, June 13, 1993, Sec. II, p.15
New York Times Biographical Service, May 1982, p.654; Jan. 1992, p.98
Newsweek, May 24, 1993, p.60; June 14, 1993, pp.56, 60, and 64
Omni, July 1993, p.50
People, July 20, 1981, p.74
Teen, Nov. 1982, p.51
Time, July 15, 1985, pp.54, 62; Apr. 26, 1993, p.49

ADDRESS

Amblin Entertainment
Universal Pictures
100 Universal Plaza
Universal City, CA 91608

Patrick Stewart 1940-
English Actor and Writer
Stars as Jean-Luc Picard on "Star Trek: The Next Generation"

BIRTH

Patrick Stewart was born July 13, 1940, in Mirfield, England, a small mill town in the northern portion of the British Isles known as Yorkshire. His father, Alfred, was a sergeant major in World War II (1939-1945) and was later a house painter. His mother, Gladys, was a weaver who worked in a mill in the town. Stewart has two older brothers.

YOUTH

Stewart does not say much about his younger years, except to note that they were touched by poverty and violence. "Life was scary," he recalls. His father was a brutal man, with an uncontrollable temper. "I wasn't beaten, but there was violence in the house. My father would get very angry. He would lose control."

EARLY MEMORIES

Even though Mirfield is a small town with a population of only 9,000, there were 11 amateur drama clubs, as well as choirs, bands, and orchestras, when Patrick was growing up. These offered him an early and welcome outlet from an unhappy home life. "I could say, 'I'm going to rehearsal,' when they asked where I was going. It cauterized the fear and the hurt and the pain. Being able to go somewhere else and say 'What if' or 'Once upon a time' was comforting."

He also remembers exploring the rugged terrain around his home. "I was brought up looking at the crests of hilltops all around me. From the first time my parents would allow me to wander off on my own, to get to the top of those hills and look beyond, it's always held a particular fascination for me. I was one of those children who read Robert Louis Stevenson and Joseph Conrad when I was growing up, so I would pore over maps of the South China Sea with names like Java and Sumatra, which were always thrilling to me."

EDUCATION AND FIRST JOBS

Stewart attended the local grade schools and left at the age of 15, the minimum age for quitting school in England. He had done well in writing and landed a job with the local paper, the *Mirfield Reporter*. By this time, he was performing with four different theater groups, and he often had a friend cover the event he was to write about, or he would even make up the story he was to report. His editor at the paper gave him an ultimatum: he could either give up his acting or lose his job. He quit.

CHOOSING A CAREER

Stewart remembers that final confrontation with his editor: "I was 17, and I left out of spite. I objected to being told how I should lead my life. I went home and told my parents I'd left and they were very upset. They asked what I was going to do, and I said, 'I'm going to become an actor.' I made the decision only to annoy the editor of the newspaper."

CAREER HIGHLIGHTS

But the decision was the right one, and Stewart entered his chosen profession with enthusiasm and ambition. In 1957, after being involved in dozens of regional theater productions, Stewart won a two-year scholarship to the Bristol Old Vic, an outstanding theater company that has trained generations of fine English actors. He toured with the troop for several years, performing in Australia, New Zealand, and South America.

ROYAL SHAKESPEARE COMPANY

In 1966, Stewart joined the Royal Shakespeare Company (RSC), the most distinguished theater company in the world devoted to performing the works of Shakespeare and other dramatists of world renown. Over the next 25 years, he gained a reputation as an outstanding actor, winning praise for his performance in a number of roles. Some of his most famous parts with the RSC include: Enobarbus in *Anthony and Cleopatra*, Oberon in *Midsummer Night's Dream*, Shylock in *The Merchant of Venice*, Leontes in *The Winter's Tale*, the title roles in *Titus Andronicus, Henry IV, Part One* and *Part Two*, and *Henry V*. He also starred in non-Shakespearean roles, winning acclaim for his interpretation of Eilert Lovberg in Henrik Ibsen's *Hedda Gabler*, King David in Peter Shaffer's *Yonadab*, and George in Edward Albee's *Who's Afraid of Virginia Woolf?*

Several of his performances have won major awards for Stewart, including an Olivier Award (the most prestigious honor in British theater) for his portrayal of Enobarbus in *Anthony and Cleopatra* in 1979, as well as an Olivier nomination that same year for his Shylock in *The Merchant of Venice*. For his performance in *Who's Afraid of Virginia Woolf?* he won the London Fringe Award for Best Actor in 1987.

To supplement his rather skimpy salary with the RSC, Stewart also did a number of film roles, appearing in *Excaliber* (1981), *Dune* (1984), and *Lifeforce* (1985). Stewart's television roles first brought him to the attention of the American audience. In 1977, he appeared as Sejanus in the BBC/Masterpiece Theater production of *I, Claudius*. He also captivated audiences with his interpretation of the role of Karla, the fictitious head of the Soviet KGB, in the TV adaptations of John Le Carre's novels *Tinker Tailor, Soldier, Spy* (1979) and *Smiley's People* (1982).

In addition to his acting roles with the RSC, Stewart was the associate director of a group called Alliance for Creative Theatre, Education, and Research (ACTER), and as part of his job he began visiting American colleges and universities in the 1970s to talk to students about performing Shakespeare. He returned several times over the years to the University of California at Santa Barbara.

"STAR TREK: THE NEXT GENERATION"

While visiting California in 1986, Stewart assisted a friend by reading some dramatic excerpts at a literary lecture. In the audience that night was

Robert Justman, one of the producers for a new television show, "Star Trek: The Next Generation." The new show was to be the follow-up to the original "Star Trek" show of the 1960s, which by then had achieved the status of a cult classic. The producers were casting the show at that time, and Justman supposedly turned to his wife and said, "We've found our captain."

Stewart read for the part three times, and six months later, he donned the uniform of the United Federation of Planets to become Jean-Luc Picard, Captain of the starship Enterprise. Stewart had no idea at that time of the popularity of the show. He remembers seeing snippets of the earlier program. "It used to air in England on Saturday afternoons, and when I was working for the RSC in Stratford, I could get home between a matinee and an evening show and have tea with my family. Sometimes that meant watching whatever was on TV with my children, and very often it would be 'Star Trek.'" The next day, his children would act out their favorite parts of the episodes for their father.

Now in its seventh season, "Star Trek: The Next Generation" is one of the most popular shows on television, and the highest-rated weekly syndicated series in America. The series takes place aboard the Enterprise in the 24th century, 100 years after the voyages of the original show.

Captain Picard is joined by a diverse crew, many of whom are distinguished stage actors in their own right. They include Jonathan Frakes as Commander Will Riker, Gates McFadden as Dr. Beverly Crusher, LeVar Burton as Lieutenant Commander Geordi La Forge, Marina Sirtis as Counselor Deanna Troi, Michael Dorn as Lieutenant Worf, and Brent Spiner as Data.

Another member of the cast is Whoopi Goldberg, who plays Guinan, the centuries-old host of the ship's lounge. Goldberg, a well-known star of TV and movies, actively campaigned for the part of Guinan when the show was first being cast. She remembered the original "Star Trek," which also featured a diverse crew, including Nichelle Nichols as Uhura, the ship's communication's officer. "Not only was Uhura proof that black folks would make it into the future, she was beautiful, smart, and had power," remembers Goldberg.

When the show first aired, there were the inevitable comparisons between the earlier and the current versions. The original "Star Trek" boasts millions of fans worldwide, many of whom were skeptical of the newcomer. But most viewers found that the new show had a depth and ingenuity that the first show lacked, and the critics agreed. And it had a special effects budget, rumored to be about a half millions dollars per episode, that brought the show a state-of-the-art look comparable to such sci-fi movies as *Star Wars*. In its first year of syndication, "Star Trek: The Next Generation" won a Peabody Award, a prestigious award for excellence in broadcasting.

Like the earlier show, "Star Trek: The Next Generation" centers on the ship's mission: "to boldly go where no one has gone before," and to follow the Prime Directive, which, in the words of Stewart, "requires that the beliefs, customs, and ideologies of a society or citizen should be sacrosanct." Stewart is widely credited with setting high standards and bringing a greater credibility to the show. Unlike the brash Captain Kirk of the earlier show, his character is a wise, thoughtful commander, more likely to choose diplomacy than a punch in an alien encounter. Stewart is rather sensitive about his baldness, but even that aspect lends his persona as Captain Picard a certain mature and distinguished quality. He thinks the fans see Picard as he does: "A visionary, dreamer, adventurer and compassionate man. And he is a cultured, literate man."

Stewart was irritated with some in the theater community who rejected his work in a television series, calling it "slumming." He adamantly opposes this view, saying: "that not only was it not slumming, but all of my years speaking blank verse and sitting on thrones and wearing tights and striding the stage of the RSC was nothing but a preparation for sitting in the captain's chair of the starship Enterprise."

Playing the role of Picard made Stewart even more interested in an aspect of many of the characters he's played: the nature and meaning of power. To explore this concept further, he created a one-man show, "Uneasy Lies the Head," a group of monologues, or speeches given by one character alone on the stage, spoken by different leaders throughout history.

The fame the role of Picard has brought him continues to surprise Stewart. "It seems incredible to me that more than 30 million people watched our pilot episode, which is certainly more people than have ever seen me on stage in my whole career." The Star Trek conventions that take place several times a year and are attended by thousands of adoring fans are another aspect of his fame. Stewart says he was totally unprepared for the reaction at his first Trekkie convention: "I came back thinking I had just experienced what it must be like to be Sting or Michael Jackson."

Several years into the series, Stewart began to miss the stage and was worried that his creative "juices weren't flowing." So he decided to stage Charles Dickens's *A Christmas Carol*—as a one-man show. He first performed the show in California in 1990, portraying 39 characters from Dickens's immortal classic. He concentrates on the vibrant language and ingenious characterizations of the original work, returning to the "grim, powerful, potent tale of redemption" of Dickens's original, which he felt had been obscured in sugar-coated interpretations.

In another departure from the TV series, Stewart directed several of his "Star Trek" co-stars in a revival of Tom Stoppard's *Every Good Boy Deserves Favour* in 1992. It is a work he knows well, having been part of the world premiere in England in 1977. It is a fascinating play, taking place in a Soviet hospital and focusing on the lives of two inmates—one a political prisoner and one truly mad. The revival has done well on tours across the country, and perhaps indicates the next step the "Next Generation" cast will take. The 1993-94 season will most likely be the last for the series, and since the actors work so well as an ensemble, they will probably work together again.

In addition to his famous television role, Stewart is a well-known voice to TV audiences. His deep, rich voice has been heard in commercials for such products as RCA televisions and Pontiac cars. He also served as host and narrator for a PBS series on early explorers and the mapping of the planet. He very much enjoyed the work: "as an actor with a classical background, I was particularly intrigued by the episodes that deal with the great periods of expansion and exploration in the 14th through 16th centuries, when the map-maker was one of the most important individuals in a society."

Stewart has plans already in the works for his post-Star Trek days. He recently completed writing an adaptation drawn from Mikhail Bulgakov's *The Master and Margarita*, in which he plays Pontius Pilate. His endless curiosity to explore new roles will continue to take him on to new challenges, and back to his first love, Shakespeare. He has written several scholarly pieces on the playwright, and has also written and given a lecture-demonstration on the character of Shylock, from *The Merchant of Venice*.

ON SHAKESPEARE

Stewart always tries to perform some Shakespeare at the Star Trek conventions, and he is pleased with the result. Many fans have said that after hearing Stewart they have been inspired to read Shakespeare for the first time, or to return to him after years. "It might be said to be a sort of missionary work," he says.

He is eager to return to the RSC after an absence of nine years. "The excitement of performing Shakespeare is that you never open the final door on any major role. Performing and studying Shakespeare is a process of constant revelation."

HOBBIES AND OTHER INTERESTS

Stewart is an active supporter of Amnesty International, which has received proceeds from some of his performances. He also enjoys "fell-walking," or mountain hiking, a term for hiking in the rough, ragged terrain of his Yorkshire upbringing. He is determined to learn to scuba dive, and when this final season of "Star Trek" ends, he will try to overcome his lifelong fear of the water and pursue this new interest with Brent Spiner, who plays the android, Data, in "Next Generation."

MARRIAGE AND FAMILY

Stewart married Sheila Falconer, a choreographer, on March 3, 1966. They are now divorced. They have two children, Daniel, born in 1968, who is a recent graduate of the California School of the Arts and an actor and director, and Sophie, born in 1974, who is also studying acting. And what does their father think about that? "I didn't encourage either one to take up this profession, because 90-odd percent of all actors don't work. I know a lot of very unhappy and frustrated actors for that reason, and I didn't want that for my children. As for me, well, I'm absolutely obsessed with acting and have nothing to replace it with."

CREDITS

THEATER

Anthony and Cleopatra, 1972, 1973, 1979
Midsummer Night's Dream, 1977
Every Good Boy Deserves Favour, 1977 and 1991
Merchant of Venice, 1978
Henry IV, Parts One and *Two,* 1982-83
Henry V, 1984
Who's Afraid of Virginia Woolf? 1985
Yonadab, 1985
A Christmas Carol, 1990-92

TELEVISION

I, Claudius, 1977
Tinker, Tailor, Soldier, Spy, 1979

Smiley's People, 1982
"Star Trek: The Next Generation," 1987-

FILMS

Excaliber, 1981
Dune, 1984
Lifeforce, 1985
Lady Jane, 1986

HONORS AND AWARDS

Olivier Award: 1979
London Fringe Best Actor Award: 1987

FURTHER READING

BOOKS

Contemporary Theatre, Film, and Television, Vol. 7

PERIODICALS

Baltimore Sun, Sep. 27, 1990, p.F1
Boston Herald, Dec. 15, 1990, p.B1
Chicago Tribune, Apr. 4, 1993, p.C7
Los Angeles Times, Mar. 11, 1986, p.F1; Feb. 14, 1992, p.24
New York Daily News, July 2, 1990, p.B7; Dec. 15, 1991, p.E12
New York Post, Dec. 16, 1991, F10
Newsday, Dec. 16, 1991, p.B38
Philadelphia Inquirer, Jul. 28, 1991, p.8
San Francisco Examiner, Feb. 16, 1992, p.D8
The Times (London), Jan. 7, 1977, p.6
TV Guide, Aug. 31, 1991, p.5; July 18, 1992, p.7; July 31, 1993, p.8
USA Today, June 15, 1989, p.D3
Washington Times, Dec. 6, 1991, p.F4

ADDRESS

ICM
8899 Beverly Blvd.
Los Angeles, CA 90048

R.L. Stine 1943-
American Writer for Children and Young Adults
Popular Author of the "Goosebumps" and "Fear Street" Series

BIRTH

Robert Lawrence (R.L.) Stine, prolific author of two series of scary stories for young readers, was born on October 8, 1943, in Columbus, Ohio, to Lewis, a shipping clerk, and Anne (Feinstein) Stine.

YOUTH

Very little is known about Stine's childhood, except for his early and consistent dedication to writing. Stine was was so single-minded growing up, as he admits in Jim Roginski's *Behind the Covers*, a collection of interviews with authors of children's books, that he never made much time for anything except writing. He started writing at the age of nine, when he hauled an old typewriter out of the attic and started pounding out little joke books. He'd spend entire summers typing, keeping every word, and his wife jokes now that "If he read it today, he would probably still think it was hilarious!" Stine's parents wondered why he didn't try to get a summer job when he was in high school, but his response was always, "I can't this summer. I'm writing a novel."

EARLY INFLUENCES

It was the discovery of *Mad* comics that piqued Stine's interest in zany humor, one day while he was waiting his turn at the barbershop. "I discovered *Mad* comics one day when I was 11 or 12. They absolutely blew me away. I couldn't believe anything could be so funny," he recalls. His parents would not allow him to bring the magazine into the house, though, saying it was trashy reading, "So, I used to get a haircut every two weeks," he continues, "just to make sure I didn't miss an issue." Years later, and by then a successful and immensely popular humorist, the author would defend this kind of light reading for children by contending that there's nothing wrong with a book that's "just for fun."

EDUCATION

Stine attended Ohio State University, where he edited the school's humor magazine, *The Sundial*. It was there that he created his first pen name, Jovial Bob Stine. "To help sales, I decided to create some kind of persona," he says now by way of explanation. Later, Stine added the pseudonyms Eric Affabee and Zachary Blue.

After earning his bachelor of arts degree in 1965, he did graduate work at New York University, and then returned briefly to Ohio to teach social studies in the public school system. From there, it was off to New York again because, he says, "I figured that's where writers lived."

FIRST JOBS

Stine started out his writing career in magazine publishing. He went to work for *Junior Scholastic* in 1968, writing news and history articles. Three years later he started editing *Search*, a creative magazine for remedial readers of junior high school age. The new publication, a departure from *Scholastic's* traditional image, spawned two more innovative and immensely successful publications under Stine's guidance. In 1974 he started *Dynamite*, for fourth and fifth graders, which quickly became the largest children's magazine in the country. Soon after he created the companion magazine, *Bananas*, geared toward teenagers.

Teenage humor, according to Stine, is based on recognition: "Things they recognize from their own lives," he says. "We had a feature called, 'It Never Fails!' For example, 'It never fails [that] when you get in the shower, the phone rings.' 'It never fails that when the teacher asks the one question you don't know, she calls on you.'" During his years as a magazine creator and editor (he also piloted *Maniac* in 1984 and 1985), Stine continued to write children's books—a mixture of wacky humor and tales of suspense—and became head writer for "Eureeka's Castle" on Nickelodeon.

For Stine, humor has an important role to play in children's books. "The whole problem with doing humor for children comes from adults. A lot of people seem to think that if a book or magazine is just funny, it's trash. Adults have their right to read or watch trash. Adults have their right to pick out a book that's just for entertainment, nothing else. But many adults seem to feel that every children's book has to teach them something, has to be uplifting in some way. My theory is a children's book doesn't have to teach them anything. It can be just for fun." Legions of young fans confirm Stine's sentiments by consistently keeping his paperback books among the top 50 on bestseller lists.

CAREER HIGHLIGHTS

By the mid 1980s, he turned his pen almost exclusively to stories with scary themes. Suddenly, suspense had become popular among young readers, from children in elementary school to teens who devoured the Christopher Pike and Stephen King tales of horror. Stine moved quickly from humor to spooky stories of werewolves and swamps. Today, he reigns as one of the country's most popular writers for kids.

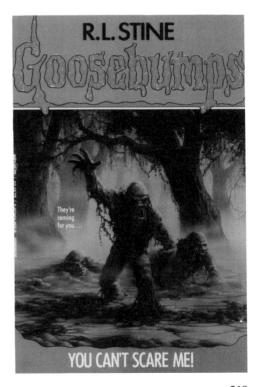

To date, Stine has penned more than 150 books in all, but "never a word for adults," he says. Each day, he spins out 15 to 20 pages of material on a rigorous schedule of self-discipline. "Someone . . . called me the Jekyll and Hyde of children's books," he remarks, referring to the fictional split-personality character made famous a century ago by Robert Louis Stevenson, "and I guess that's about right. I wrote about 30 or 40 joke books and humor books before I slipped into my horror identity. These days, I'm scary all the time."

Stine churns out two hair-raising novels each month for his "Goosebumps" and "Fear Street" series (the former for eight-to-ten-year- olds, the latter for kids ten to thirteen), and constantly appears among the fifty best-selling authors on the weekly list (for adults and children) computed by *USA Today*. "Every week, his mailbox groans with 400 [fan] letters," says the newspaper, which also notes that his biggest challenge in writing for children is making his fictional kids sound real. Stine takes it all in stride, though, as he dashes off still another book of terror. "Kids aren't really eloquent," he says. "They never speak in paragraphs."

Stine currently has at least a half-dozen new stories in production, including the two newest "Goosebumps" titles, *The Scarecrow Walks at Midnight* and *Go Eat Worms*, due out in June 1994, and several new "Fear Street" books due to be published this summer. A number of other stories are in development.

While some have criticized the recent emphasis on horror for young readers, Stine disagrees. "Part of the appeal is they're safe scares," he explains. "You're home in your room and reading. The books are not nearly as scary as the real world." The challenge, he says, is "to find new cheap thrills" for his readers. "I mean disgusting, gross things to put in the book that they'll like: the cat is boiled in the spaghetti, a girl pours honey over a boy and sets ants on him. They like the gross stuff."

MARRIAGE AND FAMILY

R.L. Stine works at home in New York without a staff, although he has help on the "Fear Street" series from his wife, the former Jane Waldhorn, to whom he has been married since 1969. Jane is an experienced editor of children's books and magazines, and she co-authored some of her husband's books of humor. The Stines have a son Matthew, age 13, who claims not to read his father's books.

FAVORITE BOOKS

Stine says that his favorite scary book is *Something Wicked This Way Comes* by Ray Bradbury.

SELECTED TITLES

UNDER THE NAME JOVIAL BOB STINE

How To Be Funny: An Extremely Silly Guidebook, 1978
The Absurdly Silly Encyclopedia and Flyswatter, 1978

The Complete Book of Nerds, 1979
Going Out! Going Steady! Going Bananas!, 1980
The Sick of Being Sick Book, 1980 (with Jane Stine)
Don't Stand in the Soup, 1982
Everything You Need to Survive, 1983 (four books, with subtitles: *Brothers and Sisters, First Dates, Homework,* and *Money Problems,* all written with Jane Stine)
Jovial Bob's Computer Joke Book, 1985

SUSPENSE STORIES

The Time Raider, 1982
Horrors of the Haunted Museum, 1984
Indiana Jones and the Cult of the Mummy's Crypt, 1985
Cavern of the Phantoms, 1986
Attack on the King, 1986 (under pseudonym Eric Affabee)
The Petrova Twist, 1987 (under pseudonym Zachary Blue)
Phone Calls, 1990

"FEAR STREET" SERIES

The New Girl, 1989
The Surprise Party, 1989
The Overnight, 1989
Missing, 1990
The Wrong Number, 1990
The Sleepwalker, 1990
Haunted, 1990
Halloween Party, 1990
The Stepsister, 1990
Ski Weekend, 1991
The Fire Game, 1991
Lights Out, 1991
Fear Street Super Chiller: Party Summer, 1991
The Secret Bedroom, 1991
Fear Street Super Chiller: Silent Night, 1991
The Knife, 1992
Prom Queen, 1992
First Date, 1992
Fear Street Super Chiller: Goodnight Kiss, 1992
Fear Street Cheerleaders: The First Evil, 1992
Fear Street Cheerleaders: The Second Evil, 1992
Fear Street Cheerleaders: The Third Evil, 1992
The Best Friend, 1992
Fear Street Super Chiller: Broken Hearts, 1993
The Cheater, 1993

Sunburn, 1993
The Fear Street Saga: The Betrayal, 1993
The Fear Street Saga: The Secret, 1993
The Fear Street Saga: The Burning, 1993
Fear Street Super Chiller: Silent Night 2, 1993
The New Boy, 1994
The Dare, 1994
Bad Dreams, 1994
Double Date, 1994

"GOOSEBUMPS" SERIES

Welcome to Dead House, 1992
Stay Out of the Basement, 1992
Monster Blood, 1992
Say Cheese & Die! 1992
The Curse of the Mummy's Tomb, 1993
Let's Get Invisible! 1993
Night of the Living Dummy, 1993
The Girl Who Cried Monster, 1993
Welcome to Camp Nightmare, 1993
The Ghost Next Door, 1993
The Haunted Mask, 1993
Be Careful What You Wish For . . . 1993
Piano Lessons Can Be Murder, 1993
The Werewolf of Fever Swamp, 1993
You Can't Scare Me!, 1994
One Day at Horror Land, 1994
Why I'm Afraid of Bees, 1994
Monster Blood II, 1994

FURTHER READING

BOOKS

Roginski, Jim. *Behind the Covers: Interviews With Authors and Illustrators of Books for Children and Young Adults*, 1985

PERIODICALS

Contemporary Authors, New Revision Series, Vol. 22
Detroit Free Press, Oct. 23, 1991, p.F1
Newsday, Jan. 2, 1994, Section 2, p.1
USA Today, Dec. 2, 1993, p.C1

ADDRESS

Scholastic Books
555 Broadway
New York, NY 10012

BRIEF ENTRY—OBITUARY

Lewis Thomas   1913-1993
American Scientist, Educator, Writer, and Physician

EARLY LIFE AND CAREER

Lewis Thomas was born in Flushing, New York, on November 25, 1913, to Joseph Simon Thomas, a doctor, and Grace Peck Thomas, a nurse. He grew up accompanying his father on house calls. He was the fourth of five children, with one brother and three sisters.

Thomas attended a private school for boys, McBurney, in New York City. After he graduated in 1929, he attended Princeton

University, where he studied biology and received his B.S. in 1933. He went on to medical school at Harvard University, receiving his M.D. in 1937. After interning at Boston City Hospital, he did his residency at the Neurological Institute of New York.

Thomas was drawn to the laboratory rather than the practice of medicine, and he began a life of combined research, teaching, and writing in the 1940s that continued into the 1980s. During World War II (1939-1945), he worked on research into infectious diseases. He was dean of the Schools of Medicine at Yale and at New York University in the 1960s and 1970s, and he later served as the president of the Memorial Sloan-Kettering Cancer Center in New York City, considered one of the best research and treatment facilities for cancer in the world.

MAJOR ACCOMPLISHMENTS

One of Thomas's many accomplishments was his series of essays on science for the nonspecialist. Such works as *The Lives of a Cell* (1974), which won the National Book Award and sold hundreds of thousands of copies, were praised for their elegant prose and concise, lucid content. Called "evolution's most accomplished prose stylist," Thomas educated and delighted thousands of readers, and his scientific insights provided the ideas and direction for researchers in such diverse areas as cancer, heart disease, and drug addiction.

Lewis and his wife, Beryl Thomas, had three daughters, Abigail, Judith, and Eliza. In addition to his lifelong pursuit of scientific inquiry, Thomas also loved music, particularly the music of Johann Sebastian Bach. He died December 3, 1993, of Waldenstrom's disease, a condition that is similar to cancer.

He is remembered as a man of scientific rigor, vision, and eloquence. He was recalled by one colleague this way: "His great talent was to identify things of interest and enthuse others. He discovered the power of shared fascination. He was called a poet of science. He made science into a literature."

Thomas thought and wrote often of the interrelationship of humankind and nature. In *Lives of a Cell* he said this: "We are told that the trouble with Modern Man is that he has been trying to detach himself from nature. He sits on the topmost tiers of polymer, glass, and steel, dangling his pulsing legs, surveying at a distance the writhing life of the planet. In this scenario, Man comes on as a stupendous lethal force, and the earth is pictured as something delicate, like rising bubbles at the surface of a country pond, or flights of fragile birds. But it is an illusion to think that there is anything fragile about the life of the earth; surely this is the toughest membrane imaginable in the universe, opaque to probability, impermeable to death. We are the delicate part, transient and vulnerable as cilia."

SELECTED WRITINGS

The Lives of a Cell, 1974
The Medusa and the Snail, 1979
Late Thoughts on Listening to Mahler's Ninth Symphony, 1983
Could I Ask You Something, 1984
The Fragile Species, 1992

FURTHER READING

Current Biography Yearbook 1975
New York Times, Dec. 4, 1993, p.A11
New York Times Magazine, Nov. 21, 1993, p.50

Barbara Walters 1931-
American Broadcast Journalist
Host of ABC News Magazine "20/20" and the "Barbara Walters Specials"

BIRTH

Barbara Walters was born on September 25, 1931, in Boston, Massachusetts. She was the third child of Louis Edward Walters, a theatrical producer and founder of the famous Latin Quarter nightclubs, and Dena Selett (originally Seletsky) Walters. The couple's other children were a son, Burton, who died of pneumonia in 1922 at the age of fourteen months, and a daughter, Jacqueline, born mentally retarded in 1926.

Author Jerry Oppenheimer's *Barbara Walters: An Unauthorized Biography* gives the newswoman's birth year as 1929, but no other available information seems to support that claim.

YOUTH

By her own admission, Walters's childhood was lonely. She tells of "moving too much, always being in new schools, among new people, resentful that my situation wasn't like the other kids." Both parents were involved with the nightclub business, and to be with them—especially with the father who was rarely at home during her waking hours—Barbara would spend her free time at the clubs either doing homework, reading, or meeting the famous patrons who had become part of her extended family circle. Author Mary Malone, in *Barbara Walters: TV Superstar*, writes that "on school holidays, she had nowhere to go but the club, where she liked to climb up to the lighting booth and look down on the stage below." She was a shy and sensitive little girl whose sole playmate was her retarded sister, toward whom she felt fiercely protective during the six decades of Jacqueline's life.

Friends and relatives from those earliest days confirm Barbara Walters's self-proclaimed shyness and vulnerability (then and now), a surprising trait in one who has lived so much of her life in the public eye. They suggest that her carefully guarded private life has its roots in her unconventional childhood. Lou Walters was a compulsive gambler whose business risks eventually led to bankruptcy, and young Barbara grew up too soon, sharing her mother's worries about their unreliable financial future. "I was an adult at nine," she sadly acknowledges.

EARLY MEMORIES

Barbara Walters is reticent about her earliest years. "I don't have any favorite memories of my childhood," she once told a magazine interviewer. "I recall that I really couldn't communicate with my sister as a child, so I used to think that this was the way it had to be, that everyone's sister was retarded. It was frustrating and lonely; it left a mark. That's why my heroes have always been people who look after the handicapped. They are admirable."

EDUCATION

From Brookline (near Boston), where she entered first grade, to Miami Beach, then back and forth between Florida and New York City, Walters's school years took her on a zigzagging journey up and down the east coast. For short periods, she attended prestigious private schools in New York, Fieldston in Riverdale (The Bronx) and Birch Wathen in Manhattan, graduating from the latter in 1949. She was awarded an A.B. degree four years later from Sarah Lawrence College, also in Riverdale. Surprisingly, friends from college days do not remember Walters being especially concerned with current events—interests that would be an integral part of her career in subsequent years. She excelled in English, dramatics, and creative writing, but had no clear vision of a profession. "I didn't think that I had a great compelling career in my future," Walters says now. She knew, though, that she would have to support herself, since family finances rose and fell dramatically with her father's uncertain business deals. "Dad made and lost lots of money . . . I always felt it would be over tomorrow," she says.

CHOOSING A CAREER

Walters's skill with words, supported by a speedwriting course, landed her a part-time job as a copywriter for a New York advertising agency. She went from there to a local television station, WNBC-TV, where she prepared releases for the various shows on the daily schedule. As the TV station developed more of its own programming, she was made a producer, learning "to edit film and do voice-overs," she recalls. "To this day, I can still do it and write and edit. . . .It was very solid background."

CAREER HIGHLIGHTS

The television industry was just beginning to expand, and Walters felt that she had found her niche. She moved over to the CBS network, mainly as a news writer who was given only occasional on-camera appearances. The slight speech impediment that she retains to this day put her at a disadvantage for on-air work. "I was the kind nobody thought could make it," she recalls. "I had a funny Boston accent. I couldn't pronounce my *R*'s. I wasn't a beauty." Then, in 1961, her first real break came when she was hired by NBC's highly rated "Today Show." The new job was only an entry-level staff position, but Walters had set an agenda for success and was determined to make it happen. "If you want to get ahead," she advises now, "you must work, longer, harder, and more compulsively than the other guy. I don't know of any shortcuts." After proving her mettle as reporter, interviewer, editor, and writer, she was put on camera as a substitute for a departing colleague. The 13-week assignment lasted for 15 years, from 1961 to 1976. In addition to her work on "Today," she also hosted a popular NBC syndicated series, "Not for Women Only," for several years. Barbara Walters had made a breakthrough, not only for herself, but for her gender, in what was then a man's game.

Walters soon became a celebrity in her own right as she traveled the world for stories and personal profiles. Among her high-visibility assignments on "Today" were interviews with U.S. presidents and government dignitaries, foreign leaders (Anwar Sadat, Menachem Begin, Muammar

Qaddafi, Fidel Castro), and luminaries of stage, screen, and opera. She was with the NBC team that went to China to cover the visits of President Richard Nixon in 1972 and President Gerald Ford in 1975. In those years with NBC, Walters also covered the investiture of the Prince of Wales, went to London for Queen Elizabeth's silver jubilee, and was personally invited to the lavish celebration of the 2500th anniversary of the Persian Empire.

However, Walters's growing prestige was not without controversy. Many male reporters resented her aggressiveness and the special status and relationships she seemed to enjoy—she wryly says that they saw her as pushy and abrasive in situations where her male counterparts would be perceived as confident and assertive. One of the "Today Show" hosts, the late Frank McGee, a respected television journalist, was especially unhappy at sharing the morning desk with Walters. Their cool relationship was a difficult time for both, and ended, sadly, with McGee's death from cancer in 1974. It was only then that Walters became official co-host of "Today," a position never before held on any network by a woman.

THE MILLION-DOLLAR MOVE TO ABC

Barbara Walters was, by this time, the most visible woman on television. Some said that she had become "as famous as many of her guests." Her ratings were high enough for ABC to lure her away in 1976 from her home network with an unheard of contract—a staggering million dollars a year for five years, and a co-anchoring position with Harry Reasoner on the "ABC Evening News." She became the highest paid journalist ever, but was soon forced to defend that salary. Her outraged detractors failed to understand then that her contract was not only for the anchor position (another first for a woman), but also for the four specials that she would develop and present each year. The focus in the all-male bastion quickly switched to money. As author Malone writes, "Reasoner . . . and the anchormen of the other two networks' evening news programs all received hefty salary raises in the wake of Barbara's record-breaking contract." Today, such immense figures are standard in the industry.

The envy among Walters's colleagues was rampant. She was roundly criticized for her "lack of journalistic credentials" and for "crossing the line between news and show business." Worst of all, though, was the treatment she received from Reasoner. He was affronted by her equal status and treated her with "patronizing tolerance," says one ABC news executive. "He viewed her as an interloper." As a team, they failed in the ratings. In 1978, Walters was reassigned to the special reports and interviews that were her greatest strength, Reasoner returned to CBS, his former network, and ABC reorganized its news format to three-city coverage, with Frank Reynolds in Washington, Peter Jennings in London, and (the late) Max

Robinson in Chicago. Ultimately, the news desk was given to Peter Jennings, who holds it today.

Following her experience on the "ABC Evening News," Walters began working with Hugh Downs, her old friend and co-host from the "Today" show, on ABC's "20/20," a newsmagazine they have built together into a solid and well-respected program. Her numerous and timely interviews on "20/20" and on the "Barbara Walters Specials" read, says one publication, like a "Who's Who" of newsmakers. She has interviewed every president since Richard Nixon, and made journalism history in 1977 by arranging the first joint interview with Egypt's President Anwar Sadat and Israel's Prime Minister Menachem Begin. Another of her accomplishments was securing a prime-time conversation with Cuban President Fidel Castro, whom she had interviewed in a visit to his country several years earlier. Walters has talked on-screen to Russian Federation President Boris Yeltsin; to Dr. Jack Kevorkian, the controversial Michigan proponent of assisted suicide; to Abbie Hoffman, the 1960s radical fugitive; and to stars and authors and poets, many of whom had never before granted television interviews. Her style is conversational, but her questioning often is seen by detractors as crossing the line into privacy. She is labeled as manipulative by many, but her drive and personality have brought her legions of admirers, too. In a sharply competitive business, Barbara Walters continues to do what *Cosmopolitan* credited her with a decade ago: she has "scooped the most erudite men on her beat."

MEMORABLE EXPERIENCES

One especially touching episode stands out in Walters's memories of the countless ABC specials she has hosted over nearly two decades. The Shah and Empress of Iran were being featured and, Walters relates, "the Shah, in one of the most compelling moments I can remember in any of our interviews, looked at his beautiful and [educated] empress and said she wasn't fit to rule if he died, because women were equal in human rights but not in intelligence or ability. I will never forget her face or the tears in her eyes."

Walters has indelible personal memories, too, from her early days at ABC, and spoke as recently as 1992 about her negative experiences after joining that network: "Back then everybody was gunning for me. They criticized me for everything . . . my salary, the way I pronounce my R's [referring, in particular, to the late comedienne Gilda Radner's 'Baba Wawa' parody on 'Saturday Night Live.'] Who is this terrible person on with this serious newsman, Harry Reasoner? I felt very wounded. I had a mother, a father, a retarded sister and a daughter I was supporting. . . . I was drowning. I was not only drowning, I was reading every day about people who were willing to put my head under the water. . . ."

MAJOR INFLUENCES

Walters has said that she has no mentor, but cherishes the support of loyal friends. She does reveal, however, that the distinguished actress Katherine Hepburn, whom she has profiled twice on television, has been her greatest inspiration. Walters describes her as "dogmatic, opinionated, brave, and smart. I remember her saying, 'I have lived like a man. I have earned my own living and I wore pants and I did whatever I damn well wanted to do' . . . If you asked me, was there anybody I was in awe of, I would probably say Hepburn."

Walters also admits to having a personal hero—Mike Wallace, CBS journalist and coeditor of "60 Minutes." She shows her admiration for his energy and endurance as she speaks of how he is "still traveling all over the world, playing tennis, doing great work at age 75."

MARRIAGE AND FAMILY

Barbara Walters has been married three times. She and her first husband, New York businessman Robert Henry Katz, separated soon after their 1955 marriage, and that union was annulled. In December 1963, she wed theatrical producer Lee Guber (now deceased), a man whose energies and show-business enterprises mirrored those of her father in his most productive days. In June 1968, they adopted an infant girl whom they named Jacqueline Dena, after Walters's sister and mother. Walters and Guber stayed together for about eight years and were divorced four years after their initial separation. After the breakup, they maintained an unusually cordial relationship that gave their growing child a sense of security.

Professional obligations and the added strain of bicoastal living are said to have scuttled Walters's most recent marriage. She was wed to Californian Marvin Lee Adelson, a television and movie impresario, from 1986 to 1992. Today, she lives in a spacious Fifth Avenue apartment overlooking Manhattan's Central Park. Her adult daughter disdains a celebrity existence and lives quietly in the Pacific Northwest.

HOBBIES AND OTHER INTERESTS

Although she says that she has reached a point in her life where she would like to slow down, Walters's relentless drive rarely extends to activities outside her career. When she reads, it is almost always in preparation for her interviews. Her social life is often intertwined with celebrity appearances, and what little personal time she is able to carve out of her frenzied days she spends at home or with old friends. Walters laughingly estimates that she belongs to more health clubs (that she doesn't use) than anyone else in New York and, apparently, lack of time has moved her workout schedule away from the clubs and into her apartment. A *New York Times* profile reports that, in the middle of her library, she keeps "two enormous exercise machines, a Stair Master and a treadmill."

WRITINGS

How To Talk With Practically Anybody About Practically Anything, 1971

HONORS AND AWARDS

Woman of the Decade (*Ladies Home Journal*): 1970 (one of 10)
Woman of the Year in Communications: 1974
One of 200 Leaders of the Future (*Time*): 1974
Emmy Award (National Academy of Television Arts and Sciences): 1975
Broadcaster of the Year (International Radio and Television Society): 1975
Mass Media Award (American Jewish Committee, Institute of Human Relations): 1975
Barbara Walters College Scholarship in Broadcast Journalism (established in her name by the Illinois Broadcasters Association): 1975
Matrix Award (New York Women in Communications): 1977
Hubert H. Humphrey Freedom Prize (Anti-Defamation League of B'nai B'rith): 1978 (shared with Walter Cronkite and John Chancellor)
President's Award (Overseas Press Club): 1988
Museum of Broadcasting Honor (with retrospective on her career): 1988
Lowell Thomas Award (Marist College): 1990, 1994 (for journalism excellence)
Hall of Fame (National Academy of Television Arts and Sciences): 1990
American Museum of Moving Images Salute: 1992
Broadcasting & Cable Hall of Fame: 1993
Lifetime Achievement Award (Women's Projects and Productions): 1993
Newsperson of the Decade [for the 1980s (*TV Guide*)]: 1993
Hall of Fame (International Women's Forum): 1994

FURTHER READING

BOOKS

Gilbert, Lynn, and Gaylen Moore. *Particular Passions: Talks With Women Who Have Shaped Our Times*, 1981
Malone, Mary. *Barbara Walters: TV Superstar* (Contemporary Women Series), 1990
Oppenheimer, Jerry. *Barbara Walters: An Unauthorized Biography*, 1991
Who's Who in America, 1994

PERIODICALS

Cosmopolitan, May 1990, p.356

Good Housekeeping, Jan. 1992, p.56
Harper's Magazine, Nov. 1989, p.40
Ladies Home Journal, June 1986, p.32; Mar. 1988, p.124; Nov. 1990, p.199
The Nation, Mar. 29, 1987, p.383
New York Times Magazine, Sep. 10, 1992, p.40; Mar. 19, 1994, p.12
People, Summer 1989 (special TV anniversary issue), p.66; Jan. 22, 1990, p.42
TV Guide, Sep. 27, 1991, p.35; Mar. 28, 1992, p.17; Mar. 19, 1994, p.12
Vogue, Feb. 1992, p.218

ADDRESS

"20/20", ABC News
47 West 66th Street
New York, NY 10023

BRIEF ENTRY

Charlie Ward 1970-
American Football and Basketball Player
Winner of the 1993 Heisman Trophy

EARLY LIFE

Charlie Ward, Jr., was born October 12, 1970, in Thomasville, Georgia, to Charlie and Willard Ward. He was the third of their seven children. Charlie Senior is a history teacher, and Willard is a school librarian. The Wards are a close-knit and deeply religious family, and Charlie Ward stands out almost as much for his soft-spoken demeanor and clean living as for his achievements as one of the most accomplished college athletes in history.

"Being a real straight arrow is something a lot of people are offended by I guess," he says. "But that's the way I've been all my life. It's just fun to be one of a kind."

While Ward earned good grades in high school and played so well that he was named Georgia's top prep quarterback in 1987, his ACT scores were too low to get him into the school of his choice, Florida State University. So he went to Tallahassee Community College for a year, brought up his test scores, and got into Florida State.

MAJOR ACCOMPLISHMENTS

Ward was an outstanding player in two sports at a major football and basketball powerhouse. As a football player, and as FSU's first black quarterback, he led the Seminoles to a national title in 1993, and even though he only played for two years, he set seven single-season records and seven career records. In his final season at FSU, Ward completed nearly 70% of his passes for a total of 3,032 yards and 27 touchdowns. On the basketball court as a point guard, Ward helped the team to a 22-10 record in the 1991-92 season, and to a 25-10 record in 1992-93.

In December 1993, Ward received the Heisman trophy as the outstanding collegiate football player in the U.S. The ceremony takes place each year at the Downtown Athletic Club in New York City. He got 91 percent of the first-place votes, making his one of largest margins of victory for the award in history. He dedicated the award to his late grandfathers, and, after thanking everyone, said to his teammates: "Guys, thanks to you everything's possible."

Ward graduated from FSU in December 1993, with a bachelor's degree in therapeutic recreation. His plans for the future, while guaranteed to be bright, are not clear as of this writing. Ward will probably be the only athlete in history to be drafted in the first round by both the NFL and the NBA, and he will make his career decision sometime later in 1994. Or, he could play professional baseball: although he didn't play baseball at the college level, this outstanding athlete was drafted last year by the Milwaukee Brewers. "I might just do it for the heck of it," Ward said.

Ward is active in a number of charities, including the Children's Miracle Network, the United Way, the Muscular Dystrophy Foundation, the March of Dimes, the American Heart Association, and the Police Athletic League. In addition, he takes part in the adopt-a-brother program in Tallahassee, and he speaks regularly at school and churches to kids.

HONORS AND AWARDS

Heisman Trophy: 1993
Player of the Year (*Sporting News*): 1993
Sullivan Award: 1993

FURTHER READING

People, Nov. 15, 1993, p.135
Sporting News, Dec. 20, 1993, p.23
Sports Illustrated, Oct. 5, 1992, p.32; Dec. 27, 1993, p.28

ADDRESS

Florida State University Sports Information
P.O. Drawer 2195
Tallahassee, FL 32316

Steve Young 1961-
American Professional Football Player
MVP Quarterback for the San Francisco 49ers

BIRTH

Jon Steven Young was born October 11, 1961, in Salt Lake City, the youngest of four sons and one daughter of LeGrande Young, a corporate lawyer, and Sherry Young, a homemaker. The family is directly descended from religious leader Brigham Young, who founded the Mormon religion and led his followers to Utah in the middle of the nineteenth century.

YOUTH

LeGrande Young, a running back at Brigham Young University (BYU) in the 1950s, was known by the nickname "Grit" on the football field, and he took that same attitude in his household. "My father is a black-and-white guy," Steve says. "If I was one minute late, he'd be at the doorstep waiting for me . . . . He never hit any of us. He didn't have to. He'd just give that look, the one where you'd disappointed him."

The day began early for the Youngs, a faithfully observant Mormon family living in Greenwich, Connecticut, where LeGrande had been transferred in 1967, and where Steve grew up. They nearly always were up at 5 a.m. for a half-hour drive to Scarsdale, New York, where they worshipped at the nearest (Mormon) Church of Jesus Christ of Latter-Day Saints. LeGrande would then drop Sherry off at home and the children at school before going to his office. It was a structured way of life for the active young family.

Steve's mother remembers Steve as a "heavy" child, always serious. He used to sit and watch football games with intense concentration, twirling his hair with one finger. "I think he always wanted to be a professional football player," Sherry says. Steve's dad discounts the importance of this: "Aw, that's every kid's dream," he says. "I wanted to be one, too."

EARLY MEMORIES

Young learned early from his father the importance of being active. "He was the kind of guy," Steve says, "that when I'd wake up Saturday mornings at, say, nine o'clock and was supposed to mow the lawn, the lawn mower would be going. He would want me to come sprinting out so he could say, 'I can't wait all day.' . . .My dad wanted you to do everything perfectly. And he wanted to keep you humble."

EDUCATION

Young was a National Merit Scholar at Greenwich High, a nationally recognized school, where he compiled a 3.7 grade-point average, including an A in advanced-placement calculus. He was a three-sport star (football, baseball, basketball) and, upon graduation, accepted a football scholarship at Brigham Young in Provo, Utah. There, he excelled in the classroom as well as on the football field, majoring in international relations and finance. "He'd worry like the other players," recalls football secretary Shirley Johnson. " 'Oh, I just did terrible on it' or 'That was a terrible paper,' and then he'd get the highest grade in the class."

After graduating from BYU in 1984, Young went on to graduate school. Never one to settle, or to refuse a challenge, he decided to earn a law degree while playing pro football, since he did not want to merely reflect on his glory days when the time came to retire. "I don't know what kind of law I want to practice, but it won't be corporate law, I know that," he says. Continuing his law studies in the offseason, Young graduated from BYU law school in 1993.

CAREER HIGHLIGHTS

COLLEGE FOOTBALL

By the time he was in college, it was clear that Steve Young was a fine enough athlete to compete professionally. But he had to wait two years behind future pro star Jim McMahon at BYU. At last, in 1982, Young emerged as the nation's premier quarterback. The Cougars went 11-1, including a Holiday Bowl victory over Missouri as Young passed for more than 300 yards in ten games. Gil Brandt, the renowned NFL (National Football League) scout, called him "the most accurate passer I've ever seen. Period." Young also ran well, gaining 418 rushing yards for the season. He led the NCAA (National Collegiate Athletic Association) in total offense by more than 100 yards per game, and finished second in the balloting for the coveted Heisman Trophy in 1983, an award given annually to the best college football player.

STARTING IN THE PROS—
THE EXPRESS AND THE OVERWHELMING CONTRACT

Young graduated in 1984 at a time when the NFL was trying to hold the line on salaries. This was especially difficult because of the upstart spring circuit, the United States Football League (USFL). Although Young had always wanted to be an NFL star, he agonized about competing contract offers. He finally decided that the new league's promises were more appealing. The Los Angeles Express gave him a chance to start immediately—and a $42 million contract, spread out until the year 2027. He called the contract process "sheer madness," and worried about fan reaction to the colossal deal. "I'm worrying about my values," he said at the time, and the day after the signing he was so upset and embarrassed about the enormity of the contract, reported the *New York Times*, that he even suggested to his agent that he should give back all the money, "except for a salary equal to the average salary of the other football players [on the team] and enough money to rent an apartment in Los Angeles and buy four new tires for his 1965 Oldsmobile." He was not then, nor is he yet, comfortable with the affluence his career has brought.

Young played well in two seasons with the Express, but did nothing spectacular. Rick Reilly of *Sports Illustrated* observed that he had "distinguished himself more as a scrambler than as a passer." The league, meanwhile, labored in obscurity and declining fortunes. When the 1985 USFL season was over, Young decided that enough was enough. He spent more than a million dollars to buy out his contract with Los Angeles and signed with the Tampa Bay Buccaneers. His two years there, however, were a disaster. The Bucs went 4-28 over that time, and Young was constrained by a conservative offensive philosophy and a weak offensive line. During the two seasons, he threw for only 11 touchdowns while giving up 21 interceptions.

THE SAN FRANCISCO YEARS

Steve Young got the break he needed when Tampa Bay traded him to the San Francisco 49ers in April 1987. Although he would be consigned to the bench backing up the legendary Joe Montana, he finally would be involved in an offense that could stress his talents and in an organization with a fine history of player development. Young played in 35 games over the next four years, but started in only ten. He was widely regarded as the best backup quarterback in the league, a status that had to be unsatisfying to such a fierce competitor. A highlight of those years, though, was a 49-yard touchdown run against Minnesota in 1988. He eluded eight Vikings on the run and provided the Niners with the margin of victory in what NFL Films' Steve Sabol called "the best football over the past 25 years."

Some reporters noted that Young and Montana had a chilly relationship during that time, but Steve always held his tongue, even when Montana and receiver Jerry Rice occasionally swiped at him in the press. "Young will not criticize Montana," writes Peter King, as painful as the star's treatment of him must have been.

A torn tendon placed Montana on the injured reserve list at the start of the 1991 season, finally giving Steve Young a chance to lead a top-caliber team through an NFL season. Although Bay Area (San Francisco) fans who had seen Montana capture four Super Bowls were not satisfied, Young performed beautifully. Playing in 11 games, and starting 10 before sustaining an injury, he rolled up 3,465 yards and a league-leading passing efficiency rating of 101.8. The Niners missed the playoffs, however, and Young continued to be compared unfavorably to Montana. Ann Killion, writing in the *San Jose Mercury News*, said that "[Steve] won't criticize the healthy portion of the public that doesn't accept him simply because he's not Joe. He just shrugs his shoulders. It's part of the territory."

It would take one more year, his tenth professional season, for Steve Young's talents to be fully appreciated. With Montana on the disabled list for most of the season, Young took the NFL by storm in 1992, completing 67 percent of his passes for 6,021 yards with 25 touchdowns and only seven interceptions. His 107.0 passer rating marked the first time in football history that a quarterback achieved the 100 mark for two consecutive years. Young led the Niners to the NFL championship game, which they lost to the eventual Super Bowl champions, the Dallas Cowboys. He won the league title that year of Most Valuable Player.

San Francisco lost Joe Montana to the Kansas City Chiefs during the off season in 1993. His departure leaves the team's future in the hands of Young, a man the Rams' defensive coach calls "a defensive coach's nightmare." *Petersen's Pro Football Preview* praised Young for his "ability both to run for yardage and also to escape from pass rushers," adding that he "has a strong arm, is effective downfield, and has developed a nice sense of when to run or not run, and also when to stop running and throw on the run." Now that he is out from under Montana's looming presence and after a decade in the pros, Steve Young is getting the recognition he has worked so hard to win.

MAJOR INFLUENCES

Young did not rebel against his strict father. "I think in some ways my father is too harsh about life, but I truly respect him," Steve says. "I can't tell you how grateful I am for the way I was raised, and it wasn't easy. I was the oldest of the kids and if there was a fight, I was always responsible. Yet as tough as my father was, he was always fair." Young credits his dad for providing him with a strong work ethic and a disdain for luxury.

One humorous anecdote from 1984 points up the prevailing philosophy in the Young household. Just after Steve signed his record contract with the now-defunct USFL, he went home to Greenwich with a pocketful of money. But LeGrande, reported *Sports Illustrated*, "made sure his son didn't lose perspective. He had him mow the lawn, clean out the garage, do the dishes and help his [then] 14-year-old brother, Tommy, deliver the *Greenwich Times*."

MARRIAGE AND FAMILY

Steve Young remains single at the age of 32. "I'd love to get married," he says. "I think that would be something that would be great." Despite a couple of serious relationships, however, he apparently has not yet found the right match. He keeps a home in Mountain View, California, near San Jose, and splits his off-season time between a tiny house in Provo and a ski lodge in Park City, Utah.

HOBBIES AND OTHER INTERESTS

Young lives simply and is casual and unpretentious. He no longer wheels around in an old car littered with fast-food wrappers, but in spite of his enormous wealth, he is happy driving the Jeep Cherokee he bought on impulse some years ago from a former BYU teammate. "I don't like [fancy] cars, I swear to you," he has said. "I've always wanted a really fast car. I don't care what it looks like on the outside. One of these days I'm going to get me a fast car."

Steve Young is known as a generous benefactor. Foremost among his many charities is his own Forever Young Foundation, which directs money to troubled children in the Bay Area, to his alma mater in Provo, and to charitable organizations near his Connecticut hometown. The foundation will receive more than $1 million over the period of the record five-year, $26.75 million contract he signed with the 49ers in July 1993. Young also does charitable work with Navajo Indians in Utah and other western states, and makes dozens of motivational speeches to Mormon youth every year during the off season. Keenly interested in politics as well, he calls himself a "liberal Republican," although he campaigned for moderate Democrat Dianne Feinstein (now U.S. Senator Feinstein) in her successful run for governor of California several years ago.

Young looks forward to eventually fulfilling his Mormon mission of two years overseas, a commitment made by most devout Mormon men, and one he delayed at the beginning of his career.

HONORS AND AWARDS

Consensus All-American: 1983
All-NFL Team: 1992
All-Pro: 1992
NFL Most Valuable Player: 1992
Sporting News Player of the Year: 1992
Miller Lite Player of the Year: 1992
Len Eshmont Award (given by teammates for inspirational play): 1992
Pro Bowl Award: 1993

FURTHER READING

PERIODICALS

Current Biography, Oct. 1993, p.54
Los Angeles Times, Aug. 2, 1992, p.C3

New York Times, May 27, 1993, p.B14
People, Nov. 8, 1982, p.134
San Francisco Chronicle, Sep. 23, 1991, p.D3
San Jose Mercury News, Aug. 28, 1988, p.W4
Sport, December 1985, p.55; Aug. 1993, p.29
Sports Illustrated, Sep. 19, 1988, p.44; Sep.30, 1991, p.24; May 13, 1993, p.69

ADDRESS

San Francisco 49ers
4949 Centennial Boulevard
Santa Clara, CA 95054

Kim Zmeskal 1976-
American Gymnast
Two-Time World Champion, Three-Time National Champion, and Olympic Bronze Medalist

BIRTH

Kim Zmeskal (zuh-MESS-kal) was born February 6, 1976, in Houston, Texas. Her mother, Clarice, is a contract manager for Mobil Oil, and her father, David, is a manager of a welding parts store. She has a younger brother, Eric, and a younger sister, Melissa.

YOUTH

Kim's interest in gymnastics started early. Both of her parents worked, and she spent several hours each week watching her babysitter's daughter take gymnastics. By the time she was six, she'd been bitten by the bug. "She just got in the car one day when I picked her up and started talking about cartwheels and stuff," Clarice Zmeskal recalls. "She said, 'Oh, it's really neat, mom. Can I do it?'" Despite her enthusiasm, Kim admits that she was scared at first. "I used to be the scardest thing," she recalls. "I wouldn't do anything. I used to cry all the time because I didn't want to do it. My mom used to say, 'If you're going to sit there and cry then we're going to have to take you out.' I didn't want to do that, so I started working out."

A YOUNG GYMNAST

At that time, Bela Karolyi, the well-known gymnastics coach who had guided Nadia Comaneci of Romania to an Olympic gold medal in 1976, had emigrated to the U.S. He decided to open a gymnastics club in Houston, coincidentally located just down the street from the Zmeskal home. He was training an elite group of gymnasts from around the country, one of whom was Mary Lou Retton, who would go on to win the Olympic gold medal in 1984. Compact, muscular, and fiery, Retton was one of the first U.S. gymnasts to capture the hearts of the American public and the imaginations of young would-be gymnasts. She became a role model for a generation of girls who longed to compete in a sport that until that point had been dominated by teams from Eastern Europe.

Although Zmeskal began training at the gym in 1982, she didn't begin to work with Karolyi until 1987. But he knew who she was. Zmeskal was part of a group of seven- and eight-year-olds called "The Pumpkin Federation," with Zmeskal as Pumpkin President. Even then, Karolyi recognized her potential. "She was this little, jumping, pumping thing who exploded every time she moved," he recalls. "Her little feet would be moving a hundred miles an hour. It's hard at that age to get a true measure of what these little tigers might be like. But you could predict big things for Kim. She had great physical capabilities. She was an itty bitty girl with a great big heart."

EDUCATION

Zmeskal attended public schools in Houston until she was 14, when her training intensified and she began to attend a private school, Northland Christian, which allowed her to go to class for three-and-a-half hours only. At that time, she would go to the gym first thing in the morning, work out for a few hours, go to school from 11 to 2:30, go home for dinner and a nap, then go back to the gym from 4:30 to 8. She'd return home for homework and bed. Despite all the effort she put into her sport, Zmeskal was always a straight-A student, and she particularly liked math.

CAREER HIGHLIGHTS

Zmeskal got used to hearing how much she looked and moved like Retton, which was fine with her, for Retton was her idol. Retton also represented changes in the ideal gymnasts' body type and in the sport itself. In the 1980s, gymnastic judges began to favor the power and athletic ability of someone like Retton over the elegant, balletic movements that typified former champions. Like Retton, Zmeskal is small: 4'7" and 80 pounds. Although she competes in all the gymnastic events—floor exercise, uneven parallel bars, the balance beam, and the vault—Zmeskal's favorite event is floor exercise, where her speed and strength are shown to best advantage. Her weakest event is the uneven parallels, where gymnasts with longer bodies look better and score better.

Zmeskal's dedication and intensity paid off early. She began to compete in junior division championships in 1988 at the age of 12, and by the time she was 13 she was winning national championships. In 1989, she won the U.S. all-around championship for junior girls. The all-around competition combines scores from floor exercise, uneven parallels, vault, and beam. She followed her victory in the junior division one year later with a win in the all-around competition for senior women. At the age of 14, she was the youngest national champion, male or female, to win the title. It was to be the first of three consecutive U.S. titles for Zmeskal. That same year, 1990, she won the McDonald's American Cup, scoring a first in the all-around, the vault, and the floor exercise. She also competed in the Goodwill Games, where she placed sixth in the all-around.

By this time, her training had increased so much that she began to take her high school classes through correspondence courses. She also attracted a great deal of media attention, bearing up well under the close scrutiny that continued until her Olympic debut two year later. Many noted her unbending concentration and dedication, including Retton, who said, "she has a steel stomach and an iron heart." Karolyi, who often refers to his gymnasts as different animals, called her a "lion."

Zmeskal's determination impressed many people, even her parents. "In many ways, she pushed *us*," her parents say. She has even refused to let her parents in the gym during her work outs. "Sometimes I guess I sound like I don't want my parents around. I know they have been a big part of what I'm doing. But this is my thing. Gymnastics is something *I've* always wanted. It's something that I can get into and get away from everything else. I enjoy it, for myself." And with the commitment comes sacrifice. While in training, Zmeskal never ate pizza, ice cream, or other sweets, and she had to watch her weight all the time. But, she says, the sacrifices were always worth it.

THE WORLD CHAMPIONSHIPS

In 1991 at the World Championships in Indianapolis, Indiana, Zmeskal stunned the sports world by becoming the world champion in the all-around. Once again she was in the record books: she was the first U.S. woman ever to win first place in the event at the World's. She won over the favored athlete, Svetlana Boguinskaia of the USSR. Boguinskaia claimed that the U.S. judges were biased, and that Zmeskal didn't deserve the medal. She even refused to shake Zmeskal's hand after the competition. Karolyi responded in defense of his protege: "This is the end of an era of Soviet domination. This is a beautiful world champion, Svetlana Boguinskaia. All the respect and admiration go to her, but her time is over. The championship went to the right person."

Any doubts about Zmeskal's ability were silenced the following year, when she won two more world gymnastics titles, in floor exercise and balance beam, at the World Championships in Paris. Now her attention, and the media's, centered on the Olympics, to be held in July 1992 in Barcelona, Spain.

1992 OLYMPICS

Beginning in early 1992, the press began a deluge of articles about Zmeskal, predicting her dominance in the 1992 Olympic games. She was on the cover of *Time* magazine and was featured in an HBO special. The stage was set for what many commentators thought would be a sweep by Zmeskal. The pressure was enormous. But something went wrong. On her first event, Zmeskal lost her footing on the balance beam and fell. It was during a routine move, a back handspring, something she had done thousands of times before. She couldn't believe what was happening. "I came off the podium thinking, 'That wasn't the Olympics,'" she recalled. "I was worried I'd let everybody down. Bela. The team. The American people. How could I not? The television camera was right in my face." It was a face that, in the words of one commentator, "showed shock, and that pained frightened expression seldom left Zmeskal's countenance for the rest of the competition."

Her mistake cost her dearly, and nearly knocked her out of the competition altogether. Later, during her floor exercise routine, she momentarily stepped out of bounds on her landing. These small mistakes cost Zmeskal her much-anticipated gold medals. She had to settle for a bronze as part of the U.S. team effort, which most saw as a consolation prize.

Zmeskal's fall from glory caused another storm of media attention. Many writers felt that Zmeskal and all the young gymnasts were simply under too much pressure, at too young an age. They claimed that the kids had been robbed of their childhoods, burdened with expectations they couldn't possibly fulfill. Karolyi especially came under fire. Several of his former athletes came forward and accused him of being a bully, of forcing them to perform when they were injured, and of emphasizing the importance of slimness until they developed eating disorders. Karolyi announced his retirement. Zmeskal, pursued by reporters, went home to Houston, where she returned to public school and the normal routine of a high school junior. She jogged to stay in shape, worked out two hours instead of eight each day, and stayed out of competition and the limelight.

In the spring of 1993, she was asked to compete in an invitational tournament sponsored by Subaru. She was one of four contestants, and she did a tremendous job, winning the event. But she did not return to the world of competition. She attended the world championships in 1993 as a spectator. She also plans to see the 1996 Olympics "from the stands." Gymnastics is still a part, but a much smaller part, of her life. She now takes part in training demonstrations with Karolyi and other former competitors like Comaneci and Bart Carter.

With gymnastics no longer the center of her life, Zmeskal has had time to put her experience in perspective. "For so long my goal had been the

'92 Olympics. It never seemed like it would be here. Then, all of a sudden it was over and it was like, 'What now?' All I ever knew was the gym, and it was a shock to my system to go to school. At first, my feelings about myself were based on what other people thought. But I learned to put things in perspective. I learned that winning a gold medal isn't the only thing that makes you feel like you've won."

FAMILY

Many commentators have noted that Zmeskal seems to have been spared the emotional trauma that often goes with becoming an international star at such a young age, and most say the credit goes to her family. Unlike many young sports hopefuls who have to live away from their families to train, Zmeskal lives one block from Karolyi's gym. The family had arranged vacations, birthday parties, and all kinds of events around Zmeskal's schedule for years, and they continue to be supportive of her decisions regarding gymnastics and her future.

HOBBIES AND OTHER INTERESTS

Zmeskal is a fan of the daytime soap opera "Days of Our Lives," likes Arsenio Hall and Boyz II Men, and collects bottles, pins, and t-shirts.

She also tries to answer all of her fan mail personally, and she is always willing to oblige fans who come up to her in restaurants and ask her to sign a napkin. But not everyone recognizes her. Recently, she went to a restaurant with her family, and because of her small size, the waitress gave her crayons and a coloring book.

HONORS AND AWARDS

U.S. National Champion: 1990, 1991, 1992
McDonald's American Cup: 1990, 1991, 1992
World Gymnastics Champion: 1991, 1992
Olympic Bronze Medal: Women's Team, 1992

FURTHER READING

PERIODICALS

Houston Chronicle, July 19, 1992, p.A11
Houston Post, Apr. 22, 1992, p.G8; Dec. 6, 1992, p.B5
International Gymnast, Sep. 1990, p.17; Dec. 1990, p.25; May 1993, p.16
Los Angeles Times, July 7, 1992, p.F14
Miami Herald, June 12, 1992, p.C6; Sep. 7, 1993, p.C2
New York Times, July 30, 1989, p. H1; June 11, 1990. p.C9

Newsweek, July 27, 1992, p.54; Aug. 10, 1992, p.20
People, Oct. 28, 1991, p.111
Seventeen, June 1992, p.86
Sports Illustrated, Sep. 23, 1991, p.40; July 22, 1992, p.54; Dec. 14, 1992, p.70
Time, July 27, 1992, p.56

ADDRESS

IMG
22 E. 71st Street
New York, NY 10021

Photo and Illustration Credits

Tim Allen/Photos: Copyright © 1992,1993 Touchstone Pictures & Television.

Marian Anderson/Photo: UPI/Bettmann.

Ned Andrews/Photo: Mark Bowen

Yasir Arafat/Photos: AP/Wide World Photos.

Mayim Bialik/Photo: NBC Photo.

Bonnie Blair/Photos: Rick Stewart/ALLSPORT; Simon Bruty/ ALLSPORT.

Mary Chapin Carpenter/Photo: Caroline Greyshock

Connie Chung/Photo: Tony Esparza.

Beverly Cleary/Photo: Margaret Miller. Cover: A Dell Yearling title by Beverly Cleary.

Kurt Cobain/Photo: Copyright © Charile Hoselton/Retna Ltd.

F. W. de Klerk/Photo: AP/Wide World Photos.

Rita Dove/Photo: Fred Viebahn.

Linda Ellerbee/Photo: Gittings/Skipworth, Inc.

Zlata Filipovic/Photo: AP/Wide World Photos.

Ruth Bader Ginsburg/Photo: Martin Simon.

Tonya Harding/Photos: Mike Powell/ALLSPORT: Annie O'Neill/ Copyright © 1994 *The Detroit News*

Melissa Joan Hart/Photo: NICKELODEON/Tom Hurst.

Geoff Hooper/Photo: Mark Bowen.

Dan Jansen/Photos: Cy White.

Nancy Kerrigan/Photos: Bill Frakes/*Sports Illustrated*; Heinz Kluetmeier/ *Sports Illustrated*

Charlotte Lopez/Photo: Charles Bush.

Wilma Mankiller/Photo: James Schnepf.

Shannon Miller/Photo: USA Gymnastics photo copyright © Dave Black.

Toni Morrison/Photo: Copyright © Kate Kunz.

Richard Nixon/Photos: AP Wide World Photos.

Greg Norman/Photos: AP/Wide World Photos; Jacqueline Duvoisin/ *Sports Illustrated*

Severo Ochoa/Photo: AP/Wide World Photos.

River Phoenix/Photo: Alan Derek/Rnagefinders/Globe Photos.

Richard Scarry/Cover: Illustration by Richard Scarry from CARS AND TRUCKS AND THINGS THAT GO. Copyright © 1974 by Richard Scarry. Used by permission of Western Publishing Company, Inc.

Will Smith/Photo: Myles Aronowitz; NBC Photo.

Steven Spielberg/Photo: Murray Close.

R.L. Stine/Cover: Scholastic, Inc.

Charlie Ward/Photos: FSU Sports Information.

Kim Zmeskal/Photos: U.S.G.F. Photo Copyright © Dave Black

Appendix

This Appendix contains updates for individuals profiled in Volumes 1, 2, and 3 of *Biography Today*.

* YASIR ARAFAT *

For his efforts in 1993 in negotiating peace between the Palestine Liberation Organization and Israel, PLO Chairman Yasir Arafat was awarded the Nobel Peace Prize on October 14, 1994. He shares the honor with Israeli Prime Minister Yitzhak Rabin and Israeli Foreign Minister Shimon Peres. In announcing their decision, the Nobel committee stated that "Arafat, Peres, and Rabin have made substantial contributions to a historic process through which peace and cooperation can replace war and hate." The choice of Arafat was controversial: one member of the Nobel committee resigned in protest, because of Arafat's connections with active terrorist groups. On the day the award was announced, the extremist Palestinian group Hamas murdered an Israeli soldier they had kidnapped. The actions of Hamas tragically overshadowed Arafat's receipt of the prize; how these recent events will affect the on-going negotiations between the PLO and Israel is not clear.

* FIDEL CASTRO *

In the past year, Fidel Castro's nation of Cuba has been racked with internal dissent and external pressures to change. A recent crisis in which thousands of Cubans attempted to flee their country and seek asylum in the U.S. ended in the U.S. decision to admit up to 20,000 Cuban immigrants a year and to temporarily detain those who wish to leave at the U.S. naval base at Guantanamo Bay in Cuba. Also, Cuba is under pressure from Spain to negotiate with Cuban exiles living in the U.S. who want to oust Castro from power and bring democracy and a market economy to Cuba. Whether or not Castro's regime can withstand the domestic and outside forces remains a question.

* BENJAMIN CHAVIS *

Benjamin Chavis was fired from his job as executive director of the NAACP on August 19, 1994, after allegations of sexual harassment and financial mismanagement came to light. In an out-of-court settlement, Chavis paid $82,000 to a former aide, Mary E. Stansel, who had threatened him with a sexual harassment and a sex discrimination suit. Of that amount, $64,000 came from NAACP funds, and the settlement could cost the group up to $332,000. Also, it was announced that the organization had a deficit of almost $3 million, which some members blamed on Chavis's extravagant spending. These problems were compounded by Chavis's overtures to the controversial leader of the Nation of Islam, Lewis Farrakhan, a move that many NAACP members opposed. After he was fired, Chavis claimed he had been "crucified" and threatened to sue the organization. Chavis is now chairman of the African-American Leadership Summit, which was formed to analyze political, economic, and social concerns of the African-American community.

* BILL CLINTON *

Three of Bill Clinton's major legislative efforts during his second year in office included the successful passage of NAFTA (North American Free Trade Agreement) and the Crime Bill, as well as the failure of his comprehensive health care bill. In foreign policy, Clinton committed U.S. troops to Haiti to reestablish the presidency of Jean Bertrand Aristide and to the Persian Gulf to counter the attempt of Saddam Hussein to once again invade Kuwait. Clinton's rating in the polls is low; as of October 1994, only 42 percent of the American people believed he was doing his job well. Commentators cite his main problems as his frequent reversals on domestic and foreign policy issues, the damage done to his credibility and reputation brought about by the continuing investigation into the Whitewater financial scandal (that implicates both Bill and Hillary Clinton), and the anti-Washington mood in the country.

* HILLARY CLINTON *

As the Clinton administration's central spokesperson for health care reform, Hillary Clinton was much in the news in the past year. But legislation on health care reform and national insurance was not passed in the U.S. Congress this year. She believes that the administration was not successful in getting its plan understood by the American people, and that the administration also underestimated the opposition to its proposals. Still, Hillary Clinton does not believe that health care reform is a dead issue. "What's important is what went right and what's going to go on in the future, because health care reform is now on the national agenda. And that is a big step forward for our country."

* F.W. DE KLERK *

In April 1994, F.W. de Klerk lost his bid for reelection to the presidency of South Africa as the National Party candidate. The presidency went to Nelson Mandela, whose ANC party won with 60 percent of the vote; de Klerk received 30 percent. De Klerk continues to serve the government as a member of Mandela's cabinet in the position of executive deputy president.

* SHANNEN DOHERTY *

Shannen Doherty left the cast of the popular television show "Beverly Hills 90210" at the end of the 1993-1994 season. She claims she quit, even though reports from the show's producers indicate that she was fired for chronic lateness. In September 1993, Doherty married Ashley Hamilton. The couple separated in February and Doherty filed for divorce April 7, 1994.

* SERGEI FEDOROV *

Sergei Fedorov ended the 1994 NHL Hockey season as the most honored player in the league, becoming the first Russian-born player to win the Hart Trophy as the league's most valuable player. He also received the Selke Trophy as the best defensive forward, and the Pearson Award as the best player in the NHL, an honor awarded by his fellow players. "It's the greatest time I have ever had," said Fedorov.

* POPE JOHN PAUL II *

After the Pope canceled his much-anticipated trip to the United States in September 1994, concern regarding his state of health began to arise. The Pope had broken his leg and undergone surgery in April, and he had appeared frail and unsteady in his recent public appearances. He had planned to travel to the U.S. in October until his condition caused his doctors to recommend that he postpone his trip. Despite the Pope's physical frailty, Vatican officials are denying that anything is seriously wrong with him and say that he plans to visit the U.S. in 1995.

* MICHAEL JORDAN *

After retiring from basketball in the fall of 1993, Jordan stunned the sports world again by deciding to play for a minor league baseball team, the Birmingham Barons, who are part of the Chicago White Sox baseball organization. The transition to a new sport has not been easy, and Jordan has not played that well, ending his first season with a .202 batting average. As of this writing, Jordan plans to play in the minors again in 1995. He also appeared again in a Chicago Bulls uniform, playing in a charity basketball game organized by former teammate Scottie Pippin in September 1994. Jordan delighted the crowd, scoring 52 points in the game. It was the final game played in the old Chicago Bulls Stadium, and Jordan kissed the floor as a final tribute to the place where he and the Bulls had won three straight NBA championships.

* NELSON MANDELA *

In 1993, Nelson Mandela received the Nobel Peace Prize, which he shared with F.W. de Klerk. In 1994, he became the first black man elected to the office of President of South Africa, defeating former President F.W. de Klerk in elections held in April. As *Chicago Tribune* writer Liz Sly wrote, Mandela assumed "the presidency of the country that imprisoned him for 27 years for advocating the democratic system of government that came into existence" with his election. Six months into his term, Mandela leads a country that is struggling to make economic and social gains and to enter the world economy. In October of 1994 Mandela spoke to both the United Nations and the U.S. Congress, thanking them for their support for the struggle of his people.

* WALTER DEAN MYERS *

In February 1994 Walter Dean Myers won the Lifetime Achievement Award given by the Association for Library Service to Children. The awarding group is part of the American Library Association.

* MARTINA NAVRATILOVA *

Martina Navratilova retired from tennis in November 1994, playing her final match in the Virginia Slims Championships in New York City. Considered by many to be the greatest woman's tennis player of all time, Navratilova won more tournaments than any other player in the history of the sport. Her records include 18 Grand Slam titles, 167 tournaments, and a ranking in the top five for the last 20 years. "Friends say, 'Oh, don't' retire, don't retire,'" says Navratilova, "and you know I'm not retiring. I'm just not going to play tennis. I'm going to have a blast." Now, she is looking forward to finishing her new home in Aspen, Colorado, and to trying new sports, like helicopter skiing.

* ROSA PARKS *

In August 1994, civil rights pioneer Rosa Parks was brutally beaten during a robbery in her Detroit home. The assailant, Joseph Skipper, was arrested and charged with the crime. Parks was treated and released from a Detroit hospital and is fully recovered. She has participated in the investigation into the incident: "I'm trying to do everything I can to cooperate to see that justice will be done," she said. She plans to continue her work with the Rosa and Raymond Parks Institute for Self Development.

* YITZHAK RABIN *

With PLO Chairman Yasir Arafat and Israeli Foreign Minister Simon Peres, Yitzhak Rabin was awarded the Nobel Peace Prize on October 14, 1994, for his work in negotiating peace between the Israeli and Palestinian peoples. The Nobel committee said the award was intended to "honor a political act which called for great courage on both sides, and which has opened up opportunities for a new development towards fraternity in the Middle East." But the receipt of the award was marred by tragedy. On the day the prize was announced, the Palestinian extremist group

Hamas murdered an Israeli soldier they had kidnapped; another Israeli soldier and several Hamas members also died in the Israeli effort to free the captive soldier. At a news conference Rabin said, "I would gladly give up the Nobel prize if I could bring the two fallen soldiers back to life." What affect the incident will have on the continuing PLO—Israeli talks is not known.

* STEVEN SPIELBERG *

Spielberg's film *Schindler's List* was released in late 1993, and it proved to be a great popular and critical success. In the United States and Europe, the movie stirred renewed interest, particularly among younger viewers, in learning about the Holocaust. At the Academy Awards ceremony on March 21, 1994, Spielberg was honored with the award for Best Director, and the movie won six additional Oscars, including the awards for Best Picture, Adapted Screenplay, Cinematography, Film Editing, Original Score, and Art Direction. In addition, his hit *Jurassic Park* won several Oscars for its technical achievements, including the awards for Best Sound, Sound Effects Editing, and Visual Effects.

Name Index

Listed below are the names of all individuals profiled in *Biography Today,* followed by the date of the issue in which they appear.

Abdul, Paula 92/Jan
Agassi, Andre 92/Jul
Allen, Tim 94/Apr
Alley, Kirstie 92/Jul
Anderson, Marian 94/Jan
Anderson, Terry 92/Apr
Andretti, Mario 94/Sep
Andrews, Ned 94/Sep
Angelou, Maya 93/Apr
Arafat, Yasir 94/Sep;
   94/Update
Arnold, Roseanne 92/Oct
Ashe, Arthur 93/Sep
Asimov, Isaac 92/Jul
Avi 93/Jan
Babbitt, Bruce 94/Jan
Baker, James 92/Oct
Barkley, Charles 92/Apr
Barr, Roseanne
   see Arnold, Roseanne 92/Oct
Battle, Kathleen 93/Jan
Bergen, Candice 93/Sep
Bialik, Mayim 94/Jan
Bird, Larry 92/Jan
Blair, Bonnie 94/Apr
Blume, Judy 92/Jan
Blythe, William J. IV
   see Clinton, Bill 92/Jul
Bollea, Terry J.
   see Hogan, Hulk 92/Apr
Boutros-Ghali, Boutros 93/Apr
Bradley, Ed 94/Apr
Breathed, Berke 92/Jan
Breathed, Guy Berkeley
   see Breathed, Berke .. 92/Jan
Brooks, Garth 92/Oct
Burke, Chris 93/Sep
Burrell, Stanley Kirk
   see Hammer 92/Jan
Bush, Barbara 92/Jan
Bush, George 92/Jan
Candy, John 94/Sep
Carpenter, Mary Chapin 94/Sep
Carvey, Dana 93/Jan

Castro, Fidel . 92/Jul;94/Update
Chavez, Cesar 93/Sep
Chavis, Benjamin 94/Jan;
   94/Update
Chung, Connie 94/Jan
Cisneros, Henry 93/Sep
Cleary, Beverly 94/Apr
Clinton, Bill 92/Jul;
   94/Update
Clinton, Hillary
   Rodham .. 93/Apr;94/Update
Cobain, Kurt 94/Sep
Cosby, Bill 92/Jan
Cosby, William Henry, Jr.
   see Cosby, Bill 92/Jan
Cousteau, Jacques 93/Jan
Crawford, Cindy 93/Apr
Culkin, Macaulay 93/Sep
de Klerk, F.W. 94/Apr;
   94/Update
Diana, Princess of Wales 92/Jul
Dick, Tim Allen
   see Allen, Tim 94/Apr
Doherty, Shannen 92/Apr;
   94/Update
Dole, Elizabeth Hanford 92/Jul
Dove, Rita 94/Jan
Duke, David 92/Apr
Duncan, Lois 93/Sep
Edelman, Marian
   Wright 93/Apr
Ellerbee, Linda 94/Apr
Estefan, Gloria 92/Jul
Fedorov, Sergei 94/Apr;
   94/Update
Fielder, Cecil 93/Sep
Filipovic, Zlata 94/Sep
Fresh Prince
   see Smith, Will 94/Sep
Fuentes, Daisy 94/Jan
Gates, Bill 93/Apr
Geisel, Theodor Seuss
   see Seuss, Dr. 92/Jan
Gilbert, Sara 93/Apr

NAME INDEX

Gillespie, Dizzy 93/Apr
Gillespie, John Birks
  see Gillespie, Dizzy .. 93/Apr
Ginsburg, Ruth Bader . 94/Jan
Goldberg, Whoopi 94/Apr
Gorbachev, Mikhail ... 92/Jan;
  94/Update
Gore, Al 93/Jan
Graf, Steffi 92/Jan
Gretzky, Wayne 92/Jan;
  93/Update
Groening, Matt 92/Jan
Guisewite, Cathy 93/Sep
Guy, Jasmine 93/Sep
Haley, Alex 92/Apr
Hammer 92/Jan
Handford, Martin 92/Jan
Harding, Tonya 94/Sep
Hart, Melissa Joan 94/Jan
Hawking, Stephen 92/Apr
Hill, Anita 93/Jan
Hogan, Hulk 92/Apr
Hooper, Geoff 94/Jan
Horowitz, Winona Laura
  see Ryder, Winona ... 93/Jan
Houston, Whitney 94/Sep
Hussein, Saddam 92/Jul
Iacocca, Lee A. 92/Jan
Ice-T 93/Apr
Jackson, Bo 92/Jan;
  93/Update
Jackson, Vincent Edward
  see Jackson, Bo 92/Jan
Jansen, Dan 94/Apr
Jemison, Mae 92/Oct
Jennings, Peter 92/Jul
Jobs, Steven 92/Jan
John Paul II . 92/Oct;94/Update
Johnson, Caryn
  see Goldberg, Whoopi 94/Apr
Johnson, Earvin (Magic)
  see Johnson, Magic .. 92/Apr
Johnson, Magic 92/Apr
Johnson, Marguerite
  see Angelou, Maya .. 93/Apr

Jordan, Michael 92/Jan;
  93/Update;94/Update
Joyner-Kersee, Jackie 92/Oct
Kerrigan, Nancy 94/Apr
Kistler, Darci 93/Jan
Lalas, Alexi 94/Sep
lang, k.d. 93/Sep
Lang, Katherine Dawn
  see lang, k.d. 93/Sep
Lee, Shelton J.
  see Lee, Spike 92/Apr
Lee, Spike 92/Apr
Lemieux, Mario 92/Jul;
  93/Update
L'Engle, Madeleine 92/Jan
Leno, James Douglas Muir
  see Leno, Jay 92/Jul
Leno, Jay 92/Jul
Lopez, Charlotte 94/Apr
Ma, Yo-Yo 92/Jul
Mandela, Nelson 92/Jan;
  94/Update
Mankiller, Wilma 94/Apr
Marino, Dan 93/Apr
Marrow, Tracy
  see Ice-T 93/Apr
Marsalis, Wynton 92/Apr
Marshall, Thurgood 92/Jan;
  93/Update
Martin, Ann M. 92/Jan
McClintock, Barbara 92/Oct
McCully, Emily Arnold . 92/Jul;
  93/Update
Menchu, Rigoberta 93/Jan
Miller, Shannon 94/Sep
Morrison, Toni 94/Jan
Myers, Walter Dean 93/Jan;
  94/Update
Navratilova, Martina ... 93/Jan;
  94/Update
Naylor, Phyllis Reynolds 93/Apr
Nixon, Richard 94/Sep
Norman, Greg 94/Jan
Novello, Antonia 92/Apr;
  93/Update
Nureyev, Rudolf 93/Apr

NAME INDEX

Ochoa, Severo 94/Jan
O'Connor, Sandra Day . 92/Jul
O'Neal, Shaquille 93/Sep
Owens, Dana
  see Queen Latifah ... 92/Apr
Parks, Rosa . 92/Apr;94/Update
Pauley, Jane 92/Oct
Perot, H. Ross 92/Apr;
  94/Update
Perry, Luke 92/Jan
Phoenix, River 94/Apr
Pine, Elizabeth Michele 94/Jan
Pippen, Scottie 92/Oct
Powell, Colin 92/Jan;93/Update
Priestley, Jason 92/Apr
Queen Latifah 92/Apr
Rabin, Yitzhak 92/Oct;
  93/Update;94/Update
Reno, Janet 93/Sep
Rice, Jerry 93/Apr
Ride, Sally 92/Jan
Robinson, Mary 93/Sep
Rose, Pete 92/Jan
Ryan, Nolan 92/Oct;93/Update
Ryder, Winona 93/Jan
Salk, Jonas 94/Jan
Scarry, Richard 94/Sep
Schwarzkopf, H.
  Norman 92/Jan
Seinfeld, Jerry 92/Oct
Seuss, Dr. 92/Jan
Smith, Emmitt 94/Sep
Smith, Will 94/Sep

Spencer, Diana
  see Diana, Princess of
  Wales 92/Jul
Spielberg, Steven 94/Jan;
  94/Update
Spinelli, Jerry 93/Apr
Steinem, Gloria 92/Oct
Stewart, Patrick 94/Jan
Stine, R.L. 94/Apr
Thomas, Clarence 92/Jan
Thomas, Lewis 94/Apr
Van Allsburg, Chris 92/Apr
Voigt, Cynthia 92/Oct
Walters, Barbara 94/Sep
Ward, Charlie 94/Apr
Washington, Denzel 93/Jan
Watterson, Bill 92/Jan
Watterson, William B. II
  see Watterson, Bill 92/Jan
Wayans, Keenen Ivory ... 93/Jan
Williams, Robin 92/Apr
Winfield, Dave 93/Jan
Winfrey, Oprah 92/Apr
Wojtyla, Karol Josef
  see John Paul II 92/Oct
Wortis, Avi
  see Avi 93/Jan
Yamaguchi, Kristi 92/Apr
Yeltsin, Boris 92/Apr;
  93/Update
Young, Steve 94/Jan
Zmeskal, Kim 94/Jan

General Index

This index includes subjects, occupations, organizations, and ethnic and minority origins that pertain to individuals profiled in *Biography Today*.

"ABC World News Tonight"
  Jennings, Peter, 92/Jul
activists
  Arafat, Yasir, 94/Sep;94/Update
  Ashe, Arthur, 93/Sep
  Chavez, Cesar, 93/Sep
  Chavis, Benjamin, 94/Jan;
    94/Update
  Edelman, Marian Wright, 93/Apr
  Mandela, Nelson, 92/Jan;
    94/Update
  Mankiller, Wilma, 94/Apr
  Menchu, Rigoberta, 93/Jan
  Parks, Rosa, 92/Apr;94/Update
  Steinem, Gloria, 92/Oct
actors/actresses
  Allen, Tim, 94/Apr
  Alley, Kirstie, 92/Jul
  Arnold, Roseanne, 92/Oct
  Bergen, Candice, 93/Sep
  Bialik, Mayim, 94/Jan
  Burke, Chris, 93/Sep
  Candy, John, 94/Sep
  Carvey, Dana, 93/Jan
  Culkin, Macaulay, 93/Sep
  Doherty, Shannen, 92/Apr;
    94/Update
  Gilbert, Sara, 93/Apr
  Goldberg, Whoopi, 94/Apr
  Hart, Melissa Joan, 94/Jan
  Lee, Spike, 92/Apr
  Perry, Luke, 92/Jan
  Phoenix, River, 94/Apr
  Priestley, Jason, 92/Apr
  Ryder, Winona, 93/Jan
  Smith, Will, 94/Sep
  Stewart, Patrick, 94/Jan
  Washington, Denzel, 93/Jan
  Wayans, Keenen Ivory, 93/Jan
  Williams, Robin, 92/Apr
  Winfrey, Oprah, 92/Apr

AIDS (acquired immuno-deficiency syndrome)
  Ashe, Arthur, 93/Sep
  Johnson, Magic, 92/Apr
  Nureyev, Rudolf, 93/Apr
Afrikaners
  de Klerk, F.W., 94/Apr;
    94/Update
**Ambassador to the
United Nations**
  Bush, George, 92/Jan
American Red Cross
  Dole, Elizabeth Hanford, 92/Jul
**amyotrophic lateral
sclerosis (ALS)**
  Hawking, Stephen, 92/Apr
**ANC (African National
Congress)**
  de Klerk, F.W., 94/Apr
  Mandela, Nelson, 92/Jan;
    94/Update
apartheid
  de Klerk, F.W., 94/Apr;
    94/Update
  Mandela, Nelson, 92/Jan;
    94/Update
Apple Computer
  Jobs, Steven, 92/Jan
Aqua-lung
  Cousteau, Jacques, 93/Jan
Arizona, Governor of
  Babbitt, Bruce, 94/Jan
Arkansas, Governor of
  Clinton, Bill, 92/Jul
Army, U.S.
  Ashe, Arthur, 93/Sep
  Asimov, Isaac, 92/Jul
  Gore, Al, 93/Jan
  Ice-T, 93/Apr
  Myers, Walter Dean, 93/Jan
  Powell, Colin, 92/Jan

GENERAL INDEX

Scarry, Richard, 94/Sep
Schwarzkopf, H. Norman, 92/Jan
Seuss, Dr., 92/Jan
Asian-American
Chung, Connie, 94/Jan
Ma, Yo-Yo, 92/Jul
Yamaguchi, Kristi, 92/Apr
Associated Press
Anderson, Terry, 92/Apr
astronauts
Jemison, Mae, 92/Oct
Ride, Sally, 92/Jan
athletes
Agassi, Andre, 92/Jul
Ashe, Arthur, 93/Sep
Barkley, Charles, 92/Apr
Bird, Larry, 92/Jan
Blair, Bonnie, 94/Apr
Fedorov, Sergei, 94/Apr; 94/Update
Graf, Steffi, 92/Jan
Gretzky, Wayne, 92/Jan; 93/Update
Harding, Tonya, 94/Sep
Jackson, Bo, 92/Jan;93/Update
Jansen, Dan, 94/Apr
Johnson, Magic, 92/Apr
Jordan, Michael, 92/Jan; 93/Update;94/Update
Joyner-Kersee, Jackie, 92/Oct
Kerrigan, Nancy, 94/Apr
Lalas, Alexi, 94/Sep
Lemieux, Mario, 92/Jul; 93/Update
Marino, Dan, 93/Apr
Miller, Shannon, 94/Sep
Navratilova, Martina, 93/Jan; 94/Update
O'Neal, Shaquille, 93/Sep
Pippen, Scottie, 92/Oct
Rice, Jerry, 93/Apr
Rose, Pete, 92/Jan
Ryan, Nolan, 92/Oct;93/Update
Smith, Emmitt, 94/Sep
Ward, Charlie, 94/Apr
Winfield, Dave, 93/Jan
Yamaguchi, Kristi, 92/Apr
Zmeskal, Kim, 94/Jan
Attorney General, U.S.
Reno, Janet, 93/Sep
Australian
Norman, Greg, 94/Jan
authors
Angelou, Maya, 93/Apr
Ashe, Arthur, 93/Sep
Asimov, Isaac, 92/Jul
Avi, 93/Jan
Bergen, Candice, 93/Sep
Blume, Judy, 92/Jan
Boutros-Ghali, Boutros, 93/Apr
Cleary, Beverly, 94/Apr
Cosby, Bill, 92/Jan
Cousteau, Jacques, 93/Jan
Dove, Rita, 94/Jan
Duncan, Lois, 93/Sep
Filipovic, Zlata, 94/Sep
Gore, Albert, Jr., 93/Jan
Haley, Alex, 92/Apr
Handford, Martin, 92/Jan
Iacocca, Lee A., 92/Jan
L'Engle, Madeleine, 92/Jan
Martin, Ann M., 92/Jan
McCully, Emily Arnold, 92/Jul; 93/Update
Morrison, Toni, 94/Jan
Myers, Walter Dean, 93/Jan; 94/Update
Naylor, Phyllis Reynolds, 93/Apr
Nixon, Richard, 94/Sep
Salk, Jonas, 94/Jan
Scarry, Richard, 94/Sep
Seuss, Dr., 92/Jan
Spinelli, Jerry, 93/Apr
Steinem, Gloria, 92/Oct
Stewart, Patrick, 94/Jan
Stine, R.L., 94/Apr
Thomas, Lewis, 94/Apr
Van Allsburg, Chris, 92/Apr

GENERAL INDEX

Voigt, Cynthia, 92/Oct
automobile executive
   Iacocca, Lee A., 92/Jan
automobile racer
   Andretti, Mario, 94/Sep
ballet
   Kistler, Darci, 93/Jan
   Nureyev, Rudolf, 93/Apr
baseball players
   Fielder, Cecil, 93/Sep
   Jackson, Bo, 92/Jan;93/Update
   Jordan, Michael, 94/Update
   Rose, Pete, 92/Jan
   Ryan, Nolan, 92/Oct;93/Update
   Winfield, Dave, 93/Jan
basketball players
   Barkley, Charles, 92/Apr
   Bird, Larry, 92/Jan
   Johnson, Magic, 92/Apr
   Jordan, Michael, 92/Jan;
    93/Update;94/Update
   O'Neal, Shaquille, 93/Sep
   Pippen, Scottie, 92/Oct
   Ward, Charlie, 94/Apr
"Beverly Hills, 90210"
   Doherty, Shannen, 92/Apr;
    94/Update
   Perry, Luke, 92/Jan
   Priestley, Jason, 92/Apr
Beloved
   Morrison, Toni, 94/Jan
biology
   McClintock, Barbara, 92/Oct
   Ochoa, Severo, 94/Jan
black
  activists
    Ashe, Arthur, 93/Sep
    Chavis, Benjamin, 94/Jan;
     94/Update
    Edelman, Marian Wright,
     93/Apr
    Mandela, Nelson, 92/Jan;
     94/Update
    Parks, Rosa, 92/Apr;
     94/Update

actors/actresses
   Goldberg, Whoopi, 94/Apr
   Guy, Jasmine, 93/Sep
   Lee, Spike, 92/Apr
   Smith, Will, 94/Sep
   Washington, Denzel, 93/Jan
   Wayans, Keenen Ivory, 93/Jan
   Winfrey, Oprah, 92/Apr
astronauts
   Jemison, Mae, 92/Oct
athletes
   Ashe, Arthur, 93/Sep
   Fielder, Cecil, 93/Sep
   Harding, Tonya, 94/Sep
   Jackson, Bo, 92/Jan;93/Update
   Johnson, Magic, 92/Apr
   Jordan, Michael, 92/Jan;
    93/Update;94/Update
   Joyner-Kersee, Jackie, 92/Oct
   O'Neal, Shaquille, 93/Sep
   Pippen, Scottie, 92/Oct
   Rice, Jerry, 93/Apr
   Smith, Emmitt, 94/Sep
   Ward, Charlie, 94/Apr
   Winfield, Dave, 93/Jan
authors
   Angelou, Maya, 93/Apr
   Ashe, Arthur, 93/Sep
   Cosby, Bill, 92/Jan
   Dove, Rita, 94/Jan
   Haley, Alex, 92/Apr
   Morrison, Toni, 94/Jan
   Myers, Walter Dean, 93/Jan;
    94/Update
film directors
   Lee, Spike, 92/Apr
   Wayans, Keenen Ivory, 93/Jan
general, U.S. Army
   Powell, Colin, 92/Jan;
    93/Update
journalists
   Bradley, Ed, 94/Apr
jurists
   Marshall, Thurgood, 92/Jan;
    93/Update

GENERAL INDEX

Thomas, Clarence, 92/Jan
musicians
　Gillespie, Dizzy, 93/Apr
　Marsalis, Wynton, 92/Apr
public figures
　Hill, Anita, 93/Jan
singers
　Anderson, Marian, 94/Jan
　Battle, Kathleen, 93/Jan
　Hammer, 92/Jan
　Houston, Whitney, 94/Sep
　Ice-T, 93/Apr
　Queen Latifah, 92/Apr
　Smith, Will, 94/Sep
television
　Cosby, Bill, 92/Jan
　Goldberg, Whoopi, 94/Apr
　Guy, Jasmine, 93/Sep
　Smith, Will, 94/Sep
　Wayans, Keenan Ivory, 93/Jan
　Winfrey, Oprah, 92/Apr
"Blossom"
　Bialik, Mayim, 94/Jan
Bosnian
　Filipovic, Zlata, 94/Sep
Boston Celtics
　Bird, Larry, 92/Jan
Boy Scouts
　Anderson, Terry, 92/Apr
　Perot, H. Ross, 92/Apr
　Spielberg, Steven, 94/Jan
Brief History of Time, A
　Hawking, Stephen, 92/Apr
business leaders
　Gates, Bill, 93/Apr
　Iacocca, Lee A., 92/Jan
　Jobs, Steven, 92/Jan
　Perot, H. Ross, 92/Apr;
　　93/Update
Calvin and Hobbes
　Watterson, Bill, 92/Jan
Camp Fire Girls
　Cleary, Beverly, 94/Apr
Canadian
　Candy, John, 94/Sep

Gretzky, Wayne, 92/Jan;
　93/Update
Jennings, Peter, 92/Jul
lang, k.d., 93/Sep
Lemieux, Mario, 92/Jul;
　93/Update
Priestley, Jason, 92/Apr
Cars and Trucks and Things That Go
　Scarry, Richard, 94/Sep
cartoonists
　Breathed, Berke, 92/Jan
　Guisewite, Cathy, 93/Sep
　Groening, Matt, 92/Jan
　Watterson, Bill, 92/Jan
Cat in the Hat, The
　Seuss, Dr., 92/Jan
Cathy
　Guisewite, Cathy, 93/Sep
"CBS Evening News"
　Chung, Connie, 94/Jan
Chairman, Joint Chiefs of Staff
　Powell, Colin, 92/Jan;93/Update
"Cheers"
　Alley, Kirstie, 92/Jul
Cherokee
　Mankiller, Wilma, 94/Apr
Chicago Bulls
　Jordan, Michael, 92/Jan;
　　93/Update;94/Update
　Pippen, Scottie, 92/Oct
Chicago White Sox
　Jackson, Bo, 92/Jan;93/Update
children's authors
　Asimov, Isaac, 92/Jul
　Avi, 93/Jan
　Blume, Judy, 92/Jan
　Cleary, Beverly, 94/Apr
　Duncan, Lois, 93/Sep
　Handford, Martin, 92/Jan
　L'Engle, Madeleine, 92/Jan
　Martin, Ann M., 92/Jan
　McCully, Emily Arnold, 92/Apr;
　　93/Update

GENERAL INDEX

Myers, Walter Dean, 93/Jan; 94/Update
Naylor, Phyllis Reynolds, 93/Apr
Scarry, Richard, 94/Sep
Seuss, Dr., 92/Jan
Spinelli, Jerry, 93/Apr
Stine, R.L., 94/Apr
Van Allsburg, Chris, 92/Apr
Voigt, Cynthia, 92/Oct

Children's Defense Fund (CDF)
Edelman, Marian Wright, 93/Apr

choreographers
Abdul, Paula, 92/Jan
Nureyev, Rudolf, 93/Apr

Chrysler Corporation
Iacocca, Lee A., 92/Jan

CIA, director of the
Bush, George, 92/Jan

Civil Rights Movement
Chavis, Benjamin, 94/Jan; 94/Update
Edelman, Marian Wright, 93/Apr
Marshall, Thurgood, 92/Jan; 93/Update
Parks, Rosa, 92/Apr;94/Update

"Clarissa Explains It All"
Hart, Melissa Joan, 94/Jan

clergy
Chavis, Benjamin, 94/Jan; 94/Update

Coast Guard, U.S.
Haley, Alex, 92/Apr

comedians
Allen, Tim, 94/Apr
Arnold, Roseanne, 92/Oct
Candy, John, 94/Sep
Carvey, Dana, 93/Jan
Cosby, Bill, 92/Jan
Goldberg, Whoopi, 94/Apr
Leno, Jay, 92/Jul
Seinfeld, Jerry, 92/Oct
Wayans, Keenen Ivory, 93/Jan
Williams, Robin, 92/Apr

Communists
Castro, Fidel, 92/Jul;94/Update
Gorbachev, Mikhail, 92/Jan
Yeltsin, Boris, 92/Apr; 93/Update

computers
Gates, Bill, 93/Apr
Jobs, Steven, 92/Jan
Perot, H. Ross, 92/Apr

"Cosby Show, The"
Cosby, Bill, 92/Jan

cosmology
Hawking, Stephen, 92/Apr

Cousteau Society
Cousteau, Jacques, 93/Jan

Cuba, president of
Castro, Fidel, 92/Jul;94/Update

Cuban
Castro, Fidel, 92/Jul;94/Update

Cuban-American
see also Hispanic-American
Estefan, Gloria, 92/Jul
Fuentes, Daisy, 94/Jan

Cuban Revolution
Castro, Fidel, 92/Jul;94/Update

Czechoslovakian
Navratilova, Martina, 93/Jan; 94/Update

Dallas Cowboys
Smith, Emmitt, 94/Sep

dancers
Abdul, Paula, 92/Jan
Estefan, Gloria, 92/Jul
Hammer, 92/Jan
Kistler, Darci, 93/Jan
Nureyev, Rudolf, 93/Apr

David and Jonathan
Voigt, Cynthia, 92/Oct

Dear Mr. Henshaw
Cleary, Beverly, 94/Apr

Deenie
Blume, Judy, 92/Jan

Democratic Party
Clinton, Bill, 92/Jul
Gore, Al, 93/Jan

GENERAL INDEX

Desert Shield/Desert Storm commander
  Schwarzkopf, H. Norman, 92/Jan
Detroit Red Wings
  Fedorov, Sergei, 94/Apr; 94/Update
Detroit Tigers
  Fielder, Cecil, 93/Sep
Dicey's Song
  Voigt, Cynthia, 92/Oct
"A Different World"
  Guy, Jasmine, 93/Sep
diplomats
  Boutros-Ghali, Boutros, 93/Apr
disabled
  Hawking, Stephen, 92/Apr
doctors
  Jemison, Mae, 92/Oct
  Novello, Antonia, 92/Apr
  Salk, Jonas, 94/Jan
Down's Syndrome
  Burke, Chris, 93/Sep
Edmonton Oilers
  Gretzky, Wayne, 92/Jan
EDS (Electronic Data Systems)
  Perot, H. Ross, 92/Apr
Egyptian
  Boutros-Ghali, Boutros, 93/Apr
English
  Diana, Princess of Wales, 92/Jul
  Handford, Martin, 92/Jan
  Hawking, Stephen, 92/Apr
  Stewart, Patrick, 94/Jan
environmentalists
  Babbitt, Bruce, 94/Jan
  Cousteau, Jacques, 93/Jan
  Gore, Al, 93/Jan
"Eye to Eye with Connie Chung"
  Chung, Connie, 94/Jan
Fear Street
  Stine, R.L., 94/Apr

female
  activists
    Edelman, Marian Wright, 93/Apr
    Mankiller, Wilma, 94/Apr
    Menchu, Rigoberta, 93/Jan
    Parks, Rosa, 92/Apr;94/Update
    Steinem, Gloria, 92/Oct
  actresses
    Alley, Kirstie, 92/Jul
    Arnold, Roseanne, 92/Oct
    Bergen, Candice, 93/Sep
    Bialik, Mayim, 94/Jan
    Doherty, Shannen, 92/Apr; 94/Update
    Gilbert, Sara, 93/Apr
    Goldberg, Whoopi, 94/Apr
    Guy, Jasmine, 93/Sep
    Hart, Melissa Joan, 94/Jan
    Ryder, Winona, 93/Jan
    Winfrey, Oprah, 92/Apr
  astronauts
    Jemison, Mae, 92/Oct
    Ride, Sally, 92/Jan
  athletes
    Blair, Bonnie, 94/Apr
    Graf, Steffi, 92/Jan
    Harding, Tonya, 94/Sep
    Joyner-Kersee, Jackie, 92/Oct
    Kerrigan, Nancy, 94/Apr
    Miller, Shannon, 94/Sep
    Navratilova, Martina, 93/Jan; 94/Update
    Yamaguchi, Kristi, 92/Apr
    Zmeskal, Kim, 94/Jan
  authors
    Angelou, Maya, 93/Apr
    Bergen, Candice, 93/Sep
    Blume, Judy, 92/Jan
    Cleary, Beverly, 94/Apr
    Dove, Rita, 94/Jan
    Duncan, Lois, 93/Sep
    Filipovic, Zlata, 94/Sep
    L'Engle, Madeleine, 92/Jan
    McCully, Emily Arnold, 92/Jul; 93/Update

Morrison, Toni, 94/Jan
Naylor, Phyllis Reynolds, 93/Apr
Steinem, Gloria, 92/Oct
Voigt, Cynthia, 92/Oct
cartoonists
Guisewite, Cathy, 93/Sep
dancers
Abdul, Paula, 92/Jan
Estefan, Gloria, 92/Jul
Kistler, Darci, 93/Jan
doctors
Jemison, Mae, 92/Oct
Novello, Antonia, 92/Apr; 93/Update
journalists
Chung, Connie, 94/Jan
Ellerbee, Linda, 94/Apr
Pauley, Jane, 92/Oct
Walters, Barbara, 94/Sep
jurists
Ginsburg, Ruth Bader, 94/Jan
O'Connor, Sandra Day, 92/Jul
models (professional)
Crawford, Cindy, 93/Apr
public figures
Bush, Barbara, 92/Jan
Clinton, Hillary Rodham, 93/Apr
Diana, Princess of Wales, 92/Apr
Dole, Elizabeth Hanford, 92/Jul
Fuentes, Daisy, 94/Jan
Hill, Anita, 93/Jan
Lopez, Charlotte, 94/Apr
Reno, Janet, 93/Sep
Robinson, Mary, 93/Sep
scientists
Jemison, Mae, 92/Oct
McClintock, Barbara, 92/Oct
Ride, Sally, 92/Jan
singers
Abdul, Paula, 92/Jan
Anderson, Marian, 94/Jan
Battle, Kathleen, 93/Jan

Carpenter, Mary Chapin, 94/Sep
Estefan, Gloria, 92/Jul
Guy, Jasmine, 93/Sep
Houston, Whitney, 94/Sep
lang, k.d., 93/Sep
Queen Latifah, 92/Apr
feminists
Ginsburg, Ruth Bader, 94/Jan
Steinem, Gloria, 92/Oct
film directors
Lee, Spike, 92/Oct
Spielberg, Steven, 94/Jan; 94/Update
Wayans, Keenen Ivory, 93/Jan
film producers
Cousteau, Jacques, 93/Jan
First Lady of the United States
Bush, Barbara, 92/Jan
Clinton, Hillary Rodham, 93/Apr
football players
Jackson, Bo, 92/Jan; 93/Update
Marino, Dan, 93/Apr
Rice, Jerry, 93/Apr
Smith, Emmitt, 94/Sep
Ward, Charlie, 94/Apr
Young, Steve, 94/Jan
Forever
Blume, Judy, 92/Jan
Forever Young Foundation
Young, Steve, 94/Jan
foster children
Lopez, Charlotte, 94/Apr
Foundation
Asimov, Isaac, 92/Jul
French
Cousteau, Jacques, 93/Jan
French-Canadian
Abdul, Paula, 92/Jan
Lemieux, Mario, 92/Jul
"Fresh Prince of Bel-Air"
Smith, Will, 94/Sep

GENERAL INDEX

general, U.S. Army
　Powell, Colin, 92/Jan; 93/Update
　Schwarzkopf, H. Norman, 92/Jan
genetics
　McClintock, Barbara, 92/Oct
　Ochoa, Severo, 94/Jan
German
　Graf, Steffi, 92/Jan
Girl Scouts
　Clinton, Hillary Rodham, 93/Apr
golf
　Norman, Greg, 94/Jan
Goosebumps
　Stine, R.L., 94/Apr
Governor of Arizona
　Babbitt, Bruce, 94/Jan
Governor of Arkansas
　Clinton, Bill, 92/Jul
"grand slam" of tennis, winner
　Graf, Steffi, 92/Jan
　Navratilova, Martina, 93/Jan
Green Eggs and Ham
　Seuss, Dr., 92/Jan
Guatemalan
　Menchu, Rigoberta, 93/Jan
gymnasts
　Miller, Shannon, 94/Sep
　Zmeskal, Kim, 94/Jan
Harpo Productions
　Winfrey, Oprah, 92/Apr
Heisman Trophy
　Jackson, Bo, 92/Jan
　Ward, Charlie, 94/Apr
Henry Huggins
　Cleary, Beverly, 94/Apr
heptathlon
　Joyner-Kersee, Jackie, 92/Oct
Hispanic-American
　Chavez, Cesar, 93/Sep
　Cisneros, Henry, 93/Sep
　Estefan, Gloria, 92/Jul
　Fuentes, Daisy, 94/Jan
　Lopez, Charlotte, 94/Apr
　Novello, Antonia, 92/Apr
　Ochoa, Severo, 94/Jan
hockey players
　Fedorov, Sergei, 94/Apr; 94/Update
　Gretzky, Wayne, 92/Jan; 93/Update
　Lemieux, Mario, 92/Jul; 93/Update
Hodgkin's disease
　Lemieux, Mario, 93/Update
Homecoming
　Voigt, Cynthia, 92/Oct
"Home Improvement"
　Allen, Tim, 94/Apr
hostages
　Anderson, Terry, 92/Apr
I, Robot
　Asimov, Isaac, 92/Jul
illustrators
　Handford, Martin, 92/Jan
　McCully, Emily Arnold, 92/Apr; 93/Update
　Scarry, Richard, 94/Sep
　Seuss, Dr., 92/Jan
　Van Allsburg, Chris, 92/Apr
"In Living Color"
　Wayans, Keenen Ivory, 93/Jan
inventors
　Cousteau, Jacques, 93/Jan
Iraq, President of
　Hussein, Saddam, 92/Jul
Iraqi
　Hussein, Saddam, 92/Jul
Ireland, President of
　Robinson, Mary, 93/Sep
Irish
　Robinson, Mary, 93/Sep
Israel, Prime Minister of
　Rabin, Yitzhak, 92/Oct; 93/Update;94/Update
Israeli
　Rabin, Yitzhak, 92/Oct; 93/Update;94/Update

GENERAL INDEX

Italian
    Andretti, Mario, 94/Sep
Jazz
    Morrison, Toni, 94/Jan
Joint Chiefs of Staff, Chairman of
    Powell, Colin, 92/Jan; 93/Update
journalists
    Anderson, Terry, 92/Apr
    Bradley, Ed, 94/Apr
    Chung, Connie, 94/Jan
    Ellerbee, Linda, 94/Apr
    Jennings, Peter, 92/Jul
    Pauley, Jane, 92/Oct
    Walters, Barbara, 94/Sep
Jurassic Park
    Spielberg, Steven, 94/Jan; 94/Update
jurists
    Ginsburg, Ruth Bader, 94/Jan
    Marshall, Thurgood, 92/Jan; 93/Update
    O'Connor, Sandra Day, 92/Jul
    Thomas, Clarence, 92/Jan
justices, United States Supreme Court
    Ginsburg, Ruth Bader, 94/Jan
    Marshall, Thurgood, 92/Jan
    O'Connor, Sandra Day, 92/Jul
    Thomas, Clarence, 92/Jan
Ku Klux Klan
    Duke, David, 92/Apr
Labor Party (Israel)
    Rabin, Yitzhak, 92/Oct; 93/Update;94/Update
Laker Girl
    Abdul, Paula, 92/Jan
lawyers
    Babbitt, Bruce, 94/Jan
    Boutros-Ghali, Boutros, 93/Apr
    Clinton, Hillary Rodham, 93/Apr
    Reno, Janet, 93/Sep

librarians
    Avi, 93/Jan
    Cleary, Beverly, 94/Apr
"Life Goes On"
    Burke, Chris, 93/Sep
literacy, promotion of
    Bush, Barbara, 92/Jan
Los Angeles Kings
    Gretzky, Wayne, 92/Jan; 93/Update
Los Angeles Lakers
    Johnson, Magic, 92/Apr
Los Angeles Raiders
    Jackson, Bo, 92/Jan;93/Update
Lou Gehrig's disease
    see amyotrophic lateral sclerosis
Maniac Magee
    Spinelli, Jerry, 93/Apr
Marine Corps
    Anderson, Terry, 92/Apr
    Baker, James, 92/Oct
Miami Dolphins
    Marino, Dan, 93/Apr
Microsoft Corp.
    Gates, Bill, 93/Apr
military service, France
    Cousteau, Jacques, 93/Jan
military service, Israel
    Rabin, Yitzhak, 92/Oct
military service, U.S.
    Army
        Ashe, Arthur, 93/Sep
        Asimov, Isaac, 92/Jul
        Gore, Al, 93/Jan
        Ice-T, 93/Apr
        Myers, Walter Dean, 93/Jan
        Powell, Colin, 92/Jan; 93/Update
        Scarry, Richard, 94/Sep
        Schwarzkopf, H. Norman, 92/Jan
        Seuss, Dr., 92/Jan
    Coast Guard
        Haley, Alex, 92/Apr

GENERAL INDEX

Marine Corps
  Anderson, Terry, 92/Apr
  Baker, James, 92/Oct
Navy
  Bush, George, 92/Jan
  Chavez, Cesar, 93/Sep
  Cosby, Bill, 92/Jan
  Nixon, Richard, 94/Sep
  Perot, H. Ross, 92/Apr
  Spinelli, Jerry, 93/Apr
Minnesota Twins
  Winfield, Dave, 93/Jan
Mirette on the High Wire
  McCully, Emily Arnold, 93/Update
Miss Teen USA
  Lopez, Charlotte, 94/Apr
models (professional)
  Crawford, Cindy, 93/Apr
"Mork and Mindy"
  Williams, Robin, 92/Jul
Mouse and the Motorcycle, The
  Cleary, Beverly, 94/Apr
***Ms.* magazine**
  Steinem, Gloria, 92/Oct
MTV
  Crawford, Cindy, 93/Apr
  Fuentes, Daisy, 94/Jan
"Murphy Brown"
  Bergen, Candice, 93/Sep
musicians
  Gillespie, Dizzy, 93/Apr
  Ma, Yo-Yo, 92/Jul
  Marsalis, Wynton, 92/Apr
National Association for the Advancement of Colored People (NAACP)
  Angelou, Maya, 93/Apr
  Chavis, Benjamin, 94/Jan;94/Update
  Marshall, Thurgood, 92/Jan
  Parks, Rosa, 92/Apr
National Association for the Advancement of White People (NAAWP)
  Duke, David, 92/Apr

National Party (South Africa)
  de Klerk, F.W., 94/Apr; 94/Update
National Spelling Bee, Scripps Howard
  Andrews, Ned, 94/Sep
  Hooper, Geoff, 94/Jan
native peoples
  Mankiller, Wilma, 94/Apr
  Menchu, Rigoberta, 93/Jan
Navy, U.S.
  Bush, George, 92/Jan
  Chavez, Cesar, 93/Sep
  Cosby, Bill, 92/Jan
  Nixon, Richard, 94/Sep
  Perot, H. Ross, 92/Apr
  Spinelli, Jerry, 93/Apr
Nazism
  Duke, David, 92/Apr
New York City Ballet
  Kistler, Darci, 93/Jan
"Nick News"
  Ellerbee, Linda, 94/Apr
Nightfall
  Asimov, Isaac, 92/Jul
Nirvana
  Cobain, Kurt, 94/Sep
Nobel Prize
  Arafat, Yasir, 94/Update
  de Klerk, F.W., 94/Apr
  Gorbachev, Mikhail, 92/Jan
  Mandela, Nelson, 94/Update
  McClintock, Barbara, 92/Oct
  Menchu, Rigoberta, 93/Jan
  Morrison, Toni, 94/Jan
  Ochoa, Severo, 94/Jan
  Rabin, Yitzhak, 94/Update
Oakland Athletics, batboy
  Hammer, 92/Jan
obituaries
  Anderson, Marian, 94/Jan
  Ashe, Arthur, 93/Sep
  Asimov, Isaac, 92/Jul
  Candy, John, 94/Sep
  Chavez, Cesar, 93/Sep

GENERAL INDEX

Cobain, Kurt, 94/Sep
Gillespie, Dizzy, 93/Apr
Haley, Alex, 92/Apr
Marshall, Thurgood, 93/Update
McClintock, Barbara, 92/Oct
Nixon, Richard, 94/Sep
Nureyev, Rudolf, 93/Apr
Ochoa, Severo, 94/Jan
Phoenix, River, 94/Apr
Scarry, Richard, 94/Sep
Seuss, Dr., 92/Jan
Thomas, Lewis, 94/Apr
Oh, the Places You'll Go!
   Seuss, Dr., 92/Jan
oil executive
   Bush, George, 92/Jan
Olympics
   Blair, Bonnie, 94/Apr
   Harding, Tonya, 94/Sep
   Jansen, Dan, 94/Apr
   Joyner-Kersee, Jackie, 92/Oct
   Kerrigan, Nancy, 94/Apr
   Miller, Shannon, 94/Sep
   Yamaguchi, Kristi, 92/Apr
   Zmeskal, Kim, 94/Jan
opera
   Anderson, Marian, 94/Jan
   Battle, Kathleen, 93/Jan
"Oprah Winfrey Show, The"
   Winfrey, Oprah, 92/Apr
Orfe
   Voigt, Cynthia, 92/Oct
Orlando Magic
   O'Neal, Shaquille, 93/Sep
Palestinian
   Arafat, Yasir, 94/Sep;94/Update
Perot Systems Corp.
   Perot, H. Ross, 92/Apr
Philadelphia 76ers
   Barkley, Charles, 92/Apr
Phoenix Suns
   Barkley, Charles, 92/Apr
Pittsburgh Penguins
   Lemieux, Mario, 92/Jul;
   93/Update

PLO (Palestinian Liberation Organization)
   Arafat, Yasir, 94/Sep;94/Update
Poet Laureate of the United States
   Dove, Rita, 94/Jan
Polar Express, The
   Van Allsburg, Chris, 92/Apr
polio vaccine
   Salk, Jonas, 94/Jan
Polish
   John Paul II, 92/Oct;
   94/Update
politicians
   Arafat, Yasir, 94/Sep;94/Update
   Babbitt, Bruce, 94/Jan
   Baker, James, 92/Oct
   Boutros-Ghali, Boutros, 93/Apr
   Bush, George, 92/Jan
   Castro, Fidel, 92/Jul;
   94/Update
   Cisneros, Henry, 93/Sep
   Clinton, Bill, 92/Jul;
   94/Update
   de Klerk, F.W., 94/Apr;
   94/Update
   Duke, David, 92/Apr
   Gorbachev, Mikhail, 92/Jan
   Gore, Al, 93/Jan
   Hussein, Saddam, 92/Jul
   Mandela, Nelson, 92/Jan;
   94/Update
   Nixon, Richard, 94/Sep
   Perot, H. Ross, 92/Apr;
   93/Update
   Rabin, Yitzhak, 92/Oct;
   93/Update;94/Update
   Robinson, Mary, 93/Sep
   Yeltsin, Boris, 92/Apr;
   93/Update
Pope of the Roman Catholic Church
   John Paul II, 92/Oct;94/Update
President of Cuba
   Castro, Fidel, 92/Jul;94/Update

GENERAL INDEX

President of Iraq
  Hussein, Saddam, 92/Jul
President of Ireland
  Robinson, Mary, 93/Sep
President of the Republic of South Africa
  de Klerk, F.W., 94/Apr; 94/Update
  Mandela, Nelson, 94/Update
President of the Russian Federation
  Yeltsin, Boris, 92/Apr; 93/Update
President of the Soviet Union
  Gorbachev, Mikhail, 92/Jan
President of the United States
  Bush, George, 92/Jan
  Clinton, Bill, 92/Jul
  Nixon, Richard, 94/Sep
Prime Minister of Israel
  Rabin, Yitzhak, 92/Oct; 93/Update;94/Update
Principal Chief of the Cherokee Nation of Oklahoma
  Mankiller, Wilma, 94/Apr
publisher
  Seuss, Dr., 92/Jan
Puerto Rican
  see also Hispanic-American
  Lopez, Charlotte, 94/Apr
  Novello, Antonia, 92/Apr
Ramona
  Cleary, Beverly, 94/Apr
rap singers
  Hammer, 92/Jan
  Ice-T, 93/Apr
  Queen Latifah, 92/Apr
  Smith, Will, 94/Sep
recording artists
  Abdul, Paula, 92/Jan
  Anderson, Marian, 94/Jan
  Battle, Kathleen, 93/Jan
  Brooks, Garth, 92/Oct
  Carpenter, Mary Chapin, 94/Sep
  Cobain, Kurt, 94/Sep
  Cosby, Bill, 92/Jan
  Estefan, Gloria, 92/Jul
  Guy, Jasmine, 93/Sep
  Hammer, 92/Jan
  Houston, Whitney, 94/Sep
  Ice-T, 93/Apr
  lang, k.d., 93/Sep
  Ma, Yo-Yo, 92/Jul
  Marsalis, Wynton, 92/Apr
  Queen Latifah, 92/Apr
  Smith, Will, 94/Sep
Red Cross
  see American Red Cross
Republican National Committee, chairman
  Bush, George, 92/Jan
Republican Party
  Baker, James, 92/Oct
  Bush, George, 92/Jan
  Nixon, Richard, 94/Sep
Rhodes Scholar
  Clinton, Bill, 92/Jul
Richard Scarry's Best Word Book Ever
  Scarry, Richard, 94/Sep
robots
  Asimov, Isaac, 92/Jul
Roman Catholic Church
  John Paul II, 92/Oct; 94/Update
Roots
  Haley, Alex, 92/Apr
"Roseanne"
  Arnold, Roseanne, 92/Oct
  Gilbert, Sara, 93/Apr
royalty
  Diana, Princess of Wales, 92/Jul
Russian
  Fedorov, Sergei, 94/Apr; 94/Update
  Gorbachev, Mikhail, 92/Jan
  Yeltsin, Boris, 92/Apr; 93/Update

GENERAL INDEX

Russian Federation, president of
   Yeltsin, Boris, 92/Apr;93/Update
San Francisco 49ers
   Rice, Jerry, 93/Apr
   Young, Steve, 94/Jan
"Saturday Night Live"
   Carvey, Dana, 93/Jan
science fiction literature
   Asimov, Isaac, 92/Jul
Science Talent Search, Westinghouse
   Pine, Elizabeth Michele, 94/Jan
scientists
   Asimov, Isaac, 92/Jul
   Hawking, Stephen, 92/Apr
   Jemison, Mae, 92/Oct
   McClintock, Barbara, 92/Oct
   Ochoa, Severo, 94/Jan
   Ride, Sally, 92/Jan
   Salk, Jonas, 94/Jan
   Thomas, Lewis, 94/Apr
scientology
   Alley, Kirstie, 92/Jul
   Seinfeld, Jerry, 92/Oct
"SCTV"
   Candy, John, 94/Sep
Secretary General of the United Nations
   Boutros-Ghali, Boutros, 93/Apr
Secretary of Housing and Urban Development, U.S.
   Cisneros, Henry, 93/Sep
Secretary of Interior, U.S.
   Babbitt, Bruce, 94/Jan
Secretary of Labor, U.S.
   Dole, Elizabeth Hanford, 92/Jul
Secretary of State, U.S.
   Baker, James, 92/Oct
Secretary of Transportation, U.S.
   Dole, Elizabeth Hanford, 92/Jul
Secretary of Treasury, U.S.
   Baker, James, 92/Oct
"Seinfeld"
   Seinfeld, Jerry, 92/Oct

sexual harassment
   Hill, Anita, 93/Jan
Shiloh
   Naylor, Phyllis Reynolds, 93/Apr
"Simpsons, The"
   Groening, Matt, 92/Jan
singers
   Abdul, Paula, 92/Jan
   Anderson, Marian, 94/Jan
   Battle, Kathleen, 93/Jan
   Brooks, Garth, 92/Oct
   Carpenter, Mary Chapin, 94/Sep
   Cobain, Kurt, 94/Sep
   Estefan, Gloria, 92/Jul
   Guy, Jasmine, 93/Sep
   Hammer, 92/Jan
   Houston, Whitney, 94/Sep
   Ice-T, 93/Apr
   lang, k.d., 93/Sep
   Queen Latifah, 92/Apr
   Smith, Will, 94/Sep
"60 Minutes"
   Bradley, Ed, 94/Apr
skaters
   Blair, Bonnie, 94/Apr
   Harding, Tonya, 94/Sep
   Jansen, Dan, 94/Apr
   Kerrigan, Nancy, 94/Apr
   Yamaguchi, Kristi, 92/Apr
soccer
   Lalas, Alexi, 94/Sep
Song of Solomon
   Morrison, Toni, 94/Jan
S.O.R. Losers
   Avi, 93/Jan
South Africa, president of
   de Klerk, F.W., 94/Apr; 94/Update
   Mandela, Nelson, 94/Update
South African
   de Klerk, F.W., 94/Apr; 94/Update
   Mandela, Nelson, 92/Jan; 94/Update

GENERAL INDEX

Soviet Union, president of
  Gorbachev, Mikhail, 92/Jan
"Star Trek: The Next Generation"
  Goldberg, Whoopi, 94/Apr
  Stewart, Patrick, 94/Jan
Superfudge
  Blume, Judy, 92/Jan
Supreme Court justices, U.S.
  Ginsburg, Ruth Bader, 94/Jan
  Marshall, Thurgood, 92/Jan; 93/Update
  O'Connor, Sandra Day, 92/Jul
  Thomas, Clarence, 92/Jan
Surgeon General, U.S.
  Novello, Antonia, 92/Apr; 93/Update
Syrian-Brazilian
  Abdul, Paula, 92/Jan
Tartar
  Nureyev, Rudolf, 93/Apr
television
  Allen, Tim, 94/Apr
  Alley, Kirstie, 92/Jul
  Arnold, Roseanne, 92/Oct
  Bergen, Candice, 93/Sep
  Bialik, Mayim, 94/Jan
  Burke, Chris, 93/Sep
  Candy, John, 94/Sep
  Carvey, Dana, 93/Jan
  Chung, Connie, 94/Jan
  Cosby, Bill, 92/Jan
  Cousteau, Jacques, 93/Jan
  Crawford, Cindy, 93/Apr
  Ellerbee, Linda, 94/Apr
  Fuentes, Daisy, 94/Jan
  Gilbert, Sara, 93/Apr
  Goldberg, Whoopi, 94/Apr
  Groening, Matt, 92/Jan
  Guy, Jasmine, 93/Sep
  Hart, Melissa Joan, 94/Jan
  Jennings, Peter, 92/Jul
  Leno, Jay, 92/Jul
  Pauley, Jane, 92/Oct
  Seinfeld, Jerry, 92/Oct
  Smith, Will, 94/Sep
  Stewart, Patrick, 94/Jan
  Walters, Barbara, 94/Sep
  Wayans, Keenen Ivory, 93/Jan
  Williams, Robin, 92/Apr
  Winfrey, Oprah, 92/Apr
tennis players
  Agassi, Andre, 92/Jul
  Ashe, Arthur, 93/Sep
  Graf, Steffi, 92/Jan
  Navratilova, Martina, 93/Jan; 94/Update
Texas Rangers
  Ryan, Nolan, 92/Oct;93/Update
Tiger Eyes
  Blume, Judy, 92/Jan
"Today" Show, The
  Pauley, Jane, 92/Oct
  Walters, Barbara, 94/Sep
"Tonight Show with Jay Leno, The"
  Leno, Jay, 92/Jul
True Confessions of Charlotte Doyle, The
  Avi, 93/Jan
"20/20"
  Walters, Barbara, 94/Sep
United Farm Workers (UFW)
  Chavez, Cesar, 93/Sep
United Nations
  Ambassador to
    Bush, George, 92/Jan
  Secretary General
    Boutros-Ghali, Boutros, 93/Apr
United States
  Army, general
    Powell, Colin, 92/Jan;93/Update
    Schwarzkopf, H. Norman, 92/Jan
  Attorney General
    Reno, Janet, 93/Sep
  First Lady of
    Bush, Barbara, 92/Jan
    Clinton, Hillary Rodham, 93/Apr

GENERAL INDEX

Joint Chiefs of Staff Chairman of
  Powell, Colin, 92/Jan; 93/Update
Poet Laureate of
  Dove, Rita, 94/Jan
President of
  Bush, George, 92/Jan
  Clinton, Bill, 92/Jul
  Nixon, Richard, 94/Sep
Secretary of Housing and Urban Development
  Cisneros, Henry, 93/Sep
Secretary of Interior
  Babbitt, Bruce, 94/Jan
Secretary of Labor
  Dole, Elizabeth Hanford, 92/Jul
Secretary of State
  Baker, James, 92/Oct
Secretary of Transportation
  Dole, Elizabeth Hanford, 92/Jul
Secretary of Treasury
  Baker, James, 92/Oct
Supreme Court, justice of
  Ginsburg, Ruth Bader, 94/Jan
  Marshall, Thurgood, 92/Jan; 93/Update
  O'Connor, Sandra Day, 92/Jul
  Thomas, Clarence, 92/Jan
Surgeon General
  Novello, Antonia, 92/Apr; 93/Update
Vice President of
  Bush, George, 92/Jan
  Gore, Al, 93/Jan
  Nixon, Richard, 94/Sep

White House Chief of Staff
  Baker, James, 92/Oct
Vice-President of the United States
  Bush, George, 92/Jan
  Gore, Al, 93/Jan
  Nixon, Richard, 94/Sep
Watergate
  Nixon, Richard, 94/Sep
What Do People Do All Day?
  Scarry, Richard, 94/Sep
Where's Waldo?
  Handford, Martin, 92/Jan
White House Chief of Staff
  Baker, James, 92/Oct
Wimbledon winners
  Agassi, Andre, 92/Jul
  Navratilova, Martina, 93/Jan; 94/Update
Winfield Foundation, David M.
  Winfield, Dave, 93/Jan
wrestlers
  Hogan, Hulk, 92/Apr
Wrinkle in Time, A
  L'Engle, Madeleine, 92/Jan
WWF (World Wrestling Federation)
  Hogan, Hulk, 92/Apr
Zlata's Diary
  Filipovic, Zlata, 94/Sep

Places of Birth Index

The following index lists the places of birth for the individuals profiled in *Biography Today*. Places of birth are entered under state, province, and/or country.

Alabama
 Barkley, Charles (Leeds), 92/Apr
 Jackson, Bo (Bessemer), 92/Jan
 Jemison, Mae (Decatur), 92/Oct
 Parks, Rosa (Tuskegee), 92/Apr
Alberta, Canada
 lang, k.d. (Edmonton), 93/Sep
Arizona
 Chavez, Cesar (Yuma), 93/Sep
Arkansas
 Clinton, Bill (Hope), 92/Jul
 Pippen, Scottie (Hamburg), 92/Oct
Australia
 Norman, Greg (Mt. Isa, Queensland), 94/Jan
Bosnia-Herzogovina
 Filipovic, Zlata (Sarajevo), 94/Sep
British Columbia, Canada
 Priestley, Jason (Vancouver), 92/Apr
California
 Abdul, Paula (Van Nuys), 92/Jan
 Babbitt, Bruce (Los Angeles), 94/Jan
 Bergen, Candice (Beverly Hills), 93/Sep
 Bialik, Mayim (San Diego), 94/Jan
 Breathed, Berke (Encino), 92/Jan
 Fielder, Cecil (Los Angeles), 93/Sep
 Gilbert, Sara (Santa Monica), 93/Apr
 Hammer (Oakland), 92/Jan
 Jobs, Steven (San Francisco), 92/Jan
 Kistler, Darci (Riverside), 93/Jan
 Nixon, Richard (Yorba Linda), 94/Sep
 Ride, Sally (Encino), 92/Jan
 Yamaguchi, Kristi (Fremont), Apr 92
Canada
 Candy, John (Newmarket, Ontario), 94/Sep
 Gretzky, Wayne (Brantford, Ontario), 92/Jan
 Jennings, Peter (Toronto, Ontario), 92/Jul
 lang, k.d. (Edmonton, Alberta), 93/Sep
 Lemieux, Mario (Montreal, Quebec), 92/Jul
 Priestley, Jason (Vancouver, British Columbia), 92/Apr
Colorado
 Allen, Tim (Denver), 94/Apr
Connecticut
 McClintock, Barbara (Hartford), 92/Oct
Cuba
 Castro, Fidel (Mayari, Oriente), 92/Jul
 Estefan, Gloria (Havana), 92/Jul
 Fuentes, Daisy (Havana), 94/Jan
Czechoslovakia
 Navratilova, Martina (Prague), 93/Jan
Egypt
 Arafat, Yasir (Cairo), 94/Sep
 Boutros-Ghali, Boutros (Cairo), 93/Apr
England
 Diana, Princess of Wales (Norfolk), 92/Jul
 Handford, Martin (London), 92/Jan

PLACES OF BIRTH INDEX

Hawking, Stephen (Oxford), 92/Apr
Stewart, Patrick (Mirfield), 94/Jan
Florida
Reno, Janet (Miami), 93/Sep
Smith, Emmitt (Pensacola), 94/Sep
France
Cousteau, Jacques (St. Andre-de-Cubzac), 93/Jan
Ma, Yo-Yo (Paris), 92/Jul
Georgia
Hogan, Hulk (Augusta), 92/Apr
Lee, Spike (Atlanta), 92/Apr
Thomas, Clarence (Pin Point), 92/Jan
Ward, Charlie (Thomasville), 94/Apr
Germany
Graf, Steffi (Mannheim), 92/Jan
Guatemala
Menchu, Rigoberta (Chimel, El Quiche), 93/Jan
Illinois
Clinton, Hillary Rodham (Chicago), 93/Apr
Crawford, Cindy (De Kalb), 93/Apr
Joyner-Kersee, Jackie (East St. Louis), 92/Oct
McCully, Emily Arnold (Galesburg), 92/Jul
Indiana
Bird, Larry (West Baden), 92/Jan
Naylor, Phyllis Reynolds (Anderson), 93/Apr
Pauley, Jane (Indianapolis), 92/Oct
Iraq
Hussein, Saddam (al-Auja), 92/Jul
Ireland
Robinson, Mary (Ballina), 93/Sep
Israel
Rabin, Yitzhak (Jerusalem), 92/Oct

Italy
Andretti, Mario (Montona), 94/Sep
Kansas
Alley, Kirstie (Wichita), 92/Jul
Louisiana
Marsalis, Wynton (New Orleans), 92/Apr
Maryland
Marshall, Thurgood (Baltimore), 92/Jan
Massachusetts
Bush, George (Milton), 92/Jan
Guy, Jasmine (Boston), 93/Sep
Kerrigan, Nancy (Woburn), 94/Apr
Pine, Elizabeth Michele (Boston), 94/Jan
Scarry, Richard (Boston), 94/Sep
Seuss, Dr. (Springfield), 92/Jan
Voigt, Cynthia (Boston), 92/Oct
Walters, Barbara (Boston), 94/Sep
Michigan
Johnson, Magic (Lansing), 92/Apr
Lalas, Alexi (Royal Oak), 94/Sep
Van Allsburg, Chris, 92/Apr
Minnesota
Ryder, Winona (Winona), 93/Jan
Winfield, Dave (St. Paul), 93/Jan
Mississippi
Rice, Jerry (Crawford), 93/Apr
Winfrey, Oprah (Kosciusko), 92/Apr
Missouri
Angelou, Maya (St. Louis), 93/Apr
Miller, Shannon (Rolla), 94/Sep
Montana
Carvey, Dana (Missoula), 93/Jan
Nevada
Agassi, Andre (Las Vegas), 92/Jul

PLACES OF BIRTH INDEX

New Jersey
  Blume, Judy, 92/Jan
  Carpenter, Mary Chapin (Princeton), 94/Sep
  Houston, Whitney (Newark), 94/Sep
  Ice-T (Newark), 93/Apr
  Martin, Ann M. (Princeton), 92/Jan
  O'Neal, Shaquille (Newark), 93/Sep
  Queen Latifah (Newark), 92/Apr
  Schwarzkopf, H. Norman (Trenton), 92/Jan

New York State
  Avi (New York City), 93/Jan
  Blair, Bonnie (Cornwall), 94/Apr
  Burke, Chris (New York City), 93/Sep
  Bush, Barbara (New York City), 92/Jan
  Culkin, Macaulay (New York City), 93/Sep
  Ginsburg, Ruth Bader (Brooklyn), 94/Jan
  Goldberg, Whoopi (New York City), 94/Apr
  Haley, Alex (Ithaca), 92/Apr
  Hart, Melissa Joan (Smithtown), 94/Jan
  Jordan, Michael (Brooklyn), 92/Jan
  L'Engle, Madeleine (New York City), 92/Jan
  Leno, Jay (New Rochelle), 92/Jul
  Powell, Colin (New York City), 92/Jan
  Salk, Jonas (New York City), 94/Jan
  Seinfeld, Jerry (Brooklyn), 92/Oct
  Washington, Denzel (Mount Vernon), 93/Jan
  Wayans, Keenen Ivory (New York City), 93/Jan

North Carolina
  Chavis, Benjamin (Oxford), 94/Jan
  Dole, Elizabeth Hanford (Salisbury), 92/Jul

Ohio
  Anderson, Terry (Lorain), 92/Apr
  Battle, Kathleen (Portsmouth), 93/Jan
  Dove, Rita (Akron), 94/Jan
  Guisewite, Cathy (Dayton), 93/Sep
  Morrison, Toni (Lorain), 94/Jan
  Perry, Luke (Mansfield), 92/Jan
  Rose, Pete (Cincinnati), 92/Jan
  Spielberg, Steven (Cincinnati), 94/Jan
  Steinem, Gloria (Toledo), 92/Oct
  Stine, R.L. (Columbus), 94/Apr

Oklahoma
  Brooks, Garth (Tulsa), 92/Oct
  Duke, David (Tulsa), 92/Apr
  Hill, Anita (Morris), 93/Jan
  Mankiller, Wilma (Tahlequah), 94/Apr

Ontario, Canada
  Candy, John (Newmarket), 94/Sep
  Gretzky, Wayne (Brantford), 92/Jan
  Jennings, Peter (Toronto), 92/Jul

Oregon
  Cleary, Beverly (McMinnville), 94/Apr
  Groening, Matt (Portland), 92/Jan
  Harding, Tonya (Portland), 94/Sep
  Hooper, Geoff (Salem), 94/Jan
  Phoenix, River (Madras), 94/Apr

Oriente, Cuba
  Castro, Fidel (Mayari), 92/Jul

PLACES OF BIRTH INDEX

Palestine
Rabin, Yitzhak (Jerusalem), 92/Oct
Pennsylvania
Anderson, Marian (Philadelphia), 94/Jan
Bradley, Ed (Philadelphia), 94/Apr
Cosby, Bill, 92/Jan
Duncan, Lois (Philadelphia), 93/Sep
Iacocca, Lee A. (Allentown), 92/Jan
Marino, Dan (Pittsburgh), 93/Apr
Smith, Will (Philadelphia), 94/Sep
Poland
John Paul II (Wadowice), 92/Oct
Puerto Rico
Lopez, Charlotte, 94/Apr
Novello, Antonia (Fajardo), 92/Apr
Quebec, Canada
Lemieux, Mario, 92/Jul
Queensland, Australia
Norman, Greg (Mt. Isa), 94/Jan
El Quiche, Guatemala
Menchu, Rigoberta (Chimel), 93/Jan
Russia
Asimov, Isaac (Petrovichi), 92/Jul
Fedorov, Sergei (Pskov), 94/Apr
Gorbachev, Mikhail (Privolnoye), 92/Jan
Nureyev, Rudolf, 93/Apr
Yeltsin, Boris (Butka), 92/Apr
South Africa
de Klerk, F.W. (Mayfair), 94/Apr
Mandela, Nelson (Umtata), 92/Jan
South Carolina
Edelman, Marian Wright (Bennettsville), 93/Apr
Gillespie, Dizzy (Cheraw), 93/Apr
Spain
Ochoa, Severo (Luarca), 94/Jan

Stavropol, Russia
Gorbachev, Mikhail (Privolnoye), 92/Jan
Tennessee
Andrews, Ned (Oakridge), 94/Sep
Doherty, Shannen (Memphis), 92/Apr
Texas
Baker, James (Houston), 92/Oct
Cisneros, Henry (San Antonio), 93/Sep
Ellerbee, Linda (Bryan), 94/Apr
O'Connor, Sandra Day (El Paso), 92/Jul
Perot, H. Ross (Texarkana), 92/Apr
Ryan, Nolan (Refugio), 92/Oct
Zmeskal, Kim (Houston), 94/Jan
Transkei, South Africa
Mandela, Nelson (Umtata), 92/Jan
USSR (Union of Soviet Socialist Republics)
Asimov, Isaac (Petrovichi, Russia), 92/Jul
Fedorov, Sergei (Pskov, Russia), 94/Apr
Gorbachev, Mikhail (Privolnoye, Russia), 92/Jan
Nureyev, Rudolf (Russia), 93/Apr
Yeltsin, Boris (Butka, Russia), 92/Apr
Utah
Arnold, Roseanne (Salt Lake City), 92/Oct
Young, Steve (Salt Lake City), 94/Jan
Virginia
Ashe, Arthur (Richmond), 93/Sep
Washington, D.C.
Chung, Connie, 94/Jan
Gore, Al, 93/Jan

Watterson, Bill, 92/Jan
Washington state
Cobain, Kurt (Aberdeen), 94/Sep
Gates, Bill (Seattle), 93/Apr
West Virginia
Myers, Walter Dean
(Martinsburg), 93/Jan
Wisconsin
Jansen, Dan (Milwaukee), 94/Apr
Yekaterinburg, Russia
Yeltsin, Boris (Butka), 92/Apr
Yugoslavia
Filipovic, Zlata (Sarajevo,
Bosnia-Herzogovina), 94/Sep

Birthday Index

January

- 2 Asimov, Isaac (1920)
- 4 Naylor, Phyllis Reynolds (1933)
- 8 Hawking, Stephen W. (1942)
- 9 Menchu, Rigoberta (1959)
  Nixon, Richard (1913)
- 22 Chavis, Benjamin (1948)
- 25 Alley, Kirstie (1955)
- 28 Gretzky, Wayne (1961)
- 29 Winfrey, Oprah (1954)
  Gilbert, Sara (1975)
- 31 Ryan, Nolan (1947)

February

- 1 Spinelli, Jerry (1941)
  Yeltsin, Boris (1931)
- 4 Parks, Rosa (1913)
- 6 Zmeskal, Kim (1976)
- 7 Brooks, Garth (1962)
- 10 Norman, Greg (1955)
- 12 Blume, Judy (1938)
- 15 Groening, Matt (1954)
- 17 Anderson, Marian (1897)
  Jordan, Michael (1963)
- 18 Morrison, Toni (1931)
- 20 Barkley, Charles (1963)
  Cobain, Kurt (1967)
  Crawford, Cindy (1966)
- 21 Carpenter, Mary Chapin (1958)
- 24 Jobs, Steven (1955)
- 25 Voigt, Cynthia (1942)
- 28 Andretti, Mario (1940)

March

- 1 Rabin, Yitzhak (1922)
- 2 Gorbachev, Mikhail (1931)
  Seuss, Dr. (1904)
- 3 Hooper, Geoff (1979)
  Joyner-Kersee, Jackie (1962)
- 10 Guy, Jasmine (1964)

March, continued

- 10 Miller, Shannon (1977)
- 15 Ginsburg, Ruth Bader (1933)
- 16 O'Neal, Shaquille (1972)
- 17 Nureyev, Rudolf (1938)
- 18 Blair, Bonnie (1964)
  de Klerk, F.W. (1936)
- 18 Queen Latifah (1970)
- 20 Lee, Spike (1957)
- 25 Steinem, Gloria (1934)
- 26 O'Connor, Sandra Day (1930)
- 30 Hammer (1933)
- 31 Chavez, Cesar (1927)
  Gore, Al (1948)

April

- 2 Carvey, Dana (1955)
- 4 Angelou, Maya (1928)
- 5 Powell, Colin (1937)
- 12 Cleary, Beverly (1916)
  Doherty, Shannen (1971)
- 14 Rose, Pete (1941)
- 18 Hart, Melissa Joan (1976)
- 28 Baker, James (1930)
  Duncan, Lois (1934)
  Hussein, Saddam (1937)
  Leno, Jay (1950)
- 29 Agassi, Andre (1970)
  Seinfeld, Jerry (1954)

May

- 9 Bergen, Candice (1946)
- 14 Smith, Emmitt (1969)
- 18 John Paul II (1920)
- 21 Robinson, Mary (1944)
- 26 Ride, Sally (1951)

June

- 1 Lalas, Alexi (1970)
- 4 Kistler, Darci (1964)
- 5 Scarry, Richard (1919)

BIRTHDAY INDEX

June, continued

8 Bush, Barbara (1925)
  Edelman, Marian Wright (1939)
  Wayans, Keenen Ivory (1958)
11 Cousteau, Jacques (1910)
12 Bush, George (1924)
13 Allen, Tim (1953)
14 Graf, Steffi (1969)
16 McClintock, Barbara (1902)
17 Jansen, Dan (1965)
18 Van Allsburg, Chris (1949)
19 Abdul, Paula (1962)
21 Breathed, Berke (1957)
22 Bradley, Ed (1941)
23 Thomas, Clarence (1948)
27 Babbitt, Bruce (1938)
  Perot, H. Ross (1930)

July

1 Diana, Princess of Wales (1961)
  Duke, David (1950)
  McCully, Emily Arnold (1939)
2 Marshall, Thurgood (1908)
5 Watterson, Bill (1958)
10 Ashe, Arthur (1943)
11 Cisneros, Henry (1947)
12 Cosby, Bill (1937)
  Yamaguchi, Kristi (1972)
13 Stewart, Patrick (1940)
18 Mandela, Nelson (1918)
21 Reno, Janet (1938)
  Williams, Robin (1952)
29 Dole, Elizabeth Hanford (1936)
  Jennings, Peter (1938)
30 Hill, Anita (1956)

August

9 Houston, Whitney (1963)
11 Haley, Alex (1921)
  Hogan, Hulk (1953)
12 Martin, Ann M. (1955)

August, continued

12 Myers, Walter Dean (1937)
13 Battle, Kathleen (1948)
  Castro, Fidel (1927)
14 Johnson, Magic (1959)
15 Ellerbee, Linda (1944)
19 Clinton, Bill (1946)
20 Chung, Connie (1946)
22 Schwarzkopf, H. Norman (1934)
23 Novello, Antonia (1944)
24 Arafat, Yasir (1929)
23 Phoenix, River (1970)
26 Burke, Christopher (1965)
  Culkin, Macaulay (1980)
28 Dove, Rita (1952)
  Priestley, Jason (1969)

September

1 Estefan, Gloria (1958)
5 Guisewite, Cathy (1950)
15 Marino, Dan (1961)
21 Fielder, Cecil (1963)
24 Ochoa, Severo (1905)
25 Lopez, Charlotte (1976)
  Pippen, Scottie (1965)
  Smith, Will (1968)
  Walters, Barbara (1931)
27 Handford, Martin (1956)

October

3 Winfield, Dave (1951)
5 Lemieux, Mario (1965)
7 Ma, Yo-Yo (1955)
8 Stine, R.L. (1943)
11 Perry, Luke (1964?)
  Young, Steve (1961)
12 Ward, Charlie (1970)
13 Kerrigan, Nancy (1969)
  Rice, Jerry (1962)
15 Iacocca, Lee A. (1924)
17 Jemison, Mae (1956)
18 Marsalis, Wynton (1961)
  Navratilova, Martina (1956)

October, continued

21 Gillespie, Dizzy (1956)
26 Clinton, Hillary Rodham (1947)
27 Anderson, Terry (1947)
28 Gates, Bill (1955)
    Salk, Jonas (1914)
29 Ryder, Winona (1971)
31 Candy, John (1950)
    Pauley, Jane (1950)

November

2   lang, k.d. (1961)
3   Arnold, Roseanne (1952)
12 Andrews, Ned (1980)
    Harding, Tonya (1970)
13 Goldberg, Whoopi (1949)
14 Boutros-Ghali, Boutros (1922)
17 Fuentes, Daisy (1966)
18 Mankiller, Wilma (1945)
25 Thomas, Lewis (1913)
26 Pine, Elizabeth Michele (1975)
29 L'Engle, Madeleine (1918)
30 Jackson, Bo (1962)

December

3   Filipovic, Zlata (1980)
7   Bird, Larry (1956)
12 Bialik, Mayim (1975)
13 Fedorov, Sergi (1969)
18 Spielberg, Steven (1947)
23 Avi (1937)
28 Washington, Denzel (1954)

People to Appear in Future Issues

Actors
Trini Alvarado
Richard Dean
  Anderson
Dan Aykroyd
Valerie Bertinelli
Lisa Bonet
Matthew Broderick
Candice Cameron
Cher
Kevin Costner
Tom Cruise
Jamie Lee Curtis
Ted Danson
Tommy Davidson
Geena Davis
Matt Dillon
Michael Douglas
Larry Fishburne
Harrison Ford
Jody Foster
Michael J. Fox
Richard Gere
Tracey Gold
Melanie Griffith
Tom Hanks
Mark Harmon
Michael Keaton
Val Kilmer
Angela Lansbury
Christopher Lloyd
Marlee Matlin
Bette Midler
Alyssa Milano
Demi Moore
Rick Moranis
Eddie Murphy
Bill Murray
Leonard Nimoy
Ashley Olsen
Mary Kate Olsen
Sean Penn
Phylicia Rashad
Keanu Reeves
Julia Roberts
Bob Saget
Fred Savage
Arnold
  Schwarzenegger
William Shatner
Christian Slater
Jimmy Smits
Sylvester Stallone
John Travolta
Damon Wayans
Bruce Willis
B.D. Wong

Artists
Mitsumasa Anno
Graeme Base
Maya Ying Lin

Astronauts
Neil Armstrong

Authors
Jean M. Auel
Lynn Banks
Gwendolyn Brooks
John Christopher
Arthur C. Clarke
John Colville
Robert Cormier
Paula Danziger
Paula Fox
Jamie Gilson
Rosa Guy
Nat Hentoff
James Herriot
S.E. Hinton
Stephen King
Norma Klein
E.L. Konigsburg
Lois Lowry
David Macaulay
Stephen Manes
Norma Fox Mazer
Anne McCaffrey
Gloria D. Miklowitz
Joan Lowery Nixon
Marsha Norman
Robert O'Brien
Francine Pascal
Gary Paulsen
Christopher Pike
Daniel Pinkwater
Ann Rice
Louis Sachar
Carl Sagan
J.D. Salinger
John Saul
Maurice Sendak
Shel Silverstein
Amy Tan
Alice Walker
Jane Yolen
Roger Zelazny
Paul Zindel

Business
Minoru Arakawa
Michael Eisner
William Ford, Jr.
Anita Roddick
Donald Trump
Ted Turner
Lillian Vernon

Cartoonists
Lynda Barry
Roz Chast
Jim Davis
Greg Evans
Nicole Hollander
Gary Larson
Charles Schulz
Art Spiegelman
Garry Trudeau

Comedians
Dan Aykroyd
Steve Martin
Eddie Murphy
Bill Murray

Dancers
Debbie Allen
Mikhail
  Baryshnikov
Suzanne Farrell
Gregory Hines
Gelsey Kirkland
Twyla Tharp
Tommy Tune

**Directors/
  Producers**
Woody Allen
Steven Bocho
Ken Burns
Francis Ford
  Coppola
John Hughes
George Lucas
Penny Marshall
Leonard Nimoy
Rob Reiner
John Singleton

**Environmentalists/
  Animal Rights**
Marjory Stoneman
  Douglas
Kathryn Fuller
Lois Gibbs
Wangari Maathai
Linda Maraniss
Ingrid Newkirk
Pat Potter

Journalists
Tom Brokaw
Dan Rather
Nina Totenberg
Mike Wallace
Bob Woodward

Musicians
Another Bad Creation
Joshua Bell
George Benson
Black Box
Boyz II Men
Edie Brickell
James Brown
C & C Music Factory
Mariah Carey
Ray Charles
Chayanne
Natalie Cole
Cowboy Junkies
Billy Ray Cyrus
Def Leppard
Gerardo
Guns N' Roses
Ice Cube
India
Janet Jackson
Jermaine Jackson
Kitaro
Kris Kross
KRS-One
Andrew Lloyd Webber
Courtney Love
Madonna
Barbara Mandrell
Marky Mark
Branford Marsalis
Paul McCartney
Midori
N.W.A.
Sinead O'Connor
Teddy Pendergrass
Itzhak Perlman
Prince
Public Enemy
Raffi
Bonnie Raitt
Red Hot Chili Peppers

People to Appear in Future Issues

Lou Reed
R.E.M.
Kenny Rogers
Axl Rose
Run-D.M.C.
Carly Simon
Paul Simon
Michelle Shocked
Sting
TLC
Randy Travis
2 Live Crew
Vanilla Ice
Stevie Wonder

Politics/
  World Leaders
Jean-Bertrand
  Aristide
Les Aspin
Benazir Bhutto
Jesse Brown
Ronald Brown
Pat Buchanan
Jimmy Carter
Violeta Barrios
  de Chamorro
Shirley Chisolm
Jean Chretien
Warren Christopher
Edith Cresson
Mario Cuomo
Robert Dole
Mike Espy
Louis Farrakhan
Alan Greenspan
Vaclav Havel
Jesse Jackson
Jack Kemp
Bob Kerrey
Coretta Scott King
John Major
Imelda Marcos
Slobodan Milosevic
Brian Mulroney
Manuel Noriega
Hazel O'Leary
Major Owens
Leon Panetta
Federico Pena
Robert Reich
Ann Richards
Richard Riley
Phyllis Schlafly
Pat Schroeder
Aung San Suu Kyi
Donna Shalala
Desmond Tutu
Lech Walesa

Royalty
Charles, Prince of
  Wales
Duchess of York
  (Sarah Ferguson)
Queen Noor

Scientists
Sallie Baliunas
Avis Cohen
Donna Cox
Stephen Jay Gould
Mimi Koehl
Deborah Letourneau
Philippa Marrack
Helen Quinn
Carl Sagan
Barbara Smuts
Flossie Wong-Staal
Aslihan Yener
Adrienne Zihlman

Sports
Jim Abbott
Muhammad Ali
Sparky Anderson
Michael Andretti
Boris Becker
Bobby Bonilla
Jose Canseco
Jennifer Capriati
Michael Chang
Roger Clemens
Randall Cunningham
Eric Davis
Clyde Drexler
John Elway
Chris Evert
George Foreman
Zina Garrison
Florence Griffith-Joyner
Rickey Henderson
Evander Holyfield
Desmond Howard
Brett Hull
Raghib Ismail
Jim Kelly
Petr Klima
Bernie Kozar
Greg LeMond
Carl Lewis
Mickey Mantle
Willy Mays
Paul Molitor
Joe Montana
Jack Nicklaus
Joe Paterno
Kirby Puckett
Mark Rippien

David Robinson
John Salley
Barry Sanders
Monica Seles
Daryl Strawberry
Danny Sullivan
Vinnie Testaverde
Isiah Thomas
Mike Tyson
Steve Yzerman

Television
  Personalities
Downtown Julie
  Brown
Andre Brown
  (Dr. Dre)
Phil Donahue
Arsenio Hall
David Letterman
Joan Lunden
Dennis Miller
Jane Pratt
Martha Quinn
Diane Sawyer

Other
Madeleine Albright
James Brady
Johnnetta Cole
Jaimie Escalante
Jack Kevorkian
Wendy Kopp
Sister Irene Kraus
Mother Theresa
Eli Weisel
Jeanne White

BUSINESS REPLY MAIL
First Class Mail   Permit No. 174   Detroit, MI

Postage will be paid by addressee

Omnigraphics, Inc.

Attn: Order Dept.
Penobscot Building
Detroit, MI 48226

No Postage
Necessary
if Mailed
in the
United States

BUSINESS REPLY MAIL
First Class Mail   Permit No. 174   Detroit, MI

Postage will be paid by addressee

Omnigraphics, Inc.

Attn: *Biography Today,* Editor
Penobscot Building
Detroit, MI 48226

No Postage
Necessary
if Mailed
in the
United States

ON-APPROVAL ORDER FORM

Please send the following on 60-day approval:

Copies

____ BIOGRAPHY TODAY
ISSN 1058-2347 .... $45.00/year (3 issues)
____ *Standing Order*
____ 1992 Hardbound Annual 47.00
____ 1993 Hardbound Annual 47.00
____ 1994 Hardbound Annual 47.00
____ *Standing Order*
____ Annual Subscription
(3 issues and hardbound annual) 90.00
____ *Standing Order*
____ Individual Issues 15.00
____ BIOGRAPHY TODAY AUTHOR SERIES 30.00

☐ Payment enclosed, ship postpaid   ☐ Bill us, plus shipping

Institution _____

Attention _____

Address _____

City _____

State, Zip _____

Phone (___) _____

9/94

We want to cover the people *you* want to know about in *Biography Today*. Take a look at the list of people we plan to include in upcoming issues. Then use this card to list other people you want to see in *Biography Today*. If we include someone you suggest, your library wins a free issue, and you get one to keep, with our thanks.

People I'd like to see in BIOGRAPHY TODAY:

_____
_____
_____
_____
_____

Name _____

Institution _____

Address _____

City _____

State, Zip _____